More Light on the Path

To
Adam and Emily,
Holly and Jeanette,
The next generation of seekers

Other Books by David W. Baker

Obadiah, Jonah, Micah: An Introduction and Commentary (co-author)

Nahum, Habakkuk, Zephaniah: An Introduction and Commentary

Faith, Tradition, and History: Old Testament Historiography in Its Near Eastern Context (co-editor)

To Bob
God bless you in seeds
and savior.

More Light on the Path

Daily Scripture Readings
in Hebrew and Greek

David W. Baker and Elaine A. Heath
(with Morven R. Baker)

Baker Books
A Division of Baker Book House Co
Grand Rapids, Michigan 49516

© 1998 by David W. Baker and Elaine A. Heath

Published by Baker Books
a division of Baker Book House Company
Box 6287, Grand Rapids, MI 49516-6287

Second printing, June 2003

Printed in the United States of America

Library of Congress Cataloging-in-Publication Data

Baker, David W. (David Weston), 1950–
    More light on the path : daily scripture readings in Hebrew
  and Greek / David W. Baker and Elaine R. Heath (with Morven R.
  Baker).
      p. cm.
  Text in English, Greek, and Hebrew.
  Includes bibliographical references and index.
  ISBN 0-8010-2165-0 (pbk.)
    1. Bible—Devotional use. 2. Devotional calendars.
    I. Heath, Elaine A., 1954– . II. Baker, Morven R.   III. Title.
BS491.5.B35 1998   98-40712
220.4′4—dc21

For information about academic books, resources for Christian leaders, and all new releases available from Baker Book House, visit our web site:
http://www.bakerbooks.com

Foreword

LEARNING THE BIBLICAL LANGUAGES of Greek and Hebrew is arduous work—long hours of disciplined and sometimes painful study. Many of the learners have done the work without any initial liking for it; it was a requirement set by school or church and was accepted as an act of obedience. Thousands upon thousands of pastors and teachers, plus a not inconsiderable number of others of God's people in workplace and marketplace and home, have done it and continue to do it. Most of us, once having done it, do not regret the time or effort spent in the learning. We relish the experience of working with the actual languages in which God's saving revelation was first written. We acquire a taste for first-handedness, the resonating sounds and radiating meanings released into our lives by these ancient, but now new, texts.

And yet, despite the long hours spent in learning these marvelous languages and the considerable benefits experienced, more often than not these same men and women, having acquired a modest stock of vocabulary and the ability to parse verb forms, gradually lose proficiency. Post-academic life is demanding and decidedly unsympathetic to anything that doesn't provide quick and obvious returns. We are handed job descriptions in which our wonderful languages don't even rate a footnote; we acquire families who plunge us into urgencies in which Hebrew radicals provide no shortcuts; we can't keep up with all the stuff thrown at us in easy English—who has time for hard Greek? It isn't long before the languages are, as we say, "lost."

Translators do their best to keep our Holy Scriptures available and accurate for us in our mother tongue. And their "best" is the very best—no age and language has been as blessed in devout and skilled translators as ours. But there is nothing quite like working with the original languages on their own unique terms. A translation is still a translation. I have a friend, a professor of these biblical languages, who tells his students that reading a translation is like being kissed through cellophane—however ardent and well-planted the kiss, it lacks a certain immediacy.

David Baker and Elaine Heath have provided a manual for keeping these precious languages, acquired at such high cost but in constant danger of slipping into oblivion, at hand, quite literally, "handy." By providing brief readings in Hebrew and Greek in a living and believing context of meditation and prayer, those of us who learned the languages are provided an accessible means for daily access to the languages on their own terms. Here is an admirable way to keep daily company with the words and rhythms and diction that keep us current with "the news that stays news."

Eugene H. Peterson
Professor Emeritus of Spiritual Theology
Regent College, Vancouver, B.C.
November 1998

Preface

THE IMPETUS FOR THIS WORK was provided by the very helpful book by Heinrich Bitzer, *Light on the Path I* (Grand Rapids: Baker, 1982), from the original *Licht auf Dem Weg: Light on the Path: Lumen Semitae:* Φῶς ταῖς Τρίβοις: אור לנתיבה (Oekumenischer Verlag: Dr. R. F. Edel, 1969). This work provided brief daily readings from the Hebrew Old Testament and Greek New Testament. Bitzer supplements the texts with a brief morphological description of the difficult forms, along with glosses on the basic form from which they are derived in German, English, and Latin.

This work also presents daily readings from both Testaments, but with an intentional topical orientation in selecting the texts, which follow a single topic for each week. Where appropriate, these topics revolve around the Christian (e.g., Easter, Trinity Sunday, Thanksgiving) and Jewish (e.g., Succoth, Day of Atonement) calendars. They also follow themes such as the spiritual gifts and graces, stages of life, and problem areas of concern to the child of God.

Morphological analyses of the more difficult forms are also supplied. We analyze Hebrew verb forms lacking one or more radical and Greek forms that are inconsistent in their principal parts. More subjectively, we have also treated other constructions that might prove difficult. Hebrew and Greek words that occur less than fifty times in the Bible are glossed for their basic form, that is, without any prepositions, plurals, or other nominal or verbal modifications.

A unique feature, and one that we hope will add value to the readings, is the inclusion of brief prayers or devotional thoughts based on the readings of the day. These are in English, so we trust that they might be useful in family quiet times and on other occasions.

A note on the layout of the entries. Each daily reading includes the references for the two passages. Numbers in brackets indicate the English translations' verse numberings when these differ from that of the original-language text. The morphological analyses provide indications of the parts of speech and the morphology of each. An abbreviation list follows this preface. After that we have included a guide as to when each numbered week's readings should be read between the years 1998 and 2007. Since the volume will, we trust, be used year after year, we have elected not to assign a date to each reading. This method would be satisfactory for special occasions with fixed dates (e.g., Christmas), but not for those which are variable (e.g., Easter and Thanksgiving).

Several resources were invaluable in producing this work. The texts themselves are the *Biblia Hebraica Stuttgartensia* (Stuttgart: Deutsche Bibelgesellschaft, 1990) and the *Nestle Aland 26th Edition Greek New Testament* (Stuttgart: Deutsche Bibelgesellschaft, 1983). Tools that greatly aided the production include the following:

1. Sakae Kubo, *A Reader's Greek-English Lexicon of the New Testament and a Beginner's Guide for the Translation of New Testament Greek* (Andrews University Monographs 4; Berrien Springs, Mich.: Andrews University, 1975), for finding rare Greek words.
2. George M. Landes, *A Student's Vocabulary of Biblical Hebrew Listed according to Frequency and Cognate* (New York: Charles Scribner's, 1961), for finding rarer Hebrew words.
3. *Logos Bible Software 2.0c, Level 4* (Oak Harbor: Logos Research Systems, 1996), which includes morphological databases for Hebrew (copyrighted 1995 by Westminster Theological Seminary) and Greek (copyrighted 1995 by Gramcord Institute). This package was especially useful due to its relatively seamless text transfer link with the word processing package that is listed next.
4. *Microsoft Word for Windows 6* (Microsoft Corporation, 1983–94).
5. Wesley J. Perschbacher, ed., *The New Analytical Greek Lexicon* (Peabody, Mass.: Hendrickson, 1990).

At the end of this volume are two indexes. One indicates the Scripture passages used, referred to by giving the week and day in which the reading is listed (e.g., 48/7). The second is an alphabetical listing of the weekly subjects.

The daily readings were selected by both David Baker and Elaine Heath. Baker provided the morphological analysis and glosses and also composed the work. Heath wrote the daily prayers and meditations, except for weeks 44 and 47, which were written by Morven Baker, and week 53, written by David Baker. We thank Melissa Archer for choosing Greek forms needing morphological comment.

Abbreviations

1.	1st person (I/me/my/ we/us/our)	in.	infinitive
		ind.	indicative
2.	2d person (you/your)	int.	interrogative
3.	3d person (he/she/it/they/his/hers/ its/their/him/her/them)	jus.	jussive
		K.	Ketiv; form written in Masoretic text
A.	Aramaic	m.	masculine
a.	article	mid.	middle voice
ab.	absolute	N.	Nifal stem
acc.	accusative	n.	noun
act.	active	nom.	nominative
adj.	adjective	nt.	neuter
adv.	adverb	P.	Piel stem
aor.	aorist	p.	plural
c.	conversive/consecutive	para.	paragogic נ or ה
cj.	conjunction	pass.	passive
coh.	cohortative	Pe.	Peal
com.	common (masculine or feminine)	pf.	perfect (affix) form
		Pil.	Pilel
cor.	correlative	Plpl.	Pilpel
cs.	construct	plup.	pluperfect
d.	definite	Po.	Polel
dat.	dative	pr.	pronoun/pronominal
en.	energic *nun*	prep.	preposition
f.	feminine	pres.	present
fut.	future	pt.	particle
gen.	genitive	ptc.	participle
H.	Hifil stem	Pu.	Pual
Ha.	Hafel	Q.	Qal
Hisht.	Hishtafel	Qe.	Qere; form to be read in Masoretic text
Ho.	Hofal stem		
Ht.	Hitpael	rel.	relative
Htpl.	Hitpolel	sf.	suffix
impf.	imperfect (prefixed) form	sub.	subjunctive
		v.	verb
impv.	imperative (command) form		

9

Calendar of Weekly Readings

Starting Date	1998	1999	2000	2001	2002	2003	2004	2005	2006	2007
1/1	1	1	1	1	1	1	1	1	1	1
1/8	2	2	2	2	2	2	2	2	2	2
1/15	3	3	3	3	3	3	3	3	3	3
1/22	4	4	4	4	4	4	4	4	4	4
1/29	5	5	5	5	5	5	5	5	5	5
2/5	6	6	6	6	6	6	6	7	6	6
2/12	8	7	8	8	7	8	8	6	8	8
2/19	7	8	9	9	8	9	7	8	9	7
2/26	9	9	10	7	9	10	9	9	7	9
Leap Year			53/2				53/2			
3/5	10	10	7	10	10	7	10	10	10	10
3/12	11	11	11	11	11	11	11	11	11	11
3/19	12	12	12	12	12	12	12	12	12	12
3/26	14	14	14	14	13	14	14	13	14	14
4/2	15	13	15	15	14	15	13	14	15	13
4/9	13	15	16	13	15	16	15	15	16	15
4/16	16	16	17	16	16	13	16	16	13	16
4/23	17	17	13	17	17	17	17	17	17	17
4/30	18	18	18	18	18	18	18	18	18	18
5/7	19	19	19	19	19	19	19	19	19	19
5/14	20	20	20	20	21	20	20	20	20	20
5/21	23	21	23	23	22	23	21	23	23	21
5/28	21	22	24	21	20	24	22	24	21	22
6/4	22	23	21	22	23	21	23	25	22	23
6/11	24	24	22	24	24	22	24	21	24	24
6/18	25	25	25	25	25	25	25	22	25	25
6/25	26	26	26	26	26	26	26	26	26	26

Starting Date	1998	1999	2000	2001	2002	2003	2004	2005	2006	2007
7/2	27	27	27	27	27	27	27	27	27	27
7/9	28	28	28	28	28	28	28	28	28	28
7/16	29	29	29	29	29	29	29	29	29	29
7/23	30	30	30	30	30	30	30	30	30	30
7/30	31	31	31	31	31	31	31	31	31	31
8/6	32	32	32	32	32	32	32	32	32	32
8/13	33	33	33	33	33	33	33	33	33	33
8/20	34	34	34	34	34	34	34	34	34	34
8/27	35	35	35	35	35	35	35	35	35	35
9/3	36	36	36	36	36	36	36	36	36	36
9/10	37	37	37	37	41	37	37	37	37	37
9/17	38	41	38	38	42	38	38	38	38	41
9/24	41	42	39	41	43	39	41	39	39	42
10/1	42	43	40	42	37	41	42	40	41	43
10/8	43	38	41	43	38	42	43	41	42	38
10/15	39	39	42	39	39	43	39	42	43	39
10/22	40	40	43	40	40	40	40	43	40	40
10/29	44	44	44	44	44	44	44	44	44	44
11/5	45	45	45	45	45	45	45	45	45	45
11/12	46	46	46	46	46	46	46	46	46	46
11/19	47	48	47	47	47	47	48	48	47	47
11/26	48	47	48	48	48	48	47	47	48	48
12/3	49	49	49	49	49	49	49	49	49	49
12/10	50	50	50	50	50	50	50	50	50	50
12/17	51	51	51	51	51	51	51	51	51	51
12/24	52	52	52	52	52	52	52	52	52	50
12/31	53/1	53/1	53/1	53/1	53/1	53/1	53/1	53/1	53/1	53/1

Week 1

Graced Beginnings

1. Genesis 1:1–2; John 1:1–2

Wind of Love

YOU ARE MY BEGINNING, my living Word, my God. Brood across the chaos in my soul, O Wind of Love. Illumine every darkness, bring life from unknown deeps, create in me a heart that is your own.

GENESIS 1:1–2

יָּבְרֵאשִׁית בָּרָא אֱלֹהִים אֵת הַשָּׁמַיִם וְאֵת הָאָרֶץ׃
²וְהָאָרֶץ הָיְתָה תֹהוּ וָבֹהוּ וְחֹשֶׁךְ עַל־פְּנֵי תְהוֹם וְרוּחַ אֱלֹהִים
מְרַחֶפֶת עַל־פְּנֵי הַמָּיִם׃

הָיְתָה v.3.f.s.pf.Q. [הָיָה]; תֹהוּ וָבֹהוּ (formless and empty); תְהוֹם (deep);
מְרַחֶפֶת v.f.s.act.ptc.P. [רָחַף] (hover)

JOHN 1:1–2

¹Ἐν ἀρχῇ ἦν ὁ λόγος, καὶ ὁ λόγος ἦν πρὸς τὸν θεόν, καὶ θεὸς ἦν ὁ λόγος. ²οὗτος ἦν ἐν ἀρχῇ πρὸς τὸν θεόν.

ἦν v.3.s.impf.ind. [εἰμί]

2. Genesis 2:7; John 1:14, 16

The Potter and the Clay

THE POTTER HALLOWS THE SOIL, the dusty, common ground, with creatures that are somehow like their God. But there is more. The Potter becomes the clay, Incarnate Love. Full of grace and truth, the Vessel will be broken, hallowing forever all brokenness, holding forth the promise of all newness, becoming in us the recreating energy of God.

GENESIS 2:7

וַיִּיצֶר יְהוָה אֱלֹהִים אֶת־הָאָדָם עָפָר מִן־הָאֲדָמָה וַיִּפַּח
בְּאַפָּיו נִשְׁמַת חַיִּים וַיְהִי הָאָדָם לְנֶפֶשׁ חַיָּה:

וַיִּיצֶר v.c. + v.3.m.s.impf.Q. [יצר]; וַיִּפַּח v.c. + v.3.m.s.impf.Q. [נפח] (blow); נִשְׁמַת (breath); וַיְהִי v.c. + v.3.m.s.impf.Q. [היה]

JOHN 1:14, 16

¹⁴Καὶ ὁ λόγος σὰρξ ἐγένετο καὶ ἐσκήνωσεν ἐν ἡμῖν, καὶ ἐθεασάμεθα τὴν δόξαν αὐτοῦ, δόξαν ὡς μονογενοῦς παρὰ πατρός, πλήρης χάριτος καὶ ἀληθείας. ¹⁶ὅτι ἐκ τοῦ πληρώματος αὐτοῦ ἡμεῖς πάντες ἐλάβομεν καὶ χάριν ἀντὶ χάριτος·

ἐγένετο v.3.s.aor.mid.ind. [γίνομαι]; ἐσκήνωσεν (live); ἐθεασάμεθα v.1.p.aor.mid.ind. [θεάομαι] (see); μονογενοῦς (only); πλήρης (full); πληρώματος (fullness); ἐλάβομεν v.1.p.aor.ind.act. [λαμβάνω]; ἀντὶ (instead of)

3. Genesis 12:2-3; Hebrews 11:8, 12

Holy Dreams

I SCARCELY CAN IMAGINE the dreams God has for me. Or for my life. Or for my world. But with all my heart I want my life to be a resounding "Yes!"

GENESIS 12:2-3

²וְאֶעֶשְׂךָ לְגוֹי גָּדוֹל וַאֲבָרֶכְךָ וַאֲגַדְּלָה שְׁמֶךָ וֶהְיֵה בְּרָכָה:
³וַאֲבָרֲכָה מְבָרְכֶיךָ וּמְקַלֶּלְךָ אָאֹר וְנִבְרְכוּ בְךָ כֹּל מִשְׁפְּחֹת הָאֲדָמָה:

וְאֶעֶשְׂךָ cj. + v.1.com.s.impf.Q. [עשׂה] + 2.m.s.pr.sf.; וַאֲבָרֶכְךָ cj. + v.1.com.s.impf.P. [ברך] + 2.m.s.pr.sf.; וַאֲגַדְּלָה cj. + v.1.com.s.coh.P. [גדל]; וֶהְיֵה cj. + v.2.m.s.impv.Q. [היה]; אָאֹר v.1.com.s.impf.Q. [ארר]

HEBREWS 11:8, 12

⁸Πίστει καλούμενος Ἀβραὰμ ὑπήκουσεν ἐξελθεῖν εἰς τόπον ὃν ἤμελλεν λαμβάνειν εἰς κληρονομίαν, καὶ ἐξῆλθεν μὴ ἐπιστάμενος ποῦ ἔρχεται. ¹²διὸ καὶ ἀφ' ἑνὸς ἐγεννήθησαν, καὶ ταῦτα νενεκρωμένου, καθὼς τὰ ἄστρα τοῦ οὐρανοῦ τῷ πλήθει καὶ ὡς ἡ ἄμμος ἡ παρὰ τὸ χεῖλος τῆς θαλάσσης ἡ ἀναρίθμητος.

ὑπήκουσεν v.3.s.aor.act.ind. [ὑπακούω] (obey); ἤμελλεν 3.s.impf.act.ind. Attic [μέλλω]; κληρονομίαν (inheritance); ἐξῆλθεν v.3.s.aor.act.ind. [ἐξ-έρχομαι]; ἐπιστάμενος (know); νενεκρωμένου (worn out); ἄστρα (star); ἄμμος (sand); χεῖλος (shore)

15

4. Deuteronomy 26:18–19; 1 Peter 2:9–10

Living Words

LET US BE YOUR SACRED WORDS in our desperate, needy world.
Let us be your covenant of love. Let us be your mercy, Holy God.

DEUTERONOMY 26:18–19

¹⁸וַיהוָה הֶאֱמִירְךָ הַיּוֹם לִהְיוֹת לוֹ לְעַם סְגֻלָּה כַּאֲשֶׁר דִּבֶּר־
לָךְ וְלִשְׁמֹר כָּל־מִצְוֹתָיו:
¹⁹וּלְתִתְּךָ עֶלְיוֹן עַל כָּל־הַגּוֹיִם אֲשֶׁר עָשָׂה לִתְהִלָּה וּלְשֵׁם
וּלְתִפְאָרֶת וְלִהְיֹתְךָ עַם־קָדֹשׁ לַיהוָה אֱלֹהֶיךָ כַּאֲשֶׁר דִּבֵּר

סְגֻלָּה [הָיָה]; הֶאֱמִירְךָ v.3.m.s.pf.H. [אמר] + 2.m.s.pr.sf.; לִהְיוֹת prep.+in.cs.Q. [הָיָה];
(possession); וּלְתִתְּךָ cj. + prep. + v.in.cst.Q. [נתן] + 2.m.s.pr.sf.; וּלְתִפְאָרֶת
(glory); וְלִהְיֹתְךָ cj. + prep. + v.in.cst.Q. [היה] + 2.m.s.pr.sf.

1 PETER 2:9–10

⁹Ὑμεῖς δὲ γένος ἐκλεκτόν, βασίλειον ἱεράτευμα, ἔθνος ἅγιον,
λαὸς εἰς περιποίησιν, ὅπως τὰς ἀρετὰς ἐξαγγείλητε τοῦ ἐκ
σκότους ὑμᾶς καλέσαντος εἰς τὸ θαυμαστὸν αὐτοῦ φῶς·
¹⁰οἵ ποτε οὐ λαὸς
νῦν δὲ λαὸς θεοῦ,
οἱ οὐκ ἠλεημένοι
νῦν δὲ ἐλεηθέντες.

γένος (race); ἐκλεκτόν (chosen); βασίλειον (royal); ἱεράτευμα (priesthood); περιποίησιν (property); ἀρετὰς (virtue); ἐξαγγείλητε (report); σκότους (darkness); θαυμαστὸν (wonderful); ποτε (once); νῦν (now);
ἠλεημένοι v.m.p.nom.pf.pass.ptc. [ἐλεέω] (be shown mercy); ἐλεηθέντες
v.m.p.nom.aor.pass.ptc. [ἐλεέω]

5. Deuteronomy 8:3; John 14:21

The Beginnings of the Law

THE MOTIVE BEHIND THE LAW was life and love. But we forget. Rules, rules, rules . . . punishment, rewards . . . observing all the protocol of God. That's what we think about the Law. But Jesus doesn't think that way at all. "I can tell you really love me," he whispers, "because you live as if everything I tell you is the truth."

DEUTERONOMY 8:3

³וַיְעַנְּךָ וַיַּרְעִבֶךָ וַיַּאֲכִלְךָ אֶת־הַמָּן אֲשֶׁר לֹא־יָדַעְתָּ
וְלֹא יָדְעוּן אֲבֹתֶיךָ לְמַעַן הוֹדִעֲךָ כִּי לֹא עַל־הַלֶּחֶם לְבַדּוֹ יִחְיֶה
הָאָדָם כִּי עַל־כָּל־מוֹצָא פִי־יְהוָה יִחְיֶה הָאָדָם:

וַיְעַנְּךָ v.c. + v.3.m.s.impf.P. [ענה] + 2.m.s.pr.sf.; וַיַּרְעִבֶךָ v.c. + v.3.m.s.impf.H. [רעב] (cause hunger) + 2.m.s.pr.sf.; וַיַּאֲכִלְךָ v.c. + v.3.m.s.impf.H. [אכל] + 2.m.s.pr.sf.; הַמָּן (manna); יָדְעוּן v.3.c.p.pf.Q. [ידע] + para.; הוֹדִעֲךָ v.3.m.s.pf.H. [ידע] + 2.m.s.pr.sf.; מוֹצָא (utterance)

JOHN 14:21

²¹ὁ ἔχων τὰς ἐντολάς μου καὶ τηρῶν αὐτὰς ἐκεῖνος ἐστιν ὁ ἀγαπῶν με· ὁ δὲ ἀγαπῶν με ἀγαπηθήσεται ὑπὸ τοῦ πατρός μου, κἀγὼ ἀγαπήσω αὐτὸν καὶ ἐμφανίσω αὐτῷ ἐμαυτόν.

ἐστιν v.3.s.pres.ind. [εἰμί]; ἐμφανίσω (reveal); ἐμαυτόν (myself)

6. Isaiah 53:12; Ephesians 2:4–7

Where Healing Begins

YOUR GREAT, WOUNDED HEART BLEEDS the pain of all creation. O Jesus, in your pain my pain is healed. Your crucified love makes me whole.

ISAIAH 53:12

¹²לָכֵן אֲחַלֶּק־לוֹ בָרַבִּים וְאֶת־עֲצוּמִים יְחַלֵּק שָׁלָל תַּחַת אֲשֶׁר הֶעֱרָה לַמָּוֶת נַפְשׁוֹ וְאֶת־פֹּשְׁעִים נִמְנָה וְהוּא חֵטְא־רַבִּים נָשָׂא וְלַפֹּשְׁעִים יַפְגִּיעַ:

עֲצוּמִים (mighty); הֶעֱרָה v.3.m.s.pf.H. [ערה] (pour out); פֹּשְׁעִים (rebel); נִמְנָה (reckon); יַפְגִּיעַ: (intercede)

EPHESIANS 2:4–7

⁴ὁ δὲ θεὸς πλούσιος ὢν ἐν ἐλέει, διὰ τὴν πολλὴν ἀγάπην αὐτοῦ ἣν ἠγάπησεν ἡμᾶς, ⁵καὶ ὄντας ἡμᾶς νεκροὺς τοῖς παραπτώμασιν συνεζωοποίησεν τῷ Χριστῷ,—χάριτι ἐστε σεσωσμένοι—⁶καὶ συνήγειρεν καὶ συνεκάθισεν ἐν τοῖς ἐπουρανίοις ἐν Χριστῷ Ἰησοῦ, ⁷ἵνα ἐνδείξηται ἐν τοῖς αἰῶσιν τοῖς ἐπερχομένοις τὸ ὑπερβάλλον πλοῦτος τῆς χάριτος αὐτοῦ ἐν χρηστότητι ἐφ᾽ ἡμᾶς ἐν Χριστῷ Ἰησοῦ.

πλούσιος (rich); ἐλέει n.nt.s.dat. (mercy); παραπτώμασιν (sin); συνεζωοποίησεν v.3.s.aor.act.ind. [συζωοποιέω] (make live together); σεσωσμένοι v.m.p.nom.pf.pass.ptc. [σῴζω]; συνήγειρεν (raise together); συνεκάθισεν v.3.s.aor.act.ind. [συγκαθίζω] (make sit together); ἐνδείξηται (show); ἐπερχομένοις (approach); ὑπερβάλλον (surpassing); πλοῦτος (riches); χρηστότητι n.f.s.dat. (kindness)

7. Jeremiah 29:11–14a; Revelation 22:17

Now Is the Time to Begin

GRACE IS THE WOMB of every true beginning. "Come and find me!" calls the Seeker. "Come and drink!" invites the One who creates thirst. "Come, let us start afresh, this day, this very hour!" beckons the God of our beginnings.

JEREMIAH 29:11–14A

‏¹¹כִּי אָנֹכִי יָדַעְתִּי אֶת־הַמַּחֲשָׁבֹת אֲשֶׁר אָנֹכִי חֹשֵׁב עֲלֵיכֶם נְאֻם־
יְהוָה מַחְשְׁבוֹת שָׁלוֹם וְלֹא לְרָעָה לָתֵת לָכֶם אַחֲרִית וְתִקְוָה:
¹²וּקְרָאתֶם אֹתִי וַהֲלַכְתֶּם וְהִתְפַּלַּלְתֶּם אֵלָי וְשָׁמַעְתִּי אֲלֵיכֶם:
¹³וּבִקַּשְׁתֶּם אֹתִי וּמְצָאתֶם כִּי תִדְרְשֻׁנִי בְּכָל־לְבַבְכֶם:
¹⁴וְנִמְצֵאתִי לָכֶם נְאֻם־יְהוָה

לָתֵת prep. + v.in.cs.Q. [נתן]

REVELATION 22:17

¹⁷Καὶ τὸ πνεῦμα καὶ ἡ νύμφη λέγουσιν· Ἔρχου. καὶ ὁ ἀκούων εἰπάτω· Ἔρχου. καὶ ὁ διψῶν ἐρχέσθω, ὁ θέλων λαβέτω ὕδωρ ζωῆς δωρεάν.

νύμφη (bride); διψῶν (thirst); δωρεάν (as a gift)

19

Week 2

Epiphany

1. Genesis 49:10; Matthew 2:1–2

Kneeling at the Manger

IT IS VERY EASY FOR US TO KNEEL before the throne, but not so easy to kneel before the manger. What is our response to those around us who are weak, helpless, defenseless, dependent on others for their lives? Unless we kneel before the manger, we do not kneel before the throne.

GENESIS 49:10

לֹא־יָסוּר שֵׁבֶט מִיהוּדָה וּמְחֹקֵק מִבֵּין רַגְלָיו עַד כִּי־יָבֹא שִׁילֹה ¹⁰
וְלוֹ יִקְּהַת עַמִּים׃

וּמְחֹקֵק (ruler); יָבֹא v.3.m.s. impf.Q. [בוא]; שִׁילֹה PN./rel.pt. + 3.m.s.pr.sf. (Shiloh/that which is his); יִקְּהַת (obedience)

MATTHEW 2:1–2

¹Τοῦ δὲ Ἰησοῦ γεννηθέντος ἐν Βηθλέεμ τῆς Ἰουδαίας ἐν ἡμέραις Ἡρῴδου τοῦ βασιλέως, ἰδοὺ μάγοι ἀπὸ ἀνατολῶν παρεγένοντο εἰς Ἱεροσόλυμα ²λέγοντες, Ποῦ ἐστιν ὁ τεχθεὶς βασιλεὺς τῶν Ἰουδαίων; εἴδομεν γὰρ αὐτοῦ τὸν ἀστέρα ἐν τῇ ἀνατολῇ καὶ ἤλθομεν προσκυνῆσαι αὐτῷ.

μάγοι (wise men); ἀνατολῶν (east); παρεγένοντο (arrive); Ποῦ (where); ἐστιν v.3.s.pres.ind. [εἰμί]; τεχθεὶς v.m.s.nom.pass.ptc.aor. [τίκτω] (give birth to); εἴδομεν v.1.p.aor.act.ind. [ὁράω]; ἀστέρα (star)

2. 1 Samuel 16:1; Matthew 2:4–6

House of Bread

FROM THE "HOUSE OF BREAD" came the Bread of Life. May I, too, be a "house of bread," one who nourishes hungry pilgrims, one who gives to them the Bread of Life.

1 SAMUEL 16:1

¹וַיֹּאמֶר יְהוָה אֶל־שְׁמוּאֵל עַד־מָתַי אַתָּה מִתְאַבֵּל אֶל־שָׁאוּל וַאֲנִי
מְאַסְתִּיו מִמְּלֹךְ עַל־יִשְׂרָאֵל מַלֵּא קַרְנְךָ שֶׁמֶן וְלֵךְ אֶשְׁלָחֲךָ
אֶל־יִשַׁי בֵּית־הַלַּחְמִי כִּי־רָאִיתִי בְּבָנָיו לִי מֶלֶךְ׃

מִמְּלֹךְ prep. + 3.m.s.pr.sf.; [מאס] v.1.com.s.pf.Q. מְאַסְתִּיו (mourn); מִתְאַבֵּל
[ראה] v.1.c.s.pf. רָאִיתִי ;[הלך] v.2.m.s.impv.Q. + cj. וְלֵךְ; [מלך] ;[מלך] + v.in.cs.Q.

MATTHEW 2:4–6

⁴καὶ συναγαγὼν πάντας τοὺς ἀρχιερεῖς καὶ γραμματεῖς τοῦ
λαοῦ ἐπυνθάνετο παρ᾽ αὐτῶν ποῦ ὁ Χριστὸς γεννᾶται. ⁵οἱ δὲ
εἶπαν αὐτῷ, Ἐν Βηθλέεμ τῆς Ἰουδαίας· οὕτως γὰρ γέγραπται
διὰ τοῦ προφήτου·
    ⁶καὶ σὺ Βηθλέεμ, γῆ Ἰούδα,
        οὐδαμῶς ἐλαχίστη εἶ ἐν τοῖς ἡγεμόσιν
          Ἰούδα·
    ἐκ σοῦ γὰρ ἐξελεύσεται ἡγούμενος,
        ὅστις ποιμανεῖ τὸν λαόν μου τὸν Ἰσραήλ.

ἐπυνθάνετο (ask); ποῦ (where); εἶπαν v.3.p.aor.act.ind. [λέγω]; οὐδαμῶς
(in no way); ἐλαχίστη (least); ἡγεμόσιν (ruler); ποιμανεῖ (rule)

3. Isaiah 42:1; Mark 1:9–10

The Water of the Spirit

JESUS HAD TO BE FILLED with the Holy Spirit. If this was necessary for the very Son of God for him to carry out his ministry, can it be any less the case for us? There is no ministry apart from the washing, cleansing, overflowing Water of the Spirit.

ISAIAH 42:1

¹הֵן עַבְדִּי אֶתְמָךְ־בּוֹ בְּחִירִי רָצְתָה נַפְשִׁי נָתַתִּי רוּחִי עָלָיו מִשְׁפָּט
לַגּוֹיִם יוֹצִיא׃

אֶתְמָךְ v.1.com.s.impf.Q. [תמך] (grasp) with loss of accent; בְּחִירִי (chosen one); רָצְתָה v.3.f.s.pf.Q. [רצה]; נָתַתִּי v.1.com.s.pf.Q. [נתן]; יוֹצִיא v.3.m.s.impf.H. [יצא]

MARK 1:9–10

⁹Καὶ ἐγένετο ἐν ἐκείναις ταῖς ἡμέραις ἦλθεν Ἰησοῦς ἀπὸ Ναζαρὲτ τῆς Γαλιλαίας καὶ ἐβαπτίσθη εἰς τὸν Ἰορδάνην ὑπὸ Ἰωάννου. ¹⁰καὶ εὐθὺς ἀναβαίνων ἐκ τοῦ ὕδατος εἶδεν σχιζομένους τοὺς οὐρανοὺς καὶ τὸ πνεῦμα ὡς περιστερὰν καταβαῖνον εἰς αὐτόν·

ἐγένετο v.3.s.aor.mid.ind. [γίνομαι]; ἦλθεν v.3.s.aor.act.ind. [ἔρχομαι]; εἶδεν v.3.s.aor.act.ind. [ὁράω]; σχιζομένους (divide); περιστερὰν (dove)

4. Micah 4.1–2, John 6.45

Let All Things Be My Teachers

TEACH ME WHO YOU ARE, O Lord, through the simple and the mundane events of my life, through the painful and the impossible, the confusing and the exhausting, the surprising and the predictable. Let all things be my teachers, that I might know and love you more. Amen.

MICAH 4:1–2

¹וְהָיָה בְּאַחֲרִית הַיָּמִים יִהְיֶה הַר בֵּית־יְהוָה נָכוֹן בְּרֹאשׁ הֶהָרִים
וְנִשָּׂא הוּא מִגְּבָעוֹת וְנָהֲרוּ עָלָיו עַמִּים:
²וְהָלְכוּ גּוֹיִם רַבִּים וְאָמְרוּ לְכוּ וְנַעֲלֶה אֶל־הַר־יְהוָה וְאֶל־
בֵּית אֱלֹהֵי יַעֲקֹב וְיֹרֵנוּ מִדְּרָכָיו וְנֵלְכָה בְּאֹרְחֹתָיו כִּי
מִצִּיּוֹן תֵּצֵא תוֹרָה וּדְבַר־יְהוָה מִירוּשָׁלָם:

לְכוּ (flow); וְנָהֲרוּ [נשא] cj. + v.m.s.ptc.N.; נִשָּׂא [כון]; נָכוֹן v.m.s.ptc.N.
וְנֵלְכָה [ירה] + 3.m.s.pr.sf.; וְיֹרֵנוּ cj. + v.m.s.impf.H. [הלך]; v.2.m.p.impv.Q.
cj. + v.1.com.p.coh.Q. [הלך]; תֵּצֵא v.3.f.s.impf.Q. [יצא]

JOHN 6:45

⁴⁵ἔστιν γεγραμμένον ἐν τοῖς προφήταις· Καὶ ἔσονται πάντες διδακτοὶ θεοῦ· πᾶς ὁ ἀκούσας παρὰ τοῦ πατρὸς καὶ μαθὼν ἔρχεται πρὸς ἐμέ.

ἔστιν v.3.s.pres.ind. [εἰμί]; διδακτοὶ (taught); μαθὼν v.m.s.nom.aor.act.ptc. [μανθάνω] (learn)

23

5. Isaiah 60:1–3; Ephesians 5:14

The Time to Sing

THE TIME TO ARISE AND SHINE, to sing the beauty of God is while it is yet dark, while the air is thick with unbelief.

ISAIAH 60:1–3

¹ק֣וּמִי א֔וֹרִי כִּ֥י בָ֖א אוֹרֵ֑ךְ וּכְב֥וֹד יְהוָ֖ה עָלַ֥יִךְ זָרָֽח׃

²כִּֽי־הִנֵּ֤ה הַחֹ֨שֶׁךְ֙ יְכַסֶּה־אֶ֔רֶץ וַעֲרָפֶ֖ל לְאֻמִּ֑ים וְעָלַ֨יִךְ֙ יִזְרַ֣ח יְהוָ֔ה וּכְבוֹד֖וֹ עָלַ֥יִךְ יֵרָאֶֽה׃

³וְהָלְכ֥וּ גוֹיִ֖ם לְאוֹרֵ֑ךְ וּמְלָכִ֖ים לְנֹ֥גַהּ זַרְחֵֽךְ׃

ק֣וּמִי v.2.f.s.impv.Q. [קום]; א֔וֹרִי v.2.f.s.impv.Q. [אור] (shine); בָ֖א v.3.m.s.pf.Q. [בוא]; זָרָֽח (shine forth); וַעֲרָפֶ֖ל (darkness); לְאֻמִּ֑ים (nation); לְנֹ֥גַהּ (brightness); זַרְחֵֽךְ (shining)

EPHESIANS 5:14

¹⁴πᾶν γὰρ τὸ φανερούμενον φῶς ἐστιν. διὸ λέγει,
Ἔγειρε, ὁ καθεύδων,
  καὶ ἀνάστα ἐκ τῶν νεκρῶν,
καὶ ἐπιφαύσει σοι ὁ Χριστός.

ἐστιν v.3.s.pres.ind. [εἰμί]; καθεύδων (sheep); ἐπιφαύσει (shine)

6. Psalm 45:7–8, 10 [6–7, 9]; Hebrews 1:8

Absolute Rule

ONLY CHRIST CAN RULE with absolute authority and exact absolute obedience, without once violating his subjects. The rule of Christ is utterly "other" than any rulership we know. The closest analogy we have is the rulership of love over a man's and a woman's hearts, causing them to subsume all else to love's demands. It is a flawed analogy but a good one, nonetheless.

PSALM 45:7–8, 10 [6–7, 9]

⁷כִּסְאֲךָ אֱלֹהִים עוֹלָם וָעֶד שֵׁבֶט מִישֹׁר שֵׁבֶט מַלְכוּתֶךָ:
⁸אָהַבְתָּ צֶּדֶק וַתִּשְׂנָא רֶשַׁע עַל־כֵּן מְשָׁחֲךָ אֱלֹהִים אֱלֹהֶיךָ שֶׁמֶן שָׂשׂוֹן מֵחֲבֵרֶיךָ:
¹⁰בְּנוֹת מְלָכִים בְּיִקְּרוֹתֶיךָ נִצְּבָה שֵׁגַל לִימִינְךָ בְּכֶתֶם אוֹפִיר:

מִישֹׁר (uprightness); מְשָׁחֲךָ v.3.m.s.pf.Q. [משׁח] + 2.m.s.pr.sf.; שָׂשׂוֹן (joy); מֵחֲבֵרֶיךָ (companion); בְּיִקְּרוֹתֶיךָ prep. + adj.f.p. (precious) + 2.m.s.pr.sf.; נִצְּבָה v.3.f.s.ptc.N. [נצב]; שֵׁגַל n.f.s. (favorite wife); בְּכֶתֶם (finest gold); אוֹפִיר (Ophir)

HEBREWS 1:8

⁸πρὸς δὲ τὸν υἱόν,
ὁ θρόνος σου ὁ θεὸς εἰς τὸν αἰῶνα τοῦ
αἰῶνος,
καὶ ἡ ῥάβδος τῆς εὐθύτητος ῥάβδος τῆς
βασιλείας σου.

ῥάβδος (staff); εὐθύτητος (righteousness)

7. Psalm 67:5–8 [4–7]; Matthew 2:10–11a

Laying My Treasures at Your Feet

PERHAPS I DO NOT HAVE GOLD, frankincense, and myrrh, Jesus, but I do have treasures I want to give to you. They are the treasures of my time, my relationships, and my suffering. I do give them to you. This is my worship.

PSALM 67:5–8 [4–7]

⁵יִשְׂמְחוּ וִירַנְּנוּ לְאֻמִּים כִּי־תִשְׁפֹּט עַמִּים מִישׁוֹר וּלְאֻמִּים
בָּאָרֶץ תַּנְחֵם סֶלָה׃
⁶יוֹדוּךָ עַמִּים אֱלֹהִים יוֹדוּךָ עַמִּים כֻּלָּם׃
⁷אֶרֶץ נָתְנָה יְבוּלָהּ יְבָרְכֵנוּ אֱלֹהִים אֱלֹהֵינוּ׃
⁸יְבָרְכֵנוּ אֱלֹהִים וְיִירְאוּ אֹתוֹ כָּל־אַפְסֵי־אָרֶץ׃

וִירַנְּנוּ cj. + v.3.m.p.impf.P. [רנן]; לְאֻמִּים (nation); מִישׁוֹר (uprightness); תַּנְחֵם v.2.m.s.impf.H. [נחה] + 3.m.p.pr.sf.; יוֹדוּךָ v.3.m.p.impf.H. [ידה] + 2.m.s.pr.sf.; יְבָרְכֵנוּ v.3.m.s.impf.P. [ברך] + 1.com.p.pr.sf.; יְבוּלָהּ (produce); וְיִירְאוּ cj. + v.3.m.p.impf.Q. [ירא]; אַפְסֵי (end)

MATTHEW 2:10–11A

¹⁰ἰδόντες δὲ τὸν ἀστέρα ἐχάρησαν χαρὰν μεγάλην σφόδρα. ¹¹καὶ ἐλθόντες εἰς τὴν οἰκίαν εἶδον τὸ παιδίον μετὰ Μαρίας τῆς μητρὸς αὐτοῦ, καὶ πεσόντες προσεκύνησαν αὐτῷ

ἰδόντες v.m.p.nom.aor.act.ptc. [ὁράω]; ἀστέρα (star); σφόδρα (very much); εἶδον v.1.s.aor.act.ind. [ὁράω]; προσεκύνησαν (revere)

Week 3

Joy

1. Psalm 16:11; Acts 2:25–28

You Are My Joy

YOUR PRESENCE IS MY JOY; your face, my delight. When life gets hellish and my heart is crushed with grief, just a glance into your eyes is enough. You are my joy, my God.

PSALM 16:11

‎¹¹תּוֹדִיעֵנִי אֹרַח חַיִּים שֹׂבַע שְׂמָחוֹת אֶת־פָּנֶיךָ נְעִמוֹת בִּימִינְךָ
‎נֶצַח׃

‎תּוֹדִיעֵנִי v.2.m.s.impf.H. [‎ידע] + 1.com.s.pr.sf.; ‎שֹׂבַע n.m.s.cs. (abundance); ‎נְעִמוֹת (pleasant); ‎נֶצַח (forever)

ACTS 2:25–28

²⁵Δαυὶδ γὰρ λέγει εἰς αὐτόν,
Προορώμην τὸν κύριον ἐνώπιόν μου διὰ παντός,
ὅτι ἐκ δεξιῶν μού ἐστιν ἵνα μὴ σαλευθῶ.
²⁶διὰ τοῦτο ηὐφράνθη ἡ καρδία μου καὶ ἠγαλλιάσατο
ἡ γλῶσσά μου,
ἔτι δὲ καὶ ἡ σάρξ μου κατασκηνώσει ἐπ᾽ ἐλπίδι,
²⁷ὅτι οὐκ ἐγκαταλείψεις τὴν ψυχήν μου εἰς ᾅδην
οὐδὲ δώσεις τὸν ὅσιόν σου ἰδεῖν διαφθοράν.
²⁸ἐγνώρισάς μοι ὁδοὺς ζωῆς,
πληρώσεις με εὐφροσύνης μετὰ τοῦ
προσώπου σου.

Προορώμην (foresee); ἐνώπιον (before); ἐστιν v.3.s.pres.ind. [εἰμί]; σαλευθῶ (move); ηὐφράνθη v.3.s.aor.pass.ind. [εὐφραίνω] (be glad); ἠγαλλιάσατο (be glad); κατασκηνώσει (live); ἐγκαταλείψεις (leave); ᾅδην (Hades); ὅσιόν (pious); ἰδεῖν v.aor.act.in. [ὁράω]; διαφθοράν (corruption); ἐγνώρισας (reveal); εὐφροσύνης n.f.s.gen. (joy)

27

2. 1 Chronicles 16:31–33; Luke 2:10–11

Good News, God News!

HEAVEN AND EARTH EXPLODE with joy—good news, God news!
Angels sing what every heart will know: our God reigns!

1 CHRONICLES 16:31–33

³¹יִשְׂמְחוּ הַשָּׁמַיִם וְתָגֵל הָאָרֶץ וְיֹאמְרוּ בַגּוֹיִם יְהוָה מָלָךְ׃
³²יִרְעַם הַיָּם וּמְלֹאוֹ יַעֲלֹץ הַשָּׂדֶה וְכָל־אֲשֶׁר־בּוֹ׃
³³אָז יְרַנְּנוּ עֲצֵי הַיָּעַר מִלִּפְנֵי יְהוָה כִּי־בָא לִשְׁפּוֹט אֶת־הָאָרֶץ׃

וְתָגֵל cj. + v.3.f.s.impf.Q. [גיל] (rejoice); יִרְעַם (storm); וּמְלֹאוֹ (fullness);
יַעֲלֹץ (exult); בָא v.ptc.m.s.Q. [בוא]

LUKE 2:10–11

¹⁰καὶ εἶπεν αὐτοῖς ὁ ἄγγελος, Μὴ φοβεῖσθε, ἰδοὺ γὰρ
εὐαγγελίζομαι ὑμῖν χαρὰν μεγάλην ἥτις ἔσται παντὶ τῷ λαῷ,
¹¹ὅτι ἐτέχθη ὑμῖν σήμερον σωτὴρ ὅς ἐστιν Χριστὸς κύριος ἐν
πόλει Δαυίδ.

εἶπεν v.3.s.aor.act.ind. [λέγω]; ἔσται v.3.s.fut.ind. [εἰμί]; ἐτέχθη
v.3.s.aor.pass.ind. [τίκτω] (bear); σήμερον (today); σωτήρ (savior); ἐστιν
v.3.s.pres.ind. [εἰμί]

3. Job 33:24–26; Jude 21–25

Joy in Things Made New

THOUGH WE ARE OFTEN BEWILDERED by the Job-like sufferings of life, your will, O God, is to make all things new. Who but our God could remove our blemishes and keep us on the path? For all these things we find joy in you, God of our salvation!

JOB 33:24–26

‎²⁴וַיְחֻנֶּנּוּ וַיֹּאמֶר פְּדָעֵהוּ מֵרֶדֶת שָׁחַת מָצָאתִי כֹפֶר׃
‎²⁵רֻטֲפַשׁ בְּשָׂרוֹ מִנֹּעַר יָשׁוּב לִימֵי עֲלוּמָיו׃
‎²⁶יֶעְתַּר אֶל־אֱלוֹהַּ וַיִּרְצֵהוּ וַיַּרְא פָּנָיו בִּתְרוּעָה וַיָּשֶׁב לֶאֱנוֹשׁ צִדְקָתוֹ׃

[פדע] וַיְחֻנֶּנּוּ v.c. + v.3.m.s.impf.Q. [חנן] +3.m.s.pr.sf.; פְּדָעֵהוּ v.2.m.s.impv.Q. (rescue) + 3.m.s.pr.sf.; מֵרֶדֶת prep. + v.in.cs.Q. [ירד]; שָׁחַת (grave); כֹפֶר (ransom); רֻטֲפַשׁ v.3.m.s.pf.Pu. [רטפש] (refresh); מִנֹּעַר (youth); עֲלוּמָיו (youth); יֶעְתַּר v.3.m.s.impf.Q. [עתר] (pray); וַיִּרְצֵהוּ v.c. + v.3.m.s.impf.Q. [רצה] + 3.m.s.pr.sf.; וַיַּרְא v.c. + v.3.m.s.impf.Q. [ראה]; בִּתְרוּעָה (noise); וַיָּשֶׁב v.c. + v.3.m.s.impf.H. [שוב]

JUDE 24–25

²⁴Τῷ δὲ δυναμένῳ φυλάξαι ὑμᾶς ἀπταίστους καὶ στῆσαι κατενώπιον τῆς δόξης αὐτοῦ ἀμώμους ἐν ἀγαλλιάσει, ²⁵μόνῳ θεῷ σωτῆρι ἡμῶν διὰ Ἰησοῦ Χριστοῦ τοῦ κυρίου ἡμῶν δόξα μεγαλωσύνη κράτος καὶ ἐξουσία πρὸ παντὸς τοῦ αἰῶνος καὶ νῦν καὶ εἰς πάντας τοὺς αἰῶνας, ἀμήν.

φυλάξαι (guard); ἀπταίστους (without stumbling); κατενώπιον (in the presence of); ἀμώμους (blameless); ἀγαλλιάσει (joy); μόνῳ (only); σωτῆρι (savior); μεγαλωσύνη (majesty); κράτος (strength); πρὸ (before); νῦν (now)

4. 1 Chronicles 16:25–27; Revelation 15:3–4

No More Idols

Joy, TRUE JOY, IS BORN when idols are abandoned and when God, true God, becomes our only God.

1 CHRONICLES 16:25–27

²⁵כִּי גָדוֹל יְהוָה וּמְהֻלָּל מְאֹד וְנוֹרָא הוּא עַל־כָּל־אֱלֹהִים:
²⁶כִּי כָּל־אֱלֹהֵי הָעַמִּים אֱלִילִים וַיהוָה שָׁמַיִם עָשָׂה:
²⁷הוֹד וְהָדָר לְפָנָיו עֹז וְחֶדְוָה בִּמְקֹמוֹ:

וְנוֹרָא cj. + m.s.ptc.N. [ירא]; אֱלִילִים (idol); הוֹד (splendor); וְהָדָר (majesty)

REVELATION 15:3–4

³καὶ ᾄδουσιν τὴν ᾠδὴν Μωϋσέως τοῦ δούλου τοῦ θεοῦ καὶ τὴν ᾠδὴν τοῦ ἀρνίου λέγοντες·
    Μεγάλα καὶ θαυμαστὰ τὰ ἔργα σου,
        κύριε ὁ θεὸς ὁ παντοκράτωρ·
    δίκαιαι καὶ ἀληθιναὶ αἱ ὁδοί σου,
        ὁ βασιλεὺς τῶν ἐθνῶν·
⁴τίς οὐ μὴ φοβηθῇ, κύριε,
    καὶ δοξάσει τὸ ὄνομά σου;
ὅτι μόνος ὅσιος,
    ὅτι πάντα τὰ ἔθνη ἥξουσιν
    καὶ προσκυνήσουσιν ἐνώπιόν σου,
ὅτι τὰ δικαιώματά σου ἐφανερώθησαν.

ᾄδουσιν (sing); ᾠδήν (song); ἀρνίου (lamb); θαυμαστὰ (marvelous); παντοκράτωρ (almighty); ἀληθιναι (true); μόνος (alone); ὅσιος (holy); ἥξουσιν v.3.p.fut.act.ind. [ἥκω]; ἐνώπιόν (before); δικαιώματά (righteous deed); ἐφανερώθησαν 3.p.aor.pass.ind. [φανερόω] (show)

5. Psalm 43:4–5; Ephesians 3:16–19

With Pockets Full of Treasure

LIKE SOME GREAT FACTORY filled with grease and noise, and clocks that must be punched, and endless repetitious tasks, my life grows weary, Lord. Come into the grimy clatter with pockets full of treasures. Tell me your story once again. Come, renew my joy.

PSALM 43:4–5

⁴וְאָב֨וֹאָה ׀ אֶל־מִזְבַּ֬ח אֱלֹהִים֮ אֶל־אֵל֮ שִׂמְחַ֪ת גִּ֫ילִ֥י וְאוֹדְךָ֥ בְכִנּ֑וֹר
אֱלֹהִ֥ים אֱלֹהָֽי׃
⁵מַה־תִּשְׁתּ֬וֹחֲחִ֨י ׀ נַפְשִׁי֮ וּמַה־תֶּהֱמִ֪י עָ֫לָ֥י הוֹחִ֣ילִי לֵֽ֭אלֹהִים כִּי־
ע֣וֹד אוֹדֶ֑נּוּ יְשׁוּעֹ֥ת פָּנַ֗י וֵֽאלֹהָֽי׃

וְאָב֨וֹאָה cj. + v.1.com.s.coh.Q. [בוא]; גִּילִי (rejoicing); וְאוֹדְךָ cj. + v.1.com.s.coh.Q. [ידה] + 2.m.s.pr.sf.; בְכִנּוֹר (harp); תִּשְׁתּוֹחֲחִי v.2.f.s.impf.Hitpoal [שחח] (be depressed); תֶּהֱמִי v.2.f.s.impf.Q. [המה] (make noise); הוֹחִילִי v.2.f.s.impv.H. [יחל] (wait); אוֹדֶנּוּ v.1.com.s. impf.H. [ידה] + en. + 3.m.s.pr.sf.

EPHESIANS 3:16–19

¹⁶ἵνα δῷ ὑμῖν κατὰ τὸ πλοῦτος τῆς δόξης αὐτοῦ δυνάμει κραταιωθῆναι διὰ τοῦ πνεύματος αὐτοῦ εἰς τὸν ἔσω ἄνθρωπον, ¹⁷ κατοικῆσαι τὸν Χριστὸν διὰ τῆς πίστεως ἐν ταῖς καρδίαις ὑμῶν, ἐν ἀγάπῃ ἐρριζωμένοι καὶ τεθεμελιωμένοι, ¹⁸ἵνα ἐξισχύσητε καταλαβέσθαι σὺν πᾶσιν τοῖς ἁγίοις τί τὸ πλάτος καὶ μῆκος καὶ ὕψος καὶ βάθος, ¹⁹γνῶναί τε τὴν ὑπερβάλλουσαν τῆς γνώσεως ἀγάπην τοῦ Χριστοῦ, ἵνα πληρωθῆτε εἰς πᾶν τὸ πλήρωμα τοῦ θεοῦ.

δῷ v.3.s.aor.act.sub. [δίδωμι]; πλοῦτος (riches); κραταιωθῆναι (strengthen); ἔσω (inner); κατοικῆσαι (live); ἐρριζωμένοι v.m.p.nom.pf.pass.ptc. [ῥιζόω] (rooted); τεθεμελιωμένοι v.m.p.nom.pf.pass.ptc. [θεμελιόω] (founded); γνῶναι v.aor.act.in. [γινώσκω]

6. Psalm 40:2–4 [1–3]; James 1:2–4

Joy Born in Sorrow

I HAVE YET TO MEET A SAINT whose face beams Incarnate Joy, whose eyes do not betray stories of pain. Sanctity grows through suffering, if we let it.

PSALM 40:2–4 [1–3]

²קַוֹּה קִוִּיתִי יְהוָה וַיֵּט אֵלַי וַיִּשְׁמַע שַׁוְעָתִי:
³וַיַּעֲלֵנִי מִבּוֹר שָׁאוֹן מִטִּיט הַיָּוֵן וַיָּקֶם עַל־סֶלַע רַגְלַי
כּוֹנֵן אֲשֻׁרָי:
⁴וַיִּתֵּן בְּפִי שִׁיר חָדָשׁ תְּהִלָּה לֵאלֹהֵינוּ יִרְאוּ רַבִּים וְיִירָאוּ
וְיִבְטְחוּ בַּיהוָה:

קַוֹּה (wait); קִוִּיתִי v.1.com.s.pf.P. [קוה]; וַיֵּט v.c. + v.3.m.s.impf.Q. [נטה]; שַׁוְעָתִי (cry); וַיַּעֲלֵנִי v.c.+ v.3.m.s.impf.H. [עלה] + 1.com.s.pr.sf.; שָׁאוֹן (din); מִטִּיט (mud); הַיָּוֵן (mire); וַיָּקֶם v.c. + v.3.m.s.impf.H. [קום]; סֶלַע (rock); כּוֹנֵן v.3.m.s.pf.Pil. [כון]; אֲשֻׁרָי (step); וַיִּתֵּן v.c. + v.3.m.s.impf.Q. [נתן]; יִרְאוּ v.3.m.p. impf.Q. [ראה]

JAMES 1:2–4

²Πᾶσαν χαρὰν ἡγήσασθε, ἀδελφοί μου, ὅταν πειρασμοῖς περιπέσητε ποικίλοις, ³γινώσκοντες ὅτι τὸ δοκίμιον ὑμῶν τῆς πίστεως κατεργάζεται ὑπομονήν. ⁴ἡ δὲ ὑπομονὴ ἔργον τέλειον ἐχέτω, ἵνα ἦτε τέλειοι καὶ ὁλόκληροι ἐν μηδενὶ λειπόμενοι.

ἡγήσασθε v.2.p.aor.mid.ind. [ἡγέομαι] (consider); πειρασμοῖς (trial); περιπέσητε v.2.p.aor.act.sub. [περιπίπτω] (happen); ποικίλοις (various); δοκίμιον (testing); κατεργάζεται (produce); ὑπομονήν (patience); ὁλόκληροι (complete); λειπόμενοι (lack)

7. Jeremiah 32.40–41, Hebrews 13.20–21

Our Joy Is God's Shalom

It is God's greatest joy to give us all we need. In other words, our joy is God's joy.

Jeremiah 32:40–41

40וְכָרַתִּי לָהֶם בְּרִית עוֹלָם אֲשֶׁר לֹא־אָשׁוּב מֵאַחֲרֵיהֶם לְהֵיטִיבִי
אוֹתָם וְאֶת־יִרְאָתִי אֶתֵּן בִּלְבָבָם לְבִלְתִּי סוּר מֵעָלָי׃
41וְשַׂשְׂתִּי עֲלֵיהֶם לְהֵטִיב אוֹתָם וּנְטַעְתִּים בָּאָרֶץ הַזֹּאת
בֶּאֱמֶת בְּכָל־לִבִּי וּבְכָל־נַפְשִׁי׃

וְכָרַתִּי v.c. + v.1.com.s.pf.Q. [כרת]; לְהֵיטִיבִי prep. + v.in.cs.H. [יטב] +
1.com.s.pr.sf.; יִרְאָתִי (fear); אֶתֵּן v.1.com.s.impf.Q. [נתן]; וְשַׂשְׂתִּי v.c. +
v.1.com.s.pf.Q. [שׂושׂ] (rejoice); לְהֵטִיב prep. + v.in.cs.H.defective [יטב];
וּנְטַעְתִּים v.c. + v.1.com.s.pf.Q. [נטע] + 3.m.p.pr.sf.

Hebrews 13:20–21

20Ὁ δὲ θεὸς τῆς εἰρήνης, ὁ ἀναγαγὼν ἐκ νεκρῶν τὸν ποιμένα
τῶν προβάτων τὸν μέγαν ἐν αἵματι διαθήκης αἰωνίου, τὸν
κύριον ἡμῶν Ἰησοῦν, 21καταρτίσαι ὑμᾶς ἐν παντὶ ἀγαθῷ εἰς
τὸ ποιῆσαι τὸ θέλημα αὐτοῦ, ποιῶν ἐν ἡμῖν τὸ εὐάρεστον
ἐνώπιον αὐτοῦ διὰ Ἰησοῦ Χριστοῦ, ᾧ ἡ δόξα εἰς τοὺς αἰῶνας
[τῶν αἰώνων], ἀμήν.

ἀναγαγὼν (lead); ποιμένα (shepherd); προβάτων (sheep); διαθήκης
(covenant); καταρτίσαι (perfect); εὐάρεστον (pleasing); ἐνώπιον (before)

Week 4

Patience

1. Exodus 34:6–7; Romans 2:4

Prayer Candle

LIKE A TALL, THICK, BEESWAX PRAYER CANDLE, hand-dipped twelve, no, twenty times, God's patience burns through the night. Honey-sweet, the flame welcomes prodigals home.

EXODUS 34:6–7

⁶וַיַּעֲבֹר יְהוָה עַל־פָּנָיו וַיִּקְרָא יְהוָה יְהוָה אֵל רַחוּם וְחַנּוּן
אֶרֶךְ אַפַּיִם וְרַב־חֶסֶד וֶאֱמֶת:
⁷נֹצֵר חֶסֶד לָאֲלָפִים נֹשֵׂא עָוֹן וָפֶשַׁע וְחַטָּאָה וְנַקֵּה לֹא יְנַקֶּה
פֹּקֵד עֲוֹן אָבוֹת עַל־בָּנִים וְעַל־בְּנֵי בָנִים עַל־שִׁלֵּשִׁים וְעַל־
רִבֵּעִים:

רַחוּם (compassionate); וְחַנּוּן (gracious); אֶרֶךְ (long); וְנַקֵּה (be clean); שִׁלֵּשִׁים (great-grandchildren); רִבֵּעִים (great-great-grandchildren)

ROMANS 2:4

⁴ἢ τοῦ πλούτου τῆς χρηστότητος αὐτοῦ καὶ τῆς ἀνοχῆς καὶ τῆς μακροθυμίας καταφρονεῖς, ἀγνοῶν ὅτι τὸ χρηστὸν τοῦ θεοῦ εἰς μετάνοιαν σε ἄγει;

πλούτου (riches); χρηστότητος (kindness); ἀνοχῆς (forbearance); μακροθυμίας (patience); καταφρονεῖς (despise); χρηστόν (kindness); μετάνοιαν (repentance)

2. Nehemiah 9:16–17; Romans 3:25

Two Points of View

WHEN I THINK OF PATIENCE, I think of clenched teeth, denial, frustration, waiting in endless lines for something that should happen *now*. When God thinks of patience, he thinks of love freely given, of mended hearts, and of those for whom he gladly died. O God, purify my heart.

NEHEMIAH 9:16–17

¹⁶וְהֵם וַאֲבֹתֵינוּ הֵזִידוּ וַיַּקְשׁוּ אֶת־עָרְפָּם וְלֹא שָׁמְעוּ אֶל־
מִצְוֹתֶיךָ:
¹⁷וַיְמָאֲנוּ לִשְׁמֹעַ וְלֹא־זָכְרוּ נִפְלְאֹתֶיךָ אֲשֶׁר עָשִׂיתָ עִמָּהֶם
וַיַּקְשׁוּ אֶת־עָרְפָּם וַיִּתְּנוּ־רֹאשׁ לָשׁוּב לְעַבְדֻתָם בְּמִרְיָם
וְאַתָּה אֱלוֹהַ סְלִיחוֹת חַנּוּן וְרַחוּם אֶרֶךְ־אַפַּיִם וְרַב־חֶסֶד
וְלֹא עֲזַבְתָּם:

הֵזִידוּ v.3.m.p.pf.H. [זיד] (act presumptuously); וַיַּקְשׁוּ v.c. + v.3.m.p.impf.H.
[קשה] (be stubborn); וַיְמָאֲנוּ (refuse); נִפְלְאֹתֶיךָ (wonders); עָשִׂיתָ v.2.m.s.pf.Q.
[עשה]; עָרְפָּם (neck); וַיִּתְּנוּ v.c. + v.3.m.p.impf.Q. [נתן]; בְּמִרְיָם (rebellion);
סְלִיחוֹת (forgiveness); רַחוּם (compassionate); חַנּוּן (gracious); אֶרֶךְ (long);
עֲזַבְתָּם v.2.m.s.pf.Q. [עזב] + 3.m.p.pr.sf.

ROMANS 3:25

²⁵ὃν προέθετο ὁ θεὸς ἱλαστήριον διὰ [τῆς] πίστεως ἐν τῷ αὐτοῦ
αἵματι εἰς ἔνδειξιν τῆς δικαιοσύνης αὐτοῦ διὰ τὴν πάρεσιν
τῶν προγεγονότων ἁμαρτημάτων

προέθετο v.3.s.aor.mid.ind. [προτίθημι] (send out); ἱλαστήριον (propitiation, expiation); ἔνδειξιν (sign); πάρεσιν (leaving unpunished); προγεγονότων (done before); ἁμαρτημάτων (sin)

3. Genesis 49:18; 2 Corinthians 6:4–7

For the Cross Set Before Him

WHEN I AM TEMPTED TO COMPLAIN about the wait, beloved Jesus, because of hardship or misunderstanding or just plain old fatigue, cup my face in your strong hands. Raise my eyes to the cross and let me see what you endured. Then gently lead me back to the work to which I'm called.

GENESIS 49:18

יּⁱⁱⁱ¹⁸לִישׁוּעָתְךָ קִוִּיתִי יְהוָה׃

לִישׁוּעָתְךָ prep. + n.f.s.cs. + 2.m.s.pr.sf.; קִוִּיתִי v.1.com.s. pf.P. [קוה] (await)

2 CORINTHIANS 6:4–7

⁴ἀλλ᾽ ἐν παντὶ συνίσταντες ἑαυτοὺς ὡς θεοῦ διάκονοι, ἐν ὑπομονῇ πολλῇ, ἐν θλίψεσιν, ἐν ἀνάγκαις, ἐν στενοχωρίαις, ⁵ἐν πληγαῖς, ἐν φυλακαῖς, ἐν ἀκαταστασίαις, ἐν κόποις, ἐν ἀγρυπνίαις, ἐν νηστείαις, ⁶ἐν ἁγνότητι, ἐν γνώσει, ἐν μακροθυμίᾳ, ἐν χρηστότητι, ἐν πνεύματι ἁγίῳ, ἐν ἀγάπῃ ἀνυποκρίτῳ, ⁷ἐν λόγῳ ἀληθείας, ἐν δυνάμει θεοῦ· διὰ τῶν ὅπλων τῆς δικαιοσύνης τῶν δεξιῶν καὶ ἀριστερῶν,

διάκονοι (servant); ὑπομονῇ (patience); ἀνάγκαις (calamity); στενοχωρίαις (trouble); πληγαῖς (blow); φυλακαῖς (imprisonment); ἀκαταστασίαις (disturbance); κόποις (work); ἀγρυπνίαις (sleeplessness); νηστείαις (lack of food); ἁγνότητι (purity); μακροθυμία (forbearance); χρηστότητι (kindness); ἀνυποκρίτῳ (genuine); ὅπλων τῆς δικαιοσύνης τῶν δεξιῶν (weapons—offensive and defensive)

4. Psalm 80:15–16; James 3:17–18

Patience and Its Fruit

THE FRUIT OF GOD'S PATIENCE is reconciliation. I suspect that if I shared God's concern for reconciliation, I would also manifest his patience.

PSALM 86:15–16

¹⁵וְאַתָּה אֲדֹנָי אֵל־רַחוּם וְחַנּוּן אֶרֶךְ אַפַּיִם וְרַב־חֶסֶד וֶאֱמֶת׃
¹⁶פְּנֵה אֵלַי וְחָנֵּנִי תְּנָה־עֻזְּךָ לְעַבְדֶּךָ וְהוֹשִׁיעָה לְבֶן־אֲמָתֶךָ׃

רַחוּם (compassionate); וְחַנּוּן (gracious); אֶרֶךְ (long); וְחָנֵּנִי cj. +
v.2.m.s.impv.Q. [חנן] + 1.com.s.pr.sf.; תְּנָה v.2.m.s.impv.Q. [נתן] + para.;
וְהוֹשִׁיעָה cj. + v.3.m.s.pf.H. [ישע] + para.

JAMES 3:17–18

¹⁷ἡ δὲ ἄνωθεν σοφία πρῶτον μὲν ἁγνή ἐστιν, ἔπειτα εἰρηνική, ἐπιεικής, εὐπειθής, μεστὴ ἐλέους καὶ καρπῶν ἀγαθῶν, ἀδιάκριτος, ἀνυπόκριτος. ¹⁸καρπὸς δὲ δικαιοσύνης ἐν εἰρήνῃ σπείρεται τοῖς ποιοῦσιν εἰρήνην.

ἄνωθεν (from above); ἁγνή (pure); ἐστιν v.3.s.pres.ind. [εἰμί]; ἔπειτα
(then); εἰρηνική (peace-loving); ἐπιεικής (gentle); εὐπειθής (yielding);
μεστὴ (full); ἐλέους (mercy); ἀδιάκριτος (impartial); ἀνυπόκριτος (sincere)

5. Proverbs 25:15; Luke 18:3–5

Nagging Virtue

IT ALWAYS CATCHES ME BY SURPRISE, Lord, that you regard the importunate widow's nagging as a great virtue. It is virtuous to nag God? Well, whether we call it nagging or steely persistence (now *there's* a pious phrase), you call it patience. And it brings great reward.

PROVERBS 25:15

בְּאֹרֶךְ אַפַּיִם יְפֻתֶּה קָצִין וְלָשׁוֹן רַכָּה תִּשְׁבָּר־גָּרֶם:¹⁵

יְפֻתֶּה (be persuaded); קָצִין (ruler); רַכָּה (tender); גָּרֶם (person)

LUKE 18:3–5

³χήρα δὲ ἦν ἐν τῇ πόλει ἐκείνῃ καὶ ἤρχετο πρὸς αὐτὸν λέγουσα, Ἐκδίκησόν με ἀπὸ τοῦ ἀντιδίκου μου. ⁴καὶ οὐκ ἤθελεν ἐπὶ χρόνον. μετὰ δὲ ταῦτα εἶπεν ἐν ἑαυτῷ, Εἰ καὶ τὸν θεὸν οὐ φοβοῦμαι οὐδὲ ἄνθρωπον ἐντρέπομαι, ⁵διά γε τὸ παρέχειν μοι κόπον τὴν χήραν ταύτην ἐκδικήσω αὐτήν, ἵνα μὴ εἰς τέλος ἐρχομένη ὑπωπιάζῃ με.

χήρα (widow); ἦν v.3.s.impf.ind. [εἰμί]; Ἐκδίκησόν (avenge); ἀντιδίκου (enemy); εἶπεν v.3.s.aor.act.ind. [λέγω]; ἐντρέπομαι (have regard for); παρέχειν (give); κόπον (trouble); τέλος (end); ὑπωπιάζῃ (wear out)

6. Psalm 63:3–5 [2–4]; Colossians 1:11–12

Hidden Goodness

PATIENCE IS ONE OF THOSE VIRTUES that softly steal into one's heart, unknown to self but glorious to others.

PSALM 63:3–5 [2–4]

³כֵּן בַּקֹּדֶשׁ חֲזִיתִיךָ לִרְאוֹת עֻזְּךָ וּכְבוֹדֶךָ׃

⁴כִּי־טוֹב חַסְדְּךָ מֵחַיִּים שְׂפָתַי יְשַׁבְּחוּנְךָ׃

⁵כֵּן אֲבָרֶכְךָ בְחַיָּי בְּשִׁמְךָ אֶשָּׂא כַפָּי׃

חֲזִיתִיךָ v.1.com.s.pf.Q. [חזה] + 2.m.s.pr.sf.; לִרְאוֹת prep. + v.in.cs.Q. [ראה]; יְשַׁבְּחוּנְךָ v.3.m.p.impf.P. [שבח] (praise) + para.2.m.s.pr.sf.; אֶשָּׂא v.1.com.s.impf.Q. [נשא]

COLOSSIANS 1:11–12

¹¹ἐν πάσῃ δυνάμει δυναμούμενοι κατὰ τὸ κράτος τῆς δόξης αὐτοῦ εἰς πᾶσαν ὑπομονὴν καὶ μακροθυμίαν. μετὰ χαρᾶς ¹²εὐχαριστοῦντες τῷ πατρὶ τῷ ἱκανώσαντι ὑμᾶς εἰς τὴν μερίδα τοῦ κλήρου τῶν ἁγίων ἐν τῷ φωτί·

δυναμούμενοι (strengthen); κράτος (power); ὑπομονὴν (endurance); μακροθυμίαν (patience); εὐχαριστοῦντες (give thanks); ἱκανώσαντι (make fit); μερίδα (portion); κλήρου (lot)

7. Psalm 40:10–11 [9–10]; 2 Timothy 4:2–3

A Winning Combination

IF I WOULD WIN THE EAR OF OTHERS with my words, I must first win their hearts with my patience.

PSALM 40:10–11 [9–10]

¹⁰בִּשַּׂרְתִּי צֶדֶק בְּקָהָל רָב הִנֵּה שְׂפָתַי לֹא אֶכְלָא יְהוָה אַתָּה יָדָעְתָּ׃

¹¹צִדְקָתְךָ לֹא־כִסִּיתִי בְּתוֹךְ לִבִּי

אֱמוּנָתְךָ וּתְשׁוּעָתְךָ אָמַרְתִּי לֹא־כִחַדְתִּי חַסְדְּךָ וַאֲמִתְּךָ לְקָהָל רָב׃

בִּשַּׂרְתִּי (announce good news); אֶכְלָא (shut up); כִסִּיתִי v.1.com.s.pf.P. [כסה]; אֱמוּנָתְךָ (faithfulness); וּתְשׁוּעָתְךָ (salvation); כִחַדְתִּי (hide)

2 TIMOTHY 4:2–3

²κήρυξον τὸν λόγον, ἐπίστηθι εὐκαίρως ἀκαίρως, ἔλεγξον, ἐπιτίμησον, παρακάλεσον, ἐν πάσῃ μακροθυμίᾳ καὶ διδαχῇ. ³ἔσται γὰρ καιρὸς ὅτε τῆς ὑγιαινούσης διδασκαλίας οὐκ ἀνέξονται ἀλλὰ κατὰ τὰς ἰδίας ἐπιθυμίας ἑαυτοῖς ἐπισωρεύσουσιν διδασκάλους κνηθόμενοι τὴν ἀκοὴν

ἐπίστηθι v.2.s.aor.act.impv. [ἐφίστημι] (be ready); εὐκαίρως (appropriate time); ἀκαίρως (inappropriate time); ἔλεγξον (correct); ἐπιτίμησον (rebuke); μακροθυμίᾳ (patience); διδαχῇ (doctrine); ὑγιαινούσης (correct); διδασκαλίας (teaching); ἀνέξονται (put up with); ἐπιθυμίας (desire); ἐπισωρεύσουσιν (pile up); κνηθόμενοι (itch); ἀκοὴν (ear)

Kindness

1. Job 0:14; Galatians 0:9–10

Twofold Kindness

TRUE LOVE FOR GOD always results in kindness toward others. The two are inseparable. To harden my heart against one who needs my kindness is to turn away from the face of God.

JOB 6:14

14לַמָּס מֵרֵעֵהוּ חָסֶד וְיִרְאַת שַׁדַּי יַעֲזוֹב:

לַמָּס (despairing one); שַׁדַּי (Shaddai)

GALATIANS 6:9–10

⁹τὸ δὲ καλὸν ποιοῦντες μὴ ἐγκακῶμεν, καιρῷ γὰρ ἰδίῳ θερίσομεν μὴ ἐκλυόμενοι. ¹⁰ἄρα οὖν ὡς καιρὸν ἔχομεν, ἐργαζώμεθα τὸ ἀγαθὸν πρὸς πάντας, μάλιστα δὲ πρὸς τοὺς οἰκείους τῆς πίστεως.

ἐγκακῶμεν (lose heart); θερίσομεν (reap a harvest); ἐκλυόμενοι v.m.p.nom.pres.pass.ptc. [εκλύομαι] (grow weary); ἄρα (then); ἐργαζώμεθα (do); μάλιστα (especially); οἰκείους (household member)

2. Psalm 112:4–5; Ephesians 4:31–32

The Light of Kindness

KINDNESS IS A CHOICE I make that sheds light on darkened paths—both my own and those of others.

PSALM 112:4–5

⁴זָרַח בַּחֹשֶׁךְ אוֹר לַיְשָׁרִים חַנּוּן וְרַחוּם וְצַדִּיק׃
⁵טוֹב־אִישׁ חוֹנֵן וּמַלְוֶה יְכַלְכֵּל דְּבָרָיו בְּמִשְׁפָּט׃

זָרַח (shine); חַנּוּן (gracious); וְרַחוּם (compassionate); וּמַלְוֶה (borrow); יְכַלְכֵּל v.3.m.s.impf.Plpl. [כול] (maintain)

EPHESIANS 4:31–32

³¹πᾶσα πικρία καὶ θυμὸς καὶ ὀργὴ καὶ κραυγὴ καὶ βλασφημία ἀρθήτω ἀφ᾽ ὑμῶν σὺν πάσῃ κακίᾳ. ³²γίνεσθε [δὲ] εἰς ἀλλήλους χρηστοί, εὔσπλαγχνοι, χαριζόμενοι ἑαυτοῖς, καθὼς καὶ ὁ θεὸς ἐν Χριστῷ ἐχαρίσατο ὑμῖν.

πικρία (bitterness); θυμὸς (rage); ὀργὴ (anger); κραυγὴ (shouting); βλασφημία (blasphemy); ἀρθήτω v.3.s.aor.pass.impv. [αἴρω]; κακίᾳ (wickedness); χρηστοί (kind); εὔσπλαγχνοι (tenderhearted); ἐχαρίσατο (forgive)

3. Zechariah 7:9–10; Matthew 23:23

Being Real

IT IS FAR EASIER TO FOLLOW measured rules and assume a kindly
pose than to quietly, without ado, be kind.

ZECHARIAH 7:9–10

⁹כֹּה אָמַר יְהוָה צְבָאוֹת לֵאמֹר מִשְׁפַּט אֱמֶת שְׁפֹטוּ וְחֶסֶד וְרַחֲמִים
עֲשׂוּ אִישׁ אֶת־אָחִיו:
¹⁰וְאַלְמָנָה וְיָתוֹם גֵּר וְעָנִי אַל־תַּעֲשֹׁקוּ וְרָעַת אִישׁ אָחִיו אַל־
תַּחְשְׁבוּ בִּלְבַבְכֶם:

שְׁפֹטוּ v.2.m.p.impv.Q.pause [שפט]; וְרַחֲמִים (mercy); עֲשׂוּ v.2.m.p.impv.Q.
[עשה]; וְיָתוֹם (orphan); תַּעֲשֹׁקוּ (oppress)

MATTHEW 23:23

²³Οὐαὶ ὑμῖν, γραμματεῖς καὶ Φαρισαῖοι ὑποκριταί, ὅτι
ἀποδεκατοῦτε τὸ ἡδύοσμον καὶ τὸ ἄνηθον καὶ τὸ κύμινον
καὶ ἀφήκατε τὰ βαρύτερα τοῦ νόμου, τὴν κρίσιν καὶ τὸ ἔλεος
καὶ τὴν πίστιν· ταῦτα [δὲ] ἔδει ποιῆσαι κἀκεῖνα μὴ ἀφιέναι.

ἀποδεκατοῦτε (tithe); ἡδύοσμον (mint); ἄνηθον (dill); κύμινον (cum-
min); ἀφήκατε v.2.p.aor.act.ind. [ἀφίημι]; βαρύτερα (important); ἔλεος
(mercy)

4. Proverbs 21:21; Romans 14:18–19

Kindness as Gratitude

WHEN I THINK OF ALL THAT YOU HAVE DONE for me, dearest Lord, it is your kind heart that melts my heart the most. You have never spoken a word of correction to me that was not wrapped in tender love, nor has your gentleness been lacking when I have been afraid. No wonder, then, that my best thanks to you is in being kind to those I'll meet today.

PROVERBS 21:21

²¹רֹדֵף צְדָקָה וָחָסֶד יִמְצָא חַיִּים צְדָקָה וְכָבוֹד:

ROMANS 14:18–19

¹⁸ὁ γὰρ ἐν τούτῳ δουλεύων τῷ Χριστῷ εὐάρεστος τῷ θεῷ καὶ δόκιμος τοῖς ἀνθρώποις. ¹⁹Ἄρα οὖν τὰ τῆς εἰρήνης διώκωμεν καὶ τὰ τῆς οἰκοδομῆς τῆς εἰς ἀλλήλους.

δουλεύων (serve); εὐάρεστος (pleasing); δόκιμος (approved); Ἄρα (so); διώκωμεν (chase after); οἰκοδομῆς (building up)

5. Hosea 4.1–3, 1 Thessalonians 3:6–8

Nourishment for the World

KINDNESS IS LIKE A SPIRITUAL FOOD CHAIN—others are nourished by our kindness and in turn can pass it on. Eventually the planet itself is fed and clothed. It all begins in hiddenness, in the heart.

HOSEA 4:1–3

¹שִׁמְעוּ דְבַר־יְהוָה בְּנֵי יִשְׂרָאֵל כִּי רִיב לַיהוָה עִם־יוֹשְׁבֵי הָאָרֶץ
כִּי אֵין־אֱמֶת וְאֵין־חֶסֶד וְאֵין־דַּעַת אֱלֹהִים בָּאָרֶץ:
²אָלֹה וְכַחֵשׁ וְרָצֹחַ וְגָנֹב וְנָאֹף פָּרָצוּ וְדָמִים בְּדָמִים נָגָעוּ:
³עַל־כֵּן תֶּאֱבַל הָאָרֶץ וְאֻמְלַל כָּל־יוֹשֵׁב בָּהּ בְּחַיַּת הַשָּׂדֶה
וּבְעוֹף הַשָּׁמָיִם וְגַם־דְּגֵי הַיָּם יֵאָסֵפוּ:

אָלֹה v.in.ab.Q. (swear); וְכַחֵשׁ (deny); וְרָצֹחַ (murder); וְגָנֹב (steal); וְנָאֹף (commit adultery); וְאֻמְלַל (be feeble); תֶּאֱבַל (mourn/dry up); דְּגֵי (fish)

1 THESSALONIANS 3:6–8

⁶῎Αρτι δὲ ἐλθόντος Τιμοθέου πρὸς ἡμᾶς ἀφ᾽ ὑμῶν καὶ εὐαγγελισαμένου ἡμῖν τὴν πίστιν καὶ τὴν ἀγάπην ὑμῶν καὶ ὅτι ἔχετε μνείαν ἡμῶν ἀγαθὴν πάντοτε, ἐπιποθοῦντες ἡμᾶς ἰδεῖν καθάπερ καὶ ἡμεῖς ὑμᾶς, ⁷διὰ τοῦτο παρεκλήθημεν, ἀδελφοί, ἐφ᾽ ὑμῖν ἐπὶ πάσῃ τῇ ἀνάγκῃ καὶ θλίψει ἡμῶν διὰ τῆς ὑμῶν πίστεως, ⁸ὅτι νῦν ζῶμεν ἐὰν ὑμεῖς στήκετε ἐν κυρίῳ.

῎Αρτι (now); μνείαν (remembrance); πάντοτε (always); ἐπιποθοῦντες (long for); ἰδεῖν v.aor.act.in. [ὁράω]; καθάπερ (just as); ἀνάγκη (serious trouble); θλίψει (calamity); νῦν (now); στήκετε (stand firm)

6. Micah 6:7–8; 1 Thessalonians 3:1–3

Justice, Kindness, and Humility

LORD, MAY I BE JUST in my dealings with others, yet more than that, may I have the humility to see my own great need for mercy. Then I will truly love kindness—the kindness you show to me—and I will be your kindness to others.

MICAH 6:7–8

⁷הֲיִרְצֶה יְהוָה בְּאַלְפֵי אֵילִים בְּרִבְבוֹת נַחֲלֵי־שָׁמֶן הַאֶתֵּן בְּכוֹרִי
פִּשְׁעִי פְּרִי בִטְנִי חַטַּאת נַפְשִׁי:
⁸הִגִּיד לְךָ אָדָם מַה־טּוֹב וּמָה־יְהוָה דּוֹרֵשׁ מִמְּךָ כִּי אִם־עֲשׂוֹת
מִשְׁפָּט וְאַהֲבַת חֶסֶד וְהַצְנֵעַ לֶכֶת עִם־אֱלֹהֶיךָ:

בְּרִבְבוֹת (ten thousand); הַאֶתֵּן int.pt. + v.1.com.s.impf.Q. [נתן]; הִגִּיד
v.3.m.s.pf.H. [נגד]; עֲשׂוֹת v.in.cs.Q. [עשׂה]; וְהַצְנֵעַ cj. + v.in.ab.H. [צנע] (be
humble); לֶכֶת prep. + v.in.cs.Q. [הלך]

1 THESSALONIANS 3:1–3

¹Διὸ μηκέτι στέγοντες εὐδοκήσαμεν καταλειφθῆναι ἐν
Ἀθήναις μόνοι ²καὶ ἐπέμψαμεν Τιμόθεον, τὸν ἀδελφὸν ἡμῶν
καὶ συνεργὸν τοῦ θεοῦ ἐν τῷ εὐαγγελίῳ τοῦ Χριστοῦ, εἰς τὸ
στηρίξαι ὑμᾶς καὶ παρακαλέσαι ὑπὲρ τῆς πίστεως ὑμῶν ³τὸ
μηδένα σαίνεσθαι ἐν ταῖς θλίψεσιν ταύταις. αὐτοὶ γὰρ οἴδατε
ὅτι εἰς τοῦτο κείμεθα·

μηκέτι (no longer); στέγοντες (stand); εὐδοκήσαμεν (decide);
καταλειφθῆναι v.aor.pass.in. [καταλείπω] (stay behind); συνεργὸν (co-
worker); στηρίξαι (establish); σαίνεσθαι (trouble); θλίψεσιν (affliction);
κείμεθα v.1.p.pres.mid.ind. [κεῖμαι] (destined)

7. Isaiah 35:3–6; 1 Thessalonians 5:14–15

The Breath of God

WE HAVE YET TO REALIZE the unlimited power of kindness to melt fear, cure blindness, heal wounded hearts, sustain the weary, and strengthen the weak. Kindness is the breath of God.

ISAIAH 35:3–6

³חַזְּקוּ יָדַיִם רָפוֹת וּבִרְכַּיִם כֹּשְׁלוֹת אַמֵּצוּ:
⁴אִמְרוּ לְנִמְהֲרֵי־לֵב חִזְקוּ אַל־תִּירָאוּ הִנֵּה אֱלֹהֵיכֶם נָקָם יָבוֹא
גְּמוּל אֱלֹהִים הוּא יָבוֹא וְיֹשַׁעֲכֶם:
⁵אָז תִּפָּקַחְנָה עֵינֵי עִוְרִים וְאָזְנֵי חֵרְשִׁים תִּפָּתַחְנָה:
⁶אָז יְדַלֵּג כָּאַיָּל פִּסֵּחַ וְתָרֹן לְשׁוֹן אִלֵּם כִּי־נִבְקְעוּ בַמִּדְבָּר
מַיִם וּנְחָלִים בָּעֲרָבָה:

יָבוֹא v.3.m.s.impf.Q. [בוא]; וְיֹשַׁעֲכֶם cj. + v.3.m.s.impf.H. [ישע] + 2.m.p.pr.sf.;
וְתָרֹן cj. + v.3.f.s.impf.Q. [רנן]

1 THESSALONIANS 5:14–15

¹⁴παρακαλοῦμεν δὲ ὑμᾶς, ἀδελφοί, νουθετεῖτε τοὺς ἀτάκτους, παραμυθεῖσθε τοὺς ὀλιγοψύχους, ἀντέχεσθε τῶν ἀσθενῶν, μακροθυμεῖτε πρὸς πάντας. ¹⁵ὁρᾶτε μή τις κακὸν ἀντὶ κακοῦ τινι ἀποδῷ, ἀλλὰ πάντοτε τὸ ἀγαθὸν διώκετε [καὶ] εἰς ἀλλήλους καὶ εἰς πάντας.

νουθετεῖτε (urge); ἀτάκτους (lazy); παραμυθεῖσθε (encourage); ὀλιγοψύχους (timid); ἀντέχεσθε (help); ἀσθενῶν (weak); μακροθυμεῖτε (be patient); ἀντὶ (in place of); ἀποδῷ (pay back); πάντοτε (always); διώκετε (seek after)

Week 6

Generosity

1. Proverbs 11:24–25; Acts 2:44–47

One Clasp

COULD IT BE THAT THE SAME CLASP that opens and closes my purse, opens and closes my heart?

PROVERBS 11:24–25

²⁴יֵ֣שׁ מְ֭פַזֵּר וְנוֹסָ֣ף ע֑וֹד וְחוֹשֵׂ֥ךְ מִ֝יֹּ֗שֶׁר אַךְ־לְמַחְסֽוֹר׃
²⁵נֶֽפֶשׁ־בְּרָכָ֥ה תְדֻשָּׁ֑ן וּמַרְוֶ֗ה גַּם־ה֥וּא יוֹרֶֽא׃

וְנוֹסָ֣ף cj. + v.m.s.ptc.N. [יסף]; יוֹרֶֽא v.3.m.s.impf.H. [ירא]

ACTS 2:44–47

⁴⁴πάντες δὲ οἱ πιστεύοντες ἦσαν ἐπὶ τὸ αὐτὸ καὶ εἶχον ἅπαντα κοινὰ ⁴⁵καὶ τὰ κτήματα καὶ τὰς ὑπάρξεις ἐπίπρασκον καὶ διεμέριζον αὐτὰ πᾶσιν καθότι ἄν τις χρείαν εἶχεν· ⁴⁶καθ' ἡμέραν τε προσκαρτεροῦντες ὁμοθυμαδὸν ἐν τῷ ἱερῷ, κλῶντές τε κατ' οἶκον ἄρτον, μετελάμβανον τροφῆς ἐν ἀγαλλιάσει καὶ ἀφελότητι καρδίας ⁴⁷αἰνοῦντες τὸν θεὸν καὶ ἔχοντες χάριν πρὸς ὅλον τὸν λαόν. ὁ δὲ κύριος προσετίθει τοὺς σῳζομένους καθ' ἡμέραν ἐπὶ τὸ αὐτό.

κοινὰ (together); κτήματα (property); ὑπάρξεις (possession); ἐπίπρασκον (sell); διεμέριζον (distribute); καθότι (as much as); χρείαν (need); καθ' ἡμέραν τε prep. from κατα + n.f.s.acc. + enclitic pt. (daily); προσκαρτεροῦντες (be devoted to); ὁμοθυμαδόν (with one mind); κλῶντες (break); μετελάμβανον (share); τροφῆς (food); ἀγαλλιάσει (joy); ἀφελότητι (sincerity); αἰνοῦντες (praise); προσετίθει v.3.s.impf.act.ind. [προστίθημι]; ἐπὶ τὸ αὐτό prep. + d.a.nt.s.acc. + pr.nt.s.acc. (to it/them)

2. Deuteronomy 8:17–18; 1 Timothy 6:17–19

Spending Habits

THE WHOLE POINT OF WEALTH, from God's perspective, is to further his covenant of redemptive love. How we use physical wealth is a fairly good barometer of how we spend our spiritual self as well.

DEUTERONOMY 8:17–18

¹⁷וְאָמַרְתָּ בִּלְבָבֶךָ כֹּחִי וְעֹצֶם יָדִי עָשָׂה לִי אֶת־הַחַיִל הַזֶּה:
¹⁸וְזָכַרְתָּ אֶת־יְהוָה אֱלֹהֶיךָ כִּי הוּא הַנֹּתֵן לְךָ כֹּחַ לַעֲשׂוֹת חָיִל
לְמַעַן הָקִים אֶת־בְּרִיתוֹ אֲשֶׁר־נִשְׁבַּע לַאֲבֹתֶיךָ כַּיּוֹם הַזֶּה:

לַעֲשׂוֹת prep. + v.in.cs.Q. [עשׂה]; הָקִים v.in.ab.H. [קום]

1 TIMOTHY 6:17–19

¹⁷Τοῖς πλουσίοις ἐν τῷ νῦν αἰῶνι παράγγελλε μὴ ὑψηλοφρονεῖν μηδὲ ἠλπικέναι ἐπὶ πλούτου ἀδηλότητι ἀλλ᾽ ἐπὶ θεῷ τῷ παρέχοντι ἡμῖν πάντα πλουσίως εἰς ἀπόλαυσιν, ¹⁸ἀγαθοεργεῖν, πλουτεῖν ἐν ἔργοις καλοῖς, εὐμεταδότους εἶναι, κοινωνικούς, ¹⁹ἀποθησαυρίζοντας ἑαυτοῖς θεμέλιον καλὸν εἰς τὸ μέλλον, ἵνα ἐπιλάβωνται τῆς ὄντως ζωῆς.

πλουσίοις (rich); νῦν (now); παράγγελλε (command); ὑψηλοφρονεῖν (be proud); ἠλπικέναι v.pf.in.act. [ἐλπίζω] (trust); πλούτου (wealth); ἀδηλότητι (uncertainty); παρέχοντι (provide); πλουσίως (richly); ἀπόλαυσιν (enjoyment); ἀγαθοεργεῖν (do good); πλουτεῖν (be rich); εὐμεταδότους (generous); εἶναι v.pres.in. [εἰμί]; κοινωνικούς (sharing); ἀποθησαυρίζοντας (store up); θεμέλιον (foundation); ἐπιλάβωνται v.3.p.aor.mid.sub. [ἐπιλαμβάνομαι] (take hold of); ὄντως (real)

3. Proverbs 30:8–9; Matthew 6:11–13

Daily Bread

It is God's will for all of us to have daily bread. It is also his will for us to be the answers to that prayer when others pray it. Do I pray to *our* Father, or just to *my* Father? If I truly pray to *our* Father, consistently, generosity will follow.

Proverbs 30:8–9

⁸שָׁ֤וְא ׀ וּֽדְבַר־כָּזָ֡ב הַרְחֵ֪ק מִמֶּ֫נִּי רֵ֥אשׁ וָעֹ֗שֶׁר אַל־תִּֽתֶּן־לִ֑י הַטְרִיפֵ֗נִי
לֶ֣חֶם חֻקִּֽי׃
⁹פֶּ֤ן אֶשְׂבַּ֨ע ׀ וְכִחַ֗שְׁתִּי וְאָמַ֗רְתִּי מִ֥י יְהוָ֑ה וּפֶֽן־אִ֝וָּרֵ֗שׁ וְגָנַ֥בְתִּי
וְ֝תָפַ֗שְׂתִּי שֵׁ֣ם אֱלֹהָֽי׃

תִּתֶּן v.2.m.s.impf.Q. [נתן]; כָּזָב (lie); וָעֹשֶׁר (wealth); הַטְרִיפֵנִי v.2.m.s.impv.H. [טרף] (tear) + 1.com.s.pr.sf.; אֶשְׂבַּע (satisfy); וְכִחַשְׁתִּי (lie); אִוָּרֵשׁ v.1.com.s.impf.N. [ירשׁ]; וְגָנַבְתִּי (steal)

Matthew 6:11–13

¹¹τὸν ἄρτον ἡμῶν τὸν ἐπιούσιον δὸς ἡμῖν σήμερον·
¹²καὶ ἄφες ἡμῖν τὰ ὀφειλήματα ἡμῶν,
 ὡς καὶ ἡμεῖς ἀφήκαμεν τοῖς ὀφειλέταις ἡμῶν·
¹³καὶ μὴ εἰσενέγκῃς ἡμᾶς εἰς πειρασμόν,
 ἀλλὰ ῥῦσαι ἡμᾶς ἀπὸ τοῦ πονηροῦ.

ἐπιούσιον (daily); σήμερον (today); ὀφειλήματα (debt); ὀφειλέταις (debtor); εἰσενέγκῃς v.2.s.aor.act.sub. [εἰσφέρω] (lead); πειρασμόν (temptation); ῥῦσαι (rescue)

4. 1 Chronicles 29:11–13; 2 Corinthians 9:10–12

Fill Me, Lord

O GOD, I AM POOR AND EMPTY, lacking the strength I need for this day. As I wait quietly before you, reflecting on your beauty, remembering your grace, feed me once again. Fill me to overflowing with nourishing love. Only then will I be able to be your generous hand extended to others.

1 CHRONICLES 29:11–13

¹¹לְךָ יְהוָה הַגְּדֻלָּה וְהַגְּבוּרָה וְהַתִּפְאֶרֶת וְהַנֵּצַח
וְהַהוֹד כִּי־כֹל בַּשָּׁמַיִם וּבָאָרֶץ לְךָ יְהוָה הַמַּמְלָכָה וְהַמִּתְנַשֵּׂא
לְכֹל לְרֹאשׁ׃
¹²וְהָעֹשֶׁר וְהַכָּבוֹד מִלְּפָנֶיךָ וְאַתָּה מוֹשֵׁל בַּכֹּל וּבְיָדְךָ
כֹּחַ וּגְבוּרָה וּבְיָדְךָ לְגַדֵּל וּלְחַזֵּק לַכֹּל׃
¹³וְעַתָּה אֱלֹהֵינוּ מוֹדִים אֲנַחְנוּ לָךְ וּמְהַלְלִים לְשֵׁם תִּפְאַרְתֶּךָ׃

הַגְּדֻלָּה (greatness); וְהַתִּפְאֶרֶת (glory); וְהַנֵּצַח (eminence); וְהַהוֹד (majesty); וְהָעֹשֶׁר (riches); מוֹדִים v.m.p.act.ptc.H. [ידה]

2 CORINTHIANS 9:10–12

¹⁰ὁ δὲ ἐπιχορηγῶν σπόρον τῷ σπείροντι καὶ ἄρτον εἰς βρῶσιν χορηγήσει καὶ πληθυνεῖ τὸν σπόρον ὑμῶν καὶ αὐξήσει τὰ γενήματα τῆς δικαιοσύνης ὑμῶν. ¹¹ἐν παντὶ πλουτιζόμενοι εἰς πᾶσαν ἁπλότητα, ἥτις κατεργάζεται δι' ἡμῶν εὐχαριστίαν τῷ θεῷ· ¹²ὅτι ἡ διακονία τῆς λειτουργίας ταύτης οὐ μόνον ἐστὶν προσαναπληροῦσα τὰ ὑστερήματα τῶν ἁγίων, ἀλλὰ καὶ περισσεύουσα διὰ πολλῶν εὐχαριστιῶν τῷ θεῷ.

ἐπιχορηγῶν (give); σπείροντι (sow); βρῶσιν (food); χορηγήσει (supply); πληθυνεῖ (increase); σπόρον (seed); αὐξήσει (increase); γενήματα (harvest); πλουτιζόμενοι (enrich); ἁπλότητα (generosity); κατεργάζεται (produce); εὐχαριστίαν (thanksgiving); λειτουργίας (service); ἐστὶν v.3.s.pres.ind. [εἰμί]; προσαναπληροῦσα (supply); ὑστερήματα (lack); περισσεύουσα (abound)

5. Ezekiel 34:2–4; 1 Peter 5:1–2

Shepherds and Generosity

SURELY A SACRIFICIAL, GIVING HEART is one of the hallmarks of a true shepherd.

EZEKIEL 34:2–4

²בֶּן־אָדָם הִנָּבֵא עַל־רוֹעֵי יִשְׂרָאֵל הִנָּבֵא וְאָמַרְתָּ אֲלֵיהֶם
לָרֹעִים כֹּה אָמַר אֲדֹנָי יְהוִה הוֹי רֹעֵי־יִשְׂרָאֵל אֲשֶׁר הָיוּ רֹעִים אוֹתָם
הֲלוֹא הַצֹּאן יִרְעוּ הָרֹעִים:
³אֶת־הַחֵלֶב תֹּאכֵלוּ וְאֶת־הַצֶּמֶר תִּלְבָּשׁוּ הַבְּרִיאָה תִּזְבָּחוּ
הַצֹּאן לֹא תִרְעוּ:
⁴אֶת־הַנַּחְלוֹת לֹא חִזַּקְתֶּם וְאֶת־הַחוֹלָה לֹא־רִפֵּאתֶם וְלַנִּשְׁבֶּרֶת
לֹא חֲבַשְׁתֶּם וְאֶת־הַנִּדַּחַת לֹא הֲשֵׁבֹתֶם וְאֶת־הָאֹבֶדֶת לֹא בִקַּשְׁתֶּם
וּבְחָזְקָה רְדִיתֶם אֹתָם וּבְפָרֶךְ:

רֹעֵי v.m.p.cs.act.ptc.Q.plene [רעה]; לָרֹעִים prep. + v.m.p.act.ptc.Q. [רעה]; רֹעֵי v.m.p.cs.act.ptc.Q. [רעה]; הָיוּ v.3.c.p.Q. [היה]; יִרְעוּ v.3.m.p.impf.Q. [רעה]; הָרֹעִים d.a. + v.m.p.act.ptc.Q. [רעה]; הַצֶּמֶר (wool); הַבְּרִיאָה (fat); תִרְעוּ v.2.m.p.impf.Q. [רעה]; וְלַנִּשְׁבֶּרֶת cj. + prep. + d.a. + v.f.s.ptc.N. [שבר]; הַנִּדַּחַת d.a. + v.f.s.ptc.N. [נדח]; הֲשֵׁבֹתֶם v.2.m.p.pf.H. [שוב]; וּבְחָזְקָה (strength); רְדִיתֶם v.2.m.p.pf.Q. [רדה] (rule); וּבְפָרֶךְ (security)

1 PETER 5:1–2

¹Πρεσβυτέρους οὖν ἐν ὑμῖν παρακαλῶ ὁ συμπρεσβύτερος καὶ μάρτυς τῶν τοῦ Χριστοῦ παθημάτων, ὁ καὶ τῆς μελλούσης ἀποκαλύπτεσθαι δόξης κοινωνός· ²ποιμάνατε τὸ ἐν ὑμῖν ποίμνιον τοῦ θεοῦ [ἐπισκοποῦντες] μὴ ἀναγκαστῶς ἀλλὰ ἑκουσίως κατὰ θεόν, μηδὲ αἰσχροκερδῶς ἀλλὰ προθύμως,

συμπρεσβύτερος (fellow elder); μάρτυς (witness); παθημάτων (suffering); ἀποκαλύπτεσθαι (reveal); κοινωνός (companion); ποιμάνατε (tend); ποίμνιον (flock); ἀναγκαστῶς (under compulsion); ἑκουσίως (willingly); αἰσχροκερδῶς (liking crooked gain); προθύμως (willingly)

6. Deuteronomy 32:2; 1 Corinthians 1:18–19

Receiving Generously

THE LAVISH GRACE OF GOD goes out to everyone, but not everyone receives the gift. The day will come, though, when the truth will all be told, the day when we finally realize that we must receive as generously as God gives, in order for the world to be made whole.

DEUTERONOMY 32:2

²יַעֲרֹף כַּמָּטָר לִקְחִי תִּזַּל כַּטַּל אִמְרָתִי כִּשְׂעִירִם עֲלֵי־דֶשֶׁא
וְכִרְבִיבִים עֲלֵי־עֵשֶׂב׃

יַעֲרֹף (drip); כַּמָּטָר (rain); לִקְחִי (teaching); תִּזַּל v.3.f.s.impf.Q. [נזל] (trickle); כַּטַּל (dew); אִמְרָתִי (saying); דֶשֶׁא (grass); וְכִרְבִיבִים (downpour); עֵשֶׂב (young plant)

1 CORINTHIANS 1:18–19

¹⁸Ὁ λόγος γὰρ ὁ τοῦ σταυροῦ τοῖς μὲν ἀπολλυμένοις μωρία ἐστίν, τοῖς δὲ σῳζομένοις ἡμῖν δύναμις θεοῦ ἐστιν.
    ¹⁹γέγραπται γάρ,
    Ἀπολῶ τὴν σοφίαν τῶν σοφῶν
        καὶ τὴν σύνεσιν τῶν συνετῶν ἀθετήσω.

σταυροῦ (cross); μωρία (foolishness); Ἀπολῶ v.1.s.fut.act.ind. [ἀπόλλυμι]; σύνεσιν (wisdom); συνετῶν (wise); ἀθετήσω (reject)

7. 2 Samuel 9:6–7; 1 Thessalonians 3:9–10

The Harder Path

FOR SOME OF US IT IS MUCH EASIER to be generous with our purses than with our prayers. God deliver us from stinginess, whatever its form may be.

2 SAMUEL 9:6–7

⁶וַיָּבֹא מְפִיבֹשֶׁת בֶּן־יְהוֹנָתָן בֶּן־שָׁאוּל אֶל־דָּוִד וַיִּפֹּל עַל־
פָּנָיו וַיִּשְׁתָּחוּ וַיֹּאמֶר דָּוִד מְפִיבֹשֶׁת וַיֹּאמֶר הִנֵּה עַבְדֶּךָ׃
⁷וַיֹּאמֶר לוֹ דָוִד אַל־תִּירָא כִּי עָשֹׂה אֶעֱשֶׂה עִמְּךָ חֶסֶד בַּעֲבוּר
יְהוֹנָתָן אָבִיךָ וַהֲשִׁבֹתִי לְךָ אֶת־כָּל־שְׂדֵה שָׁאוּל אָבִיךָ וְאַתָּה
תֹּאכַל לֶחֶם עַל־שֻׁלְחָנִי תָּמִיד׃

וַיָּבֹא v.c. + 3.m.s.impf.Q. [בוא]; וַיִּפֹּל v.c. + 3.m.s.impf.Q. [נפל]; וַיִּשְׁתָּחוּ v.c. + v.3.m.s.impf.Hisht. [חוה]; בַּעֲבוּר (on account of); וַהֲשִׁבֹתִי v.c. + v.1.com.s.pf.H. [שוב]

1 THESSALONIANS 3:9–10

⁹τίνα γὰρ εὐχαριστίαν δυνάμεθα τῷ θεῷ ἀνταποδοῦναι περὶ ὑμῶν ἐπὶ πάσῃ τῇ χαρᾷ ᾗ χαίρομεν δι᾽ ὑμᾶς ἔμπροσθεν τοῦ θεοῦ ἡμῶν, ¹⁰νυκτὸς καὶ ἡμέρας ὑπερεκπερισσοῦ δεόμενοι εἰς τὸ ἰδεῖν ὑμῶν τὸ πρόσωπον καὶ καταρτίσαι τὰ ὑστερήματα τῆς πίστεως ὑμῶν;

εὐχαριστίαν (thanks); ἀνταποδοῦναι (return); ἔμπροσθεν (in the presence of); ὑπερεκπερισσοῦ (earnestly); δεόμενοι (pray); ἰδεῖν v.aor.act.in. [ὁράω]; καταρτίσαι (complete); ὑστερήματα (lack)

Lent (Penitence)

1. Genesis 3:8–9; Romans 1:20–21

Where Are You?

THE WHOLE TIME WE ARE HIDING in our sin God cries like a mother who's lost her child: "Where are you? Where are you?"

GENESIS 3:8–9

⁸וַיִּשְׁמְע֞וּ אֶת־ק֨וֹל יְהוָ֧ה אֱלֹהִ֛ים מִתְהַלֵּ֥ךְ בַּגָּ֖ן לְר֣וּחַ הַיּ֑וֹם
וַיִּתְחַבֵּ֨א הָֽאָדָ֜ם וְאִשְׁתּ֗וֹ מִפְּנֵי֙ יְהוָ֣ה אֱלֹהִ֔ים בְּת֖וֹךְ עֵ֥ץ
הַגָּֽן׃
⁹וַיִּקְרָ֛א יְהוָ֥ה אֱלֹהִ֖ים אֶל־הָֽאָדָ֑ם וַיֹּ֥אמֶר ל֖וֹ אַיֶּֽכָּה׃

וַיִּתְחַבֵּא (hide); אַיֶּכָּה int.adv. (where) + 2.m.s.pr.sf.

ROMANS 1:20–21

²⁰τὰ γὰρ ἀόρατα αὐτοῦ ἀπὸ κτίσεως κόσμου τοῖς ποιήμασιν νοούμενα καθορᾶται, ἥ τε ἀΐδιος αὐτοῦ δύναμις καὶ θειότης, εἰς τὸ εἶναι αὐτοὺς ἀναπολογήτους, ²¹διότι γνόντες τὸν θεὸν οὐχ ὡς θεὸν ἐδόξασαν ἢ ηὐχαρίστησαν, ἀλλ᾽ ἐματαιώθησαν ἐν τοῖς διαλογισμοῖς αὐτῶν καὶ ἐσκοτίσθη ἡ ἀσύνετος αὐτῶν καρδία.

ἀόρατα (invisible); ποιήμασιν (creation); νοούμενα v.nt.p.nom.pres.pass.ptc. [νοέω] (understand); καθορᾶται (notice); ἀΐδιος (eternal); θειότης (divinity); τὸ εἶναι αὐτοὺς d.a.nt.s.acc. + v.pres.in. [εἰμί] + pr.m.p.acc. (so that they be); ἀναπολογήτους (without excuse); διότι (therefore); ηὐχαρίστησαν (give thanks); ἐματαιώθησαν (be foolish); διαλογισμοῖς (thought); ἐσκοτίσθη (darken); ἀσύνετος (foolish)

2. Isaiah 64:5 [6]; 1 Peter 2:24–25

Fading Leaves

THIS YEAR THERE WASN'T ENOUGH RAIN, they say, and that is why instead of flaming a last autumn good-bye the leaves merely faded into brown death. All of them. Our souls are like the leaves. Unless we come to the Fountain, whether we go out brilliantly or slowly fade away, we will die. All of us.

ISAIAH 64:5 [6]

⁵וַנְּהִי כַטָּמֵא כֻּלָּנוּ וּכְבֶגֶד עִדִּים כָּל־צִדְקֹתֵינוּ וַנָּבֶל
כֶּעָלֶה כֻּלָּנוּ וַעֲוֹנֵנוּ כָּרוּחַ יִשָּׂאֻנוּ:

וַנְּהִי v.c. + v.1.com.p.impf.Q.shortened [היה]; עִדִּים (menstruation); וַנָּבֶל v.c. + v.1.com.p.impf.H. [נבל] (wither); כֶּעָלֶה (leaf); יִשָּׂאֻנוּ v.3.m.p.impf.Q. [נשׂא] + 1.com.p.pr.sf.

1 PETER 1:24–25

²⁴διότι
πᾶσα σὰρξ ὡς χόρτος
    καὶ πᾶσα δόξα αὐτῆς ὡς ἄνθος χόρτου·
ἐξηράνθη ὁ χόρτος
    καὶ τὸ ἄνθος ἐξέπεσεν·
²⁵τὸ δὲ ῥῆμα κυρίου μένει εἰς τὸν αἰῶνα. τοῦτο δέ
    ἐστιν τὸ ῥῆμα τὸ εὐαγγελισθὲν εἰς ὑμᾶς.

διότι (because); χόρτος/χόρτου (grass); ἄνθος (flower); ἐξηράνθη v.3.s.aor.pass.ind. [ξηραίνω] (wither); ἐξέπεσεν v.3.s.aor.act.ind. [ἐκπίπτω] (fall off)

3. Isaiah 53:6; Galatians 3:22

Penitence, Not Penance

YOU HAVE TAKEN MY INIQUITY, so willingly, so completely. Why do I try to take it back and carry it myself? Why do I insist on paying a debt that is no longer there? What you really want is for me to let go of it, to let you have it forever. Penitence, not payment—that is what you want.

ISAIAH 53:6

⁶כֻּלָּנוּ כַּצֹּאן תָּעִינוּ אִישׁ לְדַרְכּוֹ פָּנִינוּ וַיהוָה הִפְגִּיעַ בּוֹ
אֵת עֲוֹן כֻּלָּנוּ׃

הִפְגִּיעַ v.1.com.p.pf.Q. [תעה]; פָּנִינוּ v.1.com.p.pf.Q. [פנה]; תָּעִינוּ (encounter)

GALATIANS 3:22

²²ἀλλὰ συνέκλεισεν ἡ γραφὴ τὰ πάντα ὑπὸ ἁμαρτίαν, ἵνα ἡ ἐπαγγελία ἐκ πίστεως Ἰησοῦ Χριστοῦ δοθῇ τοῖς πιστεύουσιν.

συνέκλεισεν v.3.s.aor.act.ind. [συγκλείω] (imprison); δοθῇ v.3.s.aor.pass.sub. [δίδωμι]

4. Leviticus 5:14–15a; Galatians 3:23–24

A Mirror That Does Not Lie

THE LAW SHOWS US that whether we mean to be or not, we are sinners, and salvation cannot come from within. For this reason the law is our friend, a companion pointing us toward home, a mirror that does not lie.

LEVITICUS 5:14–15A

¹⁴וַיְדַבֵּר יְהוָה אֶל־מֹשֶׁה לֵּאמֹר:

¹⁵נֶפֶשׁ כִּי־תִמְעֹל מַעַל וְחָטְאָה בִּשְׁגָגָה מִקָּדְשֵׁי יְהוָה וְהֵבִיא
אֶת־אֲשָׁמוֹ לַיהוָה

תִּמְעֹל (be unfaithful); מַעַל (unfaithfulness); בִּשְׁגָגָה (inadvertence); וְהֵבִיא v.c. + v.3.m.s.pf.H. [בוא]; אֲשָׁמוֹ (guilt offering)

GALATIANS 3:23–24

²³Πρὸ τοῦ δὲ ἐλθεῖν τὴν πίστιν ὑπὸ νόμον ἐφρουρούμεθα συγκλειόμενοι εἰς τὴν μέλλουσαν πίστιν ἀποκαλυφθῆναι, ²⁴ὥστε ὁ νόμος παιδαγωγὸς ἡμῶν γέγονεν εἰς Χριστόν, ἵνα ἐκ πίστεως δικαιωθῶμεν·

Πρὸ (before); ἐφρουρούμεθα v.1.p.impf.pass.ind. [φρουρέω] (guard); συγκλειόμενοι (imprison); ἀποκαλυφθῆναι (reveal); παιδαγωγὸς (guardian); δικαιωθῶμεν (justify)

5. Isaiah 53:5; Matthew 27:46

The Forsakenness of God

THERE IS NOTHING MORE SURE than this: that God took into himself at the cross the God-forsakenness of us all. Each bleeding stripe is God's offer of promised life.

ISAIAH 53:5

⁵וְהוּא מְחֹלָל מִפְּשָׁעֵנוּ מְדֻכָּא מֵעֲוֹנֹתֵינוּ מוּסַר שְׁלוֹמֵנוּ עָלָיו וּבַחֲבֻרָתוֹ נִרְפָּא־לָנוּ׃

מְחֹלָל (wound); מְדֻכָּא (crush); וּבַחֲבֻרָתוֹ (wound)

MATTHEW 27:46

⁴⁶περὶ δὲ τὴν ἐνάτην ὥραν ἀνεβόησεν ὁ Ἰησοῦς φωνῇ μεγάλῃ λέγων, Ηλι ηλι λεμα σαβαχθανι; τοῦτ᾽ ἔστιν· Θεέ μου θεέ μου, ἱνατί με ἐγκατέλιπες;

ἀνεβόησεν v.3.s.aor.act.ind. [ἀναβοάω] (cry out); Ηλι ηλι λεμα σαβαχθανι Transliteration from Aramaic אֵלִי אֵלִי לְמָה שְׁבַקְתָּנִי "My God, my God, why did you abandon me?"; ἔστιν v.3.s.pres.ind. [εἰμί]; ἱνατί (why); ἐγκατέλιπες (abandon)

6. Isaiah 55:7; Mark 1:14–15

Run to Mercy!

RUN TO HIM, MY SOUL! Run fast with your head thrown back and your heart wide open! Run to Mercy! Run from life-as-if-God-wasn't-there! Run now!

ISAIAH 55:7

⁷יַעֲזֹב רָשָׁע דַּרְכּוֹ וְאִישׁ אָוֶן מַחְשְׁבֹתָיו וְיָשֹׁב אֶל־יְהוָה
וִירַחֲמֵהוּ וְאֶל־אֱלֹהֵינוּ כִּי־יַרְבֶּה לִסְלוֹחַ:

וְיָשֹׁב cj. + v.3.m.s.impf.Q. [שׁוב]; יְרַחֲמֵהוּ v.3.m.s.impf.P. [רחם] (have compassion) + 3.m.s.pr.sf.; לִסְלוֹחַ (forgive)

MARK 1:14–15

¹⁴Μετὰ δὲ τὸ παραδοθῆναι τὸν Ἰωάννην ἦλθεν ὁ Ἰησοῦς εἰς τὴν Γαλιλαίαν κηρύσσων τὸ εὐαγγέλιον τοῦ θεοῦ ¹⁵καὶ λέγων ὅτι Πεπλήρωται ὁ καιρὸς καὶ ἤγγικεν ἡ βασιλεία τοῦ θεοῦ· μετανοεῖτε καὶ πιστεύετε ἐν τῷ εὐαγγελίῳ.

ἦλθεν v.3.s.aor.act.ind. [ἔρχομαι]; ἤγγικεν v.3.s.pf.act.ind. [ἐγγίζω] (come near); μετανοεῖτε (repent)

7. Psalm 51:3–4 [1–2]; Luke 18:13–14

Justified by Mercy

JUSTIFIED BY *MERCY*. Not by argument or retribution, not by extracting the last farthing, not by tit for tat. Only by the mercy of God. This is what my heart needs to know. Mercy will set things right.

PSALM 51:3–4 [1–2]

³חָנֵּנִי אֱלֹהִים כְּחַסְדֶּךָ כְּרֹב רַחֲמֶיךָ מְחֵה פְשָׁעָי׃
⁴הֶרֶב כַּבְּסֵנִי מֵעֲוֺנִי וּמֵחַטָּאתִי טַהֲרֵנִי׃

חָנֵּנִי v.2.m.s.impv.Q. [חנן] + 1.com.s.pr.sf.; רַחֲמֶיךָ (mercy); מְחֵה (wipe away); הֶרֶב read as v.2.m.s.impv.Q. [רבה]; כַּבְּסֵנִי v.2.m.s.impv. [כבס] + 1.com.s.pr.sf.; טַהֲרֵנִי v.2.m.s.impv.P. [טהר] + 1.com.s.pr.sf.

LUKE 18:13–14

¹³ὁ δὲ τελώνης μακρόθεν ἑστὼς οὐκ ἤθελεν οὐδὲ τοὺς ὀφθαλμοὺς ἐπᾶραι εἰς τὸν οὐρανόν, ἀλλ᾽ ἔτυπτεν τὸ στῆθος αὐτοῦ λέγων, Ὁ θεός, ἱλάσθητί μοι τῷ ἁμαρτωλῷ. ¹⁴λέγω ὑμῖν, κατέβη οὗτος δεδικαιωμένος εἰς τὸν οἶκον αὐτοῦ παρ᾽ ἐκεῖνον· ὅτι πᾶς ὁ ὑψῶν ἑαυτὸν ταπεινωθήσεται, ὁ δὲ ταπεινῶν ἑαυτὸν ὑψωθήσεται.

τελώνης (tax collector); μακρόθεν (from a distance); οὐκ ἤθελεν neg.adv. before vowel + v.3.s.impf.act.ind. [ἐθελώ]; ἐπᾶραι (lift up); ἔτυπτεν (beat); στῆθος (breast); ἱλάσθητί v.2.s.aor.pass.impv. [ἱλάσκομαι] (be merciful); κατέβη v.3.s.aor.act.ind. [καταβαίνω]; δεδικαιωμένος (justify); ὑψῶν (raise up); ταπεινωθήσεται (humble); ὑψωθήσεται (exalt)

Week 8

Gentleness

1. Job 4:3–4; Galatians 6:1–2

The Gentle Servant

IN GENTLENESS THE SUFFERING SERVANT CAME, bearing the right-eousness of God to us, bearing the weight of our sin. So it is that when we approach one another over some wound we are to come gently, as servants, with forgiveness and restoration in our hearts.

JOB 4:3–4

³הִנֵּה יִסַּרְתָּ רַבִּים וְיָדַיִם רָפוֹת תְּחַזֵּק:
⁴כּוֹשֵׁל יְקִימוּן מִלֶּיךָ וּבִרְכַּיִם כֹּרְעוֹת תְּאַמֵּץ:

יִסַּרְתָּ (discipline); רָפוֹת (slack); יְקִימוּן v.3.m.p.impf.H. [קוּם] + para.; וּבִרְכַּיִם (knee); כֹּרְעוֹת (bend); תְּאַמֵּץ (be strong)

GALATIANS 6:1–2

¹Ἀδελφοί, ἐὰν καὶ προλημφθῇ ἄνθρωπος ἔν τινι παραπτώματι, ὑμεῖς οἱ πνευματικοὶ καταρτίζετε τὸν τοιοῦτον ἐν πνεύματι πραΰτητος, σκοπῶν σεαυτὸν μὴ καὶ σὺ πειρασθῇς. ²Ἀλλήλων τὰ βάρη βαστάζετε καὶ οὕτως ἀναπληρώσετε τὸν νόμον τοῦ Χριστοῦ.

προλημφθῇ v.3.s.aor.pass.sub. [προλαμβάνω] (overcome); παραπτώματι (sin); πνευματικοὶ (spiritual); καταρτίζετε (restore); πραΰτητος (gentleness); σκοπῶν (notice); πειρασθῇς (tempt); βάρη (burden); βαστάζετε (bear); ἀναπληρώσετε (fulfill)

2. Isaiah 42:2-3; 2 Corinthians 10:1-2

Gentle Strength

GENTLENESS SHOWS ITS TUNGSTEN STRENGTH in faithfulness rather than force.

ISAIAH 42:2-3

²לֹא יִצְעַק וְלֹא יִשָּׂא וְלֹא־יַשְׁמִיעַ בַּחוּץ קוֹלוֹ׃
³קָנֶה רָצוּץ לֹא יִשְׁבּוֹר וּפִשְׁתָּה כֵהָה לֹא יְכַבֶּנָּה לֶאֱמֶת יוֹצִיא
מִשְׁפָּט׃

יִשָּׂא v.3.m.s.impf.Q. [נשא]; רָצוּץ (crush); וּפִשְׁתָּה (wick); כֵהָה (dim); יְכַבֶּנָּה v.3.m.s.impf.P. [כבה] (be quenched) + 3.f.s.pr.sf.; יוֹצִיא v.3.m.s.impf.H. [יצא]

2 CORINTHIANS 10:1-2

¹Αὐτὸς δὲ ἐγὼ Παῦλος παρακαλῶ ὑμᾶς διὰ τῆς πραΰτητος καὶ ἐπιεικείας τοῦ Χριστοῦ, ὃς κατὰ πρόσωπον μὲν ταπεινὸς ἐν ὑμῖν, ἀπὼν δὲ θαρρῶ εἰς ὑμᾶς· ²δέομαι δὲ τὸ μὴ παρὼν θαρρῆσαι τῇ πεποιθήσει ᾗ λογίζομαι τολμῆσαι ἐπί τινας τοὺς λογιζομένους ἡμᾶς ὡς κατὰ σάρκα περιπατοῦντας.

πραΰτητος (meekness); ἐπιεικείας (gentleness); ταπεινὸς (subservient); ἀπὼν v.m.s.nom.pres.ptc. [ἄπειμι] (be absent); θαρρῶ (be confident); παρὼν v.m.s.nom.ptc. [πάρειμι] (be present); λογιζομένους (consider)

3. Numbers 12:1–3; Ephesians 4:1–3

How We Hear

THE ONLY THING MOSES HEARD when his siblings turned against him was their desperate need for prayer. So he prayed. And Miriam was healed. This is the power of gentleness.

NUMBERS 12:1–3

¹וַתְּדַבֵּר מִרְיָם וְאַהֲרֹן בְּמֹשֶׁה עַל־אֹדוֹת הָאִשָּׁה הַכֻּשִׁית אֲשֶׁר לָקָח כִּי־אִשָּׁה כֻשִׁית לָקָח:

²וַיֹּאמְרוּ הֲרַק אַךְ־בְּמֹשֶׁה דִּבֶּר יְהוָה הֲלֹא גַּם־בָּנוּ דִבֵּר וַיִּשְׁמַע יְהוָה:

³וְהָאִישׁ מֹשֶׁה עָנָיו מְאֹד מִכֹּל הָאָדָם אֲשֶׁר עַל־פְּנֵי הָאֲדָמָה:

עַל־אֹדוֹת (because of); עָנָיו (Qe. humble)

EPHESIANS 4:1–3

¹Παρακαλῶ οὖν ὑμᾶς ἐγὼ ὁ δέσμιος ἐν κυρίῳ ἀξίως περιπατῆσαι τῆς κλήσεως ἧς ἐκλήθητε, ²μετὰ πάσης ταπεινοφροσύνης καὶ πραΰτητος, μετὰ μακροθυμίας, ἀνεχόμενοι ἀλλήλων ἐν ἀγάπῃ, ³σπουδάζοντες τηρεῖν τὴν ἑνότητα τοῦ πνεύματος ἐν τῷ συνδέσμῳ τῆς εἰρήνης·

δέσμιος (prisoner); ἀξίως (worthy); κλήσεως (calling); ταπεινοφρο-σύνης (humility); πραΰτητος (gentleness); μακροθυμίας (patience); ἀνεχό-μενοι (endure); σπουδάζοντες (be eager); ἑνότητα (unity); συνδέσμῳ (band)

4. Isaiah 40:11, 1 Thessalonians 2:7–8

Models for Ministry

WHAT WOULD THE CHURCH BE LIKE if pastors were taught to regard nursing mothers as their model for ministry?

ISAIAH 40:11

ּ‎11 כְּרֹעֶה עֶדְרוֹ יִרְעֶה בִּזְרֹעוֹ יְקַבֵּץ טְלָאִים וּבְחֵיקוֹ יִשָּׂא עָלוֹת
יְנַהֵל׃

עֶדְרוֹ (flock); טְלָאִים (lamb); וּבְחֵיקוֹ (bosom); יִשָּׂא v.3.m.s.impf.Q. [נשׂא];
עָלוֹת v.f.p.ptc.Q. [עוּל] (suck); יְנַהֵל (lead)

1 THESSALONIANS 2:7–8

⁷δυνάμενοι ἐν βάρει εἶναι ὡς Χριστοῦ ἀπόστολοι. ἀλλὰ ἐγενήθημεν νήπιοι ἐν μέσῳ ὑμῶν, ὡς ἐὰν τροφὸς θάλπῃ τὰ ἑαυτῆς τέκνα, ⁸οὕτως ὁμειρόμενοι ὑμῶν εὐδοκοῦμεν μεταδοῦναι ὑμῖν οὐ μόνον τὸ εὐαγγέλιον τοῦ θεοῦ ἀλλὰ καὶ τὰς ἑαυτῶν ψυχάς, διότι ἀγαπητοὶ ἡμῖν ἐγενήθητε.

ἐν βάρει εἶναι (act authoritatively); εἶναι v.pres.in. [εἰμί]); ἐγενήθημεν v.1.p.aor.pass.ind. [γίνομαι]; νήπιοι (kind); τροφὸς (nurse); θάλπῃ (comfort); ὁμειρόμενοι (long for); εὐδοκοῦμεν (resolve); μεταδοῦναι (share); διότι (because); ἐγενήθητε v.2.p.aor.pass.ind. [γίνομαι]

5. Proverbs 24:21–22; Titus 3:1–2

The Test

THE FAILPROOF TEST OF GENTLENESS comes when we have to report to someone less capable or intelligent or, particularly, less spiritual than we think we are.

PROVERBS 24:21–22

²¹יְרָא־אֶת־יְהוָה בְּנִי וָמֶלֶךְ עִם־שׁוֹנִים אַל־תִּתְעָרָב׃
²²כִּי־פִתְאֹם יָקוּם אֵידָם וּפִיד שְׁנֵיהֶם מִי יוֹדֵעַ׃

שׁוֹנִים v.m.p.ptc.Q. [שׁנה] (differ); תִּתְעָרָב (have fellowship); פִתְאֹם (suddenly); אֵידָם (calamity); וּפִיד (ruin)

TITUS 3:1–2

¹Ὑπομίμνῃσκε αὐτοὺς ἀρχαῖς ἐξουσίαις ὑποτάσσεσθαι, πειθαρχεῖν, πρὸς πᾶν ἔργον ἀγαθὸν ἑτοίμους εἶναι, ²μηδένα βλασφημεῖν, ἀμάχους εἶναι, ἐπιεικεῖς, πᾶσαν ἐνδεικνυμένους πραΰτητα πρὸς πάντας ἀνθρώπους.

Ὑπομίμνῃσκε (remind); ὑποτάσσεσθαι (subject); πειθαρχεῖν (obey); ἑτοίμους (ready); εἶναι v.pres.in. [εἰμί]; βλασφημεῖν (blaspheme); ἀμάχους (peaceful); ἐπιεικεῖς (gentle); ἐνδεικνυμένους (show); πραΰτητα (consideration)

6. Proverbs 15:1; 1 Peter 3.8–9

When I Am Squeezed

LORD, FILL MY HEART WITH GENTLE LOVE so that when it is squeezed by trouble or hurt or someone else's anger, gentleness will come out.

PROVERBS 15:1

¹מַעֲנֶה־רַּךְ יָשִׁיב חֵמָה וּדְבַר־עֶצֶב יַעֲלֶה־אָף׃

רַּ (tender); יָשִׁיב v.3.m.s.impf.H. [שׁוב]; עֶצֶב (hurt)

1 PETER 3:8–9

⁸Τὸ δὲ τέλος πάντες ὁμόφρονες, συμπαθεῖς, φιλάδελφοι, εὔσπλαγχνοι, ταπεινόφρονες, ⁹μὴ ἀποδιδόντες κακὸν ἀντὶ κακοῦ ἢ λοιδορίαν ἀντὶ λοιδορίας, τοὐναντίον δὲ εὐλογοῦντες ὅτι εἰς τοῦτο ἐκλήθητε ἵνα εὐλογίαν κληρονομήσητε.

τέλος (finally); ὁμόφρονες (like-minded); συμπαθεῖς (sympathetic); φιλάδελφοι (brother lover); εὔσπλαγχνοι (compassionate); ταπεινόφρονες (humble); ἀποδιδόντες (repay); ἀντὶ (in place of); λοιδορίαν (abuse); τοὐναντίον (on the contrary); εὐλογοῦντες (bless); κληρονομήσητε v.2.p.aor.act.sub. [κληρονομέω] (inherit)

7. Proverbs 15:18; 1 Peter 3:15–16

Gentle Presence

THE GENTLE SOUL HAS A WAY of speaking peace into others'
storms, not with words, but with presence.

PROVERBS 15:18

18אִישׁ חֵמָה יְגָרֶה מָדוֹן וְאֶרֶךְ אַפַּיִם יַשְׁקִיט רִיב:

יְגָרֶה (stir up); מָדוֹן (strife); יַשְׁקִיט (quiet)

1 PETER 3:15–16

15κύριον δὲ τὸν Χριστὸν ἁγιάσατε ἐν ταῖς καρδίαις ὑμῶν,
ἕτοιμοι ἀεὶ πρὸς ἀπολογίαν παντὶ τῷ αἰτοῦντι ὑμᾶς λόγον
περὶ τῆς ἐν ὑμῖν ἐλπίδος, 16ἀλλὰ μετὰ πραΰτητος καὶ φόβου,
συνείδησιν ἔχοντες ἀγαθήν, ἵνα ἐν ᾧ καταλαλεῖσθε
καταισχυνθῶσιν οἱ ἐπηρεάζοντες ὑμῶν τὴν ἀγαθὴν ἐν
Χριστῷ ἀναστροφήν.

ἁγιάσατε (sanctify); ἕτοιμοι (ready); ἀεὶ (always); ἀπολογίαν (defense);
πραΰτητος (gentleness); φόβου (fear); συνείδησιν (conscience); καταλαλεῖσθε (defame); καταισχυνθῶσιν (dishonor); ἐπηρεάζοντες (abuse);
ἀναστροφήν (behavior)

Self-Control

1. Proverbs 16:32; James 1:19–20

Listening

O GOD, MAY I LISTEN with all my might, to you and to others, and may my mouth be your instrument of peace.

PROVERBS 16:32

³²טוֹב אֶרֶךְ אַפַּיִם מִגִּבּוֹר וּמֹשֵׁל בְּרוּחוֹ מִלֹּכֵד עִיר׃

JAMES 1:19–20

¹⁹Ἴστε, ἀδελφοί μου ἀγαπητοί· ἔστω δὲ πᾶς ἄνθρωπος ταχὺς εἰς τὸ ἀκοῦσαι, βραδὺς εἰς τὸ λαλῆσαι, βραδὺς εἰς ὀργήν· ²⁰ὀργὴ γὰρ ἀνδρὸς δικαιοσύνην θεοῦ οὐκ ἐργάζεται.

Ἴστε v.2.p.pf.act.impv. [οἶδα]; ταχὺς (quick); βραδὺς (slow); ὀργὴν (anger); ἐργάζεται (accomplish)

2. Psalm 37:3–4; 2 Peter 3:17–18

Self-Control and Trust

HOW LONG WILL IT TAKE, beloved Lord, until I will truly believe that you are not going to trick me somehow, that you really do want me to feel secure and blessed and daily kissed by grace? How long until I trust without reserve?

PSALM 37:3–4

³בְּטַח בַּיהוָה וַעֲשֵׂה־טוֹב שְׁכָן־אֶרֶץ וּרְעֵה אֱמוּנָה׃
⁴וְהִתְעַנַּג עַל־יְהוָה וְיִתֶּן־לְךָ מִשְׁאֲלֹת לִבֶּךָ׃

וְיִתֶּן cj. + v.3.m.s.impf.Q. [נתן]; וְהִתְעַנַּג (delight); מִשְׁאָלֹת (request)

2 PETER 3:17–18

¹⁷Ὑμεῖς οὖν, ἀγαπητοί, προγινώσκοντες φυλάσσεσθε, ἵνα μὴ τῇ τῶν ἀθέσμων πλάνῃ συναπαχθέντες ἐκπέσητε τοῦ ἰδίου στηριγμοῦ, ¹⁸αὐξάνετε δὲ ἐν χάριτι καὶ γνώσει τοῦ κυρίου ἡμῶν καὶ σωτῆρος Ἰησοῦ Χριστοῦ. αὐτῷ ἡ δόξα καὶ νῦν καὶ εἰς ἡμέραν αἰῶνος. ⌜ἀμήν.⌝

προγινώσκοντες (know before); φυλάσσεσθε (watch); ἀθέσμων (lawless); πλάνῃ (error); συναπαχθέντες v.m.p.nom.aor.pass.ptc. [συναπάγω] (led away); ἐκπέσητε v.2.p.aor.act.sub. [ἐκπίπτω] (fall off); στηριγμοῦ (firmness); αὐξάνετε (grow); γνώσει (knowledge); σωτῆρος (savior); νῦν (now)

9. Proverbs 5:18–21; 1 Thessalonians 4:3–6a

Fidelity

THE CHOICES THAT LEAD to marital fidelity are numerous and mostly subtle. But each choice to reverence my spouse's body, soul, history, or needs, is a choice to reverence Christ.

PROVERBS 5:18–21

¹⁸יְהִי־מְקוֹרְךָ בָרוּךְ וּשְׂמַח מֵאֵשֶׁת נְעוּרֶךָ:
¹⁹אַיֶּלֶת אֲהָבִים וְיַעֲלַת־חֵן דַּדֶּיהָ יְרַוֻּךָ בְכָל־עֵת בְּאַהֲבָתָהּ
תִּשְׁגֶּה תָמִיד:
²⁰וְלָמָּה תִשְׁגֶּה בְנִי בְזָרָה וּתְחַבֵּק חֵק נָכְרִיָּה:
²¹כִּי נֹכַח עֵינֵי יְהוָה דַּרְכֵי־אִישׁ וְכָל־מַעְגְּלֹתָיו מְפַלֵּס:

יְהִי v.3.m.s.jus.Q. [היה]; מְקוֹרְךָ (well); נְעוּרֶךָ (youth); וְיַעֲלַת (she-goat = wife); דַּדֶּיהָ (breast); יְרַוֻּךָ v.3.m.p.impf.P. [רוה] (satiate) + 2.m.s.pr.sf.; חֵק (bosom); נָכְרִיָּה (foreigner); נֹכַח (in front of); מַעְגְּלֹתָיו (course); מְפַלֵּס (smooth)

1 THESSALONIANS 4:3–6A

³Τοῦτο γάρ ἐστιν θέλημα τοῦ θεοῦ, ὁ ἁγιασμὸς ὑμῶν, ἀπέχεσθαι ὑμᾶς ἀπὸ τῆς πορνείας, ⁴εἰδέναι ἕκαστον ὑμῶν τὸ ἑαυτοῦ σκεῦος κτᾶσθαι ἐν ἁγιασμῷ καὶ τιμῇ, ⁵μὴ ἐν πάθει ἐπιθυμίας καθάπερ καὶ τὰ ἔθνη τὰ μὴ εἰδότα τὸν θεόν, ⁶τὸ μὴ ὑπερβαίνειν καὶ πλεονεκτεῖν ἐν τῷ πράγματι τὸν ἀδελφὸν αὐτοῦ,

ἐστιν v.3.s.pres.ind. [εἰμί]; ἁγιασμὸς (holiness); ἀπέχεσθαι (keep away); πορνείας (immorality); σκεῦος (vessel/body); κτᾶσθαι v.pres.mid.in. [κτάο-μαι] (possess); τιμῇ (honor); πάθει (passion); ἐπιθυμίας (desire); καθάπερ (just as)

4. Proverbs 25:28; 1 Corinthians 7:5

Guarding Against Excess

EVEN PRAYER MAY BECOME AN AVENUE for sin, if not exercised in moderation, with self-control.

PROVERBS 25:28

²⁸עִיר פְּרוּצָה אֵין חוֹמָה אִישׁ אֲשֶׁר אֵין מַעְצָר לְרוּחוֹ׃

מַעְצָר (restrain)

1 CORINTHIANS 7:5

⁵μὴ ἀποστερεῖτε ἀλλήλους, εἰ μήτι ἂν ἐκ συμφώνου πρὸς καιρόν, ἵνα σχολάσητε τῇ προσευχῇ καὶ πάλιν ἐπὶ τὸ αὐτὸ ἦτε, ἵνα μὴ πειράζῃ ὑμᾶς ὁ Σατανᾶς διὰ τὴν ἀκρασίαν ὑμῶν.

ἀποστερεῖτε (deprive); συμφώνου (agreement); σχολάσητε v.2.p.aor.act.sub. [σχολάζω] (devote oneself); προσευχῇ (prayer); ἐπὶ τὸ αὐτὸ prep. + d.a.nt.s.acc. + pr.nt.s.acc. (as [you were]); πειράζῃ (tempt); Σατανᾶς (Satan); ἀκρασίαν (lack of self-control)

5. Proverbs 2.6–8, 2 Timothy 1.6–7

Choosing Faith Instead of Fear

THIS COMES AS A SURPRISE, Lord, both in a chastening and liberating sense, the awareness that I have the power to choose whether to be fearful or faith-full.

PROVERBS 2:6–8

6כִּי־יְהֹוָה יִתֵּן חָכְמָה מִפִּיו דַּעַת וּתְבוּנָה׃
7יִצְפֹּן לַיְשָׁרִים תּוּשִׁיָּה מָגֵן לְהֹלְכֵי תֹם׃
8לִנְצֹר אָרְחוֹת מִשְׁפָּט וְדֶרֶךְ חֲסִידָיו יִשְׁמֹר׃

יִתֵּן v.3.m.s.impf.Q. [נתן]; וּתְבוּנָה (understanding); יִצְפֹּן (treasure); תּוּשִׁיָּה (wisdom); תֹם (completeness)

2 TIMOTHY 1:6–7

⁶δι᾽ ἣν αἰτίαν ἀναμιμνήσκω σε ἀναζωπυρεῖν τὸ χάρισμα τοῦ θεοῦ, ὅ ἐστιν ἐν σοὶ διὰ τῆς ἐπιθέσεως τῶν χειρῶν μου. ⁷οὐ γὰρ ἔδωκεν ἡμῖν ὁ θεὸς πνεῦμα δειλίας ἀλλὰ δυνάμεως καὶ ἀγάπης καὶ σωφρονισμοῦ.

αἰτίαν (therefore); ἀναμιμνήσκω (remind); ἀναζωπυρεῖν (kindle); χάρισμα (gift); ἐστιν v.3.s.pres.ind. [εἰμί]; ἐπιθέσεως (laying on [hands]); ἔδωκεν v.3.s.aor.act.ind. [δίδωμι]; δειλίας (timidity); σωφρονισμοῦ (self-discipline)

6. Psalm 34:13–17 [12–16]; 1 Peter 3:10–12

Where Is the Danger?

THE PART OF THE BODY that is most threatening to one's integrity
is the mouth.

PSALM 34:13–17 [12–16]

13מִי־הָאִישׁ הֶחָפֵץ חַיִּים אֹהֵב יָמִים לִרְאוֹת טוֹב:
14נְצֹר לְשׁוֹנְךָ מֵרָע וּשְׂפָתֶיךָ מִדַּבֵּר מִרְמָה:
15סוּר מֵרָע וַעֲשֵׂה־טוֹב בַּקֵּשׁ שָׁלוֹם וְרָדְפֵהוּ:
16עֵינֵי יְהוָה אֶל־צַדִּיקִים וְאָזְנָיו אֶל־שַׁוְעָתָם:
17פְּנֵי יְהוָה בְּעֹשֵׂי רָע לְהַכְרִית מֵאֶרֶץ זִכְרָם:

לִרְאוֹת prep. + v.in.cs.Q. [ראה]; מִרְמָה (deceit); וְרָדְפֵהוּ cj. + v.2.m.s.impv.Q.
[רדף] + 3.m.s.pr.sf.; שַׁוְעָתָם (cry for help); בְּעֹשֵׂי prep. + v.m.p.cs.act.ptc.Q.
[עשׂה]; זִכְרָם (remembrance)

1 PETER 3:10–12

¹⁰ὁ γὰρ θέλων ζωὴν ἀγαπᾶν
    καὶ ἰδεῖν ἡμέρας ἀγαθὰς
παυσάτω τὴν γλῶσσαν ἀπὸ κακοῦ
    καὶ χείλη τοῦ μὴ λαλῆσαι δόλον,
¹¹ἐκκλινάτω δὲ ἀπὸ κακοῦ καὶ ποιησάτω
ἀγαθόν,
    ζητησάτω εἰρήνην καὶ διωξάτω αὐτήν·
¹²ὅτι ὀφθαλμοὶ κυρίου ἐπὶ δικαίους
    καὶ ὦτα αὐτοῦ εἰς δέησιν αὐτῶν,
πρόσωπον δὲ κυρίου ἐπὶ ποιοῦντας κακά.

ἰδεῖν v.aor.act.in. [ὁράω]; παυσάτω v.3.s.aor.act.impv. [παύω] (cease);
χείλη (lip); δόλον (deceit); ἐκκλινάτω (turn away); διωξάτω
v.3.p.pres.act.sub. [διώκω] (pursue); ὦτα (ear); δέησιν (prayer)

7. Psalm 37.7b–9, 2 Peter 1.5–7

The Context Makes All the Difference

O GOD, MAY I EXERCISE SELF-CONTROL only in the context of steadfast faith in you and affectionate concern for others. Without those safeguards self-control will just turn into another form of idolatry.

PSALM 37:7B–9

⁷אַל־תִּתְחַר בְּמַצְלִיחַ דַּרְכּוֹ בְּאִישׁ
עֹשֶׂה מְזִמּוֹת:
⁸הֶרֶף מֵאַף וַעֲזֹב חֵמָה אַל־תִּתְחַר אַךְ־לְהָרֵעַ:
⁹כִּי־מְרֵעִים יִכָּרֵתוּן וְקֹוֵי יְהוָה הֵמָּה יִירְשׁוּ־אָרֶץ:

[רפה] v.2.m.s.impv.H. הֶרֶף; (evil thing) מְזִמּוֹת; [חרה] v.2.m.s.impf.Ht. תִּתְחַר
(abandon); [רעע] v.in.cs.H. לְהָרֵעַ prep. + [רעע]; מְרֵעִים v.m.p.act.ptc.H. [רעע];
[כרת] v.3.m.impf.N. יִכָּרֵתוּן + para.; וְקֹוֵי cj. + v.m.p.cs.act.ptc.Q. [קוה]

2 PETER 1:5–7

⁵καὶ αὐτὸ τοῦτο δὲ σπουδὴν πᾶσαν παρεισενέγκαντες ἐπιχορηγήσατε ἐν τῇ πίστει ὑμῶν τὴν ἀρετήν, ἐν δὲ τῇ ἀρετῇ τὴν γνῶσιν, ⁶ἐν δὲ τῇ γνώσει τὴν ἐγκράτειαν, ἐν δὲ τῇ ἐγκρατείᾳ τὴν ὑπομονήν, ἐν δὲ τῇ ὑπομονῇ τὴν εὐσέβειαν, ⁷ἐν δὲ τῇ εὐσεβείᾳ τὴν φιλαδελφίαν, ἐν δὲ τῇ φιλαδελφίᾳ τὴν ἀγάπην.

σπουδὴν παρεισενέγκαντες v.m.p.nom.aor.act.ptc [παρεισφέρω] (make an effort); ἐπιχορηγήσατε (provide); ἀρετήν (virtue); γνῶσιν (knowledge); ἐγκράτειαν (self-control); ὑπομονήν (patience); εὐσέβειαν (godliness); φιλαδελφίαν (brother lover)

Week 10

Perseverance in Faith

1. Psalm 51:11–13 [10–12]; Galatians 5:1

Be My Perseverance

EVEN THOUGH MY PERSEVERANCE flags at times, Lord, yours is infinitely strong. Be my perseverance. Draw me to your heart when my heart is faint. Only in you can I persevere.

PSALM 51:11–13 [10–12]

י¹¹הַסְתֵּר פָּנֶיךָ מֵחֲטָאָי וְכָל־עֲוֹנֹתַי מְחֵה׃

¹²לֵב טָהוֹר בְּרָא־לִי אֱלֹהִים וְרוּחַ נָכוֹן חַדֵּשׁ בְּקִרְבִּי׃

¹³אַל־תַּשְׁלִיכֵנִי מִלְּפָנֶיךָ וְרוּחַ קָדְשְׁךָ אַל־תִּקַּח מִמֶּנִּי׃

מְחֵה v.2.s.m.s.impv.Q. [מחה] (wipe away); חַדֵּשׁ (be new); תַּשְׁלִיכֵנִי v.2.m.s.impf.H. [שלך] + 1.com.s.pr.sf.; תִּקַּח v.2.m.s.impf.Q. [לקח]

GALATIANS 5:1

¹Τῇ ἐλευθερίᾳ ἡμᾶς Χριστὸς ἠλευθέρωσεν· στήκετε οὖν καὶ μὴ πάλιν ζυγῷ δουλείας ἐνέχεσθε.

ἐλευθερίᾳ (freedom); ἠλευθέρωσεν (set free); στήκετε (stand); ζυγῷ (yoke); δουλείας (slavery); ἐνέχεσθε v.2.p.pres.pass.impv. [ἐνέχω] (be subject)

2. Daniel 3:16–18; Luke 1:37–38

Ordinary Saints—Extraordinary Power

THE SAINTS—the Meshachs and Marys of our day—are those ordinary souls who persevere in faith when the odds are impossible, the call unthinkable, the price too high. Their great power is invisible to most of us.

DANIEL 3:16–18 (A.)

16עֲנוֹ שַׁדְרַךְ מֵישַׁךְ וַעֲבֵד נְגוֹ וְאָמְרִין לְמַלְכָּא נְבוּכַדְנֶצַּר
לָא־חַשְׁחִין אֲנַחְנָה עַל־דְּנָה פִּתְגָם לַהֲתָבוּתָךְ׃
17הֵן אִיתַי אֱלָהַנָא דִּי־אֲנַחְנָא פָלְחִין יָכִל לְשֵׁיזָבוּתַנָא מִן־אַתּוּן
נוּרָא יָקִדְתָּא וּמִן־יְדָךְ מַלְכָּא יְשֵׁיזִב׃
18וְהֵן לָא יְדִיעַ לֶהֱוֵא־לָךְ מַלְכָּא דִּי לֵאלָהָיִךְ לָא־אִיתַנָא
פָלְחִין וּלְצֶלֶם דַּהֲבָא דִּי הֲקֵימְתָּ לָא נִסְגֻּד׃

לַהֲתָבוּתָךְ prep. + v.in.cs.Ha. [תוב] + 2.m.s.pr.sf.; לְשֵׁיזָבוּתַנָא prep. +
v.in.cs.Shafel [יזב] + 1.com.p.pr.sf.; יָקִדְתָּא v.f.s.ptc.act.Pe. [יקד] + d.a.; הֲקֵימְתָּ
v.2.m.s.pf.Aphel [קום]

LUKE 1:37–38

37ὅτι οὐκ ἀδυνατήσει παρὰ τοῦ θεοῦ πᾶν ῥῆμα. 38εἶπεν δὲ
Μαριάμ· Ἰδοὺ ἡ δούλη κυρίου· γένοιτό μοι κατὰ τὸ ῥῆμα
σου. καὶ ἀπῆλθεν ἀπ᾽ αὐτῆς ὁ ἄγγελος.

ἀδυνατήσει (be impossible); εἶπεν v.3.s.aor.act.ind. [λέγω]; δούλη
(female servant); γένοιτό v.3.s.aor.mid.optative [γίνομαι]; ἀπῆλθεν
v.3.s.aor.act.ind. [ἀπέρχομαι]

3. Isaiah 1:16–17; 1 Peter 4:1–2

The Source of Persevering Faith

LEARNING TO DO GOOD and to keep on doing it takes the kind of perseverance that comes from having done wrong over and over, and from having been broken by that grievous pattern, and then having been healed by the persevering love of Christ.

ISAIAH 1:16–17

רַחֲצוּ הִזַּכּוּ הָסִירוּ רֹעַ מַעַלְלֵיכֶם מִנֶּגֶד עֵינָי חִדְלוּ הָרֵעַ: ¹⁶

לִמְדוּ הֵיטֵב דִּרְשׁוּ מִשְׁפָּט אַשְּׁרוּ חָמוֹץ שִׁפְטוּ יָתוֹם רִיבוּ אַלְמָנָה: ¹⁷

הִזַּכּוּ v.2.m.p.impv.Ht. [זכך] (be pure); הָסִירוּ v.2.m.p.impv.H. [סור]; רֹעַ (wickedness); מַעַלְלֵיכֶם (deed); הָרֵעַ v.in.ab.H. [רעע]; אַשְּׁרוּ (go straight); חָמוֹץ (ruthless); יָתוֹם (orphan); אַלְמָנָה (widow)

1 PETER 4:1–2

¹Χριστοῦ οὖν παθόντος σαρκὶ καὶ ὑμεῖς τὴν αὐτὴν ἔννοιαν ὁπλίσασθε, ὅτι ὁ παθὼν σαρκὶ πέπαυται ἁμαρτίας ²εἰς τὸ μηκέτι ἀνθρώπων ἐπιθυμίαις ἀλλὰ θελήματι θεοῦ τὸν ἐπίλοιπον ἐν σαρκὶ βιῶσαι χρόνον.

ἔννοιαν (attitude); ὁπλίσασθε v.2.p.aor.mid.impv. [ὁπλίζω] (arm); πέπαυται v.3.s.pf.pass.ind. [παύω] (cease); μηκέτι (no longer); ἐπιθυμίαις (desire); ἐπίλοιπον (left); βιῶσαι (live)

4. Deuteronomy 32.4–6, Galatians 3:1–3

Spiritual Quicksand

A SOBERING THOUGHT IT IS, that we can choose to wander into the swamp of self, any time we want. It makes no difference whether the carnality is religious or sensuous—it is quicksand to the soul.

DEUTERONOMY 32:4–6

⁴הַצּוּר תָּמִים פָּעֳלוֹ כִּי כָל־דְּרָכָיו מִשְׁפָּט אֵל אֱמוּנָה וְאֵין עָוֶל צַדִּיק וְיָשָׁר הוּא:

⁵שִׁחֵת לוֹ לֹא בָּנָיו מוּמָם דּוֹר עִקֵּשׁ וּפְתַלְתֹּל:

⁶הֲלַיהוָה תִּגְמְלוּ־זֹאת עַם נָבָל וְלֹא חָכָם הֲלוֹא־הוּא אָבִיךָ קָּנֶךָ הוּא עָשְׂךָ וַיְכֹנְנֶךָ:

פָּעֳלוֹ (deed); אֱמוּנָה (faithfulness); עָוֶל (unrighteousness); מוּמָם (blemish); עִקֵּשׁ (perverted); וּפְתַלְתֹּל cj. + adj.m.s. (twisted); תִּגְמְלוּ (repay); נָבָל (stupid); קָּנֶךָ v.m.s.ptc.Q. [קנה] + 2.m.s.pr.sf.; עָשְׂךָ v.3.m.s.pf.Q. [עשה] + 2.m.s.pr.sf.; וַיְכֹנְנֶךָ v.c. + v.3.m.s.impf.Pil. [כון] + 2.m.s.pr.sf.

GALATIANS 3:1–3

¹Ὦ ἀνόητοι Γαλάται, τίς ὑμᾶς ἐβάσκανεν, οἷς κατ' ὀφθαλμοὺς Ἰησοῦς Χριστὸς προεγράφη ἐσταυρωμένος; ²τοῦτο μόνον θέλω μαθεῖν ἀφ' ὑμῶν· ἐξ ἔργων νόμου τὸ πνεῦμα ἐλάβετε ἢ ἐξ ἀκοῆς πίστεως; ³οὕτως ἀνόητοι ἐστε, ἐναρξάμενοι πνεύματι νῦν σαρκὶ ἐπιτελεῖσθε;

ἀνόητοι (foolish); ἐβάσκανεν (bewitch); προεγράφη (publicly display); ἐσταυρωμένος (crucify); μαθεῖν v.aor.act.in. [μανθάνω] (learn); ἀκοῆς (hearing); ἐναρξάμενοι v.m.p.nom.aor.mid.part. [ἐνάρχομαι] (begin); νῦν (now); ἐπιτελεῖσθε (complete)

79

5. Job 2:3; Philippians 3:12–14

Belonging

O Jesus, how can I describe the joy I feel when I remember that *you* have made me your own? It is this truth that enables me to persevere. I am your own. And you are mine.

Job 2:3

³וַיֹּאמֶר יְהוָה אֶל־הַשָּׂטָן הֲשַׂמְתָּ לִבְּךָ אֶל־עַבְדִּי אִיּוֹב כִּי
אֵין כָּמֹהוּ בָּאָרֶץ אִישׁ תָּם וְיָשָׁר יְרֵא אֱלֹהִים וְסָר מֵרָע וְעֹדֶנּוּ
מַחֲזִיק בְּתֻמָּתוֹ וַתְּסִיתֵנִי בוֹ לְבַלְּעוֹ חִנָּם׃

הַשָּׂטָן (adversary); הֲשַׂמְתָּ int. + v.2.m.s.pf.Q. [שׂים]; תָּם (whole); וְסָר cj. +
v.m.s.act.ptc.Q. [סור]; בְּתֻמָּתוֹ (integrity); וַתְּסִיתֵנִי v.c. + v.2.m.s.impf.H. [סות]
(allure) + 1.com.s.pr.sf.; לְבַלְּעוֹ (swallow); חִנָּם (in vain)

Philippians 3:12–14

¹²Οὐχ ὅτι ἤδη ἔλαβον ἢ ἤδη τετελείωμαι, διώκω δὲ εἰ καὶ
καταλάβω, ἐφ᾽ ᾧ καὶ κατελήμφθην ὑπὸ Χριστοῦ [Ἰησοῦ].
¹³ἀδελφοί, ἐγὼ ἐμαυτὸν οὐ λογίζομαι κατειληφέναι· ἓν δέ, τὰ
μὲν ὀπίσω ἐπιλανθανόμενος τοῖς δὲ ἔμπροσθεν ἐπεκτεινόμενος,
¹⁴κατὰ σκοπὸν διώκω εἰς τὸ βραβεῖον τῆς ἄνω κλήσεως τοῦ
θεοῦ ἐν Χριστῷ Ἰησοῦ.

τετελείωμαι (finish); διώκω (press on); καταλάβω (seize); κατελήμφθην v.1.s.aor.pass.ind. [καταλαμβάνω]; λογίζομαι (consider); κατειληφέ-
ναι v.pf.act.in. [καταλαμβάνω]; ὀπίσω (behind); ἐπιλανθανόμενος (forget); ἔμπροσθεν (before); ἐπεκτεινόμενος (strain ahead); σκοπὸν (good);
διώκω (pursue); βραβεῖον (prize); ἄνω (upward); κλήσεως (calling)

6. Psalm 37:5–7a; 1 Peter 4:17–19

The Snare of Vindication

FOR SOME OF US THE DESIRE TO VINDICATE ourselves is much more damaging to our perseverance than outright cowardice or a fickle heart.

PSALM 37:5–7A

⁵גּוֹל עַל־יְהוָה דַּרְכֶּךָ וּבְטַח עָלָיו וְהוּא יַעֲשֶׂה:

⁶וְהוֹצִיא כָאוֹר צִדְקֶךָ וּמִשְׁפָּטֶךָ כַּצָּהֳרָיִם:

⁷דּוֹם לַיהוָה וְהִתְחוֹלֵל לוֹ

גּוֹל v.2.m.s.impv.Q.plene [גלל] (roll); וְהוֹצִיא v.c. + v.3.m.s.pf.H. [יצא];
כַּצָּהֳרָיִם (noon); דּוֹם v.2.m.s.impv.Q. [דמם] (be silent); וְהִתְחוֹלֵל v.c. +
v.3.m.s.pf.Ht. [חול] (await)

1 PETER 4:17–19

¹⁷ὅτι [ὁ] καιρὸς τοῦ ἄρξασθαι τὸ κρίμα ἀπὸ τοῦ οἴκου τοῦ
θεοῦ· εἰ δὲ πρῶτον ἀφ᾽ ἡμῶν, τί τὸ τέλος τῶν ἀπειθούντων τῷ
τοῦ θεοῦ εὐαγγελίῳ;
¹⁸καὶ

εἰ ὁ δίκαιος μόλις σῴζεται,
ὁ ἀσεβὴς καὶ ἁμαρτωλὸς ποῦ φανεῖται;
¹⁹ὥστε καὶ οἱ πάσχοντες κατὰ τὸ θέλημα τοῦ θεοῦ πιστῷ
κτίστῃ παρατιθέσθωσαν τὰς ψυχὰς αὐτῶν ἐν ἀγαθοποιίᾳ.

ἄρξασθαι v.aor.mid.in. [ἄρχω]; κρίμα (judgment); τέλος (outcome);
ἀπειθούντων (disobey); μόλις (scarcely); ἀσεβὴς (ungodly); ἁμαρτωλὸς
(sinner); φανεῖται (appear); κτίστῃ (creator); παρατιθέσθωσαν (commit
oneself); ἀγαθοποιία (doing good)

7. Proverbs 10:12; 1 Peter 4:7–8

Persevering Love

MORE THAN ANYTHING ELSE, I want to persevere in love, Beloved God. For that is how you captured my heart.

PROVERBS 10:12

¹²שִׂנְאָה תְּעוֹרֵר מְדָנִים וְעַל כָּל־פְּשָׁעִים תְּכַסֶּה אַהֲבָה:

שִׂנְאָה (hatred); תְּעוֹרֵר v.3.f.s.impf.Po. [עור]; מְדָנִים (strife); אַהֲבָה (love)

1 PETER 4:7–8

⁷Πάντων δὲ τὸ τέλος ἤγγικεν. σωφρονήσατε οὖν καὶ νήψατε εἰς προσευχάς· ⁸πρὸ πάντων τὴν εἰς ἑαυτοὺς ἀγάπην ἐκτενῆ ἔχοντες, ὅτι ἀγάπη καλύπτει πλῆθος ἁμαρτιῶν.

τέλος (end); ἤγγικεν (approach); σωφρονήσατε (be serious); νήψατε (be sober); προσευχάς (prayer); πρὸ (above); ἐκτενῆ (earnestly); καλύπτει (hide); πλῆθος (multitude)

Integrity

1. Psalm 92:12–16; Colossians 1:21–23

The Hope of an Undivided Heart

THE HOPE OF THE GOSPEL is also my hope for integrity. All I need to do is look back over my shoulder at the way things used to be to understand that. And what is integrity but an undivided heart, a single eye, a yielded soul?

PSALM 92:13–16

¹³צַדִּיק כַּתָּמָר יִפְרָח כְּאֶרֶז בַּלְּבָנוֹן יִשְׂגֶּה:

¹⁴שְׁתוּלִים בְּבֵית יְהוָה בְּחַצְרוֹת אֱלֹהֵינוּ יַפְרִיחוּ:

¹⁵עוֹד יְנוּבוּן בְּשֵׂיבָה דְּשֵׁנִים וְרַעֲנַנִּים יִהְיוּ:

¹⁶לְהַגִּיד כִּי־יָשָׁר יְהוָה צוּרִי וְלֹא־עַוְלָתָה בּוֹ:

כַּתָּמָר (date palm); יִפְרָח (sprout); יִשְׂגֶּה (grow); שְׁתוּלִים (plant); יְנוּבוּן v.3.m.p.impf.Q. [נוב] (bear fruit) + para.; בְּשֵׂיבָה (old age); דְּשֵׁנִים (fat); וְרַעֲנַנִּים (luxuriant); יִהְיוּ v.3.c.p.impf.Q. [היה]; לְהַגִּיד prep. + v.in.cs.H. [נגד]; עַוְלָתָה (wickedness)

COLOSSIANS 1:21–23

²¹Καὶ ὑμᾶς ποτε ὄντας ἀπηλλοτριωμένους καὶ ἐχθροὺς τῇ διανοίᾳ ἐν τοῖς ἔργοις τοῖς πονηροῖς, ²²νυνὶ δὲ ἀποκατήλλαξεν ἐν τῷ σώματι τῆς σαρκὸς αὐτοῦ διὰ τοῦ θανάτου παραστῆσαι ὑμᾶς ἁγίους καὶ ἀμώμους καὶ ἀνεγκλήτους κατενώπιον αὐτοῦ, ²³εἴ γε ἐπιμένετε τῇ πίστει τεθεμελιωμένοι καὶ ἑδραῖοι καὶ μὴ μετακινούμενοι ἀπὸ τῆς ἐλπίδος τοῦ εὐαγγελίου οὗ ἠκούσατε, τοῦ κηρυχθέντος ἐν πάσῃ κτίσει τῇ ὑπὸ τὸν οὐρανόν, οὗ ἐγενόμην ἐγὼ Παῦλος διάκονος.

ποτε (once); ἀπηλλοτριωμένους v.m.p.acc.pf.pass.ptc. [ἀπαλλοτριόω] (be alienated); ἐχθροὺς (enemy); διανοίᾳ (mind); νυνὶ (now); ἀποκατήλλαξεν (reconcile); παραστῆσαι (present); ἀμώμους (faultless); ἀνεγκλήτους (blameless); κατενώπιον (before); ἐπιμένετε (continue); τεθεμελιωμένοι v.m.p.nom.pf.pass.ptc. [θεμελιόω] (establish); ἑδραῖοι (firm); μετακινούμενοι (move); κτίσει (creature); διάκονος (servant)

2. Ezekiel 18:23–24; 1 John 2:19

Fragmentation Is a Choice

MY GOD, I CAN SCARCELY COMPREHEND the agony of your heart when you see us choose fragmentation and death.

EZEKIEL 18:23–24

²³הֶחָפֹץ אֶחְפֹּץ מוֹת רָשָׁע נְאֻם אֲדֹנָי יְהוִה הֲלוֹא בְּשׁוּבוֹ מִדְּרָכָיו
וְחָיָה:
²⁴וּבְשׁוּב צַדִּיק מִצִּדְקָתוֹ וְעָשָׂה עָוֶל כְּכֹל הַתּוֹעֵבוֹת אֲשֶׁר־
עָשָׂה הָרָשָׁע יַעֲשֶׂה וָחָי כָּל־צִדְקֹתָיו אֲשֶׁר־עָשָׂה לֹא תִזָּכַרְנָה
בְּמַעֲלוֹ אֲשֶׁר־מָעַל וּבְחַטָּאתוֹ אֲשֶׁר־חָטָא בָּם יָמוּת:

בְּשׁוּבוֹ prep. + v.in.cs.Q. [שׁוּב] + 3.m.s.pr.sf.; וְחָי עָוֶל (unrighteousness);
v.c. + v.3.m.s.pf.Q.pause [חיה]; בְּמַעֲלוֹ (unfaithfulness); מָעַל (be unfaithful)

1 JOHN 2:19

¹⁹ἐξ ἡμῶν ἐξῆλθαν ἀλλ᾽ οὐκ ἦσαν ἐξ ἡμῶν· εἰ γὰρ ἐξ ἡμῶν
ἦσαν, μεμενήκεισαν ἂν μεθ᾽ ἡμῶν· ἀλλ᾽ ἵνα φανερωθῶσιν
ὅτι οὐκ εἰσὶν πάντες ἐξ ἡμῶν.

ἐξῆλθαν v.3.p.aor.act.ind. [ἐξέρχομαι]; ἦσαν v.3.p.impf.ind. [εἰμί]; φανερωθῶσιν (reveal)

9. Habakkuk 2:3–4; Hebrews 10:38–39

Shrinking Back

HOW CAN I RESIST THE CRINGING FEAR that shrinks life into death?
Only through you, my God, only by the power of your faithfulness to me.

HABAKKUK 2:3–4

3 כִּי עוֹד חָזוֹן לַמּוֹעֵד וְיָפֵחַ לַקֵּץ וְלֹא יְכַזֵּב אִם־יִתְמַהְמָהּ
חַכֵּה־לוֹ כִּי־בֹא יָבֹא לֹא יְאַחֵר:
4 הִנֵּה עֻפְּלָה לֹא־יָשְׁרָה נַפְשׁוֹ בּוֹ וְצַדִּיק בֶּאֱמוּנָתוֹ יִחְיֶה:

חָזוֹן (vision); וְיָפֵחַ v.3.m.s.impf.H. [פוח] (breathe); יְכַזֵּב (lie); יִתְמַהְמָהּ
v.3.m.impf.Hitpalpel [מהה] (linger); חַכֵּה v.2.m.s.impv.P. [חכה] (wait); בֹא
v.in.ab.Q. [בוא]; יָבֹא v.3.m.s.impf.Q. [בוא]; יְאַחֵר (tarry); עֻפְּלָה (swell); בֶּאֱמוּנָתוֹ
(faithfulness)

HEBREWS 10:38–39

38 ὁ δὲ δίκαιος μου ἐκ πίστεως ζήσεται,
καὶ ἐὰν ὑποστείληται,
  οὐκ εὐδοκεῖ ἡ ψυχή μου ἐν αὐτῷ.
39 ἡμεῖς δὲ οὐκ ἐσμὲν ὑποστολῆς εἰς ἀπώλειαν ἀλλὰ πίστεως
εἰς περιποίησιν ψυχῆς.

ὑποστείληται v.3.s.aor.mid.sub. [ὑποστέλλω] (withdraw); εὐδοκεῖ
(delight in); ὑποστολῆς (withdrawing); ἀπώλειαν (destruction); περιποίησιν
(saving)

4. Hosea 6:3–4; Matthew 13:20–21

Beyond Limitation

WHO AMONG US could ever be more than the morning dew or a tentative, rootless plant, were it not for the integrity of God?

HOSEA 6:3–4

³וְנֵדְעָה נִרְדְּפָה לָדַעַת אֶת־יְהוָה כְּשַׁחַר נָכוֹן מוֹצָאוֹ וְיָבוֹא
כַגֶּשֶׁם לָנוּ כְּמַלְקוֹשׁ יוֹרֶה אָרֶץ׃
⁴מָה אֶעֱשֶׂה־לְּךָ אֶפְרַיִם מָה אֶעֱשֶׂה־לְּךָ יְהוּדָה וְחַסְדְּכֶם כַּעֲנַן־
בֹּקֶר וְכַטַּל מַשְׁכִּים הֹלֵךְ׃

וְנֵדְעָה cj. + v.1.com.p.coh.Q. [ידע]; לָדַעַת prep. + v.in.cs. [ידע]; כְּשַׁחַר (dawn); נָכוֹן v.m.s.ptc.N. [כון]; כַגֶּשֶׁם (rain); כְּמַלְקוֹשׁ (spring shower); יוֹרֶה v.3.m.s.impf.H. [ירה] (rain); וְכַטַּל (dew)

MATTHEW 13:20–21

²⁰ὁ δὲ ἐπὶ τὰ πετρώδη σπαρείς, οὗτος ἐστιν ὁ τὸν λόγον ἀκούων καὶ εὐθὺς μετὰ χαρᾶς λαμβάνων αὐτόν, ²¹οὐκ ἔχει δὲ ῥίζαν ἐν ἑαυτῷ ἀλλὰ πρόσκαιρός ἐστιν, γενομένης δὲ θλίψεως ἢ διωγμοῦ διὰ τὸν λόγον εὐθὺς σκανδαλίζεται.

πετρώδη (rocky); ἐστιν v.3.s.pres.ind. [εἰμί]; εὐθὺς (immediately); ῥίζαν (root); πρόσκαιρός (temporary); θλίψεως (affliction); διωγμοῦ (persecution)

5. Isaiah 29:13–15; Colossians 2:20–23

True Self

WE HAVE INTEGRITY when our inside self matches our outside self, and when our deepest self is Christ.

ISAIAH 29:13–15

¹³וַיֹּאמֶר אֲדֹנָי יַעַן כִּי נִגַּשׁ הָעָם הַזֶּה בְּפִיו וּבִשְׂפָתָיו
כִּבְּדוּנִי וְלִבּוֹ רִחַק מִמֶּנִּי וַתְּהִי יִרְאָתָם אֹתִי מִצְוַת אֲנָשִׁים
מְלֻמָּדָה:
¹⁴לָכֵן הִנְנִי יוֹסִף לְהַפְלִיא אֶת־הָעָם־הַזֶּה הַפְלֵא וָפֶלֶא וְאָבְדָה
חָכְמַת חֲכָמָיו וּבִינַת נְבֹנָיו תִּסְתַּתָּר:
¹⁵הוֹי הַמַּעֲמִיקִים מֵיהוָה לַסְתִּר עֵצָה וְהָיָה בְמַחְשָׁךְ מַעֲשֵׂיהֶם
וַיֹּאמְרוּ מִי רֹאֵנוּ וּמִי יוֹדְעֵנוּ:

נִגַּשׁ v.3.m.s.pf.N. [נגשׁ]; כִּבְּדוּנִי v.2.m.p.impv.P. [כבד] + 1.com.s.pr.sf.; וַתְּהִי v.c. + v.3.f.s.impf.Q. [היה]; יִרְאָתָם (reverence); יוֹסִף v.3.m.s.impf.H. [יסף]; הַפְלֵא v.in.ab.H. [פלא]; וָפֶלֶא (wonder); וּבִינַת (understanding); נְבֹנָיו v.m.p.ptc.N. [בין] + 3.m.s.pr.sf.; תִּסְתַּתָּר v.3.f.s.impf.Ht.pause and metathesis [סתר]; הַמַּעֲמִיקִים (deepen); לַסְתִּר prep. + v.in.cs.H.defective and contracted [סתר]; בְמַחְשָׁךְ (dark place); רֹאֵנוּ v.m.s.act.ptc.Q. [ראה] + 1.com.p.pr.sf.; יוֹדְעֵנוּ v.m.s.act.ptc.Q. [ידע] + 1.com.p.pr.sf.

COLOSSIANS 2:20–23

²⁰Εἰ ἀπεθάνετε σὺν Χριστῷ ἀπὸ τῶν στοιχείων τοῦ κόσμου, τί ὡς ζῶντες ἐν κόσμῳ δογματίζεσθε; ²¹μὴ ἅψῃ μηδὲ γεύσῃ μηδὲ θίγῃς, ²²ἅ ἐστιν πάντα εἰς φθορὰν τῇ ἀποχρήσει, κατὰ τὰ ἐντάλματα καὶ διδασκαλίας τῶν ἀνθρώπων, ²³ἅτινά ἐστιν λόγον μὲν ἔχοντα σοφίας ἐν ἐθελοθρησκίᾳ καὶ ταπεινοφροσύνῃ [καὶ] ἀφειδίᾳ σώματος, οὐκ ἐν τιμῇ τινι πρὸς πλησμονὴν τῆς σαρκός.

στοιχείων (basic principle); δογματίζεσθε (submit to rules); ἅψῃ v.2.s.aor.mid.sub. [ἅπτω] (grab); γεύσῃ (taste); θίγῃς v.2.s.aor.act.sub. [θιγγάνω] (touch); ἐστιν v.3.s.pres.ind. [εἰμί]; φθορὰν (destruction); ἀποχρήσει (abuse); ἐντάλματα (command); διδασκαλίας (teaching); ἐθελοθρησκία (self-made worship); ταπεινοφροσύνη (humility); ἀφειδίᾳ (severe handling); τιμῇ (price); πλησμονὴν (satisfaction)

6. Psalm 78:5–8; Colossians 2:5–7

Rugged Choices

EVEN IF WE WERE CATECHIZED by the Apostle Paul himself, integrity would still require the rugged choice of faith, moment by mundane moment in our workaday world.

PSALM 78:5–8

⁵וַיָּקֶם עֵדוּת בְּיַעֲקֹב וְתוֹרָה שָׂם בְּיִשְׂרָאֵל אֲשֶׁר צִוָּה אֶת־
אֲבוֹתֵינוּ לְהוֹדִיעָם לִבְנֵיהֶם׃
⁶לְמַעַן יֵדְעוּ דּוֹר אַחֲרוֹן בָּנִים יִוָּלֵדוּ יָקֻמוּ וִיסַפְּרוּ לִבְנֵיהֶם׃
⁷וְיָשִׂימוּ בֵאלֹהִים כִּסְלָם וְלֹא יִשְׁכְּחוּ מַעַלְלֵי־אֵל וּמִצְוֹתָיו
יִנְצֹרוּ׃
⁸וְלֹא יִהְיוּ כַּאֲבוֹתָם דּוֹר סוֹרֵר וּמֹרֶה דּוֹר לֹא־הֵכִין לִבּוֹ
וְלֹא־נֶאֶמְנָה אֶת־אֵל רוּחוֹ׃

וַיָּקֶם v.c. + v.3.m.s.impf.H. [קום]; שָׂם v.3.m.s.pf.Q. [שים]; לְהוֹדִיעָם prep. + v.in.cs.H. [ידע] + 3.m.p.pr.sf.; יֵדְעוּ v.3.m.p.impf.Q. [ידע]; יִוָּלֵדוּ v.3.m.p.impf.N.pause [ילד]; יָקֻמוּ v.3.m.p.impf.Q.def. [קום]; וִיסַפְּרוּ cj. + v.3.m.p.impf.P. [ספר]; כִּסְלָם (confidence); מַעַלְלֵי (deed); יִהְיוּ v.3.m.p.impf.Q. [היה]; הֵכִין v.3.m.s.pf.H. [כון]

COLOSSIANS 2:5–7

⁵εἰ γὰρ καὶ τῇ σαρκὶ ἄπειμι, ἀλλὰ τῷ πνεύματι σὺν ὑμῖν εἰμι, χαίρων καὶ βλέπων ὑμῶν τὴν τάξιν καὶ τὸ στερέωμα τῆς εἰς Χριστὸν πίστεως ὑμῶν. ⁶Ὡς οὖν παρελάβετε τὸν Χριστὸν Ἰησοῦν τὸν κύριον, ἐν αὐτῷ περιπατεῖτε, ⁷ἐρριζωμένοι καὶ ἐποικοδομούμενοι ἐν αὐτῷ καὶ βεβαιούμενοι τῇ πίστει καθὼς ἐδιδάχθητε, περισσεύοντες ἐν εὐχαριστίᾳ.

ἄπειμι (be away); τάξιν (good order); στερέωμα (steadfastness); παρελάβετε v.2.p.aor.act.ind. [παραλαμβάνω] (receive); ἐρριζωμένοι (root); ἐποικοδομούμενοι (build upon); βεβαιούμενοι (establish); περισσεύοντες (abound); εὐχαριστία (thanksgiving)

7. Exodus 14:13–14; Galatians 2:4–5

Subtle War

GOD GRANT ME A QUIET HEART in the midst of subtle war, that I might recognize both war and Victor.

EXODUS 14:13–14

‏¹³וַיֹּאמֶר מֹשֶׁה אֶל־הָעָם אַל־תִּירָאוּ הִתְיַצְּבוּ וּרְאוּ אֶת־יְשׁוּעַת
יְהוָה אֲשֶׁר־יַעֲשֶׂה לָכֶם הַיּוֹם כִּי אֲשֶׁר רְאִיתֶם אֶת־מִצְרַיִם הַיּוֹם
לֹא תֹסִפוּ לִרְאֹתָם עוֹד עַד־עוֹלָם:
¹⁴יְהוָה יִלָּחֵם לָכֶם וְאַתֶּם תַּחֲרִישׁוּן:‏

‏הִתְיַצְּבוּ‏ (stand); ‏וּרְאוּ‏ v.c. + v.3.c.p.pf.Q. [‏רָאה‏]; ‏רְאִיתֶם‏ v.2.m.p.pf.Q. [‏רָאה‏];
‏תֹסִפוּ‏ v.2.m.p.impf.H.defective [‏יסף‏]; ‏לִרְאֹתָם‏ prep. + v.in.cs.Q. [‏רָאה‏] +
3.m.p.pr.sf.; ‏תַּחֲרִישׁוּן‏ v.2.m.p.impf.H. [‏חרשׁ‏] (be silent) + para.

GALATIANS 2:4–5

⁴διὰ δὲ τοὺς παρεισάκτους ψευδαδέλφους, οἵτινες παρεισῆλθον κατασκοπῆσαι τὴν ἐλευθερίαν ἡμῶν ἣν ἔχομεν ἐν Χριστῷ Ἰησοῦ, ἵνα ἡμᾶς καταδουλώσουσιν, ⁵οἷς οὐδὲ πρὸς ὥραν εἴξαμεν τῇ ὑποταγῇ, ἵνα ἡ ἀλήθεια τοῦ εὐαγγελίου διαμείνῃ πρὸς ὑμᾶς.

παρεισάκτους (secretly); ψευδαδέλφους (false brother); παρεισῆλθον v.3.p.aor.act.ind. [παρεισέρχομαι] (sneak in); κατασκοπῆσαι (spy out); ἐλευθερίαν (freedom); καταδουλώσουσιν (enslave); εἴξαμεν (yield); ὑποταγῇ (subjection); διαμείνῃ (remain)

Week 12

Sorrow and Grief

1. Genesis 43:30–31; John 11:35–36

The Tears of God

FOR GOD, TOO, THERE ARE TIMES when tears are necessary, when nothing else will do.

GENESIS 43:30–31

³⁰וַיְמַהֵר יוֹסֵף כִּי־נִכְמְרוּ רַחֲמָיו אֶל־אָחִיו וַיְבַקֵּשׁ לִבְכּוֹת
וַיָּבֹא הַחַדְרָה וַיֵּבְךְּ שָׁמָּה:
³¹וַיִּרְחַץ פָּנָיו וַיֵּצֵא וַיִּתְאַפַּק וַיֹּאמֶר שִׂימוּ לָחֶם:

וַיָּבֹא ;[בכה] (grow warm); רַחֲמָיו (mercy); לִבְכּוֹת prep. + v.in.cs.Q. [בכה]; נִכְמְרוּ
v.c. + v.3.m.s.impf.Q. [בוא]; הַחַדְרָה d.a. + n.m.s. (room) + directive; וַיֵּבְךְּ v.c.
+ v.3.m.s.impf.Q. [בכה]; וַיֵּצֵא v.c. + v.3.m.s.impf.Q. [יצא]; וַיִּתְאַפַּק (control);
שִׂימוּ v.2.m.p.impv.Q. [שׂים]

JOHN 11:35–36

³⁵ἐδάκρυσεν ὁ Ἰησοῦς. ³⁶ἔλεγον οὖν οἱ Ἰουδαῖοι, Ἴδε πῶς ἐφίλει αὐτόν.

ἐδάκρυσεν (weep)

90

2. Psalm 56:9 [8]; Revelation 7:17

Counting My Tears

YOU ARE THE ONE WHO COUNTS MY TEARS, then gently and softly kisses them away.

PSALM 56:9 [8]

‎⁹נֹדִי סָפַרְתָּה אָתָּה שִׂימָה דִמְעָתִי בְנֹאדֶךָ הֲלֹא בְּסִפְרָתֶךָ׃

‎נֹדִי (wandering); סָפַרְתָּה v.2.m.s.pf.Q.plene [ספר]; דִמְעָתִי (tear); בְנֹאדֶךָ (bottle); בְּסִפְרָתֶךָ (account)

REVELATION 7:17

¹⁷ὅτι τὸ ἀρνίον τὸ ἀνὰ μέσον τοῦ θρόνου ποιμανεῖ
  αὐτούς
  καὶ ὁδηγήσει αὐτοὺς ἐπὶ ζωῆς πηγὰς ὑδάτων,
καὶ ἐξαλείψει ὁ θεὸς πᾶν δάκρυον ἐκ τῶν ὀφθαλμῶν
  αὐτῶν.

ἀρνίον (lamb); μέσον (center); ποιμανεῖ (tend); ὁδηγήσει (guide); πηγὰς (spring); ἐξαλείψει (wipe away); δάκρυον (tear)

3. 2 Samuel 12:22–23; 1 Thessalonians 4:13–14

Watching with Broken Hands

IN THE KEENING HOUR OF SORROW, in the dark night, Jesus watches with us. He cups us in broken hands, weeping as we weep. Thus we grieve, but not as those who are without hope.

2 SAMUEL 12:22–23

²²וַיֹּאמֶר בְּעוֹד הַיֶּלֶד חַי צַמְתִּי וָאֶבְכֶּה כִּי אָמַרְתִּי מִי יוֹדֵעַ
יְחַנַּנִי יְהוָה וְחַי הַיָּלֶד:
²³וְעַתָּה מֵת לָמָּה זֶּה אֲנִי צָם הַאוּכַל לַהֲשִׁיבוֹ עוֹד אֲנִי הֹלֵךְ אֵלָיו
וְהוּא לֹא־יָשׁוּב אֵלָי:

צַמְתִּי v.1.com.s.pf.Q. [צום] (fast); יְחַנַּנִי v.c. + v.3.m.s.pf.Q. [חנן] + 1.c.s.pr.sf.; מֵת v.3.m.s.pf.Q. [מות]; צָם v.m.s.act.ptc.Q. [צום]; הַאוּכַל int. + v.1.com.s.impf.Q. [יכל]; לַהֲשִׁיבוֹ prep. + v.in.cs.H. [שוב] + 3.m.s.pr.sf.

1 THESSALONIANS 4:13–14

¹³Οὐ θέλομεν δὲ ὑμᾶς ἀγνοεῖν, ἀδελφοί, περὶ τῶν κοιμωμένων, ἵνα μὴ λυπῆσθε καθὼς καὶ οἱ λοιποὶ οἱ μὴ ἔχοντες ἐλπίδα. ¹⁴εἰ γὰρ πιστεύομεν ὅτι Ἰησοῦς ἀπέθανεν καὶ ἀνέστη, οὕτως καὶ ὁ θεὸς τοὺς κοιμηθέντας διὰ τοῦ Ἰησοῦ ἄξει σὺν αὐτῷ.

ἀγνοεῖν (be ignorant); κοιμωμένων (sleep); λυπῆσθε (grieve)

4. Psalm 80:4–5, 7 [3–4, 6]; John 16:20–21

Grief Fulfilled

WE NEED TO GRIEVE—hard sometimes—to face the ugliness within and let our souls weep. But our grief is meant to lead to Easter. Only then does grief complete its work.

PSALM 80:4–5, 7 [3–4, 6]

⁴אֱלֹהִים הֲשִׁיבֵנוּ וְהָאֵר פָּנֶיךָ וְנִוָּשֵׁעָה׃
⁵יְהוָה אֱלֹהִים צְבָאוֹת עַד־מָתַי עָשַׁנְתָּ בִּתְפִלַּת עַמֶּךָ׃
⁷תְּשִׂימֵנוּ מָדוֹן לִשְׁכֵנֵינוּ וְאֹיְבֵינוּ יִלְעֲגוּ־לָמוֹ׃

הֲשִׁיבֵנוּ v.3.m.s.pf.H. [שׁוב] + 1.com.s.pr.sf.; וְהָאֵר cj. + 2.m.s.impv.H. [אור] (be light); וְנִוָּשֵׁעָה cj. + v.1.com.p.coh.N. [ישׁע]; עַד־מָתַי (how long?); עָשַׁנְתָּ (be angry); תְּשִׂימֵנוּ v.2.m.s.impf.Q. [שׂים] + 1.com.p.pr.sf.; מָדוֹן (strife); לִשְׁכֵנֵינוּ (inhabitant); יִלְעֲגוּ (mock)

JOHN 16:20–21

²⁰ἀμὴν ἀμὴν λέγω ὑμῖν ὅτι κλαύσετε καὶ θρηνήσετε ὑμεῖς, ὁ δὲ κόσμος χαρήσεται· ὑμεῖς λυπηθήσεσθε, ἀλλ᾽ ἡ λύπη ὑμῶν εἰς χαρὰν γενήσεται. ²¹ἡ γυνὴ ὅταν τίκτῃ λύπην ἔχει, ὅτι ἦλθεν ἡ ὥρα αὐτῆς· ὅταν δὲ γεννήσῃ τὸ παιδίον, οὐκέτι μνημονεύει τῆς θλίψεως διὰ τὴν χαρὰν ὅτι ἐγεννήθη ἄνθρωπος εἰς τὸν κόσμον.

κλαύσετε (cry); θρηνήσετε (lament); λυπηθήσεσθε (become distressed); λύπη (grief); τίκτῃ (bear); ἦλθεν v.3.s.aor.act.ind. [ἔρχομαι]; οὐκέτι (no longer); μνημονεύει (remember); θλίψεως (affliction)

5. Psalm 30:5; 2 Corinthians 4:17

A Glimpse from Above

GOD OF MY HEART, please lift the veil, however briefly. Catch me up from my small moment to your great Now. Let me see with the clear, calm eyes of Jesus, that I may remain true in this cold season of grief.

PSALM 30:5

זַמְּרוּ לַיהוָה חֲסִידָיו וְהוֹדוּ לְזֵכֶר קָדְשׁוֹ:

זַמְּרוּ (sing praise); חֲסִידָיו (pious one); וְהוֹדוּ cj. + v.m.s.impv.H. [ידה]; לְזֵכֶר (remembrance)

2 CORINTHIANS 4:17

¹⁷τὸ γὰρ παραυτίκα ἐλαφρὸν τῆς θλίψεως ἡμῶν καθ' ὑπερβολὴν εἰς ὑπερβολὴν αἰώνιον βάρος δόξης κατεργάζεται ἡμῖν,

παραυτίκα (transient); ἐλαφρὸν (affliction); θλίψεως (affliction); καθ' ὑπερβολὴν εἰς ὑπερβολὴν (go beyond); βάρος (weight); κατεργάζεται (produce)

6. Job 1.20–21, 1 Timothy 6.6–7

Enough

MAY IT BE THAT WHEN I AM STRIPPED of health or friends or honor, when my name is a joke, when my children no longer respect me, I still worship you, God of my life. May I know then, more than ever, that you are enough.

JOB 1:20–21

²⁰וַיָּקָם אִיּוֹב וַיִּקְרַע אֶת־מְעִלוֹ וַיָּגָז אֶת־רֹאשׁוֹ וַיִּפֹּל אַרְצָה
וַיִּשְׁתָּחוּ׃
²¹וַיֹּאמֶר עָרֹם יָצָאתִי מִבֶּטֶן אִמִּי וְעָרֹם אָשׁוּב שָׁמָה יְהוָה
נָתַן וַיהוָה לָקָח יְהִי שֵׁם יְהוָה מְבֹרָךְ׃

וַיָּקָם v.c. + v.3.m.s.impf.Q. [קום]; מְעִלוֹ (coat); וַיָּגָז v.c. + v.3.m.s.impf.Q. [גזז] (cut); וַיִּפֹּל v.c. + v.3.m.s.impf.Q. [נפל]; וַיִּשְׁתָּחוּ v.c. + v.3.m.s.impf.Hisht. [חוה]; וְעָרֹם (naked); יְהִי v.3.m.s.jus.Q. [היה]

1 TIMOTHY 6:6–7

⁶ἔστιν δὲ πορισμὸς μέγας ἡ εὐσέβεια μετὰ αὐταρκείας· ⁷οὐδὲν γὰρ εἰσηνέγκαμεν εἰς τὸν κόσμον, ὅτι οὐδὲ ἐξενεγκεῖν τι δυνάμεθα·

πορισμὸς (gain); εὐσέβεια (piety); αὐταρκείας (contentment); εἰση-νέγκαμεν v.1.p.aor.act.ind. [εἰσφέρω] (bring); ἐξενεγκεῖν (take out)

7. Psalm 31:9–10 [8–9]; Mark 14:33–35

Gethsemane

GRIPPED IN THE NIGHT of their Gethsemane, souls around me weep. "Will anyone watch with me?" they groan. Is there any pain like this, when even our soul friends sleep?

PSALM 31:9–10 [8–9]

⁹וְלֹא הִסְגַּרְתַּנִי בְּיַד־אוֹיֵב הֶעֱמַדְתָּ בַמֶּרְחָב רַגְלָי׃
¹⁰חָנֵּנִי יְהוָה כִּי צַר־לִי עָשְׁשָׁה בְכַעַס עֵינִי נַפְשִׁי וּבִטְנִי׃

הִסְגַּרְתַּנִי v.2.m.s.pf.H. [סגר] + 1.com.s.pr.sf.; בַמֶּרְחָב (roomy place); חָנֵּנִי
v.2.m.s.impv.Q. [חנן] + 1.com.s.pr.sf.; צַר (narrow); עָשְׁשָׁה (waste); בְכַעַס
(anger)

MARK 14:33–35

³³καὶ παραλαμβάνει τὸν Πέτρον καὶ [τὸν] Ἰάκωβον καὶ [τὸν] Ἰωάννην μετ᾽ αὐτοῦ καὶ ἤρξατο ἐκθαμβεῖσθαι καὶ ἀδημονεῖν ³⁴καὶ λέγει αὐτοῖς, Περίλυπός ἐστιν ἡ ψυχή μου ἕως θανάτου· μείνατε ὧδε καὶ γρηγορεῖτε. ³⁵καὶ προελθὼν μικρὸν ἔπιπτεν ἐπὶ τῆς γῆς καὶ προσηύχετο ἵνα εἰ δυνατόν ἐστιν παρέλθῃ ἀπ᾽ αὐτοῦ ἡ ὥρα,

παραλαμβάνει (take with); ἤρξατο v.3.s.aor.mid.ind. [ἄρχω]; ἐκθαμ-βεῖσθαι (be distressed); ἀδημονεῖν (be anxious); Περίλυπός (very troub-led); ἐστιν v.3.s.pres.ind. [εἰμί]; γρηγορεῖτε (keep awake); προελθὼν v.m.s.nom.aor.act.ptc. [προέρχομαι] (go before); μικρὸν (short); δυνατόν (possible); παρέλθῃ v.3.s.aor.act.sub. [παρέρχομαι] (pass)

Easter

1. Genesis 22:7–8; Revelation 5:6a, 7–8a, 9

Behold the Lamb!

LAMB OF GOD, I CANNOT LOOK AT YOU except with tears, with trembling songs and a broken heart and astonishment that Almighty God *is* the Lamb.

GENESIS 22:7–8

⁷וַיֹּאמֶר יִצְחָק אֶל־אַבְרָהָם אָבִיו וַיֹּאמֶר אָבִי וַיֹּאמֶר הִנֶּנִּי בְנִי וַיֹּאמֶר הִנֵּה
הָאֵשׁ וְהָעֵצִים וְאַיֵּה הַשֶּׂה לְעֹלָה:
⁸וַיֹּאמֶר אַבְרָהָם אֱלֹהִים יִרְאֶה־לּוֹ
הַשֶּׂה לְעֹלָה בְּנִי וַיֵּלְכוּ שְׁנֵיהֶם יַחְדָּו:

וְאַיֵּה (where?); הַשֶּׂה (lamb); וַיֵּלְכוּ v.c. + v.3.m.p.impf.Q. [הלך]

REVELATION 5:6A, 7–8A, 9

⁶Καὶ εἶδον ἐν μέσῳ τοῦ θρόνου καὶ τῶν τεσσάρων ζῴων καὶ ἐν μέσῳ τῶν πρεσβυτέρων ἀρνίον ... ⁷καὶ ἦλθεν καὶ εἴληφεν ἐκ τῆς δεξιᾶς τοῦ καθημένου ἐπὶ τοῦ θρόνου. ⁸Καὶ ὅτε ἔλαβεν τὸ βιβλίον, τὰ τέσσαρα ζῷα καὶ οἱ εἴκοσι τέσσαρες πρεσβύτεροι ἔπεσαν ἐνώπιον τοῦ ἀρνίου ... , ⁹καὶ ᾄδουσιν ᾠδὴν καινὴν λέγοντες·

"Άξιος εἶ λαβεῖν τὸ βιβλίον
    καὶ ἀνοῖξαι τὰς σφραγῖδας αὐτοῦ,
ὅτι ἐσφάγης καὶ ἠγόρασας τῷ θεῷ ἐν τῷ αἵματι σου
    ἐκ πάσης φυλῆς καὶ γλώσσης καὶ λαοῦ καὶ ἔθνους,

εἶδον v.1.s.aor.act.ind. [ὁράω]; τεσσάρων (four); ζῴων (living creature); ἀρνίον/ἀρνίου (lamb); ἦλθεν v.3.s.aor.act.ind. [ἔρχομαι]; εἴληφεν v.3.s.pf.acf.ind. [λαμβάνω]; ἐνώπιον (before); ᾄδουσιν (sing); ᾠδὴν n.f.s.acc.; καινὴν (new); "Άξιος (worthy); σφραγῖδας (seal); ἐσφάγης v.2.s.aor.pass.ind. [σφάζω] (slay); ἠγόρασας (buy); φυλῆς (tribe)

2. Isaiah 53:4–6; 2 Corinthians 1:3–4

The Unlovely One

WE WERE HOPING FOR YOUR COMING, hoping with a wild des-
peration that you'd overthrow our enemies and make everything new. What we didn't know was that if you came the way
we wanted, no one would survive. We did not know our need.

ISAIAH 53:4–6

⁴אָכֵן חֲלָיֵנוּ
הוּא נָשָׂא וּמַכְאֹבֵינוּ סְבָלָם וַאֲנַחְנוּ חֲשַׁבְנֻהוּ נָגוּעַ מֻכֵּה אֱלֹהִים וּמְעֻנֶּה׃
⁵וְהוּא מְחֹלָל
מִפְּשָׁעֵנוּ מְדֻכָּא מֵעֲוֹנֹתֵינוּ מוּסַר שְׁלוֹמֵנוּ עָלָיו וּבַחֲבֻרָתוֹ נִרְפָּא־לָנוּ׃
⁶כֻּלָּנוּ כַּצֹּאן תָּעִינוּ אִישׁ לְדַרְכּוֹ פָּנִינוּ וַיהוָה הִפְגִּיעַ בּוֹ אֵת עֲוֹן כֻּלָּנוּ׃

חֲלָיֵנוּ n.m.p. (sickness) + 1.com.p.pr.sf.; וּמַכְאֹבֵינוּ (pain); סְבָלָם
v.3.m.s.pf.Q. [סבל] (carry) + 3.m.p.pr.sf.; חֲשַׁבְנֻהוּ v.1.com.p.pf.Q. [חשב] +
3.m.s.pr.sf.; מֻכֵּה v.m.s.pass.ptc.Hof. [נכה]; מְחֹלָל v.m.s.pass.ptc.Po. [חלל];
מְדֻכָּא (pierce); וּבַחֲבֻרָתוֹ (wound); תָּעִינוּ v.1.com.p.pf.Q. [תעה]; פָּנִינוּ
v.1.com.p.pf.Q. [פנה]

2 CORINTHIANS 1:3–4

³Εὐλογητὸς ὁ θεὸς καὶ πατὴρ τοῦ κυρίου ἡμῶν Ἰησοῦ Χριστοῦ,
ὁ πατὴρ τῶν οἰκτιρμῶν καὶ θεὸς πάσης παρακλήσεως, ⁴ὁ
παρακαλῶν ἡμᾶς ἐπὶ πάσῃ τῇ θλίψει ἡμῶν εἰς τὸ δύνασθαι
ἡμᾶς παρακαλεῖν τοὺς ἐν πάσῃ θλίψει διὰ τῆς παρακλήσεως
ἧς παρακαλούμεθα αὐτοὶ ὑπὸ τοῦ θεοῦ.

Εὐλογητὸς (blessed); οἰκτιρμῶν (compassion); παρακλήσεως (encouragement); θλίψει (affliction)

3. Isaiah 54:10; John 3:16

The Uncursing

AS SURELY AS OUR SIN SEPARATES US FROM YOU, from ourselves, and from one another, O God, your covenant of peace uncurses us.

ISAIAH 54:10

‏¹⁰כִּי הֶהָרִים יָמוּשׁוּ וְהַגְּבָעוֹת תְּמוּטֶנָה וְחַסְדִּי מֵאִתֵּךְ לֹא־
יָמוּשׁ וּבְרִית שְׁלוֹמִי לֹא תָמוּט אָמַר מְרַחֲמֵךְ יְהוָה:‏

יָמוּשׁוּ (depart); תְּמוּטֶנָה v.3.f.p.impf.Q. [מוט] (totter); מֵאִתֵּךְ prep. [מִן] + prep. [אֵת] + 2.f.s.pr.sf.; מְרַחֲמֵךְ v.m.s.act.ptc.P. [רחם] + 2.f.s.pr.sf.

JOHN 3:16

¹⁶Οὕτως γὰρ ἠγάπησεν ὁ θεὸς τὸν κόσμον, ὥστε τὸν υἱὸν τὸν μονογενῆ ἔδωκεν, ἵνα πᾶς ὁ πιστεύων εἰς αὐτὸν μὴ ἀπόληται ἀλλ᾽ ἔχῃ ζωὴν αἰώνιον.

μονογενῆ (only); ἔδωκεν v.3.s.aor.act.ind. [δίδωμι]

99

4. Ezekiel 36:22–23; John 17:11–12

Watchers

SOMETIMES WE FORGET in our egocentric zeal that your salvation is not only for *our* sake. There's a big world watching. And a Name that will be true. Grant us broader vision, Holy Father, that we might watch with you.

EZEKIEL 36:22–23

²²לָכֵן אֱמֹר
לְבֵית־יִשְׂרָאֵל כֹּה אָמַר אֲדֹנָי יְהוִה לֹא לְמַעַנְכֶם אֲנִי עֹשֶׂה בֵּית יִשְׂרָאֵל
כִּי אִם־לְשֵׁם־קָדְשִׁי אֲשֶׁר חִלַּלְתֶּם בַּגּוֹיִם אֲשֶׁר־בָּאתֶם שָׁם:
²³וְקִדַּשְׁתִּי
אֶת־שְׁמִי הַגָּדוֹל הַמְחֻלָּל בַּגּוֹיִם אֲשֶׁר חִלַּלְתֶּם בְּתוֹכָם וְיָדְעוּ הַגּוֹיִם
כִּי־אֲנִי יְהוָה נְאֻם אֲדֹנָי יְהוִה בְּהִקָּדְשִׁי בָכֶם לְעֵינֵיהֶם:

בָּאתֶם v.2.m.p.pf.Q. [בוא]; בְּהִקָּדְשִׁי prep. + v.in.cs.N. [קדש] + 1.com.s.pr.sf.

JOHN 17:11–12

¹¹καὶ οὐκέτι εἰμὶ ἐν τῷ κόσμῳ, καὶ αὐτοὶ ἐν τῷ κόσμῳ εἰσίν, καγὼ πρὸς σὲ ἔρχομαι. Πάτερ ἅγιε, τήρησον αὐτοὺς ἐν τῷ ὀνόματι σου ᾧ δέδωκάς μοι, ἵνα ὦσιν ἓν καθὼς ἡμεῖς. ¹²ὅτε ἤμην μετ' αὐτῶν ἐγὼ ἐτήρουν αὐτοὺς ἐν τῷ ὀνόματι σου ᾧ δέδωκας μοι, καὶ ἐφύλαξα, καὶ οὐδεὶς ἐξ αὐτῶν ἀπώλετο εἰ μὴ ὁ υἱὸς τῆς ἀπωλείας, ἵνα ἡ γραφὴ πληρωθῇ.

οὐκέτι (no longer); εἰσίν v.3.p.pres.ind. [εἰμί]; δέδωκάς v.2.s.pf.act.ind. [δίδωμι]; ἐφύλαξα (keep); ἀπωλείας (destruction)

5. Zechariah 4.6, 10a, Acts 1:7-8

Resurrection Power

REMIND ME AGAIN AND AGAIN TODAY, Lord, no matter how many times I forget, that it is by your Spirit, not mine, and by your power, not mine, that resurrection life is poured out in this world.

ZECHARIAH 4:6, 10A

⁶וַיַּעַן וַיֹּאמֶר אֵלַי לֵאמֹר זֶה דְּבַר־יְהוָה אֶל־זְרֻבָּבֶל לֵאמֹר לֹא
בְחַיִל וְלֹא בְכֹחַ כִּי אִם־בְּרוּחִי אָמַר יְהוָה צְבָאוֹת:
¹⁰כִּי מִי בַז לְיוֹם
קְטַנּוֹת וְשָׂמְחוּ וְרָאוּ אֶת־הָאֶבֶן הַבְּדִיל בְּיַד זְרֻבָּבֶל:

[וַיַּעַן v.c. + v.3.m.s.impf.Q. [עַנָה]; בַז v.3.m.s.pf.Q. [בוז] (despise); קְטַנּוֹת (small thing); וְרָאוּ v.c. + v.3.c.p.pf.Q. [ראה]; הַבְּדִיל (lead) [הָאֶבֶן הַבְּדִיל plumb stone]

ACTS 1:7-8

⁷εἶπεν δὲ πρὸς αὐτοὺς Οὐχ ὑμῶν ἐστιν γνῶναι χρόνους ἢ καιροὺς οὓς ὁ πατὴρ ἔθετο ἐν τῇ ἰδίᾳ ἐξουσίᾳ, ⁸ἀλλὰ λήμψεσθε δύναμιν ἐπελθόντος τοῦ ἁγίου πνεύματος ἐφ᾽ ὑμᾶς καὶ ἔσεσθε μου μάρτυρες ἔν τε Ἰερουσαλὴμ καὶ [ἐν] πάσῃ τῇ Ἰουδαίᾳ καὶ Σαμαρείᾳ καὶ ἕως ἐσχάτου τῆς γῆς.

εἶπεν v.3.s.aor.act.ind. [λέγω]; ἐστιν v.3.s.pres.ind. [εἰμί]; γνῶναι v.aor.act.in. [γινώσκω]; ἔθετο v.3.s.aor.mid.ind. [τίθημι]; λήμψεσθε v.2.p.fut.mid.ind. [λαμβάνω]; ἐπελθόντος v.nt.s.gen.aor.act.ptc. [ἐπέρχομαι] (come); ἔσεσθε v.2.p.fut.ind. [εἰμί]; μάρτυρες (witness)

6. Zechariah 12:10–11; Luke 23:32–34

Mourning before the Dawn

IT IS WHEN WE FINALLY HEAR, with our hearts, your words "Father, forgive them . . ." that we begin to suspect the enormity of our sin. That is when we mourn not for ourselves, but for you, Jesus, for the agony we caused you. May we mourn the full extent through the night of your abandonment. Then afterward may Easter dawn in us.

ZECHARIAH 12:10–11

‏¹⁰וְשָׁפַכְתִּי
עַל־בֵּית דָּוִיד וְעַל יוֹשֵׁב יְרוּשָׁלַ͏ִם רוּחַ חֵן וְתַחֲנוּנִים וְהִבִּיטוּ אֵלַי אֵת
אֲשֶׁר־דָּקָרוּ וְסָפְדוּ עָלָיו כְּמִסְפֵּד עַל־הַיָּחִיד וְהָמֵר עָלָיו כְּהָמֵר
עַל־הַבְּכוֹר:
¹¹בַּיּוֹם הַהוּא יִגְדַּל הַמִּסְפֵּד בִּירוּשָׁלַ͏ִם כְּמִסְפַּד הֲדַד־רִמּוֹן
בְּבִקְעַת מְגִדּוֹן:

‏וְתַחֲנוּנִים (supplication); וְהִבִּיטוּ [נבט].v.c. + v.3.c.p.pf.H; דָּקָרוּ (pierce); וְסָפְדוּ (lament); כְּמִסְפֵּד (lamentation); הַיָּחִיד (solitary); וְהָמֵר cj. + v.in.ab.H. [מרר] (be bitter); כְּהָמֵר prep. + v.in.ab.H. [מרר]; בְּבִקְעַת (valley)

LUKE 23:32–34

³²Ἤγοντο δὲ καὶ ἕτεροι κακοῦργοι δύο σὺν αὐτῷ ἀναιρεθῆναι. ³³καὶ ὅτε ἦλθον ἐπὶ τὸν τόπον τὸν καλούμενον Κρανίον, ἐκεῖ ἐσταύρωσαν αὐτὸν καὶ τοὺς κακούργους, ὃν μὲν ἐκ δεξιῶν ὃν δὲ ἐξ ἀριστερῶν. ³⁴⟦ὁ δὲ Ἰησοῦς ἔλεγεν, Πάτερ, ἄφες αὐτοῖς, οὐ γὰρ οἴδασιν τί ποιοῦσιν.⟧ διαμεριζόμενοι δὲ τὰ ἱμάτια αὐτοῦ ἔβαλον κλήρους.

Ἤγοντο v.3.p.impf.pass.ind. [ἄγω]; κακοῦργοι (criminal); ἀναιρεθῆ-ναι (execute); ἦλθον v.3.p.aor.act.ind. [ἔρχομαι]; ἀριστερῶν (left); ἄφες v.2.s.aor.act.imv. [ἀφίημι]; διαμεριζόμενοι (distribute); κλήρους (lot)

7. Psalm 71:20–21; Mark 16:3–6

Roll the Stone Away!

COME ROLL THE STONE AWAY from our hearts, Risen Lord! You have risen, you are alive! Stride to the tomb within! Roll that stone away—convince us, Holy Lamb, that you are God!

PSALM 71:20–21

²⁰אֲשֶׁר הִרְאִיתַנוּ צָרוֹת רַבּוֹת וְרָעוֹת תָּשׁוּב תְּחַיֵּינִי וּמִתְּהֹמוֹת הָאָרֶץ
תָּשׁוּב תַּעֲלֵנִי:
²¹תֶּרֶב גְּדֻלָּתִי וְתִסֹּב תְּנַחֲמֵנִי:

הִרְאִיתַנוּ v.2.m.s.pf.H. [ראה] + 1.com.s.pr.sf.Qe.; תְּחַיֵּינִי v.2.m.s.impf.P.
[חיה] + 1.com.s.pr.sf.; וּמִתְּהֹמוֹת (deep); תַּעֲלֵנִי v.2.m.s.impf.H. [עלה] +
1.com.s.pr.sf.; תֶּרֶב v.2.m.s.impf.H. [רבה]; גְּדֻלָּתִי (greatness); וְתִסֹּב cj. +
v.2.m.s.impf.Q. [סבב]; תְּנַחֲמֵנִי v.2.m.s.impf.P. [נחם] + 1.com.s.pr.sf.

MARK 16:3–6

³καὶ ἔλεγον πρὸς ἑαυτάς, Τίς ἀποκυλίσει ἡμῖν τὸν λίθον ἐκ
τῆς θύρας τοῦ μνημείου; ⁴καὶ ἀναβλέψασαι θεωροῦσιν ὅτι
ἀποκεκύλισται ὁ λίθος· ἦν γὰρ μέγας σφόδρα. ⁵Καὶ
εἰσελθοῦσαι εἰς τὸ μνημεῖον εἶδον νεανίσκον καθήμενον ἐν
τοῖς δεξιοῖς περιβεβλημένον στολὴν λευκήν, καὶ
ἐξεθαμβήθησαν. ⁶ὁ δὲ λέγει αὐταῖς, Μὴ ἐκθαμβεῖσθε· Ἰησοῦν
ζητεῖτε τὸν Ναζαρηνὸν τὸν ἐσταυρωμένον· ἠγέρθη, οὐκ ἔστιν
ὧδε· ἴδε ὁ τόπος ὅπου ἔθηκαν αὐτόν.

ἀποκυλίσει/ἀποκεκύλισται (roll away); θύρας (door); μνημείου
(tomb); ἀναβλέψασαι (look up); ἦν v.3.s.impf.ind. [εἰμί]; σφόδρα (very);
εἶδον v.1.s.aor.act.ind. [ὁράω]; νεανίσκον (young man); καθήμενον (sit);
περιβεβλημένον v.m.s.acc.pf.pass.ptc. [περιβάλλω]; στολὴν (robe); λευκήν
(white); ἐξεθαμβήθησαν (be distressed); ἐσταυρωμένον (crucify); ἠγέρθη
v.3.s.aor.pass.ind. [ἐγείρω]; ἔστιν v.3.s.pres.ind [εἰμί]; ἔθηκαν
v.3.p.aor.act.ind. [τίθημι]

Week 14

Hope

1. Psalm 62:5–8 [4–7]; John 6:67–69

Where Hope Rests

My hope, O God, is not in these brief and shifting circumstances. Who knows what tomorrow might bring? No, my hope
rests in you, for you are my life.

Psalm 62:5–8 [4–7]

⁵אַ֤ךְ מִשְּׂאֵת֨וֹ ׀ יָעֲצ֣וּ לְהַדִּיחַ֮ יִרְצ֪וּ כָ֫זָ֥ב בְּפִ֥יו יְבָרֵ֑כוּ וּ֝בְקִרְבָּ֗ם
יְקַלְלוּ־סֶֽלָה׃

⁶אַ֣ךְ לֵ֭אלֹהִים דּ֣וֹמִּי נַפְשִׁ֑י כִּי־מִ֝מֶּ֗נּוּ תִּקְוָתִֽי׃

⁷אַךְ־ה֣וּא צ֭וּרִי וִישׁוּעָתִ֑י מִ֝שְׂגַּבִּ֗י לֹ֣א אֶמּֽוֹט׃

⁸עַל־אֱ֭לֹהִים יִשְׁעִ֣י וּכְבוֹדִ֑י צוּר־עֻזִּ֥י מַ֝חְסִ֗י בֵּֽאלֹהִֽים׃

מִשְּׂאֵת֨וֹ (exaltation); לְהַדִּיחַ prep. + v.in.cs.H. [נדח]; יִרְצ֪וּ v.3.m.p.impf.Q.
[רצה]; כָזָב (lie); דּ֣וֹמִּי v.2.f.s.impv.Q. [דמם] (be still); תִּקְוָתִֽי (hope); מִ֝שְׂגַּבִּ֗י
(refuge); אֶמּֽוֹט v.1.com.s.impf.N. [מוט] (totter)

John 6:67–69

⁶⁷εἶπεν οὖν ὁ Ἰησοῦς τοῖς δώδεκα, Μὴ καὶ ὑμεῖς θέλετε
ὑπάγειν; ⁶⁸ἀπεκρίθη αὐτῷ Σίμων Πέτρος, Κύριε, πρὸς τίνα
ἀπελευσόμεθα; ῥήματα ζωῆς αἰωνίου ἔχεις, ⁶⁹καὶ ἡμεῖς
πεπιστεύκαμεν καὶ ἐγνώκαμεν ὅτι σὺ εἶ ὁ ἅγιος τοῦ θεοῦ.

εἶπεν v.3.s.aor.act.ind. [λέγω]; ἀπελευσόμεθα v.1.p.fut.mid.ind. [ἀπέρ-
χομαι]; ἐγνώκαμεν v.1.p.pf.act.ind. [γινώσκω]

2. Jeremiah 14:5–8; Romans 8:19–21

A Universe Full of Hope

NOT FOR OURSELVES ALONE do we hope in you, God our Salvation. We hope on behalf of all creatures and all life, for all of creation. And because of your faithfulness we will not be disappointed.

JEREMIAH 14:5–8

‏⁵כִּי גַם־אַיֶּלֶת בַּשָּׂדֶה יָלְדָה וְעָזוֹב כִּי לֹא־הָיָה דֶּשֶׁא:
‏⁶וּפְרָאִים עָמְדוּ עַל־שְׁפָיִם שָׁאֲפוּ רוּחַ כַּתַּנִּים כָּלוּ עֵינֵיהֶם כִּי־אֵין עֵשֶׂב:
‏⁷אִם־עֲוֹנֵינוּ עָנוּ בָנוּ יְהוָה עֲשֵׂה לְמַעַן שְׁמֶךָ כִּי־רַבּוּ מְשׁוּבֹתֵינוּ לְךָ חָטָאנוּ:
‏⁸מִקְוֵה יִשְׂרָאֵל מוֹשִׁיעוֹ בְּעֵת צָרָה לָמָּה תִהְיֶה כְּגֵר בָּאָרֶץ וּכְאֹרֵחַ נָטָה לָלוּן:

דֶּשֶׁא (grass); וּפְרָאִים (wild donkey); שְׁפָיִם (height); שָׁאֲפוּ (pant after); כַּתַּנִּים (jackal); כָּלוּ v.3.c.p.pf.Q. [כלה]; עֵשֶׂב (pasture); עָנוּ v.3.c.p.pf.Q. [ענה]; רַבּוּ v.3.c.p.pf.Q. [רבב] (be many); מְשׁוּבֹתֵינוּ (backsliding); מִקְוֵה (hope); מוֹשִׁיעוֹ v.m.s.act.ptc.H. [ישע] + 3.m.s.pr.sf.

ROMANS 8:19–21

¹⁹ἡ γὰρ ἀποκαραδοκία τῆς κτίσεως τὴν ἀποκάλυψιν τῶν υἱῶν τοῦ θεοῦ ἀπεκδέχεται. ²⁰τῇ γὰρ ματαιότητι ἡ κτίσις ὑπετάγη, οὐχ ἑκοῦσα ἀλλὰ διὰ τὸν ὑποτάξαντα, ἐφ᾽ ἐλπίδι ²¹ὅτι καὶ αὐτὴ ἡ κτίσις ἐλευθερωθήσεται ἀπὸ τῆς δουλείας τῆς φθορᾶς εἰς τὴν ἐλευθερίαν τῆς δόξης τῶν τέκνων τοῦ θεοῦ.

ἀποκαραδοκία (eager expectation); κτίσεως/κτίσις (creation); ἀποκάλυψιν (revelation); ἀπεκδέχεται (eagerly await); ματαιότητι n.f.s.dat. (frustration); ἑκοῦσα (willingly); ὑποτάξαντα v.3.s.aor.pass.ind. [ὑποτάσσω]; ἐλευθερωθήσεται (free); φθορᾶς (decay); ἐλευθερίαν (freedom)

3. Psalm 25:2–5; Philippians 1:19–20

Hoping in What Is True

IT SEEMS ALMOST TOO GOOD TO BE TRUE, but it is true nonetheless. You are determined that your holy life will succeed in me. Whether I am sick or well, at ease or in trouble, you are steadily at work delivering me from shame, purely for love's sake. This is hope—to believe what you said you are doing in me!

PSALM 25:2–5

²אֱלֹהַי בְּךָ בָטַחְתִּי אַל־אֵבוֹשָׁה אַל־יַעַלְצוּ אֹיְבַי לִי:
³גַּם כָּל־קֹוֶיךָ לֹא יֵבֹשׁוּ יֵבֹשׁוּ הַבּוֹגְדִים רֵיקָם:
⁴דְּרָכֶיךָ יְהוָה הוֹדִיעֵנִי אֹרְחוֹתֶיךָ לַמְּדֵנִי:
⁵הַדְרִיכֵנִי בַאֲמִתֶּךָ וְלַמְּדֵנִי כִּי־אַתָּה אֱלֹהֵי יִשְׁעִי אוֹתְךָ קִוִּיתִי
כָּל־הַיּוֹם:

אֵבוֹשָׁה v.1.com.s.coh.Q. [בוש]; יַעַלְצוּ (rejoice); קֹוֶיךָ v.m.p.act.ptc.Q. [קוה]
(hope) + 2.m.s.pr.sf.; יֵבֹשׁוּ v.3.m.p.impf.Q. [בוש]; רֵיקָם (unsuccessfully);
הוֹדִיעֵנִי v.3.m.s.pf.H. [ידע] + 1.com.s.pr.sf.; הַדְרִיכֵנִי v.2.m.s.impv.H. [דרך] +
1.com.s.pr.sf.; קִוִּיתִי v.1.com.s.pf.P. [קוה]

PHILIPPIANS 1:19–20

¹⁹οἶδα γὰρ ὅτι τοῦτό μοι ἀποβήσεται εἰς σωτηρίαν διὰ τῆς
ὑμῶν δεήσεως καὶ ἐπιχορηγίας τοῦ πνεύματος Ἰησοῦ
Χριστοῦ ²⁰κατὰ τὴν ἀποκαραδοκίαν καὶ ἐλπίδα μου, ὅτι ἐν
οὐδενὶ αἰσχυνθήσομαι ἀλλ᾽ ἐν πάσῃ παρρησίᾳ ὡς πάντοτε
καὶ νῦν μεγαλυνθήσεται Χριστὸς ἐν τῷ σώματί μου, εἴτε διὰ
ζωῆς εἴτε διὰ θανάτου.

ἀποβήσεται (lead); σωτηρίαν (salvation); δεήσεως (prayer); ἐπιχορηγίας (help); ἀποκαραδοκίαν (eager expectation); αἰσχυνθήσομαι
(be ashamed); παρρησίᾳ (confidence); πάντοτε (always); νῦν (now); μεγαλυνθήσεται (magnify)

4. Isaiah 62:1–3; 1 Thessalonians 2:17–20

The Smile of Hope

NOTHINGS FOSTERS HOPE more surely than to see the smile of Christ in the eyes of a friend.

ISAIAH 62:1–3

¹לְמַעַן צִיּוֹן לֹא אֶחֱשֶׁה וּלְמַעַן יְרוּשָׁלַם לֹא אֶשְׁקוֹט עַד־יֵצֵא
כַנֹּגַהּ צִדְקָהּ וִישׁוּעָתָהּ כְּלַפִּיד יִבְעָר:
²וְרָאוּ גוֹיִם צִדְקֵךְ וְכָל־מְלָכִים כְּבוֹדֵךְ וְקֹרָא לָךְ שֵׁם חָדָשׁ
אֲשֶׁר פִּי יְהוָה יִקֳבֶנּוּ:
³וְהָיִית עֲטֶרֶת תִּפְאֶרֶת בְּיַד־יְהוָה וּצְנִיף מְלוּכָה בְּכַף־
אֱלֹהָיִךְ:

אֶחֱשֶׁה (keep silent); אֶשְׁקוֹט (be quiet); יֵצֵא v.3.m.s.impf.Q. [יצא]; כַנֹּגַהּ (brightness); כְּלַפִּיד (torch); וְרָאוּ v.c. + v.3.c.p.pf.Q. [ראה]; וְקֹרָא v.c. + v.3.m.s.pf.Pu. [קרא]; יִקֳבֶנּוּ v.3.m.impf.Q. [נקב] (designate) + para. + 3.m.s.pr.sf.; וְהָיִית v.c. + v.2.f.s.pf.Q. [היה]; עֲטֶרֶת (crown); תִּפְאֶרֶת (glory); וּצְנִיף (turban)

1 THESSALONIANS 2:17–20

¹⁷Ἡμεῖς δέ, ἀδελφοί, ἀπορφανισθέντες ἀφ᾽ ὑμῶν πρὸς καιρὸν ὥρας, προσώπῳ οὐ καρδίᾳ, περισσοτέρως ἐσπουδάσαμεν τὸ πρόσωπον ὑμῶν ἰδεῖν ἐν πολλῇ ἐπιθυμίᾳ. ¹⁸διότι ἠθελήσαμεν ἐλθεῖν πρὸς ὑμᾶς, ἐγὼ μὲν Παῦλος καὶ ἅπαξ καὶ δίς, καὶ ἐνέκοψεν ἡμᾶς ὁ Σατανᾶς. ¹⁹τίς γὰρ ἡμῶν ἐλπὶς ἢ χαρὰ ἢ στέφανος καυχήσεως– ἢ οὐχὶ καὶ ὑμεῖς– ἔμπροσθεν τοῦ κυρίου ἡμῶν Ἰησοῦ ἐν τῇ αὐτοῦ παρουσίᾳ; ²⁰ὑμεῖς γάρ ἐστε ἡ δόξα ἡμῶν καὶ ἡ χαρά.

ἀπορφανισθέντες (make an orphan); περισσοτέρως (abundantly); ἐσπουδάσαμεν (make every effort); ἰδεῖν v.aor.act.in. [ὁράω]; ἐπιθυμία (longing); ἅπαξ καὶ δίς (again and again); ἐνέκοψεν v.3.s.aor.act.ind. [ἐγκόπτω] (hinder); στέφανος (crown); καυχήσεως (boasting); ἔμπροσθεν (in the presence of); παρουσία (coming)

5. Jeremiah 17:7–8; Ephesians 1:11–13

Why Hope?

WE ARE ALL FAILURES AND FRAUDS, every one of us. Even so, we can rejoice in hope because our sanctity is the result of God's integrity—without exception!

JEREMIAH 17:7–8

‏⁷בָּרוּךְ הַגֶּבֶר אֲשֶׁר יִבְטַח בַּיהוָה וְהָיָה יְהוָה מִבְטַחוֹ׃
‏⁸וְהָיָה כְּעֵץ שָׁתוּל עַל־מַיִם וְעַל־יוּבַל יְשַׁלַּח שָׁרָשָׁיו וְלֹא
‏יִרְאֶה כִּי־יָבֹא חֹם וְהָיָה עָלֵהוּ רַעֲנָן וּבִשְׁנַת בַּצֹּרֶת לֹא
‏יִדְאָג וְלֹא יָמִישׁ מֵעֲשׂוֹת פֶּרִי׃

‏מִבְטַחוֹ (trust); ‏שָׁתוּל (plant); ‏יוּבַל (stream); ‏שָׁרָשָׁיו (root); ‏יָבֹא
v.3.m.s.impf.Q.def. [‏בוא]; ‏חֹם (heat); ‏עָלֵהוּ (leaf); ‏רַעֲנָן (luxuriant); ‏בַּצֹּרֶת
(drought); ‏יִדְאָג (fear); ‏יָמִישׁ (cease); ‏מֵעֲשׂוֹת prep. + v.in.cst.Q. [‏עשׂה]

EPHESIANS 1:11–13

¹¹’εν ᾧ καὶ ἐκληρώθημεν προορισθέντες κατὰ πρόθεσιν τοῦ τὰ πάντα ἐνεργοῦντος κατὰ τὴν βουλὴν τοῦ θελήματος αὐτοῦ ¹²εἰς τὸ εἶναι ἡμᾶς εἰς ἔπαινον δόξης αὐτοῦ τοὺς προηλπικότας ἐν τῷ Χριστῷ. ¹³’εν ᾧ καὶ ὑμεῖς ἀκούσαντες τὸν λόγον τῆς ἀληθείας, τὸ εὐαγγέλιον τῆς σωτηρίας ὑμῶν, ἐν ᾧ καὶ πιστεύσαντες ἐσφραγίσθητε τῷ πνεύματι τῆς ἐπαγγελίας τῷ ἁγίῳ,

ἐκληρώθημεν (choose by lot); προορισθέντες (decide beforehand); πρόθεσιν (plan); ἐνεργοῦντος (work); βουλὴν (purpose); εἶναι v.pres.in. [εἰμί]; ἔπαινον (praise); προηλπικότας v.m.p.acc.pf.act.ptc. [προελπίζω] (be first to help); σωτηρίας (salvation); ἐσφραγίσθητε (seal)

6. Jeremiah 33:2-3; Luke 11:9-10

Hope in the Pursuit

LIKE A SHY, IMPASSIONED LOVER, God invites my undeterred pursuit. Ask! Seek! Knock! He invites, wanting with all his might to answer, and to be found, and to open himself to me.

JEREMIAH 33:2-3

²כֹּה־אָמַר יְהוָה עֹשָׂהּ יְהוָה יוֹצֵר אוֹתָהּ לַהֲכִינָהּ יְהוָה שְׁמוֹ׃
³קְרָא אֵלַי וְאֶעֱנֶךָ וְאַגִּידָה לְּךָ גְּדֹלוֹת וּבְצֻרוֹת לֹא יְדַעְתָּם׃

עֹשָׂהּ v.m.s.act.ptc.Q. [עשׂה] + 3.f.s.pr.sf.; לַהֲכִינָהּ prep. + v.in.cs.H. [כון] + 3.f.s.pr.sf.; וְאֶעֱנֶךָ cj. + v.1.com.s.impf.Q. [ענה] + 2.m.s.pr.sf.; וְאַגִּידָה cj. + v.1.com.s.coh.H. [נגד]; יְדַעְתָּם v.2.m.s.pf.Q. [ידע] + 3.m.p.pr.sf.

LUKE 11:9-10

⁹Καγὼ ὑμῖν λέγω, αἰτεῖτε καὶ δοθήσεται ὑμῖν, ζητεῖτε καὶ εὑρήσετε, κρούετε καὶ ἀνοιγήσεται ὑμῖν· ¹⁰πᾶς γὰρ ὁ αἰτῶν λαμβάνει καὶ ὁ ζητῶν εὑρίσκει καὶ τῷ κρούοντι ἀνοιγ[ήσ]εται.

εὑρήσετε v.2.p.fut.act.ind. [εὑρίσκω]; κρούοντι (knock)

7. Psalm 33:18–20; 1 Thessalonians 1:9–10

Hope Reborn

MY HEART IS TROUBLED, O God. Let me see your tender eye resting on me, that I may hope again.

PSALM 33:18–20

18הִנֵּה עֵין יְהוָה אֶל־יְרֵאָיו לַמְיַחֲלִים לְחַסְדּוֹ׃
19לְהַצִּיל מִמָּוֶת נַפְשָׁם וּלְחַיּוֹתָם בָּרָעָב׃
20נַפְשֵׁנוּ חִכְּתָה לַיהוָה עֶזְרֵנוּ וּמָגִנֵּנוּ הוּא׃

יְרֵאָיו adj.m.p. + 3.m.s.pr.sf.; לַמְיַחֲלִים (wait); לְהַצִּיל prep. + v.in.cs.H. [נצל]; וּלְחַיּוֹתָם cj. + prep. + v.in.cs.P. [חיה] + 3.m.p.pr.sf.; חִכְּתָה v.3.f.s.pf.P. [חכה] (await); וּמָגִנֵּנוּ v.c. + n.m.s. + 1.com.p.pr.sf.

1 THESSALONIANS 1:9–10

⁹αὐτοὶ γὰρ περὶ ἡμῶν ἀπαγγέλλουσιν ὁποίαν εἴσοδον ἔσχομεν πρὸς ὑμᾶς, καὶ πῶς ἐπεστρέψατε πρὸς τὸν θεὸν ἀπὸ τῶν εἰδώλων δουλεύειν θεῷ ζῶντι καὶ ἀληθινῷ ¹⁰καὶ ἀναμένειν τὸν υἱὸν αὐτοῦ ἐκ τῶν οὐρανῶν, ὃν ἤγειρεν ἐκ [τῶν] νεκρῶν, Ἰησοῦν τὸν ῥυόμενον ἡμᾶς ἐκ τῆς ὀργῆς τῆς ἐρχομένης.

ἀπαγγέλλουσιν (report); ὁποίαν (what sort); εἴσοδον (entrance); ἔσχομεν v.1.p.aor.act.ind. [ἔχω]; ἐπεστρέψατε v.2.p.aor.act.ind. [ἐπιστρέφω] (turn); εἰδώλων (idol); δουλεύειν (serve); ἀληθινῷ (true); ἀναμένειν (await); ῥυόμενον (deliverer); ὀργῆς (anger)

Uncertainty

1. Zephaniah 2:1, 3; 2 Timothy 2:24–25

Perhaps

THERE IS A "PERHAPS" ATTACHED TO GRACE—not because of a tight-fisted God but because of our unwillingness to yield.

ZEPHANIAH 2:1, 3

¹הִתְקוֹשְׁשׁוּ וָקוֹשׁוּ הַגּוֹי לֹא נִכְסָף׃
³בַּקְּשׁוּ אֶת־יְהוָה כָּל־עַנְוֵי הָאָרֶץ אֲשֶׁר מִשְׁפָּטוֹ פָּעָלוּ בַּקְּשׁוּ־
צֶדֶק בַּקְּשׁוּ עֲנָוָה אוּלַי תִּסָּתְרוּ בְּיוֹם אַף־יְהוָה׃

הִתְקוֹשְׁשׁוּ v.2.m.p.impv.Ht. [קשׁשׁ] (gather); וָקוֹשׁוּ cj. + v.2.m.p.impv.Q. [קשׁשׁ]; נִכְסָף (long for); עֲנָוֵי (poor); אוּלַי (perhaps)

2 TIMOTHY 2:24–25

²⁴δοῦλον δὲ κυρίου οὐ δεῖ μάχεσθαι ἀλλὰ ἤπιον εἶναι πρὸς πάντας, διδακτικόν, ἀνεξίκακον, ²⁵ἐν πραΰτητι παιδεύοντα τοὺς ἀντιδιατιθεμένους, μήποτε δῴη αὐτοῖς ὁ θεὸς μετάνοιαν εἰς ἐπίγνωσιν ἀληθείας

μάχεσθαι (quarrel); ἤπιον (gentle); εἶναι v.pres.in. [εἰμί]; διδακτικόν (skilled in teaching); ἀνεξίκακον (not resentful); πραΰτητι (gentleness); παιδεύοντα (correct); ἀντιδιατιθεμένους (be opposed); μήποτε (lest); δῴη v.3.s.aor.act.sub. [δίδωμι]; μετάνοιαν (repentance); ἐπίγνωσιν (knowledge)

2. Deuteronomy 6:10–12; Matthew 19:23–24

The Illusion

THE GREAT SNARE OF MATERIAL WEALTH is its accompanying illusion of certainty.

DEUTERONOMY 6:10–12

¹⁰וְהָיָה כִּי יְבִיאֲךָ יְהוָה אֱלֹהֶיךָ אֶל־הָאָרֶץ אֲשֶׁר נִשְׁבַּע לַאֲבֹתֶיךָ
לְאַבְרָהָם לְיִצְחָק וּלְיַעֲקֹב לָתֶת לָךְ עָרִים גְּדֹלֹת וְטֹבֹת אֲשֶׁר
לֹא־בָנִיתָ:
¹¹וּבָתִּים מְלֵאִים כָּל־טוּב אֲשֶׁר לֹא־מִלֵּאתָ וּבֹרֹת חֲצוּבִים אֲשֶׁר
לֹא־חָצַבְתָּ כְּרָמִים וְזֵיתִים אֲשֶׁר לֹא־נָטָעְתָּ וְאָכַלְתָּ וְשָׂבָעְתָּ:
¹²הִשָּׁמֶר לְךָ פֶּן־תִּשְׁכַּח אֶת־יְהוָה אֲשֶׁר הוֹצִיאֲךָ מֵאֶרֶץ מִצְרַיִם
מִבֵּית עֲבָדִים:

יְבִיאֲךָ v.3.m.s.impf.H. [בוא] + 2.m.s.pr.sf.; לָתֶת prep. + v.in.cs.Q. [נתן];
בָנִיתָ v.1.com.s.pf.Q. [בנה]; טוּב (good thing); חֲצוּבִים (hew); וְזֵיתִים (olive tree); הוֹצִיאֲךָ v.3.m.s.pf.H. [יצא]+ 2.m.s.pr.sf.

MATTHEW 19:23–24

²³Ὁ δὲ Ἰησοῦς εἶπεν τοῖς μαθηταῖς αὐτοῦ, Ἀμὴν λέγω ὑμῖν ὅτι πλούσιος δυσκόλως εἰσελεύσεται εἰς τὴν βασιλείαν τῶν οὐρανῶν. ²⁴πάλιν δὲ λέγω ὑμῖν, εὐκοπώτερόν ἐστιν κάμηλον διὰ τρυπήματος ῥαφίδος διελθεῖν ἢ πλούσιον εἰσελθεῖν εἰς τὴν βασιλείαν τοῦ θεοῦ.

εἶπεν v.3.s.aor.act.ind. [λέγω]; πλούσιος (rich); δυσκόλως (barely); εἰσελεύσεται v.3.s.fut.mid.ind. [εἰσέρχομαι]; εὐκοπώτερον (easy); ἐστιν v.3.s.pres.ind. [εἰμί]; κάμηλον (camel); τρυπήματος (hole, eye); ῥαφίδος (needle); διελθεῖν v.aor.act.in. [διέρχομαι]; εἰσελθεῖν v.aor.act.in. [εἰσέρχομαι]

3. Daniel 3:21–22; James 1:17

Certain Goodness

THERE IS BUT ONE CERTAINTY OF GOODNESS, and that is God. Though hidden from us at times because of our own blindness, his goodness is pervasive nonetheless. In the end this will be clear.

DANIEL 3:21–22 (A.)

²¹בֵּאדַיִן גֻּבְרַיָּא אִלֵּךְ כְּפִתוּ בְּסַרְבָּלֵיהוֹן פַּטְּשֵׁיהוֹן
וְכַרְבְּלָתְהוֹן וּלְבֻשֵׁיהוֹן וּרְמִיו לְגוֹא־אַתּוּן נוּרָא יָקִדְתָּא׃
²²כָּל־קֳבֵל דְּנָה מִן־דִּי מִלַּת מַלְכָּא מַחְצְפָה וְאַתּוּנָא אֵזֵה יַתִּירָא
גֻּבְרַיָּא אִלֵּךְ דִּי הַסִּקוּ לְשַׁדְרַךְ מֵישַׁךְ וַעֲבֵד נְגוֹ קַטִּל הִמּוֹן
שְׁבִיבָא דִּי נוּרָא׃

יָקִדְתָּא ,v.f.s.ptc.Pe. [יקד] + d.a.; הַסִּקוּ v.3.m.p.pf.Ha. [סלק]

JAMES 1:17

¹⁷πᾶσα δόσις ἀγαθὴ καὶ πᾶν δώρημα τέλειον ἄνωθέν ἐστιν καταβαῖνον ἀπὸ τοῦ πατρὸς τῶν φώτων, παρ' ᾧ οὐκ ἔνι παραλλαγὴ ἢ τροπῆς ἀποσκίασμα.

δόσις (gift); δώρημα (present); τέλειον (perfect); ἄνωθεν (from above); ἐστιν v.3.s.pres.ind. [εἰμί]; ἔνι (there is); παραλλαγὴ (change); τροπῆς (variation); ἀποσκίασμα (shadow)

113

4. Isaiah 50:8–9; John 16:32

Fearless One

I CLING TO YOU, MY GOD, for there is no one else. Only you are untouched by the fears that, given the right set of circumstances, divide even the best of friends.

ISAIAH 50:8–9

‎8קָרוֹב מַצְדִּיקִי מִי־יָרִיב אִתִּי נַעַמְדָה יָּחַד מִי־בַעַל מִשְׁפָּטִי יִגַּשׁ
‎אֵלָי׃
‎9הֵן אֲדֹנָי יְהוִה יַעֲזָר־לִי מִי־הוּא יַרְשִׁיעֵנִי הֵן כֻּלָּם כַּבֶּגֶד
‎יִבְלוּ עָשׁ יֹאכְלֵם׃

נַעַמְדָה v.1.com.p.coh.Q. [עמד]; יִגַּשׁ v.3.m.s.impf.Q. [נגש]; יַרְשִׁיעֵנִי v.3.m.s.impf.H. [רשע] (condemn) + 1.com.s.pr.sf.; יִבְלוּ v.3.m.p.impf.Q. [בלה] (wear out); עָשׁ (moth); יֹאכְלֵם v.3.m.s.impf.Q. [אכל] + 3.m.p.pr.sf.

JOHN 16:32

32ἰδοὺ ἔρχεται ὥρα καὶ ἐλήλυθεν ἵνα σκορπισθῆτε ἕκαστος εἰς τὰ ἴδια καμὲ μόνον ἀφῆτε· καὶ οὐκ εἰμὶ μόνος, ὅτι ὁ πατὴρ μετ' ἐμοῦ ἐστιν.

ἔρχεται v.3.s.pres.mid.ind. [ἔρχομαι]; ἐλήλυθεν v.3.s.pf.act.ind. [ἔρχομαι]; σκορπισθῆτε (scatter); ἐστιν v.3.s.pres.ind. [εἰμί]

5. 1 Samuel 1:10, 17; 1 Peter 5:6–7

Hannah's Tears

LIKE HANNAH, LET US BITTERLY WEEP our fears to God and pour out our distress. We may be certain that his desire for us is ultimate exaltation. We may be certain that he cares.

1 SAMUEL 1:10, 17

¹⁰וְהִיא מָרַת נָפֶשׁ וַתִּתְפַּלֵּל עַל־יְהוָה וּבָכֹה תִבְכֶּה׃
¹⁷וַיַּעַן עֵלִי וַיֹּאמֶר לְכִי לְשָׁלוֹם וֵאלֹהֵי יִשְׂרָאֵל יִתֵּן אֶת־
שֵׁלָתֵךְ אֲשֶׁר שָׁאַלְתְּ מֵעִמּוֹ׃

מָרַת (bitter); וַיַּעַן v.c. + 3.m.s.impf.Q. [ענה]; לְכִי v.2.f.s.impv.Q. [הלך]; יִתֵּן v.3.m.s.impf.Q. [נתן]; שֵׁלָתֵךְ n.f.s. (request) contracted, losing א + 2.f.s.pr.sf.

1 PETER 5:6–7

⁶Ταπεινώθητε οὖν ὑπὸ τὴν κραταιὰν χεῖρα τοῦ θεοῦ, ἵνα ὑμᾶς ὑψώσῃ ἐν καιρῷ, ⁷πᾶσαν τὴν μέριμναν ὑμῶν ἐπιρίψαντες ἐπ᾽ αὐτόν, ὅτι αὐτῷ μέλει περὶ ὑμῶν.

Ταπεινώθητε (humble); κραταιὰν (powerful); ὑψώσῃ v.3.s.aor.act.sub. [ὑψόω] (raise up); μέριμναν (care); ἐπιρίψαντες v.m.p.nom.aor.act.ptc. [ἐπιρίπτω] (throw); μέλει (care)

6. Genesis 27:2; James 4:13–15

The Gift of Not Knowing

WE RARELY THINK of it as such but uncertainty is one of our greatest gifts. For it reminds us hour by hour that God is God and we are not.

GENESIS 27:2

²וַיֹּאמֶר הִנֵּה־נָא זָקַנְתִּי לֹא יָדַעְתִּי יוֹם מוֹתִי׃

זָקַנְתִּי (be old)

JAMES 4:13–15

¹³Ἄγε νῦν οἱ λέγοντες, Σήμερον ἢ αὔριον πορευσόμεθα εἰς τήνδε τὴν πόλιν καὶ ποιήσομεν ἐκεῖ ἐνιαυτὸν καὶ ἐμπορευσόμεθα καὶ κερδήσομεν· ¹⁴οἵτινες οὐκ ἐπίστασθε τὸ τῆς αὔριον ποία ἡ ζωὴ ὑμῶν· ἀτμὶς γάρ ἐστε ἡ πρὸς ὀλίγον φαινομένη, ἔπειτα καὶ ἀφανιζομένη. ¹⁵ἀντὶ τοῦ λέγειν ὑμᾶς, Ἐὰν ὁ κύριος θελήσῃ καὶ ζήσομεν καὶ ποιήσομεν τοῦτο ἢ ἐκεῖνο.

Ἄγε (listen); νῦν (now); Σήμερον (today); αὔριον (tomorrow); τήνδε (this); ἐνιαυτὸν (year); ἐμπορευσόμεθα (carry on business); κερδήσομεν (profit); ἐπίστασθε v.2.p.pres.pass.ind. [ἐπίσταμαι] (know); ποία (of what kind); ἀτμὶς (vapor); ὀλίγον (short); φαινομένη (appear); ἔπειτα (then); ἀφανιζομένη (perish); ἀντὶ (for)

7. Exodus 5.2, John 16:2–3

When Persecution Comes . . .

WHEN I FACE PERSECUTION by those who do it in your name, my God, let me remember that you have borne all blasphemy and yet you remain unshaken. Hold me close to your wounded side. Comfort me there with your certain love.

EXODUS 5:2

²וַיֹּאמֶר פַּרְעֹה מִי יְהוָה אֲשֶׁר אֶשְׁמַע בְּקֹלוֹ לְשַׁלַּח אֶת־יִשְׂרָאֵל לֹא יָדַעְתִּי אֶת־יְהוָה וְגַם אֶת־יִשְׂרָאֵל לֹא אֲשַׁלֵּחַ׃

JOHN 16:2–3

²ἀποσυναγώγους ποιήσουσιν ὑμᾶς· ἀλλ᾽ ἔρχεται ὥρα ἵνα πᾶς ὁ ἀποκτείνας ὑμᾶς δόξῃ λατρείαν προσφέρειν τῷ θεῷ. ³καὶ ταῦτα ποιήσουσιν ὅτι οὐκ ἔγνωσαν τὸν πατέρα οὐδὲ ἐμέ.

ἀποσυναγώγους (excommunicated); δόξῃ v.3.s.aor.act.sub. [δοκέω]; λατρείαν (service); προσφέρειν (bring)

Week 16

Doubt

1. 2 Kings 6:15–16; Matthew 28:16–17

A Posture of the Heart

IF ONLY DOUBT were strictly an empirical choice! But it is not. There are times when in the face of incontrovertible evidence we choose to mistrust God. Doubt is at its core a posture of the heart.

2 KINGS 6:15–16

‏¹⁵וַיַּשְׁכֵּם מְשָׁרֵת אִישׁ הָאֱלֹהִים לָקוּם וַיֵּצֵא וְהִנֵּה־חַיִל סוֹבֵב
אֶת־הָעִיר וְסוּס וָרָכֶב וַיֹּאמֶר נַעֲרוֹ אֵלָיו אֲהָהּ אֲדֹנִי אֵיכָה נַעֲשֶׂה:
¹⁶וַיֹּאמֶר אַל־תִּירָא כִּי רַבִּים אֲשֶׁר אִתָּנוּ מֵאֲשֶׁר אוֹתָם:‏

וַיֵּצֵא v.c. + v.3.m.s.impf.Q. [יצא]; אֲהָהּ (hey!)

MATTHEW 28:16–17

¹⁶Οἱ δὲ ἕνδεκα μαθηταὶ ἐπορεύθησαν εἰς τὴν Γαλιλαίαν εἰς τὸ ὄρος οὗ ἐτάξατο αὐτοῖς ὁ Ἰησοῦς, ¹⁷καὶ ἰδόντες αὐτὸν προσεκύνησαν, οἱ δὲ ἐδίστασαν.

ἕνδεκα (eleven); ἐτάξατο v.3.s.aor.mid.ind. [τάσσω] (order); ἰδόντες v.m.p.nom.aor.act.ptc. [ὁράω]; ἐδίστασαν (doubt)

2. Deuteronomy 28:05–00; Luke 21:25–26

Armageddon

FOR SOME OF US nothing short of Armageddon will shake us from self-sufficiency.

DEUTERONOMY 28:65–66

‏65וּבַגּוֹיִם הָהֵם לֹא תַרְגִּיעַ וְלֹא־יִהְיֶה מָנוֹחַ לְכַף־רַגְלֶךָ
וְנָתַן יְהוָה לְךָ שָׁם לֵב רַגָּז וְכִלְיוֹן עֵינַיִם וְדַאֲבוֹן נָפֶשׁ׃
‏66וְהָיוּ חַיֶּיךָ תְּלֻאִים לְךָ מִנֶּגֶד וּפָחַדְתָּ לַיְלָה וְיוֹמָם
וְלֹא תַאֲמִין בְּחַיֶּיךָ׃

תַרְגִּיעַ (bring rest); מָנוֹחַ (rest); רַגָּז (quaking); וְכִלְיוֹן (failing); וְדַאֲבוֹן (faint-ness); וְהָיוּ v.c. + v.3.c.p.pf.Q. [היה]; תְּלֻאִים (hang); וּפָחַדְתָּ (fear)

LUKE 21:25–26

²⁵Καὶ ἔσονται σημεῖα ἐν ἡλίῳ καὶ σελήνῃ καὶ ἄστροις, καὶ ἐπὶ τῆς γῆς συνοχὴ ἐθνῶν ἐν ἀπορίᾳ ἤχους θαλάσσης καὶ σάλου, ²⁶ἀποψυχόντων ἀνθρώπων ἀπὸ φόβου καὶ προσδοκίας τῶν ἐπερχομένων τῇ οἰκουμένῃ, αἱ γὰρ δυνάμεις τῶν οὐρανῶν σαλευθήσονται.

ἡλίῳ (sun); σελήνη (moon); ἄστροις (star); συνοχὴ (anguish); ἀπορίᾳ (anxiety); ἤχους (roaring); σάλου (roiling); ἀποψυχόντων (stop breathing); φόβου (fear); προσδοκίας (apprehension); ἐπερχομένων (come up); οἰκουμένη (world); σαλευθήσονται (shake)

3. Isaiah 49:4; 1 Thessalonians 3:4–5

The Alabaster Jar

GOD OF ALL COMFORT, strengthen us in the day of seeming failure, when all we have done in love for you appears to be a waste. Let our hearts remain steadfast; let us not doubt the value of a broken alabaster jar.

ISAIAH 49:4

⁴וַאֲנִי אָמַרְתִּי לְרִיק יָגַעְתִּי לְתֹהוּ וְהֶבֶל כֹּחִי כִלֵּיתִי אָכֵן
מִשְׁפָּטִי אֶת־יְהוָה וּפְעֻלָּתִי אֶת־אֱלֹהָי:

לְרִיק (emptiness); יָגַעְתִּי (toil); לְתֹהוּ (emptiness); כִלֵּיתִי v.1.com.s.pf.P. [כלה]; אָכֵן (surely); וּפְעֻלָּתִי (work)

1 THESSALONIANS 3:4–5

⁴καὶ γὰρ ὅτε πρὸς ὑμᾶς ἦμεν, προελέγομεν ὑμῖν ὅτι μέλλομεν θλίβεσθαι, καθὼς καὶ ἐγένετο καὶ οἴδατε. ⁵διὰ τοῦτο κἀγὼ μηκέτι στέγων ἔπεμψα εἰς τὸ γνῶναι τὴν πίστιν ὑμῶν, μή πως ἐπείρασεν ὑμᾶς ὁ πειράζων καὶ εἰς κενὸν γένηται ὁ κόπος ἡμῶν.

προελέγομεν (foretell); θλίβεσθαι (persecute); ἐγένετο v.3.s.aor.mid.ind. [γίνομαι]; μηκέτι (no longer); στέγων (endure); γνῶναι v.aor.act.in. [γινώσκω]; πως (in some way); ἐπείρασεν (tempt); κενὸν (useless); κόπος (labor)

4. Psalm 22.16–18 [15–17]; Mark 15:31–32

Doubting the Call

DID YOU DOUBT YOUR CALL, Jesus, in your abandonment? Could you still hear the Father's love over the blaspheming shouts? The healing of my doubt rests in your willingness to bear it for me, there, on the cross.

PSALM 22:16–18 [15–17]

16יָבֵשׁ כַּחֶרֶשׂ כֹּחִי וּלְשׁוֹנִי מֻדְבָּק מַלְקוֹחָי וְלַעֲפַר־מָוֶת תִּשְׁפְּתֵנִי׃

17כִּי סְבָבוּנִי כְּלָבִים עֲדַת מְרֵעִים הִקִּיפוּנִי כָּאֲרִי יָדַי וְרַגְלָי׃

18אֲסַפֵּר כָּל־עַצְמוֹתָי הֵמָּה יַבִּיטוּ יִרְאוּ־בִי׃

כַּחֶרֶשׂ (potsherd); מַלְקוֹחָי (jaw); תִּשְׁפְּתֵנִי v.2.m.s.impf.Q. [שׁפת] (set) + 1.com.s.pr.sf.; יִרְאוּ v.3.m.p.impf.Q. [ראה]; הִקִּיפוּנִי v.3.c.p.pf.H. [נקף] (surround) + 1.com.s.pr.sf.; יַבִּיטוּ v.3.m.p.impf.H. [נבט]

MARK 15:31–32

31ὁμοίως καὶ οἱ ἀρχιερεῖς ἐμπαίζοντες πρὸς ἀλλήλους μετὰ τῶν γραμματέων ἔλεγον, Ἄλλους ἔσωσεν, ἑαυτὸν οὐ δύναται σῶσαι· 32ὁ Χριστὸς ὁ βασιλεὺς Ἰσραὴλ καταβάτω νῦν ἀπὸ τοῦ σταυροῦ, ἵνα ἴδωμεν καὶ πιστεύσωμεν. καὶ οἱ συνεσταυρωμένοι σὺν αὐτῷ ὠνείδιζον αὐτόν.

ὁμοίως (likewise); ἐμπαίζοντες (mock); νῦν (now); σταυροῦ (cross); συνεσταυρωμένοι (crucify together); ὠνείδιζον v.3.p.impf.act.ind. [ὀνειδίζω] (reproach)

5. Psalm 22:2–3 [1–2]; Mark 15:33–34

The Question Behind All Doubt

WHEN JESUS CRIED, "My God, my God, why have you forsaken me?" he cried the primeval question behind all doubt.

PSALM 22:2–3 [1–2]

²אֵלִי אֵלִי לָמָה עֲזַבְתָּנִי רָחוֹק מִישׁוּעָתִי דִּבְרֵי שַׁאֲגָתִי׃
³אֱלֹהַי אֶקְרָא יוֹמָם וְלֹא תַעֲנֶה וְלַיְלָה וְלֹא־דוּמִיָּה לִי׃

מִישׁוּעָתִי prep. + n.f.s. + 1.com.s.pr.sf.; שַׁאֲגָתִי (roaring)

MARK 15:33–34

³³Καὶ γενομένης ὥρας ἕκτης σκότος ἐγένετο ἐφ' ὅλην τὴν γῆν ἕως ὥρας ἐνάτης. ³⁴καὶ τῇ ἐνάτῃ ὥρᾳ ἐβόησεν ὁ Ἰησοῦς φωνῇ μεγάλῃ, Ελωι ελωι λεμα σαβαχθανι· ὅ ἐστιν μεθερμηνευόμενον Ὁ θεός μου ὁ θεός μου, εἰς τί ἐγκατέλιπες με;

ἕκτης (sixth); σκότος (darkness); ἐγένετο v.3.s.aor.mid.ind. [γίνομαι]; ἐνάτης (ninth); ἐβόησεν (cry aloud); Ελωι ελωι λεμα σαβαχθανι Transliteration from Aramaic אֵלִי אֵלִי לְמָה שֵׁבַקְתַּנִי "My God, my God, why did you abandon me?"; ἐστιν v.3.s.pres.ind. [εἰμί]; μεθερμηνευόμενον (translate); ἐγκατέλιπες v.2.s.aor.act.ind. [εγκαταλείπω] (completely abandon)

6. Job 12.9–10, Romans 11:36

A Matter of Vision

O GOD, HEAL MY DOUBT until I see your hand everywhere, in all things.

JOB 12:9–10

⁹מִי לֹא־יָדַע בְּכָל־אֵלֶּה כִּי יַד־יְהוָה עָשְׂתָה זֹּאת׃
¹⁰אֲשֶׁר בְּיָדוֹ נֶפֶשׁ כָּל־חָי וְרוּחַ כָּל־בְּשַׂר־אִישׁ׃

עָשְׂתָה v.3.f.s.pf.Q. [עשׂה]

ROMANS 11:36

³⁶ὅτι ἐξ αὐτοῦ καὶ δι' αὐτοῦ καὶ εἰς αὐτὸν τὰ πάντα· αὐτῷ ἡ δόξα εἰς τοὺς αἰῶνας, ἀμήν.

7. Psalm 138:7; Matthew 14:31–32

Grace During Doubt

THANK GOD THE HAND OF JESUS reaches out to me, more during my doubt, perhaps, than any other time!

PSALM 138:7

‏⁷אִם־אֵלֵךְ בְּקֶרֶב צָרָה תְּחַיֵּנִי עַל אַף אֹיְבַי תִּשְׁלַח יָדֶךָ וְתוֹשִׁיעֵנִי‏
‏יְמִינֶךָ:‏

אֵלֵךְ v.1.com.s.impf.Q. [הלך]; תְּחַיֵּנִי v.2.m.s.impf.P. [חיה] + 1.com.s.pr.sf.; וְתוֹשִׁיעֵנִי cj. + v.2.m.s.impf.H. [ישע] + 1.com.s.pr.sf.

MATTHEW 14:31–32

³¹εὐθέως δὲ ὁ Ἰησοῦς ἐκτείνας τὴν χεῖρα ἐπελάβετο αὐτοῦ καὶ λέγει αὐτῷ, Ὀλιγόπιστε, εἰς τί ἐδίστασας; ³²καὶ ἀναβάντων αὐτῶν εἰς τὸ πλοῖον ἐκόπασεν ὁ ἄνεμος.

ἐπελάβετο (grasp); Ὀλιγόπιστε (little faith); ἐδίστασας (doubt); ἐκόπασεν (cease); ἄνεμος (wind)

Transition (Life Stages)

1. Psalm 22:9–10 [8–9], Galatians 1:15–16a

The Borning Day

AT MY BIRTH THE FIRST CONGRATULATIONS, the first tears of joy and shouts of jubilation came from you, Lord! When I think of this, I am so relieved. My days are ordered! There is purpose from beginning to end. I always have been and always shall be in your heart.

PSALM 22:9–10 [8–9]

⁹גֹּל אֶל־יְהֹוָה יְפַלְּטֵהוּ יַצִּילֵהוּ כִּי חָפֵץ בּוֹ׃
¹⁰כִּי־אַתָּה גֹחִי מִבָּטֶן מַבְטִיחִי עַל־שְׁדֵי אִמִּי׃

גֹּל v.2.m.s.impv.Q. [גלל] (roll); יְפַלְּטֵהוּ v.3.m.s.impf.P. [פלט] (secure) + 3.m.s.pr.sf.; יַצִּילֵהוּ v.3.m.s.impf.H. [נצל] + 3.m.s.pr.sf.; גֹחִי v.m.s.ptc.Q. [גוח] (draw forth); שְׁדֵי (breast)

GALATIANS 1:15–16A

¹⁵ὅτε δὲ εὐδόκησεν [ὁ θεὸς] ὁ ἀφορίσας με ἐκ κοιλίας μητρός μου καὶ καλέσας διὰ τῆς χάριτος αὐτοῦ ¹⁶ἀποκαλύψαι τὸν υἱὸν αὐτοῦ ἐν ἐμοί,

εὐδόκησεν (be pleased); ἀφορίσας (set apart); κοιλίας (womb); ἀποκαλύψαι (reveal)

2. Proverbs 1:3–4; 2 Timothy 2:22

Youthful Hunger

LET US NOURISH OUR CHILDREN with the fruits of holiness—
peace, patience, self-control, and so on—in our own lives. That
is the only way they will acquire a taste for an authentic spiritual life.

PROVERBS 1:3–4

לָקַחַת מוּסַר הַשְׂכֵּל צֶדֶק וּמִשְׁפָּט וּמֵישָׁרִים: ³
לָתֵת לִפְתָאיִם עָרְמָה לְנַעַר דַּעַת וּמְזִמָּה: ⁴

לָקַחַת prep. + v.in.cs.Q. [לקח]; הַשְׂכֵּל v.in.ab.H. [שׂכל]; וּמֵישָׁרִים (uprightness); לָתֵת prep. + v.in.cs.Q. [נתן]; לִפְתָאיִם (simple); עָרְמָה (prudence); וּמְזִמָּה
(purpose)

2 TIMOTHY 2:22

²²Τὰς δὲ νεωτερικὰς ἐπιθυμίας φεῦγε, δίωκε δὲ δικαιοσύνην
πίστιν ἀγάπην εἰρήνην μετὰ τῶν ἐπικαλουμένων τὸν κύριον
ἐκ καθαρᾶς καρδίας.

νεωτερικὰς (youthful); ἐπιθυμίας (desire); φεῦγε (flee); δίωκε (chase);
ἐπικαλουμένων (call upon); καθαρᾶς (clean)

3. Genesis 24:58, 60; Hebrews 13:4

Lovers

O GOD, DELIVER US from every practice in marriage that dimin-
ishes the union of lovers—a union that images our Triune
God.

GENESIS 24:58, 60

⁵⁸וַיִּקְרְאוּ לְרִבְקָה וַיֹּאמְרוּ אֵלֶיהָ הֲתֵלְכִי עִם־הָאִישׁ הַזֶּה
וַתֹּאמֶר אֵלֵךְ׃
⁶⁰וַיְבָרֲכוּ אֶת־רִבְקָה וַיֹּאמְרוּ לָהּ אֲחֹתֵנוּ אַתְּ הֲיִי לְאַלְפֵי רְבָבָה
וְיִירַשׁ זַרְעֵךְ אֵת שַׁעַר שֹׂנְאָיו׃

הֲתֵלְכִי int.pt. + v.2.f.s.impf.Q. [הלך]; אֵלֵךְ v.1.com.s.impf.Q. [הלך]; הֲיִי
v.2.f.s.impv.-Q. [היה]; רְבָבָה (ten thousand); וְיִירַשׁ cj. + v.3.m.s.impf.Q. [ירשׁ]

HEBREWS 13:4

⁴Τίμιος ὁ γάμος ἐν πᾶσιν καὶ ἡ κοίτη ἀμίαντος, πόρνους γὰρ
καὶ μοιχοὺς κρινεῖ ὁ θεός.

Τίμιος (honorable); γάμος (marriage); κοίτη (marriage bed); ἀμίαντος (undefiled); πόρνους (fornication); μοιχοὺς (adulterer)

4. Psalm 128:1–3; Matthew 19:13–14

Love for the Child, Within and Without

GOD, GRANT THAT WE MIGHT TREAT OUR CHILDREN with the same tender love and compassion, with the same protective care, with the same will for their wholeness, that you have for each of us. Help us delight in their uniqueness as they mature. We ask this for the children around us, and for the child within us.

PSALM 128:1–3

¹שִׁיר הַמַּעֲלוֹת אַשְׁרֵי כָּל־יְרֵא יְהוָה הַהֹלֵךְ בִּדְרָכָיו:
²יְגִיעַ כַּפֶּיךָ כִּי תֹאכֵל אַשְׁרֶיךָ וְטוֹב לָךְ:
³אֶשְׁתְּךָ כְּגֶפֶן פֹּרִיָּה בְּיַרְכְּתֵי בֵיתֶךָ בָּנֶיךָ כִּשְׁתִלֵי זֵיתִים
סָבִיב לְשֻׁלְחָנֶךָ:

אַשְׁרֵי (blessing); יְגִיעַ n.m.s.; אֶשְׁתְּךָ n.f.s. + 2.m.s.pr.sf.; פֹּרִיָּה (fruitful); כִּשְׁתִלֵי (transplanted slip); זֵיתִים (olive tree)

MATTHEW 19:13–14

¹³Τότε προσηνέχθησαν αὐτῷ παιδία ἵνα τὰς χεῖρας ἐπιθῇ αὐτοῖς καὶ προσεύξηται· οἱ δὲ μαθηταὶ ἐπετίμησαν αὐτοῖς. ¹⁴ὁ δὲ Ἰησοῦς εἶπεν, Ἄφετε τὰ παιδία καὶ μὴ κωλύετε αὐτὰ ἐλθεῖν πρός με, τῶν γὰρ τοιούτων ἐστὶν ἡ βασιλεία τῶν οὐρανῶν.

προσηνέχθησαν v.3.p.aor.pass.ind. [προσθέρω] (bring); ἐπιθῇ v.3.s.aor.act.sub. [ἐπιτίθημι] (inflict); ἐπετίμησαν (rebuke); εἶπεν v.3.s.aor.act.ind. [λέγω]; κωλύετε (forbid); ἐστὶν v.3.s.pres.ind. [εἰμί]

5. Isaiah 46:3–4; John 21:18

God Will Keep Me

MY LIFE IS IN YOUR KEEPING, LORD. Even when I am old and, like an infant, at the mercy of others, you will be my God. My soul will be secure.

ISAIAH 46:3–4

³שִׁמְעוּ אֵלַי בֵּית יַעֲקֹב וְכָל־שְׁאֵרִית בֵּית יִשְׂרָאֵל הַעֲמֻסִים מִנִּי־
בֶטֶן הַנְּשֻׂאִים מִנִּי־רָחַם:
⁴וְעַד־זִקְנָה אֲנִי הוּא וְעַד־שֵׂיבָה אֲנִי אֶסְבֹּל אֲנִי עָשִׂיתִי וַאֲנִי
אֶשָּׂא וַאֲנִי אֶסְבֹּל וַאֲמַלֵּט:

הַעֲמֻסִים (carry); מִנִּי prep. + 1.com.s.pr.sf.; שֵׂיבָה (old age); אֶסְבֹּל (carry); עָשִׂיתִי v.1.com.s.pf.Q. [עשׂה]; אֶשָּׂא v.1.com.s.impf.Q. [נשׂא]

JOHN 21:18

¹⁸ἀμὴν ἀμὴν λέγω σοι, ὅτε ἦς νεώτερος, ἐζώννυες σεαυτὸν καὶ περιεπάτεις ὅπου ἤθελες· ὅταν δὲ γηράσῃς, ἐκτενεῖς τὰς χεῖρας σου, καὶ ἄλλος σε ζώσει καὶ οἴσει ὅπου οὐ θέλεις.

νεώτερος (younger); ἐζώννυες v.2.s.impf.act.ind. [ζωννύω] (gird); γηράσῃς (grow old); ἐκτενεῖς (stretch out); οἴσει v.3.s.fut.act.ind. [φέρω]

6. Jeremiah 31:15; Matthew 2:18

God of Comfort

WHO BETTER THAN GOD UNDERSTANDS the agony we feel at a loved one's untimely death? What greater comfort is there than our risen Lord?

JEREMIAH 31:15

¹⁵כֹּה אָמַר יְהוָה קוֹל בְּרָמָה נִשְׁמָע נְהִי בְּכִי תַמְרוּרִים רָחֵל מְבַכָּה
עַל־בָּנֶיהָ מֵאֲנָה לְהִנָּחֵם עַל־בָּנֶיהָ כִּי אֵינֶנּוּ:

נְהִי n.m.s. (wailing); בְּכִי (weeping); תַמְרוּרִים (bitterness); מֵאֲנָה v.3.f.s.pf.P.
[מאן] (refuse)

MATTHEW 2:18

¹⁸Φωνὴ ἐν Ῥαμὰ ἠκούσθη,
    κλαυθμὸς καὶ ὀδυρμὸς πολύς·
Ῥαχὴλ κλαίουσα τὰ τέκνα αὐτῆς,
    καὶ οὐκ ἤθελεν παρακληθῆναι, ὅτι οὐκ εἰσίν.

κλαυθμὸς (crying); ὀδυρμὸς (mourning); κλαίουσα (weep); εἰσίν
v.3.p.pres.ind. [εἰμί]

7. Genesis 25.8–9a; Acts 13:36–37

Forever Life

GOD OF MY LIFE, as I grow older and the hour of my death draws near, may I know more and more that you are the God of life, and that because of you I will live forever.

GENESIS 25:8–9A

⁸וַיִּגְוַע וַיָּמָת אַבְרָהָם בְּשֵׂיבָה טוֹבָה זָקֵן וְשָׂבֵעַ וַיֵּאָסֶף אֶל־עַמָּיו:

⁹וַיִּקְבְּרוּ אֹתוֹ יִצְחָק וְיִשְׁמָעֵאל בָּנָיו אֶל־מְעָרַת הַמַּכְפֵּלָה

וַיִּגְוַע (expire); וַיָּמָת v.c. + v.3.m.s.impf.Q. [מות]; בְּשֵׂיבָה (old age); וְשָׂבֵעַ (sated); מְעָרַת (cave)

ACTS 13:36–37

³⁶Δαυὶδ μὲν γὰρ ἰδίᾳ γενεᾷ ὑπηρετήσας τῇ τοῦ θεοῦ βουλῇ ἐκοιμήθη καὶ προσετέθη πρὸς τοὺς πατέρας αὐτοῦ καὶ εἶδεν διαφθοράν· ³⁷ὃν δὲ ὁ θεὸς ἤγειρεν, οὐκ εἶδεν διαφθοράν.

γενεᾷ (generation); ὑπηρετήσας (serve); ἐκοιμήθη (die); προσετέθη (add); εἶδεν v.3.s.aor.act.ind. [ὁράω]; διαφθοράν (corruption)

Week 18

Mercy

1. Exodus 33:18–19; Romans 9:14–16

No Horizon

YOUR MERCY IS LARGE INDEED, God, much bigger than I thought. Each time I stand gazing into the opaque and seemingly bottomless depths of sin, you cup my chin in your hand and direct my eyes upward, to your mercy. There, I see no horizon.

EXODUS 33:18–19

18וַיֹּאמַר הַרְאֵנִי נָא אֶת־כְּבֹדֶךָ׃

19וַיֹּאמֶר אֲנִי אַעֲבִיר כָּל־טוּבִי עַל־פָּנֶיךָ וְקָרָאתִי בְשֵׁם יְהוָה
לְפָנֶיךָ וְחַנֹּתִי אֶת־אֲשֶׁר אָחֹן וְרִחַמְתִּי אֶת־אֲשֶׁר אֲרַחֵם׃

הַרְאֵנִי v.2.m.s.impv.H. [ראה] + 1.com.s.pr.sf.; טוּבִי (good thing); וְחַנֹּתִי v.c. + v.1.com.s.pf.Q. [חנן]; אָחֹן v.1.com.s.impf.Q. [חנן]

ROMANS 9:14–16

14Τί οὖν ἐροῦμεν; μὴ ἀδικία παρὰ τῷ θεῷ; μὴ γένοιτο.
15τῷ Μωϋσεῖ γὰρ λέγει·
    Ἐλεήσω ὃν ἂν ἐλεῶ
        καὶ οἰκτιρήσω ὃν ἂν οἰκτίρω.
16ἄρα οὖν οὐ τοῦ θέλοντος οὐδὲ τοῦ τρέχοντος ἀλλὰ τοῦ ἐλεῶντος θεοῦ.

ἐροῦμεν v.1.p.fut.act.ind. [λέγω]; ἀδικία (unrighteousness); γένοιτο v.3.s.aor.mid.ind. [γίνομαι]; Ἐλεήσω v.1.s.fut.act.ind. [ελεέω] (have mercy); οἰκτιρήσω (have compassion); ἄρα (then); τρέχοντος (run)

132

2. Psalm 23:5–6; 2 Corinthians 1:9–10

Unseen Companions

NO MATTER HOW DIFFICULT things have been on my journey, every time I pause and look back I see the tracks of goodness and mercy mingled with my own.

PSALM 23:5–6

⁵תַּעֲרֹךְ לְפָנַי שֻׁלְחָן נֶגֶד צֹרְרָי דִּשַּׁנְתָּ בַשֶּׁמֶן רֹאשִׁי כּוֹסִי
רְוָיָה:

⁶אַךְ טוֹב וָחֶסֶד יִרְדְּפוּנִי כָּל־יְמֵי חַיָּי וְשַׁבְתִּי בְּבֵית־יְהוָה
לְאֹרֶךְ יָמִים:

צֹרְרָי (show hostility); דִּשַּׁנְתָּ (grow fat); כּוֹסִי (cup); רְוָיָה (saturation);
יִרְדְּפוּנִי v.3.c.p.impf.Q. [רדף] + 1.com.s.pr.sf.; וְשַׁבְתִּי v.c. + v.1.com.s.pf.Q.
[ישב / שוב]

2 CORINTHIANS 1:9–10

⁹ἀλλὰ αὐτοὶ ἐν ἑαυτοῖς τὸ ἀπόκριμα τοῦ θανάτου ἐσχήκαμεν,
ἵνα μὴ πεποιθότες ὦμεν ἐφ᾽ ἑαυτοῖς ἀλλ᾽ ἐπὶ τῷ θεῷ τῷ
ἐγείροντι τοὺς νεκρούς· ¹⁰ὃς ἐκ τηλικούτου θανάτου
ἐρρύσατο ἡμᾶς καὶ ῥύσεται, εἰς ὃν ἠλπίκαμεν [ὅτι] καὶ ἔτι
ῥύσεται,

ἀπόκριμα (verdict); ἐσχήκαμεν v.1.p.aor.act.ind. [ἔχω]; τηλικούτου (so
great); ἐρρύσατο (rescue); ἠλπίκαμεν (hope)

3. Proverbs 28:13; Ephesians 1:5–8

Trusting in Your Mercy

MAY I BE QUICK TO SEE my transgressions, but even quicker to confess them, knowing that your heart is merciful and your forgiveness complete.

PROVERBS 28:13

¹³מְכַסֶּה פְשָׁעָיו לֹא יַצְלִיחַ וּמוֹדֶה וְעֹזֵב יְרֻחָם:

וּמוֹדֶה cj. + v.m.s.act.ptc.H. [ידה]

EPHESIANS 1:5–8

⁵προορίσας ἡμᾶς εἰς υἱοθεσίαν διὰ Ἰησοῦ Χριστοῦ εἰς αὐτόν, κατὰ τὴν εὐδοκίαν τοῦ θελήματος αὐτοῦ, ⁶εἰς ἔπαινον δόξης τῆς χάριτος αὐτοῦ ἧς ἐχαρίτωσεν ἡμᾶς ἐν τῷ ἠγαπημένῳ. ⁷ἐν ᾧ ἔχομεν τὴν ἀπολύτρωσιν διὰ τοῦ αἵματος αὐτοῦ, τὴν ἄφεσιν τῶν παραπτωμάτων, κατὰ τὸ πλοῦτος τῆς χάριτος αὐτοῦ ⁸ἧς ἐπερίσσευσεν εἰς ἡμᾶς, ἐν πάσῃ σοφίᾳ καὶ φρονήσει,

προορίσας (predestine); υἱοθεσίαν (adoption); εὐδοκίαν (favor); ἔπαινον (praise); ἐχαρίτωσεν (show favor); ἀπολύτρωσιν (redemption); ἄφεσιν (forgiveness); παραπτωμάτων (sin); πλοῦτος (riches); ἐπερίσσευσεν (lavish); φρονήσει (understanding)

1. Habakkuk 3.2, James 2:13

The Greater Good

FOR SOME OF US the hardest thing to believe about God's mercy is that it triumphs over judgment. May our hearts become convinced.

HABAKKUK 3:2

² יְהוָה שָׁמַעְתִּי שִׁמְעֲךָ יָרֵאתִי יְהוָה פָּעָלְךָ בְּקֶרֶב שָׁנִים חַיֵּיהוּ
בְּקֶרֶב שָׁנִים תּוֹדִיעַ בְּרֹגֶז רַחֵם תִּזְכּוֹר׃

שִׁמְעֲךָ (report); פָּעָלְךָ (deed); חַיֵּיהוּ v.2.m.s.impv.P. [חיה] + 3.m.s.pr.sf.; תּוֹדִיעַ v.2.m.s.impf.H. [ידע]; בְּרֹגֶז (agitation); רַחֵם v.in.cs.P.

JAMES 2:13

¹³ ἡ γὰρ κρίσις ἀνέλεος τῷ μὴ ποιήσαντι ἔλεος· κατακαυχᾶται ἔλεος κρίσεως.

κρίσις (judgment); ἀνέλεος (merciless); ἔλεος (mercy); κατακαυχᾶται v.3.s.pres.mid.ind. [κατακαυχάομαι] (triumph over)

5. Daniel 9:18–19; 1 Peter 1:3–5

Mercy, Not Merit

EVERY GOODNESS IN OUR LIVES is the result of your mercy, Holy One, and not our merit. Even if sin had never come into the world this would be true.

DANIEL 9:18–19

18הַטֵּה אֱלֹהַי אָזְנְךָ וּשֲׁמָע פְּקַחה עֵינֶיךָ וּרְאֵה שֹׁמְמֹתֵינוּ
וְהָעִיר אֲשֶׁר־נִקְרָא שִׁמְךָ עָלֶיהָ כִּי לֹא עַל־צִדְקֹתֵינוּ אֲנַחְנוּ מַפִּילִים
תַּחֲנוּנֵינוּ לְפָנֶיךָ כִּי עַל־רַחֲמֶיךָ הָרַבִּים׃
19אֲדֹנָי שְׁמָעָה אֲדֹנָי סְלָחָה אֲדֹנָי הַקְשִׁיבָה וַעֲשֵׂה אַל־תְּאַחַר לְמַעַנְךָ
אֱלֹהַי כִּי־שִׁמְךָ נִקְרָא עַל־עִירְךָ וְעַל־עַמֶּךָ׃

הַטֵּה v.2.m.s.impv.H. [נטה]; וּשֲׁמָע cj. + v.2.m.s.impv.Q.pause; פְּקַחה (open); מַפִּילִים v.m.p.act.ptc.H. [נפל]; תַּחֲנוּנֵינוּ n.m.p. (supplication) + 1.com.p.pr.sf.; שְׁמָעָה v.2.m.s.impv.Q. [שמע] + para.pause; סְלָחָה v.2.m.s.impv.Q. [סלח] (forgive) + para.; הַקְשִׁיבָה v.2.m.s.impv.H. [קשב] + para.; תְּאַחַר (hesitate)

1 PETER 1:3–5

³Εὐλογητὸς ὁ θεὸς καὶ πατὴρ τοῦ κυρίου ἡμῶν Ἰησοῦ Χριστοῦ, ὁ κατὰ τὸ πολὺ αὐτοῦ ἔλεος ἀναγεννήσας ἡμᾶς εἰς ἐλπίδα ζῶσαν δι᾽ ἀναστάσεως Ἰησοῦ Χριστοῦ ἐκ νεκρῶν, ⁴εἰς κληρονομίαν ἄφθαρτον καὶ ἀμίαντον καὶ ἀμάραντον, τετηρημένην ἐν οὐρανοῖς εἰς ὑμᾶς ⁵τοὺς ἐν δυνάμει θεοῦ φρουρουμένους διὰ πίστεως εἰς σωτηρίαν ἑτοίμην ἀποκαλυφθῆναι ἐν καιρῷ ἐσχάτῳ.

Εὐλογητὸς (blessed); ἔλεος (mercy); ἀναγεννήσας (cause to be reborn); ἀναστάσεως (resurrection); κληρονομίαν (inheritance); ἄφθαρτον (imperishable); ἀμίαντον (pure); ἀμάραντον (unfading); τετηρημένην v.f.s.acc.pf.pass.ptc. [τηρέω]; φρουρουμένους (guard); σωτηρίαν (salvation); ἑτοίμην (prepared); ἀποκαλυφθῆναι (reveal)

6. 2 Samuel 24:14; Titus 3:4–5, 7

Keep Me Close to My Need

O GOD, KEEP ME CLOSE to my own need for mercy, lest I forget the need of others. May this especially be true when others hurt me.

2 SAMUEL 24:14

¹⁴וַיֹּאמֶר דָּוִד אֶל־גָּד צַר־לִי מְאֹד נִפְּלָה־נָּא בְיַד־יְהוָה כִּי־
רַבִּים רַחֲמָיו וּבְיַד־אָדָם אַל־אֶפֹּלָה׃

צַר (distress); נִפְּלָה v.1.com.p.coh.Q. [נפל]; אֶפֹּלָה v.1.com.s.coh.Q.pause [נפל]

TITUS 3:4–5, 7

⁴ὅτε δὲ ἡ χρηστότης καὶ ἡ φιλανθρωπία ἐπεφάνη τοῦ σωτῆρος ἡμῶν θεοῦ, ⁵οὐκ ἐξ ἔργων τῶν ἐν δικαιοσύνῃ ἃ ἐποιήσαμεν ἡμεῖς ἀλλὰ κατὰ τὸ αὐτοῦ ἔλεος ἔσωσεν ἡμᾶς διὰ λουτροῦ παλιγγενεσίας καὶ ἀνακαινώσεως πνεύματος ἁγίου, ⁷ἵνα δικαιωθέντες τῇ ἐκείνου χάριτι κληρονόμοι γενηθῶμεν κατ᾽ ἐλπίδα ζωῆς αἰωνίου.

χρηστότης (kindness); φιλανθρωπία (beneficence); ἐπεφάνη (appear); σωτῆρος (savior); ἔλεος (mercy); λουτροῦ (washing); παλιγγενεσίας (rebirth); ἀνακαινώσεως (renewal); δικαιωθέντες (justify); κληρονόμοι (heir); γενηθῶμεν v.1.p.aor.pass.sub. [γίνομαι]

7. Hosea 6:6; Matthew 9:13

Disarmament

HOW BEAUTIFUL IN THE EYES OF GOD, how holy and pure, when we lay down our weapons in a spirit of merciful love.

HOSEA 6:6

‎6כִּי חֶסֶד חָפַצְתִּי וְלֹא־זָבַח וְדַעַת אֱלֹהִים מֵעֹלוֹת:

‎מֵעֹלוֹת prep. + n.f.p.

MATTHEW 9:13

13πορευθέντες δὲ μάθετε τί ἐστιν, Ἔλεος θέλω καὶ οὐ θυσίαν· οὐ γὰρ ἦλθον καλέσαι δικαίους ἀλλὰ ἁμαρτωλούς.

μάθετε v.2.p.aor.act.impv. [μανθάνω] (learn); ἐστιν v.3.s.pres.ind. [εἰμί]; Ἔλεος (mercy); θυσίαν (sacrifice); ἦλθον v.1.s.aor.act.ind. [ἔρχομαι]; ἁμαρτωλούς (sinner)

Work

1. Psalm 65:5–8 [4–7]; John 5:15–17

Life-Giving Work

ALL YOUR WORK IS LIFE-GIVING, LORD, creating something out of nothing, order out of chaos. And it is part of your call to me, I believe, to approach my work in the same way. How can I do my work today in life-giving ways?

PSALM 65:5–8 [4–7]

⁵אַשְׁרֵי תִּבְחַר וּתְקָרֵב יִשְׁכֹּן חֲצֵרֶיךָ נִשְׂבְּעָה בְּטוּב בֵּיתֶךָ קְדֹשׁ הֵיכָלֶךָ:
⁶נוֹרָאוֹת בְּצֶדֶק תַּעֲנֵנוּ אֱלֹהֵי יִשְׁעֵנוּ מִבְטָח כָּל־קַצְוֵי־אֶרֶץ וְיָם רְחֹקִים:
⁷מֵכִין הָרִים בְּכֹחוֹ נֶאְזָר בִּגְבוּרָה:
⁸מַשְׁבִּיחַ שְׁאוֹן יַמִּים שְׁאוֹן גַּלֵּיהֶם וַהֲמוֹן לְאֻמִּים:

אַשְׁרֵי (blessing); בְּטוּב (good thing); נוֹרָאוֹת v.f.p.ptc.N. [ירא]; מִבְטָח (trust); תַּעֲנֵנוּ v.3.f.s.impf.Q. [ענה] + 1.com.p.pr.sf.; מֵכִין v.m.s.act.ptc.H. [כון]; מַשְׁבִּיחַ (still); שְׁאוֹן (din); גַּלֵּיהֶם (wave); לְאֻמִּים (nation)

JOHN 5:15–17

¹⁵ἀπῆλθεν ὁ ἄνθρωπος καὶ ἀνήγγειλεν τοῖς Ἰουδαίοις ὅτι Ἰησοῦς ἐστιν ὁ ποιήσας αὐτὸν ὑγιή. ¹⁶καὶ διὰ τοῦτο ἐδίωκον οἱ Ἰουδαῖοι τὸν Ἰησοῦν, ὅτι ταῦτα ἐποίει ἐν σαββάτῳ. ¹⁷ὁ δὲ [Ἰησοῦς] ἀπεκρίνατο αὐτοῖς· ὁ πατήρ μου ἕως ἄρτι ἐργάζεται καγὼ ἐργάζομαι·

ἀπῆλθεν v.3.s.aor.act.ind. [ἀπέρχομαι]; ἐστιν v.3.s.pres.ind. [εἰμί]; ὑγιή (well); ἐδίωκον (persecute); ἄρτι (now); ἐργάζεται/ἐργάζομαι (work)

2. Genesis 2:15; Ephesians 4:28

The Prayer of Work

SO OFTEN WE THINK OF WORK as a result of the curse, a matter of toiling endlessly against thorns and weeds and rock-like soil. But work is integral to the holy life and is itself a form of prayer.

GENESIS 2:15

¹⁵וַיִּקַּח יְהֹוָה אֱלֹהִים אֶת־הָאָדָם וַיַּנִּחֵהוּ בְגַן־עֵדֶן לְעָבְדָהּ
וּלְשָׁמְרָהּ׃

וַיִּקַּח v.c. + v.3.m.s.impf.Q. [לקח]; וַיַּנִּחֵהוּ v.c. + v.3.m.s.impf.H. [נוח] + 3.m.s.pr.sf.; לְעָבְדָהּ prep. + v.in.cs.Q. [עבד] + 3.f.s.pr.sf.; וּלְשָׁמְרָהּ cj. + prep. + v.in.cs.Q. [שמר] + 3.f.s.pr.sf.

EPHESIANS 4:28

²⁸ὁ κλέπτων μηκέτι κλεπτέτω, μᾶλλον δὲ κοπιάτω ἐργαζόμενος ταῖς [ἰδίαις] χερσὶν τὸ ἀγαθόν, ἵνα ἔχῃ μεταδιδόναι τῷ χρείαν ἔχοντι.

κλέπτων (steal); μηκέτι (no longer); κοπιάτω (work); ἐργαζόμενος (work); μεταδιδόναι v.pres.act.in. [μεταδίδωμι] (share); χρείαν (need)

3. Exodus 20:9–11; John 9:4

Rhythms of Work and Rest

WHAT IS SABBATH BUT A DAY TO CELEBRATE the goodness of a job well done? So let us take the day to celebrate God's workmanship in us, in this world, and in the work he has given us to do! May every Sabbath point us to the final Sabbath, the Day in which the greatest work—redemption—will be complete.

EXODUS 20:9–11

⁹שֵׁשֶׁת יָמִים תַּעֲבֹד וְעָשִׂיתָ כָּל־מְלַאכְתֶּךָ׃
¹⁰וְיוֹם הַשְּׁבִיעִי שַׁבָּת לַיהוָה אֱלֹהֶיךָ לֹא־תַעֲשֶׂה כָל־מְלָאכָה אַתָּה
וּבִנְךָ־וּבִתֶּךָ עַבְדְּךָ וַאֲמָתְךָ וּבְהֶמְתֶּךָ וְגֵרְךָ אֲשֶׁר
בִּשְׁעָרֶיךָ׃
¹¹כִּי שֵׁשֶׁת־יָמִים עָשָׂה יְהוָה אֶת־הַשָּׁמַיִם וְאֶת־הָאָרֶץ אֶת־
הַיָּם וְאֶת־כָּל־אֲשֶׁר־בָּם וַיָּנַח בַּיּוֹם הַשְּׁבִיעִי עַל־כֵּן בֵּרַךְ
יְהוָה אֶת־יוֹם הַשַּׁבָּת וַיְקַדְּשֵׁהוּ׃

וַיְקַדְּשֵׁהוּ; וְעָשִׂיתָ v.c. + 2.m.s.pf.Q. [עשׂה]; וַיָּנַח v.c. + v.3.m.s.impf.Q. [נוח];
v.c. + v.3.m.s.impf.P. [קדשׁ] + 3.m.s.pr.sf.

JOHN 9:4

⁴ἡμᾶς δεῖ ἐργάζεσθαι τὰ ἔργα τοῦ πέμψαντός με ἕως ἡμέρα
ἐστίν· ἔρχεται νὺξ ὅτε οὐδεὶς δύναται ἐργάζεσθαι.

ἐργάζεσθαι (work); πέμψαντος v.m.s.gen.aor.act.ptc. [πέμπω]

4. Exodus 36:5–7; 2 Corinthians 9:8–9

Ready for the Work

How comforting it is to know that God equips me with everything I need (yes, including my limitations!) in order to do
the work to which he has called me.

Exodus 36:5–7

⁵וַיֹּאמְרוּ אֶל־מֹשֶׁה לֵּאמֹר מַרְבִּים הָעָם לְהָבִיא מִדֵּי הָעֲבֹדָה
לַמְּלָאכָה אֲשֶׁר־צִוָּה יְהוָה לַעֲשֹׂת אֹתָהּ׃
⁶וַיְצַו מֹשֶׁה וַיַּעֲבִירוּ קוֹל בַּמַּחֲנֶה לֵאמֹר אִישׁ וְאִשָּׁה אַל־
יַעֲשׂוּ־עוֹד מְלָאכָה לִתְרוּמַת הַקֹּדֶשׁ וַיִּכָּלֵא הָעָם מֵהָבִיא׃
⁷וְהַמְּלָאכָה הָיְתָה דַיָּם לְכָל־הַמְּלָאכָה לַעֲשׂוֹת אֹתָהּ וְהוֹתֵר׃

מַרְבִּים v.m.p.act.ptc.H. [רבה]; לְהָבִיא prep. + v.in.cs.H. [בוא]; מִדֵּי prep.
+ n.m.s.cs.; לַעֲשֹׂת prep. + v.in.cs.Q.defective [עשה]; וַיְצַו v.c. + v.3.m.s.impf.P.
[צוה]; יַעֲשׂוּ v.3.m.p.jus.Q. [עשה]; וַיִּכָּלֵא (restrain); מֵהָבִיא prep. + v.in.cs.H.
[בוא]; הָיְתָה v.3.f.s.pf.Q. [היה]; דַיָּם (enough); לַעֲשׂוֹת prep. + v.in.cs.Q. [עשה];
וְהוֹתֵר cj. + v.in.ab.H. [יתר]

2 Corinthians 9:8–9

⁸δυνατεῖ δὲ ὁ θεὸς πᾶσαν χάριν περισσεῦσαι εἰς ὑμᾶς, ἵνα ἐν
παντὶ πάντοτε πᾶσαν αὐτάρκειαν ἔχοντες περισσεύητε εἰς
πᾶν ἔργον ἀγαθόν, ⁹καθὼς γέγραπται·
Ἐσκόρπισεν, ἔδωκεν τοῖς πένησιν,
ἡ δικαιοσύνη αὐτοῦ μένει εἰς τὸν αἰῶνα.

δυνατεῖ (be strong); περισσεῦσαι (abound); πάντοτε (always); αὐτάρκειαν (sufficiency); Ἐσκόρπισεν (scatter); ἔδωκεν v.3.s.aor.act.ind. [δίδ-
ωμι]; πένησιν (poor)

5. Psalm 28.4–5, Romans 2:6–8

The Reason for Work

YOU HAVE CREATED IN ME A NEW HEART, O God, a new life. May that new life be the source of my work in this world, whether it is the mundane task of laundry, or the hard work of rebuilding broken trust.

PSALM 28:4–5

⁴תֶּן־לָהֶם כְּפָעֳלָם וּכְרֹעַ מַעַלְלֵיהֶם כְּמַעֲשֵׂה יְדֵיהֶם תֵּן לָהֶם הָשֵׁב גְּמוּלָם לָהֶם:

⁵כִּי לֹא יָבִינוּ אֶל־פְּעֻלֹּת יְהוָה וְאֶל־מַעֲשֵׂה יָדָיו יֶהֶרְסֵם וְלֹא יִבְנֵם:

מַעַלְלֵיהֶם v.2.m.s.impv.Q. [נתן]; כְּפָעֳלָם (deed); וּכְרֹעַ (wickedness); תֵּן / תֵּן (deed); הָשֵׁב v.2.m.s.impv.H. [שוב]; גְּמוּלָם (benefit); יָבִינוּ v.3.m.p.impf.Q. [בין]; פְּעֻלֹּת (work); יֶהֶרְסֵם v.3.m.s.impf.Q. [הרס] (tear down) + 3.m.p.pr.sf.; יִבְנֵם v.3.m.s.impf.Q. [בנה] + 3.m.p.pr.sf.

ROMANS 2:6–8

⁶ὃς ἀποδώσει ἑκάστῳ κατὰ τὰ ἔργα αὐτοῦ· ⁷τοῖς μὲν καθ᾽ ὑπομονὴν ἔργου ἀγαθοῦ δόξαν καὶ τιμὴν καὶ ἀφθαρσίαν ζητοῦσιν ζωὴν αἰώνιον, ⁸τοῖς δὲ ἐξ ἐριθείας καὶ ἀπειθοῦσι τῇ ἀληθείᾳ πειθομένοις δὲ τῇ ἀδικίᾳ ὀργὴ καὶ θυμός.

ἀποδώσει v.3.s.fut.act.ind. [ἀποδίδωμι] (reward); ὑπομονὴν (patience); τιμήν (honor); ἀφθαρσίαν (immortality); ἐριθείας (selfishness); ἀπειθοῦσι (disobey); ἀδικίᾳ (unrighteousness); ὀργή (anger); θυμός (wrath)

6. Proverbs 16:3; Matthew 6:31–33

True Vocation

WHEN I GAZE LOVINGLY and without haste into the face of God,
I cannot help but know my true vocation. It is fidelity to him
who is Love.

PROVERBS 16:3

³גֹּל אֶל־יְהוָה מַעֲשֶׂיךָ וְיִכֹּנוּ מַחְשְׁבֹתֶיךָ׃

גֹּל v.2.m.s.impv.Q. [גלל] (roll); וְיִכֹּנוּ cj. + v.3.m.p.impf.N. [כון]

MATTHEW 6:31–33

³¹μὴ οὖν μεριμνήσητε λέγοντες, Τί φάγωμεν; ἤ, Τί πίωμεν; ἤ,
Τί περιβαλώμεθα; ³²πάντα γὰρ ταῦτα τὰ ἔθνη ἐπιζητοῦσιν·
οἶδεν γὰρ ὁ πατὴρ ὑμῶν ὁ οὐράνιος ὅτι χρήζετε τούτων
ἁπάντων. ³³ζητεῖτε δὲ πρῶτον τὴν βασιλείαν [τοῦ θεοῦ] καὶ
τὴν δικαιοσύνην αὐτοῦ, καὶ ταῦτα πάντα προστεθήσεται
ὑμῖν.

μεριμνήσητε v.2.p.aor.act.sub. [μεριμνάω] (be anxious); περιβαλώμεθα
(wear); ἐπιζητοῦσιν (seek); οἶδεν v.3.s.pf.act.ind. [οἶδα]; χρήζετε (need);
ἁπάντων (all); προστεθήσεται (add)

7. Ecclesiastes 3:22; 1 Thessalonians 2:9–12

Priorities

AS IN ALL THINGS, BALANCE IS THE KEY. It is wholesome and honorable and necessary to do one's work with all one's heart. Likewise it is wholesome and honorable and necessary to lay that work aside, gratefully, knowing that although work is holy, it is not God.

ECCLESIASTES 3:22

²²וְרָאִיתִי כִּי אֵין טוֹב מֵאֲשֶׁר יִשְׂמַח הָאָדָם בְּמַעֲשָׂיו כִּי־הוּא
חֶלְקוֹ כִּי מִי יְבִיאֶנּוּ לִרְאוֹת בְּמֶה שֶׁיִּהְיֶה אַחֲרָיו:

וְרָאִיתִי v.c. + v.1.com.s.pf.Q. [רָאה]; יְבִיאֶנּוּ v.3.m.s.impf.H. [בוא] + en. + 3.m.s.pr.sf.; לִרְאוֹת prep. + v.in.cs.Q. [רָאה]

1 THESSALONIANS 2:9–12

⁹μνημονεύετε γάρ, ἀδελφοί, τὸν κόπον ἡμῶν καὶ τὸν μόχθον· νυκτὸς καὶ ἡμέρας ἐργαζόμενοι πρὸς τὸ μη ἐπιβαρῆσαί τινα ὑμῶν ἐκηρύξαμεν εἰς ὑμᾶς τὸ εὐαγγέλιον τοῦ θεοῦ. ¹⁰ὑμεῖς μάρτυρες καὶ ὁ θεός, ὡς ὁσίως καὶ δικαίως καὶ ἀμέμπτως ὑμῖν τοῖς πιστεύουσιν ἐγενήθημεν, ¹¹καθάπερ οἴδατε, ὡς ἕνα ἕκαστον ὑμῶν ὡς πατὴρ τέκνα ἑαυτοῦ ¹²παρακαλοῦντες ὑμᾶς καὶ παραμυθούμενοι καὶ μαρτυρόμενοι εἰς τὸ περιπατεῖν ὑμᾶς ἀξίως τοῦ θεοῦ τοῦ καλοῦντος ὑμᾶς εἰς τὴν ἑαυτοῦ βασιλείαν καὶ δόξαν.

μνημονεύετε (remember); κόπον (labor); μόχθον (hardship); ἐργαζόμενοι (work); ἐπιβαρῆσαι (burden); μάρτυρες (witness); ὁσίως (piously); δικαίως (uprightly); ἀμέμπτως (blamelessly); ἐγενήθημεν v.1.p.aor.pass.ind. [γίνομαι]; καθάπερ (just as); παραμυθούμενοι (encourage); ἀξίως (worthily)

Week 20

Servanthood

1. Isaiah 43:10; Mark 9:35–37

Childlike Servants

I DON'T KNOW WHICH IS MORE DIFFICULT, Lord: believing that you have chosen me to be your servant, or living into that call with childlike trust.

ISAIAH 43:10

^{10}אַתֶּם עֵדַי נְאֻם־יְהוָה וְעַבְדִּי אֲשֶׁר בָּחָרְתִּי לְמַעַן תֵּדְעוּ
וְתַאֲמִינוּ לִי וְתָבִינוּ כִּי־אֲנִי הוּא לְפָנַי לֹא־נוֹצַר אֵל וְאַחֲרַי לֹא
יִהְיֶה:

תֵּדְעוּ v.2.m.p.impf.Q. [ידע]; נוֹצַר v.3.m.s.pf.N. [יצר]

MARK 9:35–37

^{35}καὶ καθίσας ἐφώνησεν τοὺς δώδεκα καὶ λέγει αὐτοῖς, Εἴ τις θέλει πρῶτος εἶναι, ἔσται πάντων ἔσχατος καὶ πάντων διάκονος. ^{36}καὶ λαβὼν παιδίον ἔστησεν αὐτὸ ἐν μέσῳ αὐτῶν καὶ ἐναγκαλισάμενος αὐτὸ εἶπεν αὐτοῖς, ^{37}Ὃς ἂν ἓν τῶν τοιούτων παιδίων δέξηται ἐπὶ τῷ ὀνόματί μου, ἐμὲ δέχεται· καὶ ὃς ἂν ἐμὲ δέχηται, οὐκ ἐμὲ δέχεται ἀλλὰ τὸν ἀποστείλαντά με.

καθίσας (sit); ἐφώνησεν (call); εἶναι v.pres.in. [εἰμί]; ἔσται v.3.s.fut.ind. [εἰμί]; διάκονος (servant); ἔστησεν v.3.s.aor.act.ind. [ιστημι]; ἐναγκαλισάμενος v.m.s.nom.aor.mid.part. [εναγκαλίζομαι] (take into one's arms); εἶπεν v.3.s.aor.act.ind. [λέγω]; Ὃς ἂν ἓν rel.pr.m.s.nom. + pt. + numeral.nt.s.acc. (whichever one)

2. Isaiah 49:5–6; 1 Peter 4:10–11

Irreplaceable

How HONORED I AM IN YOUR EYES, Abba, for you called me to be your own when I had yet to draw my first breath! You have given me a place in this cosmos that no one else can fill. May I believe in the great and trusting love in your heart toward me, and may I respond with faithful love.

ISAIAH 49:5–6

⁵וְעַתָּה אָמַר יְהוָה יֹצְרִי מִבֶּטֶן לְעֶבֶד לוֹ לְשׁוֹבֵב יַעֲקֹב אֵלָיו
וְיִשְׂרָאֵל לֹא יֵאָסֵף וְאֶכָּבֵד בְּעֵינֵי יְהוָה וֵאלֹהַי הָיָה עֻזִּי:
⁶וַיֹּאמֶר נָקֵל מִהְיוֹתְךָ לִי עֶבֶד לְהָקִים אֶת־שִׁבְטֵי יַעֲקֹב וּנְצוּרֵי
יִשְׂרָאֵל לְהָשִׁיב וּנְתַתִּיךָ לְאוֹר גּוֹיִם לִהְיוֹת יְשׁוּעָתִי עַד־
קְצֵה הָאָרֶץ:

נָקֵל [קלל]; לְשׁוֹבֵב prep. + v.in.cs.Pil. [שוב]; לְהָקִים prep. + v.in.cs.H. [קום];
v.3.m.s.pf.N. [קלל]; מִהְיוֹתְךָ prep. + v.in.cs.Q. [היה] + 2.m.s.pr.sf.; לְהָשִׁיב prep.
+ v.in.cs.H. [שוב]; וּנְתַתִּיךָ v.1.com.s.pf.Q. + 2.m.s.pr.sf. [נתן]; לִהְיוֹת prep. +
v.in.cs.Q. [היה]

1 PETER 4:10–11

¹⁰ἕκαστος καθὼς ἔλαβεν χάρισμα εἰς ἑαυτοὺς αὐτὸ διακονοῦντες ὡς καλοὶ οἰκονόμοι ποικίλης χάριτος θεοῦ. ¹¹ εἴ τις λαλεῖ, ὡς λόγια θεοῦ· εἴ τις διακονεῖ, ὡς ἐξ ἰσχύος ἧς χορηγεῖ ὁ θεός, ἵνα ἐν πᾶσιν δοξάζηται ὁ θεὸς διὰ Ἰησοῦ Χριστοῦ, ᾧ ἐστιν ἡ δόξα καὶ τὸ κράτος εἰς τοὺς αἰῶνας τῶν αἰώνων, ἀμήν.

χάρισμα (gift); διακονοῦντες (serve); οἰκονόμοι (steward); ποικίλης (various); λόγια (saying); ἰσχύος (strength); χορηγεῖ (supply); ἐστιν v.3.s.pres.ind. [εἰμί]; κράτος (power)

3. Isaiah 41:8–9; Romans 11:1–2

Called as a People

GOD CALLS US *AS A PEOPLE* TO BE A SERVANT—to be his hands, his feet, and his open heart in this dark world. Let us come together then, trusting the one who formed us in all our diversity. In one accord let us become glad tidings of good news to all people!

ISAIAH 41:8–9

⁸וְאַתָּה יִשְׂרָאֵל עַבְדִּי יַעֲקֹב אֲשֶׁר בְּחַרְתִּיךָ זֶרַע אַבְרָהָם אֹהֲבִי:
⁹אֲשֶׁר הֶחֱזַקְתִּיךָ מִקְצוֹת הָאָרֶץ וּמֵאֲצִילֶיהָ קְרָאתִיךָ וָאֹמַר לְךָ
עַבְדִּי־אַתָּה בְּחַרְתִּיךָ וְלֹא מְאַסְתִּיךָ:

הֶחֱזַקְתִּיךָ v.1.com.s.pf.H. [חזק] + 2.m.s.pr.sf.; וּמֵאֲצִילֶיהָ (corner); וָאֹמַר v.c. + v.1.com.s.impf. [אמר]

ROMANS 11:1–2

¹Λέγω οὖν, μὴ ἀπώσατο ὁ θεὸς τὸν λαὸν αὐτοῦ; μὴ γένοιτο· καὶ γὰρ ἐγὼ Ἰσραηλίτης εἰμί, ἐκ σπέρματος Ἀβραάμ, φυλῆς Βενιαμίν. ²οὐκ ἀπώσατο ὁ θεὸς τὸν λαὸν αὐτοῦ ὃν προέγνω. ἢ οὐκ οἴδατε ἐν Ἠλίᾳ τί λέγει ἡ γραφή, ὡς ἐντυγχάνει τῷ θεῷ κατὰ τοῦ Ἰσραήλ;

ἀπώσατο v.3.s.aor.ind. [ἀπωθέω] (reject); γένοιτο v.3.s.aor.mid.ind. [γίνομαι]; σπέρματος (seed); φυλῆς (tribe); προέγνω v.3.s.aor.act.ind. [προγινώσκω] (foreknow); ἐντυγχάνει (intercede)

1. Isaiah 53.10–11; Matthew 20:26–28

Servanthood—The Paradigm for Love

THE LOVER BECOMES A SERVANT to the beloved. This is the paradigm for all true love. Wherever there is one who truly loves, there is one who truly serves.

ISAIAH 53:10–11

¹⁰וַיהוָה חָפֵץ דַּכְּאוֹ הֶחֱלִי אִם־תָּשִׂים אָשָׁם נַפְשׁוֹ יִרְאֶה זֶרַע יַאֲרִיךְ
יָמִים וְחֵפֶץ יְהוָה בְּיָדוֹ יִצְלָח:
¹¹מֵעֲמַל נַפְשׁוֹ יִרְאֶה יִשְׂבָּע בְּדַעְתּוֹ יַצְדִּיק צַדִּיק עַבְדִּי
לָרַבִּים וַעֲוֺנֹתָם הוּא יִסְבֹּל:

דַּכְּאוֹ (crush); הֶחֱלִי v.3.m.s.pf.H. [חלה]; אָשָׁם (guilt offering); יַאֲרִיךְ
(lengthen); וְחֵפֶץ (will); יִסְבֹּל (bear)

MATTHEW 20:26–28

²⁶οὐχ οὕτως ἔσται ἐν ὑμῖν, ἀλλ᾽ ὃς ἐὰν θέλῃ ἐν ὑμῖν μέγας
γενέσθαι ἔσται ὑμῶν διάκονος, ²⁷καὶ ὃς ἂν θέλῃ ἐν ὑμῖν εἶναι
πρῶτος ἔσται ὑμῶν δοῦλος· ²⁸ὥσπερ ὁ υἱὸς τοῦ ἀνθρώπου
οὐκ ἦλθεν διακονηθῆναι ἀλλὰ διακονῆσαι καὶ δοῦναι τὴν
ψυχὴν αὐτοῦ λύτρον ἀντὶ πολλῶν.

γενέσθαι v.aor.mid.in. [γίνομαι]; εἶναι v.pres.in. [εἰμί]; ἔσται
v.3.s.fut.ind. [εἰμί]; διάκονος (servant); ὥσπερ (as); ἦλθεν v.3.s.aor.act.ind.
[ἔρχομαι]; διακονηθῆναι (serve); λύτρον (ransom); ἀντὶ (for)

149

5. Psalm 35:27–28; 1 Corinthians 12:4–7

The Servant and the Servants

THERE ARE TWO THINGS WE NEED to learn about being servants in God's kingdom. First, God's utmost concern is the well-being of his servants. He gave his own life for their well-being. Second, when we serve one another out of love for God, we have served God. There's just no way to separate God from his servants.

PSALM 35:27–28

²⁷יָרֹ֥נּוּ וְיִשְׂמְח֗וּ חֲפֵצֵ֥י צִדְקִ֥י וְיֹאמְר֥וּ תָמִ֑יד יִגְדַּ֥ל יְהוָ֗ה
הֶ֝חָפֵ֗ץ שְׁל֣וֹם עַבְדּֽוֹ׃
²⁸וּ֭לְשׁוֹנִי תֶּהְגֶּ֣ה צִדְקֶ֑ךָ כָּל־הַ֝יּ֗וֹם תְּהִלָּתֶֽךָ׃

יָרֹ֥נּוּ v.3.m.p.impf.Q. [רנן]; חֲפֵצֵ֥י (delight); תֶּהְגֶּ֣ה (meditate)

1 CORINTHIANS 12:4–7

⁴Διαιρέσεις δὲ χαρισμάτων εἰσίν, τὸ δὲ αὐτὸ πνεῦμα· ⁵καὶ διαιρέσεις διακονιῶν εἰσιν, καὶ ὁ αὐτὸς κύριος· ⁶καὶ διαιρέσεις ἐνεργημάτων εἰσίν, ὁ δὲ αὐτὸς θεὸς ὁ ἐνεργῶν τὰ πάντα ἐν πᾶσιν. ⁷ἑκάστῳ δὲ δίδοται ἡ φανέρωσις τοῦ πνεύματος πρὸς τὸ συμφέρον.

Διαιρέσεις (variety); χαρισμάτων (gift); εἰσίν v.3.p.pres.ind. [εἰμί]; διακονιῶν (service); ἐνεργημάτων (activity); ἐνεργῶν (work); φανέρωσις (manifestation); συμφέρον (advantage)

6. Isaiah 49:1–3; John 15:15–16

Changing the World Forever

THE HONOR OF BEING CHOSEN to be your servant seems overwhelming in itself, Lord. But you have called me to so much more! You have called me to holy friendship, to a unity of heart and mind and will, the results of which will change the world forever. You have called me and my answer is "Yes!"

ISAIAH 49:1–3

¹שִׁמְעוּ אִיִּים אֵלַי וְהַקְשִׁיבוּ לְאֻמִּים מֵרָחוֹק יְהוָה מִבֶּטֶן קְרָאָנִי
מִמְּעֵי אִמִּי הִזְכִּיר שְׁמִי:
²וַיָּשֶׂם פִּי כְּחֶרֶב חַדָּה בְּצֵל יָדוֹ הֶחְבִּיאָנִי וַיְשִׂימֵנִי
לְחֵץ בָּרוּר בְּאַשְׁפָּתוֹ הִסְתִּירָנִי:
³וַיֹּאמֶר לִי עַבְדִּי־אָתָּה יִשְׂרָאֵל אֲשֶׁר־בְּךָ אֶתְפָּאָר:

אִיִּים (coast); לְאֻמִּים (nation); קְרָאָנִי v.3.m.s.pf.Q. [קרא] + 1.com.s.pr.sf.; מִמְּעֵי (womb); וַיָּשֶׂם v.c. + v.3.m.s.impf.Q. [שׂים]; חַדָּה (sharp); בְּצֵל (shadow); הֶחְבִּיאָנִי v.3.m.s.pf.H. [חבא] (hide) + 1.com.s.pr.sf.; וַיְשִׂימֵנִי v.c. + v.3.m.s.impf.Q. [שׂים] + 1.com.s.pr.sf.; בָּרוּר (select); בְּאַשְׁפָּתוֹ (quiver); הִסְתִּירָנִי v.3.m.s.pf.H. [סתר] + 1.com.s.pr.sf.; אֶתְפָּאָר (glorify)

JOHN 15:15–16

¹⁵οὐκέτι λέγω ὑμᾶς δούλους, ὅτι ὁ δοῦλος οὐκ οἶδεν τί ποιεῖ αὐτοῦ ὁ κύριος· ὑμᾶς δὲ εἴρηκα φίλους, ὅτι πάντα ἃ ἤκουσα παρὰ τοῦ πατρός μου ἐγνώρισα ὑμῖν. ¹⁶οὐχ ὑμεῖς με ἐξελέξασθε, ἀλλ᾽ ἐγὼ ἐξελεξάμην ὑμᾶς καὶ ἔθηκα ὑμᾶς ἵνα ὑμεῖς ὑπάγητε καὶ καρπὸν φέρητε καὶ ὁ καρπὸς ὑμῶν μένῃ, ἵνα ὅ τι ἂν αἰτήσητε τὸν πατέρα ἐν τῷ ὀνόματι μου δῷ ὑμῖν.

οὐκέτι (no longer); οἶδεν v.3.s.pf.act.ind. [οἶδα]; ἐγνώρισα (make known); ἐξελέξασθε v.2.p.aor.mid.ind. [ἐκλέγω] (choose); ἔθηκα v.1.s.aor.act.ind. [τίθημι]; ὅ τι ἂν rel.pr.nt.s.acc. + indef.pr.nt.s.acc. + pt. (whatever); δῷ v.3.s.aor.act.sub. [δίδωμι]

7. Isaiah 53:7–9; Philippians 2:5–8

Servant God

LET WORDS FLEE, THOUGHTS MELT, hearts break at the sight of our Servant, our crucified God.

ISAIAH 53:7–9

⁷נִגַּשׂ וְהוּא נַעֲנֶה וְלֹא יִפְתַּח־פִּיו כַּשֶּׂה לַטֶּבַח יוּבָל
וּכְרָחֵל לִפְנֵי גֹזְזֶיהָ נֶאֱלָמָה וְלֹא יִפְתַּח פִּיו:
⁸מֵעֹצֶר וּמִמִּשְׁפָּט לֻקָּח וְאֶת־דּוֹרוֹ מִי יְשׂוֹחֵחַ כִּי נִגְזַר
מֵאֶרֶץ חַיִּים מִפֶּשַׁע עַמִּי נֶגַע לָמוֹ:
⁹וַיִּתֵּן אֶת־רְשָׁעִים קִבְרוֹ וְאֶת־עָשִׁיר בְּמֹתָיו עַל לֹא־חָמָס עָשָׂה
וְלֹא מִרְמָה בְּפִיו:

נִגַּשׂ v.3.m.s.pf.N. [נגשׂ] (press); כַּשֶּׂה (kid); לַטֶּבַח (slaughter); יוּבָל v.3.m.s.impf.Ho. [יבל] (bring); וּכְרָחֵל (ewe); גֹזְזֶיהָ (shear); נֶאֱלָמָה v.3.f.s.pf.N. [אלם] (be dumb); מֵעֹצֶר (detention); לֻקָּח v.3.m.s.pf.Pu.pause [לקח]; יְשׂוֹחֵחַ v.3.m.s.impf.Pil. [שׂיח] (consider); נִגְזַר (cut off); וַיִּתֵּן v.3.m.s.impf.Q. [נתן]; רְשָׁעִים (wicked one); עָשִׁיר (rich); מִרְמָה (deceit)

PHILIPPIANS 2:5–8

⁵Τοῦτο φρονεῖτε ἐν ὑμῖν ὃ καὶ ἐν Χριστῷ Ἰησοῦ, ⁶ὃς ἐν μορφῇ θεοῦ ὑπάρχων οὐχ ἁρπαγμὸν ἡγήσατο τὸ εἶναι ἴσα θεῷ, ⁷ἀλλὰ ἑαυτὸν ἐκένωσεν μορφὴν δούλου λαβών, ἐν ὁμοιώματι ἀνθρώπων γενόμενος· καὶ σχήματι εὑρεθεὶς ὡς ἄνθρωπος ⁸ἐταπείνωσεν ἑαυτὸν γενόμενος ὑπήκοος μέχρι θανάτου, θανάτου δὲ σταυροῦ.

φρονεῖτε (think); μορφῇ (form); ἁρπαγμὸν (robbery); ἡγήσατο v.3.s.aor.mid.ind. [ἡγέομαι] (consider); εἶναι v.pres.in. [εἰμί]; ἴσα (equal); ἐκένωσεν (empty); λαβών v.m.s.nom.aor.act.ptc. [λαμβάνω]; ὁμοιώματι (likeness); σχήματι (appearance); εὑρεθεὶς v.m.s.nom.aor.pass.ptc. [εὑρίσκω]; ἐταπείνωσεν (humble); ὑπήκοος (obedient); μέχρι (until); σταυροῦ (cross)

Pentecost

1. Deuteronomy 16:9–11; Acts 2:1–4

Breaking Down the Walls

OLD MEN AND LITTLE CHILDREN, Tlingit fishers, monks and truckers, teachers, farmers, look heavenward and dance! For the Spirit is upon us, the Fire of Holy God! Liberation, jubilation, celebration—Babel is undone!

DEUTERONOMY 16:9–11

⁹שִׁבְעָה שָׁבֻעֹת תִּסְפָּר־לָךְ מֵהָחֵל חֶרְמֵשׁ בַּקָּמָה תָּחֵל לִסְפֹּר שִׁבְעָה שָׁבֻעוֹת:

¹⁰וְעָשִׂיתָ חַג שָׁבֻעוֹת לַיהוָה אֱלֹהֶיךָ מִסַּת נִדְבַת יָדְךָ אֲשֶׁר תִּתֵּן כַּאֲשֶׁר יְבָרֶכְךָ יְהוָה אֱלֹהֶיךָ:

¹¹וְשָׂמַחְתָּ לִפְנֵי יְהוָה אֱלֹהֶיךָ אַתָּה וּבִנְךָ וּבִתֶּךָ וְעַבְדְּךָ וַאֲמָתֶךָ וְהַלֵּוִי אֲשֶׁר בִּשְׁעָרֶיךָ וְהַגֵּר וְהַיָּתוֹם וְהָאַלְמָנָה אֲשֶׁר בְּקִרְבֶּךָ בַּמָּקוֹם אֲשֶׁר יִבְחַר יְהוָה אֱלֹהֶיךָ לְשַׁכֵּן שְׁמוֹ שָׁם:

שָׁבֻעֹת (week); תִּסְפָּר v.2.m.s.impf.Q. [ספר]; מֵהָחֵל prep. + v.in.cs.H. [חלל]; חֶרְמֵשׁ (sickle); בַּקָּמָה (standing grain); תָּחֵל v.2.m.s.impf.H. [חלל]; וְעָשִׂיתָ v.c. + v.2.m.s.pf.Q. [עשה]; מִסַּת (sufficiency); נִדְבַת (free-will offering); תִּתֵּן v.2.m.s.impf.Q. [נתן]; יְבָרֶכְךָ v.3.m.s.impf.P. [ברך] + 2.m.s.pr.sf.; וְהַיָּתוֹם (orphan)

ACTS 2:1–4

¹Καὶ ἐν τῷ συμπληροῦσθαι τὴν ἡμέραν τῆς πεντηκοστῆς ἦσαν πάντες ὁμοῦ ἐπὶ τὸ αὐτό. ²καὶ ἐγένετο ἄφνω ἐκ τοῦ οὐρανοῦ ἦχος ὥσπερ φερομένης πνοῆς βιαίας καὶ ἐπλήρωσεν ὅλον τὸν οἶκον οὗ ἦσαν καθήμενοι ³καὶ ὤφθησαν αὐτοῖς διαμεριζόμεναι γλῶσσαι ὡσεὶ πυρὸς καὶ ἐκάθισεν ἐφ᾽ ἕνα ἕκαστον αὐτῶν, ⁴καὶ ἐπλήσθησαν πάντες πνεύματος ἁγίου καὶ ἤρξαντο λαλεῖν ἑτέραις γλώσσαις καθὼς τὸ πνεῦμα ἐδίδου ἀποφθέγγεσθαι αὐτοῖς.

συμπληροῦσθαι (come); πεντηκοστῆς (Pentecost); ὁμοῦ (together); ἐγένετο v.3.s.aor.mid.ind. [γίνομαι]; ἄφνω (suddenly); ἦχος (noise); ὥσπερ (as); πνοῆς (wind); βιαίας (violent); ὤφθησαν v.3.p.aor.pass.ind. [ὁράω]; διαμεριζόμεναι (divide); ὡσεὶ (like); ἐκάθισεν (settle); ἤρξαντο v.3.p.aor.mid.ind. [ἄρχω]; ἀποφθέγγεσθαι (speak out)

2. Deuteronomy 14:24–26; Romans 5:9–11

Who Is the Gift, Who Is the Giver?

WE SQUEEZE OUR LITTLE PURSES, Giver of Gifts, wondering how we will survive if you should require our widow's mite. It never occurs to us that all along you've had a party planned, *just for us,* that you are the Host and we are your guests. You only want our "yes."

DEUTERONOMY 14:24–26

²⁴וְכִי־יִרְבֶּה מִמְּךָ הַדֶּרֶךְ כִּי לֹא תוּכַל שְׂאֵתוֹ כִּי־יִרְחַק מִמְּךָ
הַמָּקוֹם אֲשֶׁר יִבְחַר יְהוָה אֱלֹהֶיךָ לָשׂוּם שְׁמוֹ שָׁם כִּי יְבָרֶכְךָ
יְהוָה אֱלֹהֶיךָ:
²⁵וְנָתַתָּה בַּכָּסֶף וְצַרְתָּ הַכֶּסֶף בְּיָדְךָ וְהָלַכְתָּ אֶל־הַמָּקוֹם
אֲשֶׁר יִבְחַר יְהוָה אֱלֹהֶיךָ בּוֹ:
²⁶וְנָתַתָּה הַכֶּסֶף בְּכֹל אֲשֶׁר־תְּאַוֶּה נַפְשְׁךָ בַּבָּקָר וּבַצֹּאן
וּבַיַּיִן וּבַשֵּׁכָר וּבְכֹל אֲשֶׁר תִּשְׁאָלְךָ נַפְשֶׁךָ וְאָכַלְתָּ
שָׁם לִפְנֵי יְהוָה אֱלֹהֶיךָ וְשָׂמַחְתָּ אַתָּה וּבֵיתֶךָ:

יְבָרֶכְךָ ;.v.2.m.s.impf.Ho. [יכל] תוּכַל ;.v.in.cs.Q. [נשא] + 3.m.s.pr.sf שְׂאֵתוֹ
v.3.m.s.impf.P. [ברך] + 2.m.s.pr.sf.; וְנָתַתָּה v.c. + v.2.m.s.pf.Q.plene [נתן]; וְצַרְתָּ
v.c. + v.2.m.s.pf.Q. [צור] (hold); תְּאַוֶּה (desire); וּבַשֵּׁכָר (intoxicant); תִּשְׁאָלְךָ
v.3.f.s.impf.Q. [שאל] + 2.m.s.pr.sf.

ROMANS 5:9–11

⁹πολλῷ οὖν μᾶλλον δικαιωθέντες νῦν ἐν τῷ αἵματι αὐτοῦ
σωθησόμεθα δι᾽ αὐτοῦ ἀπὸ τῆς ὀργῆς. ¹⁰εἰ γὰρ ἐχθροὶ ὄντες
κατηλλάγημεν τῷ θεῷ διὰ τοῦ θανάτου τοῦ υἱοῦ αὐτοῦ,
πολλῷ μᾶλλον καταλλαγέντες σωθησόμεθα ἐν τῇ ζωῇ αὐτοῦ·
¹¹οὐ μόνον δέ, ἀλλὰ καὶ καυχώμενοι ἐν τῷ θεῷ διὰ τοῦ κυρίου
ἡμῶν Ἰησοῦ Χριστοῦ δι᾽ οὗ νῦν τὴν καταλλαγὴν ἐλάβομεν.

δικαιωθέντες (justify); νῦν (now); ὀργῆς (anger); ἐχθροὶ (enemy); ὄντες
v.m.p.nom.pr.ptc. [εἰμί]; κατηλλάγημεν v.1.p.aor.pass.ind. [καταλλάσσω]
(reconcile); καυχώμενοι (boast); καταλλαγὴν (reconciliation); ἐλάβομεν
v.1.p.aor.act.ind. [λαμβάνω]

3. Isaiah 2:2–4; John 16:8–11

Swords into Plowshares

THIS ALL LOOKS FINE ON PAPER, fine for other nations' swords and my neighbor's unbelief and the government's unright-eousness. Then I glance up and catch a glimpse of my own arsenal of spears and spiteful thoughts and, God have mercy, then where are my pious words? Disarmament starts at home.

ISAIAH 2:2–4

²וְהָיָה בְּאַחֲרִית הַיָּמִים נָכוֹן יִהְיֶה הַר בֵּית־יְהוָה בְּרֹאשׁ
הֶהָרִים וְנִשָּׂא מִגְּבָעוֹת וְנָהֲרוּ אֵלָיו כָּל־הַגּוֹיִם׃
³וְהָלְכוּ עַמִּים רַבִּים וְאָמְרוּ לְכוּ וְנַעֲלֶה אֶל־הַר־יְהוָה אֶל־בֵּית
אֱלֹהֵי יַעֲקֹב וְיֹרֵנוּ מִדְּרָכָיו וְנֵלְכָה בְּאֹרְחֹתָיו כִּי מִצִּיּוֹן
תֵּצֵא תוֹרָה וּדְבַר־יְהוָה מִירוּשָׁלִָם׃
⁴וְשָׁפַט בֵּין הַגּוֹיִם וְהוֹכִיחַ לְעַמִּים רַבִּים וְכִתְּתוּ חַרְבוֹתָם
לְאִתִּים וַחֲנִיתוֹתֵיהֶם לְמַזְמֵרוֹת לֹא־יִשָּׂא גוֹי אֶל־גּוֹי חֶרֶב
וְלֹא־יִלְמְדוּ עוֹד מִלְחָמָה׃

נָכוֹן v.m.s.ptc.N. [כון]; וְנִשָּׂא v.c. + v.m.s.ptc.N. [נשא]; וְנָהֲרוּ v.c. + v.3.c.p.pf.Q. [נהר] (flow); לְכוּ v.2.m.p.impv.Q. [הלך]; וְיֹרֵנוּ cj. + v.3.m.s.impf.H.defective [ירה] + 1.com.p.pr.sf.; וְנֵלְכָה cj. + v.1.com.p.coh.Q. [הלך]; תֵּצֵא v.3.f.s.impf.Q. [יצא]; וְהוֹכִיחַ v.c. + v.3.m.s.pf.H. [יכח]; וְכִתְּתוּ (crush); לְאִתִּים (plowshare); וַחֲנִיתוֹתֵיהֶם (spear); לְמַזְמֵרוֹת (pruning hook); יִשָּׂא v.3.m.s.impf.Q. [נשא]

JOHN 16:8–11

⁸καὶ ἐλθὼν ἐκεῖνος ἐλέγξει τὸν κόσμον περὶ ἁμαρτίας καὶ περὶ δικαιοσύνης καὶ περὶ κρίσεως· ⁹περὶ ἁμαρτίας μέν, ὅτι οὐ πιστεύουσιν εἰς ἐμέ· ¹⁰περὶ δικαιοσύνης δέ, ὅτι πρὸς τὸν πατέρα ὑπάγω καὶ οὐκέτι θεωρεῖτέ με· ¹¹περὶ δὲ κρίσεως, ὅτι ὁ ἄρχων τοῦ κόσμου τούτου κέκριται.

ἐλθὼν v.m.s.nom.aor.act.ptc. [ἔρχομαι]; ἐλέγξει (convict); κρίσεως (judgment); οὐκέτι (no longer); κέκριται v.3.s.pf.pass.ind. [κρίνω]

4. Jeremiah 42:2–3; James 5:16–17

Pentecostal Prayer

SURELY THE GREATEST PROOF of Pentecost is prayer that availeth much.

JEREMIAH 42:2–3

²וַיֹּאמְרוּ אֶל־יִרְמְיָהוּ הַנָּבִיא תִּפָּל־נָא תְחִנָּתֵנוּ לְפָנֶיךָ
וְהִתְפַּלֵּל בַּעֲדֵנוּ אֶל־יְהוָה אֱלֹהֶיךָ בְּעַד כָּל־הַשְּׁאֵרִית הַזֹּאת
כִּי־נִשְׁאַרְנוּ מְעַט מֵהַרְבֵּה כַּאֲשֶׁר עֵינֶיךָ רֹאוֹת אֹתָנוּ:
³וְיַגֶּד־לָנוּ יְהוָה אֱלֹהֶיךָ אֶת־הַדֶּרֶךְ אֲשֶׁר נֵלֶךְ־בָּהּ וְאֶת־
הַדָּבָר אֲשֶׁר נַעֲשֶׂה:

תִּפָּל v.3.f.s.jus.Q. [נפל]; תְחִנָּתֵנוּ (supplication); רֹאוֹת v.f.p.act.ptc.Q. [ראה];
וַיַּגֶּד cj. + v.3.m.s.impf.H. [נגד]; נֵלֶךְ v.1.com.p.impf.Q. [הלך]

JAMES 5:16–17

¹⁶ἐξομολογεῖσθε οὖν ἀλλήλοις τὰς ἁμαρτίας καὶ εὔχεσθε
ὑπὲρ ἀλλήλων ὅπως ἰαθῆτε. πολὺ ἰσχύει δέησις δικαίου
ἐνεργουμένη. ¹⁷Ἡλίας ἄνθρωπος ἦν ὁμοιοπαθὴς ἡμῖν, καὶ
προσευχῇ προσηύξατο τοῦ μὴ βρέξαι, καὶ οὐκ ἔβρεξεν ἐπὶ
τῆς γῆς ἐνιαυτοὺς τρεῖς καὶ μῆνας ἕξ·

ἐξομολογεῖσθε (confess); ἰαθῆτε v.2.p.aor.pass.sub. [ἰάομαι] (heal); ἰσχύει (be able); δέησις (prayer); ἐνεργουμένη (be effective); ἦν
v.3.s.impf.ind. [εἰμί]; ὁμοιοπαθὴς (having the same nature); προσευχῇ
(prayer); προσηύξατο (pray); βρέξαι (rain); μῆνας (month); ἕξ (six)

5. Joel 3:1–2 [2:28–29]; Acts 2:17–19a, 21

The Call and the Called

COULD THERE BE A MIGHTIER SIGN, a more astonishing wonder, than the assortment of prophets God has called? The call is the sign; the messenger is the sign; the harvest is the sign.

JOEL 3:1–2 [2:28–29]

¹וְהָיָה אַחֲרֵי־כֵן אֶשְׁפּוֹךְ אֶת־רוּחִי עַל־כָּל־בָּשָׂר וְנִבְּאוּ בְּנֵיכֶם
וּבְנוֹתֵיכֶם זִקְנֵיכֶם חֲלֹמוֹת יַחֲלֹמוּן בַּחוּרֵיכֶם חֶזְיֹנוֹת יִרְאוּ׃
²וְגַם עַל־הָעֲבָדִים וְעַל־הַשְּׁפָחוֹת בַּיָּמִים הָהֵמָּה אֶשְׁפּוֹךְ
אֶת־רוּחִי׃

וְנִבְּאוּ cj. + v.3.c.p.pf.N. [נבא]; זִקְנֵיכֶם (old); יַחֲלֹמוּן v.3.m.p.impf.Q. [חלם]
(dream) + para.; יִרְאוּ v.3.m.p.impf.Q. [ראה]; חֶזְיֹנוֹת (vision); בַּחוּרֵיכֶם (young man)

ACTS 2:17–19A, 21

¹⁷καὶ ἔσται ἐν ταῖς ἐσχάταις ἡμέραις, λέγει ὁ θεός,
ἐκχεῶ ἀπὸ τοῦ πνεύματος μου ἐπὶ πᾶσαν σάρκα,
    καὶ προφητεύσουσιν οἱ υἱοὶ ὑμῶν καὶ αἱ θυγατέρες
    ὑμῶν
καὶ οἱ νεανίσκοι ὑμῶν ὁράσεις ὄψονται
    καὶ οἱ πρεσβύτεροι ὑμῶν ἐνυπνίοις ἐνυπνιασθή
    σονται·
¹⁸ καί γε ἐπὶ τοὺς δούλους μου καὶ ἐπὶ τὰς δούλας
    μου ἐν ταῖς ἡμέραις ἐκείναις ἐκχεῶ ἀπὸ τοῦ
    πνεύματος μου,
    καὶ προφητεύσουσιν.
¹⁹καὶ δώσω τέρατα ἐν τῷ οὐρανῷ ἄνω
    καὶ σημεῖα ἐπὶ τῆς γῆς κάτω,
²¹καὶ ἔσται πᾶς ὃς ἂν ἐπικαλέσηται τὸ ὄνομα κυρίου
    σωθήσεται.

ἔσται v.3.s.fut.ind. [εἰμί]; ἐκχεῶ (shed); προφητεύσουσιν (prophecy);
θυγατέρες (daughter); νεανίσκοι (young man); ὁράσεις (vision); ὄψονται
v.3.p.fut.mid.ind. [ὁράω]; ἐνυπνίοις (dream); ἐνυπνιασθήσονται (dream);
γε (indeed); δούλας (female servant); τέρατα (wonder); ἄνω (above); κάτω
(below); ἐπικαλέσηται (call upon)

6. Genesis 8:21; Romans 15:13

A Spirit of Hope

WHEN THE WATER HAD SUBSIDED and the long night of judgment was past, tendrils of repentance mingled with the sky. And God wept, promised, and loved. Thus hope came into the world.

GENESIS 8:21

²¹וַיָּרַח יְהוָה אֶת־רֵיחַ הַנִּיחֹחַ וַיֹּאמֶר יְהוָה אֶל־לִבּוֹ לֹא־אֹסִף לְקַלֵּל עוֹד אֶת־הָאֲדָמָה בַּעֲבוּר הָאָדָם כִּי יֵצֶר לֵב הָאָדָם רַע מִנְּעֻרָיו וְלֹא־אֹסִף עוֹד לְהַכּוֹת אֶת־כָּל־חַי כַּאֲשֶׁר עָשִׂיתִי:

וַיָּרַח v.c.+v.3.m.s.impf.Q. [רִיח] (smell); הַנִּיחֹחַ (odor); אֹסִףv.1.com.s.impf.H.defective [יסף]; בַּעֲבוּר (for, though); יֵצֶר (purpose); מִנְּעֻרָיו (youth); לְהַכּוֹת prep. + v.in.cs.H. [נכה]; עָשִׂיתִי v.1.com.s.pf.Q. [עשה]

ROMANS 15:13

¹³ὁ δὲ θεὸς τῆς ἐλπίδος πληρώσαι ὑμᾶς πάσης χαρᾶς καὶ εἰρήνης ἐν τῷ πιστεύειν, εἰς τὸ περισσεύειν ὑμᾶς ἐν τῇ ἐλπίδι ἐν δυνάμει πνεύματος ἁγίου.

περισσεύειν (abound)

7. Exodus 23.16–17, Luke 2.42–43

Throw a Party!

LORD, WHO BUT YOU WOULD GIVE THE COMMAND to keep festivals without fail, no matter what? So today I'm going to throw off my infernal, brooding seriousness and I'm going to laugh and sing and dance, just for you. I'm going to gasp in wide-eyed wonder at the mystery of life. I'm going to keep a festival for you.

EXODUS 23:16–17

16וְחַג הַקָּצִיר בִּכּוּרֵי מַעֲשֶׂיךָ אֲשֶׁר תִּזְרַע בַּשָּׂדֶה וְחַג
הָאָסִף בְּצֵאת הַשָּׁנָה בְּאָסְפְּךָ אֶת־מַעֲשֶׂיךָ מִן־הַשָּׂדֶה:
17שָׁלֹשׁ פְּעָמִים בַּשָּׁנָה יֵרָאֶה כָּל־זְכוּרְךָ אֶל־פְּנֵי הָאָדֹן יְהוָה:

בִּכּוּרֵי (firstfruits); הָאָסִף (harvest); בְּצֵאת prep. + v.in.cs.Q. [יצא]; בְּאָסְפְּךָ prep. + v.in.cs.Q. [אסף] + 2.m.s.pr.sf.; יֵרָאֶה v.3.m.s.impf.N. [ראה]; זְכוּרְךָ (male)

LUKE 2:42–43

42καὶ ὅτε ἐγένετο ἐτῶν δώδεκα, ἀναβαινόντων αὐτῶν κατὰ τὸ ἔθος τῆς ἑορτῆς 43καὶ τελειωσάντων τὰς ἡμέρας, ἐν τῷ ὑποστρέφειν αὐτοὺς ὑπέμεινεν Ἰησοῦς ὁ παῖς ἐν Ἰερουσαλήμ, καὶ οὐκ ἔγνωσαν οἱ γονεῖς αὐτοῦ.

ἐγένετο v.3.s.aor.mid.ind. [γίνομαι]; ἐτῶν (year); ἔθος (custom); τελειωσάντων (be finished); ὑποστρέφειν (return); ὑπέμεινεν (remain); γονεῖς (parents)

159

Week 22

Trinity Sunday

1. Genesis 1:26; Colossians 1:15–17

"Me-ness in Christ"

HOW I LOVE THE NUANCED WONDER of those few small words: "Let us make humankind in our image"! In the beginning it was so, before the unmaking curse of sin. But thanks be to God, we have another chance. In Christ these words have come to life. I am beginning to understand that my "me-ness" is found in Christ. Unless I find me there, I will not find me at all.

GENESIS 1:26

²⁶וַיֹּאמֶר אֱלֹהִים נַעֲשֶׂה אָדָם בְּצַלְמֵנוּ כִּדְמוּתֵנוּ וְיִרְדּוּ
בִדְגַת הַיָּם וּבְעוֹף הַשָּׁמַיִם וּבַבְּהֵמָה וּבְכָל־הָאָרֶץ וּבְכָל־
הָרֶמֶשׂ הָרֹמֵשׂ עַל־הָאָרֶץ:

בְּצַלְמֵנוּ (image); כִּדְמוּתֵנוּ (likeness); וְיִרְדּוּ cj. + v.3.m.p.impf.Q. [רדה]
(rule); בִדְגַת (fish); הָרֶמֶשׂ (creeping thing); הָרֹמֵשׂ (creep)

COLOSSIANS 1:15–17

¹⁵ὅς ἐστιν εἰκὼν τοῦ θεοῦ τοῦ ἀοράτου, πρωτότοκος πάσης
κτίσεως, ¹⁶ὅτι ἐν αὐτῷ ἐκτίσθη τὰ πάντα ἐν τοῖς οὐρανοῖς καὶ
ἐπὶ τῆς γῆς, τὰ ὁρατὰ καὶ τὰ ἀόρατα, εἴτε θρόνοι εἴτε
κυριότητες εἴτε ἀρχαὶ εἴτε ἐξουσίαι· τὰ πάντα δι᾿ αὐτοῦ καὶ
εἰς αὐτὸν ἔκτισται· ¹⁷καὶ αὐτός ἐστιν πρὸ πάντων καὶ τὰ
πάντα ἐν αὐτῷ συνέστηκεν,

ἐστιν v.3.s.pres.ind. [εἰμί]; εἰκὼν (image); ἀοράτου (invisible); πρωτότοκος (firstborn); κτίσεως (creation); ἐκτίσθη (create); ὁρατὰ (visible);
κυριότητες (dominion); πρὸ (before); συνέστηκεν (exist)

160

2. Psalm 104.14–15; Luke 12:27

"Dandelions and Cows"

THANK GOD FOR DANDELIONS AND COWS! They are protection for the soul, warning against nihilism and despair. They point to life, goodness, beauty. They do all of this by simply being what they are—the good and faithful handiwork of a good and loving God.

PSALM 104:14–15

¹⁴מַצְמִיחַ חָצִיר לַבְּהֵמָה וְעֵשֶׂב לַעֲבֹדַת הָאָדָם לְהוֹצִיא לֶחֶם מִן־הָאָרֶץ:

¹⁵וְיַיִן יְשַׂמַּח לְבַב־אֱנוֹשׁ לְהַצְהִיל פָּנִים מִשָּׁמֶן וְלֶחֶם לְבַב־אֱנוֹשׁ יִסְעָד:

מַצְמִיחַ (sprout); חָצִיר (grass); וְעֵשֶׂב (herb); לְהוֹצִיא prep. + v.in.cs.H. [יצא]; יִסְעָד (sustain)

LUKE 12:27

²⁷κατανοήσατε τὰ κρίνα πῶς αὐξάνει· οὐ κοπιᾷ οὐδὲ νήθει· λέγω δὲ ὑμῖν, οὐδὲ Σολομὼν ἐν πάσῃ τῇ δόξῃ αὐτοῦ περιεβάλετο ὡς ἓν τούτων.

κατανοήσατε (consider); κρίνα (lily); νήθει (spin); περιεβάλετο (clothe)

3. Psalm 36:7–9 [6–8]; Luke 11:3

"Only Now"

ONLY FOR THIS DAY, only for this moment do I need the where-
withal to stand. Only for this hour do I need overcoming
strength. Only for the task at hand do I need to be present.
Thank you, Eternal God, for pointing me to life that is only now.

PSALM 36:7–9 [6–8]

7צִדְקָתְךָ כְּהַרְרֵי־אֵל מִשְׁפָּטֶךָ תְּהוֹם רַבָּה אָדָם־וּבְהֵמָה תוֹשִׁיעַ יְהוָה:

8מַה־יָּקָר חַסְדְּךָ אֱלֹהִים וּבְנֵי אָדָם בְּצֵל כְּנָפֶיךָ יֶחֱסָיוּן:

9יִרְוְיֻן מִדֶּשֶׁן בֵּיתֶךָ וְנַחַל עֲדָנֶיךָ תַשְׁקֵם:

תְּהוֹם (deep); תּוֹשִׁיעַ v.2.m.s.impf.H. [ישׁע]; יָקָר (precious); בְּצֵל (shadow);
יֶחֱסָיוּן v.3.m.p.impf.Q. [חסה] (seek refuge) + para.; יִרְוְיֻן v.3.m.p.impf.Q.
[רוה] (drink one's fill) + para.; מִדֶּשֶׁן (fatness); עֲדָנֶיךָ (delight); תַשְׁקֵם
v.2.m.s.impf.H. [שׁקה] + 3.m.p.pr.sf.

LUKE 11:3

3τὸν ἄρτον ἡμῶν τὸν ἐπιούσιον δίδου ἡμῖν τὸ
καθ᾽ ἡμέραν·

ἐπιούσιον (daily)

162

1. Isaiah 50:4; John 10.16

"What the Good Shepherd Will Do"

WHAT AN IMMEASURABLE COMFORT it is to know that Jesus is my *Good* Shepherd, that he *will* guide me, that he *will* give me the word I need to hear, the nourishment that I need. He will do this apart from my scrabbling or striving because the well-being of his sheep is the Shepherd's great concern. All I need to do is listen and say "yes."

ISAIAH 50:4

4אֲדֹנָי יְהוִה נָתַן לִי לְשׁוֹן לִמּוּדִים לָדַעַת לָעוּת אֶת־יָעֵף דָּבָר
יָעִיר בַּבֹּקֶר בַּבֹּקֶר יָעִיר לִי אֹזֶן לִשְׁמֹעַ כַּלִּמּוּדִים:

לִמּוּדִים (taught); לָדַעַת prep. + v.in.cs.Q. [יָדַע]; לָעוּת prep. + v.in.cs.Q. [עוּת] (help); יָעֵף (weary); יָעִיר v.3.m.s.impf.H. [עוּר] (arouse)

JOHN 10:16

16καὶ ἄλλα πρόβατα ἔχω ἃ οὐκ ἔστιν ἐκ τῆς αὐλῆς ταύτης· κἀκεῖνα δεῖ με ἀγαγεῖν καὶ τῆς φωνῆς μου ἀκούσουσιν, καὶ γενήσονται μία ποίμνη, εἷς ποιμήν.

πρόβατα (sheep); ἔστιν v.3.s.pres.ind. [εἰμί]; αὐλῆς (sheepfold); κἀκεῖνα (and that one); ποίμνη (flock)

5. Psalm 139:5–7; Philippians 4:12–13

"The Safe Place"

I WISH IT WERE OTHERWISE, O God, but I continue to struggle with this promise. You are my safe place, my home. I know this very well. Yet some part of me has yet to hear the good news or at least to believe it. Bring the rest of me home.

PSALM 139:5–7

‏ אָחוֹר וָקֶדֶם צַרְתָּנִי וַתָּשֶׁת עָלַי כַּפֶּכָה׃ ⁵

‏ פְּלִיאָה דַעַת מִמֶּנִּי נִשְׂגְּבָה לֹא־אוּכַל לָהּ׃ ⁶

‏ אָנָה אֵלֵךְ מֵרוּחֶךָ וְאָנָה מִפָּנֶיךָ אֶבְרָח׃ ⁷

אָחוֹר (behind); צַרְתָּנִי v.2.m.s.pf.Q. [צור] (besiege) + 1.com.s.pr.sf.; וַתָּשֶׁת v.c. + v.2.m.s.impf.Q. [שית]; כַּפֶּכָה n.f.s. + 2.m.s.pr.sf.plene; פְּלִיאָה n.f.s.Qe. (wonderful); נִשְׂגְּבָה (be inaccessible); אוּכַל v.1.com.s.impf.Q. [יכל]; אָנָה (to where?); אֵלֵךְ v.1.com.s.impf.Q. [הלך]

PHILIPPIANS 4:12–13

¹²οἶδα καὶ ταπεινοῦσθαι, οἶδα καὶ περισσεύειν· ἐν παντὶ καὶ ἐν πᾶσιν μεμύημαι, καὶ χορτάζεσθαι καὶ πεινᾶν καὶ περισσεύειν καὶ ὑστερεῖσθαι· ¹³πάντα ἰσχύω ἐν τῷ ἐνδυναμοῦντί με.

ταπεινοῦσθαι (humiliate); περισσεύειν (increase); μεμύημαι v.1.s.pf.pass.ind. [μυέω] (learn secrets); χορτάζεσθαι (satisfy); πεινᾶν (be hungry); ὑστερεῖσθαι (lack); ἰσχύω (be strong); ἐνδυναμοῦντι (empower)

6. Psalm 20.8–9 [7–8]; John 17:17

"A Home in My Heart"

MAKE YOURSELF AT HOME IN MY HEART, Jesus! Go ahead and help yourself to anything. Live exactly as you would in your own home. For that is what I want to be—your own home.

PSALM 20:8–9 [7–8]

⁸אֵלֶּה בָרֶכֶב וְאֵלֶּה בַסּוּסִים וַאֲנַחְנוּ בְּשֵׁם־יְהוָה אֱלֹהֵינוּ נַזְכִּיר:

⁹הֵמָּה כָּרְעוּ וְנָפָלוּ וַאֲנַחְנוּ קַמְנוּ וַנִּתְעוֹדָד:

קַמְנוּ v.1.com.p.pf.Q. [קוּם]; כָּרְעוּ (bow down); וַנִּתְעוֹדָד v.c. + v.1.com.p.impf.Htpl. [עוד] (do again)

JOHN 17:17

¹⁷ἁγίασον αὐτοὺς ἐν τῇ ἀληθείᾳ· ὁ λόγος ὁ σὸς ἀλήθεια ἐστιν.

ἁγίασον (sanctify); ἐστιν v.3.s.pres.ind. [εἰμί]

7. Joshua 1:5; Hebrews 13:5

"Contentment"

WHAT MORE COULD I EVER ASK or want than you, Beloved? And you I have, for your promise is certain, your word never fails. You are my contentment.

JOSHUA 1:5

⁵לֹא־יִתְיַצֵּב אִישׁ לְפָנֶיךָ כֹּל יְמֵי חַיֶּיךָ כַּאֲשֶׁר הָיִיתִי עִם־
מֹשֶׁה אֶהְיֶה עִמָּךְ לֹא אַרְפְּךָ וְלֹא אֶעֶזְבֶךָּ׃

יִתְיַצֵּב (stand firm); הָיִיתִי v.1.com.s.pf.Q. [היה]; אַרְפְּךָ v.1.com.s.impf.H. [רפה] (forsake) + 2.m.s.pr.sf. אֶעֶזְבֶךָּ v.1.com.s.impf.Q. [עזב] + 2.m.s.pr.sf. + en.

HEBREWS 13:5

⁵Ἀφιλάργυρος ὁ τρόπος, ἀρκούμενοι τοῖς παροῦσιν. αὐτὸς γὰρ εἴρηκεν, Οὐ μή σε ἀνῶ οὐδ᾽ οὐ μή σε ἐγκαταλίπω,

Ἀφιλάργυρος (not greedy); τρόπος (way of life); ἀρκούμενοι (be content); παροῦσιν (possession); ἀνῶ v.1.s.aor.act.sub. [ἀνίημι] (abandon); ἐγκαταλίπω (forsake)

Stewardship

1. Genesis 1:28; Luke 12:42–43

Confession

YOU GRACED US TO BE STEWARDS of your world, Elohim, nurturers of your marvelous networks of water, soil, plants, creatures of all kinds, and one another. This was your gift of love to us, your inexpressible act of trust. But our souls are stained with exploitation and contempt, for there is nothing left in this world that is not profaned with our sin. Have mercy on us, O God.

GENESIS 1:28

²⁸וַיְבָרֶךְ אֹתָם אֱלֹהִים וַיֹּאמֶר לָהֶם אֱלֹהִים פְּרוּ וּרְבוּ וּמִלְאוּ
אֶת־הָאָרֶץ וְכִבְשֻׁהָ וּרְדוּ בִּדְגַת הַיָּם וּבְעוֹף הַשָּׁמַיִם
וּבְכָל־חַיָּה הָרֹמֶשֶׂת עַל־הָאָרֶץ:

פְּרוּ v.2.m.p.impv.Q. [פרה] (be fruitful); וּרְבוּ cj. + v.2.m.p.impv.Q. [רבה];
וְכִבְשֻׁהָ v.c.+v.2.m.p.impv.Q. [כבש] (subdue) + 3.f.s.pr.sf.; וּרְדוּ cj. + v.2.m.p.impv.
[רדה] (rule); בִּדְגַת (fish); הָרֹמֶשֶׂת (creep)

LUKE 12:42–43

⁴²καὶ εἶπεν ὁ κύριος, Τίς ἄρα ἐστὶν ὁ πιστὸς οἰκονόμος ὁ
φρόνιμος, ὃν καταστήσει ὁ κύριος ἐπὶ τῆς θεραπείας αὐτοῦ
τοῦ διδόναι ἐν καιρῷ [τὸ] σιτομέτριον; ⁴³μακάριος ὁ δοῦλος
ἐκεῖνος, ὃν ἐλθὼν ὁ κύριος αὐτοῦ εὑρήσει ποιοῦντα οὕτως.

εἶπεν v.3.s.aor.act.ind. [λέγω]; ἄρα (then); ἐστὶν v.3.s.pres.ind. [εἰμί];
οἰκονόμος (steward); φρόνιμος (wise); καταστήσει (appoint); θεραπείας
(care); διδόναι v.pres.act.in. [δίδωμι]; σιτομέτριον (ration); ἐλθὼν
v.m.s.nom.aor.act.ptc. [ἔρχομαι];

2. Exodus 20:15; Luke 3:14

The Core Temptation

THE CORE TEMPTATION IN ALL STEWARDSHIP is violence—to steal, use, and ultimately destroy that which one was entrusted to protect, nourish, and love.

EXODUS 20:15

לֹא תִּגְנֹב׃¹⁵

תִּגְנֹב (steal)

LUKE 3:14

¹⁴ἐπηρώτων δὲ αὐτὸν καὶ στρατευόμενοι λέγοντες, Τί ποιήσωμεν καὶ ἡμεῖς; καὶ εἶπεν αὐτοῖς, Μηδένα διασείσητε μηδὲ συκοφαντήσητε καὶ ἀρκεῖσθε τοῖς ὀψωνίοις ὑμῶν.

ἐπηρώτων v.3.p.impf.act.ind. [ἐπερωτάω]; στρατευόμενοι (serve as a soldier); εἶπεν v.3.s.aor.act.ind. [λέγω]; διασείσητε (extort); συκοφαντ-τήσητε (harass); ἀρκεῖσθε (be satisfied); ὀψωνίοις (salary)

3. Leviticus 27:30; Luke 11:42

The Means of Abundant Life

WHEN WE TRULY EMBRACE THE EARTH as the Lord's and ourselves
as his stewards, tithes and offerings are only a start. Our whole
life becomes a gift of joyous giving. We are God's chosen means
of abundant life to one another, but that requires that we see
ourselves as stewards.

LEVITICUS 27:30

³⁰וְכָל־מַעְשַׂר הָאָרֶץ מִזֶּרַע הָאָרֶץ מִפְּרִי הָעֵץ לַיהוָה הוּא קֹדֶשׁ
לַיהוָה׃

מַעְשַׂר (tenth)

LUKE 11:42

⁴²ἀλλὰ οὐαὶ ὑμῖν τοῖς Φαρισαίοις, ὅτι ἀποδεκατοῦτε τὸ
ἡδύοσμον καὶ τὸ πήγανον καὶ πᾶν λάχανον καὶ παρέρχεσθε
τὴν κρίσιν καὶ τὴν ἀγάπην τοῦ θεοῦ· ταῦτα δὲ ἔδει ποιῆσαι
κἀκεῖνα μὴ παρεῖναι.

οὐαὶ (woe); ἀποδεκατοῦτε (tithe); ἡδύοσμον (mint); πήγανον (rue);
λάχανον (vegetable); παρέρχεσθε v.2.p.pres.mid.ind. [παρέρχομαι] (neglect); κρίσιν (judgment); παρεῖναι v.aor.act.in. [παρίημι] (neglect)

4. Numbers 18:21; 1 Corinthians 9:13–14

Workers Worthy of Hire

THE WORK OF MINISTRY is like any other work—a stewarding of particular gifts, graces, and opportunities. And so like any other work it deserves recompense, not too much and not too little. This is God's will. May it become ours as well.

NUMBERS 18:21

²¹וְלִבְנֵי לֵוִי הִנֵּה נָתַתִּי כָּל־מַעֲשֵׂר בְּיִשְׂרָאֵל לְנַחֲלָה חֵלֶף
עֲבֹדָתָם אֲשֶׁר־הֵם עֹבְדִים אֶת־עֲבֹדַת אֹהֶל מוֹעֵד:

נָתַתִּי v.1.com.s.pf.Q. [נתן]; מַעֲשֵׂר (tenth); חֵלֶף (exchange)

1 CORINTHIANS 9:13–14

¹³οὐκ οἴδατε ὅτι οἱ τὰ ἱερὰ ἐργαζόμενοι [τὰ] ἐκ τοῦ ἱεροῦ ἐσθίουσιν, οἱ τῷ θυσιαστηρίῳ παρεδρεύοντες τῷ θυσιαστηρίῳ συμμερίζονται; ¹⁴οὕτως καὶ ὁ κύριος διέταξεν τοῖς τὸ εὐαγγέλιον καταγγέλλουσιν ἐκ τοῦ εὐαγγελίου ζῆν.

ἱερὰ (holy thing); ἐργαζόμενοι (do); θυσιαστηρίῳ (altar); παρε-δρεύοντες (serve constantly); συμμερίζονται (share in); διέταξεν v.3.s.aor.act.ind. [διατάσσω] (command); καταγγέλλουσιν (proclaim)

5. 1 Samuel 1:27–28; 1 Corinthians 6:19b–20

Whose Children Are They?

IT'S ONE THING TO ACCEPT my role as steward of money, house, car, and gifts. But it's an altogether different matter with my children. What does it mean to be a good steward of my children?

1 SAMUEL 1:27–28

²⁷אֶל־הַנַּעַר הַזֶּה הִתְפַּלָּלְתִּי וַיִּתֵּן יְהוָה לִי אֶת־שְׁאֵלָתִי
אֲשֶׁר שָׁאַלְתִּי מֵעִמּוֹ:
²⁸וְגַם אָנֹכִי הִשְׁאִלְתִּהוּ לַיהוָה כָּל־הַיָּמִים אֲשֶׁר הָיָה הוּא שָׁאוּל
לַיהוָה וַיִּשְׁתַּחוּ שָׁם לַיהוָה:

וַיִּתֵּן v.c. + v.3.m.s.impf.Q. [נתן]; שְׁאֵלָתִי (request); הִשְׁאִלְתִּהוּ v.1.com.s.pf.H.
[שאל] + 3.m.s.pr.sf.; וַיִּשְׁתַּחוּ v.c. + v.3.m.s.impf.Hisht. [חוה]

1 CORINTHIANS 6:19B–20

¹⁹καὶ οὐκ ἐστὲ ἑαυτῶν; ²⁰ἠγοράσθητε γὰρ τιμῆς· δοξάσατε δὴ
τὸν θεὸν ἐν τῷ σώματι ὑμῶν.

ἠγοράσθητε v.2.p.aor.pass.ind. [ἀγοράζω] (buy); τιμῆς (price); δὴ
(therefore)

6. 2 Samuel 24:24; Mark 14:3

Alabaster Jars

WHAT IS THE JAR I AM HIDING in a safe place, the one I have been hoarding, the one that I need to open and lavish upon my Lord?

2 SAMUEL 24:24

²⁴וַיֹּאמֶר הַמֶּלֶךְ אֶל־אֲרַוְנָה לֹא כִּי־קָנוֹ אֶקְנֶה מֵאוֹתְךָ בִּמְחִיר
וְלֹא אַעֲלֶה לַיהוָה אֱלֹהַי עֹלוֹת חִנָּם וַיִּקֶן דָּוִד אֶת־הַגֹּרֶן
וְאֶת־הַבָּקָר בְּכֶסֶף שְׁקָלִים חֲמִשִּׁים:

קָנוֹ v.in.ab.Q. [קנה]; בִּמְחִיר (price); חִנָּם (in vain); וַיִּקֶן v.c. + v.3.m.s.impf.Q.
[קנה]; הַגֹּרֶן (threshing floor); חֲמִשִּׁים (fifty)

MARK 14:3

³Καὶ ὄντος αὐτοῦ ἐν Βηθανίᾳ ἐν τῇ οἰκίᾳ Σίμωνος τοῦ λεπροῦ, κατακειμένου αὐτοῦ ἦλθεν γυνὴ ἔχουσα ἀλάβαστρον μύρου νάρδου πιστικῆς πολυτελοῦς, συντρίψασα τὴν ἀλάβαστρον κατέχεεν αὐτοῦ τῆς κεφαλῆς.

λεπροῦ (leper); κατακειμένου (recline); ἦλθεν v.3.s.aor.act.ind. [ἔρχο-μαι]; ἀλάβαστρον (alabaster flask); μύρου (perfume); νάρδου (nard); πισ-τικῆς (real); πολυτελοῦς (expensive); συντρίψασα v.f.s.nom.aor.act.ptc. [συντρίβω] (break); κατέχεεν v.3.s.aor.act.ind. [καταχέω] (pour)

7. Proverbs 11:28; Luke 12:19–21

Open Us

HOW SLOW WE ARE TO SEE what is ridiculously clear! Heal our fearsome blindness, merciful God. Forgive our witless clutching at your gifts. Open our fists, open our hearts, open us. Amen.

PROVERBS 11:28

²⁸בּוֹטֵחַ בְּעָשְׁרוֹ הוּא יִפֹּל וְכֶעָלֶה צַדִּיקִים יִפְרָחוּ׃

בְּעָשְׁרוֹ (wealth); יִפֹּל v.3.m.s.impf.Q. [נפל]; וְכֶעָלֶה cj. + prep. + d.a. + n.m.s. (leaf); יִפְרָחוּ (blossom)

LUKE 12:19–21

¹⁹καὶ ἐρῶ τῇ ψυχῇ μου, ψυχή, ἔχεις πολλὰ ἀγαθὰ κείμενα εἰς ἔτη πολλά· ἀναπαύου, φάγε, πίε, εὐφραίνου. ²⁰εἶπεν δὲ αὐτῷ ὁ θεός, Ἄφρων, ταύτῃ τῇ νυκτὶ τὴν ψυχήν σου ἀπαιτοῦσιν ἀπὸ σοῦ· ἃ δὲ ἡτοίμασας, τίνι ἔσται; ²¹οὕτως ὁ θησαυρίζων ἑαυτῷ καὶ μὴ εἰς θεὸν πλουτῶν.

ἐρῶ v.1.s.fut.act.ind. [λέγω]; ἔτη (year); ἀναπαύου (rest); εἶπεν v.3.s.aor.act.ind. [λέγω]; Ἄφρων (ignorant); ἀπαιτοῦσιν (ask back); ἡτοίμασας v.2.s.aor.act.ind. [ἐτοιμάζω] (prepare); θησαυρίζων (save); πλουτῶν (be rich)

Week 24

Priesthood of Believers

1. Isaiah 43:6–7; Galatians 3:28–29

Heritage

O GOD OF OUR SALVATION, transfuse my soul with the blood of
your covenant until I no longer know any of your children in
any way except as bone of my bone and flesh of my flesh. Plant
your heart in my heart until I no longer see our future in any
terms except those of family.

ISAIAH 43:6–7

⁶אֹמַר לַצָּפוֹן תֵּנִי וּלְתֵימָן אַל־תִּכְלָאִי הָבִיאִי בָנַי מֵרָחוֹק
וּבְנוֹתַי מִקְצֵה הָאָרֶץ׃
⁷כֹּל הַנִּקְרָא בִשְׁמִי וְלִכְבוֹדִי בְּרָאתִיו יְצַרְתִּיו אַף־עֲשִׂיתִיו׃

וּלְתֵימָן v.1.com.s.impf.Q. [אמר]; תֵּנִי v.2.f.s.impv.Q.pause [נתן];
(south); תִּכְלָאִי (hold back); הָבִיאִי v.2.f.s.impv.H. [בוא]; בְּרָאתִיו
v.1.com.s.pf.Q. [ברא] + 3.m.s.pr.sf.; יְצַרְתִּיו v.1.com.s.pf.Q. [יצר] + 3.m.s.pr.sf.;
עֲשִׂיתִיו v.1.com.s.pf.Q. [עשה] + 3.m.s.pr.sf.

GALATIANS 3:28–29

²⁸οὐκ ἔνι Ἰουδαῖος οὐδὲ Ἕλλην, οὐκ ἔνι δοῦλος οὐδὲ
ἐλεύθερος, οὐκ ἔνι ἄρσεν καὶ θῆλυ· πάντες γὰρ ὑμεῖς εἷς ἐστε
ἐν Χριστῷ Ἰησοῦ. ²⁹εἰ δὲ ὑμεῖς Χριστοῦ, ἄρα τοῦ Ἀβραὰμ
σπέρμα ἐστέ, κατ᾽ ἐπαγγελίαν κληρονόμοι.

ἔνι (there is); ἄρσεν (male); θῆλυ (female); ἄρα (then); σπέρμα (seed);
κληρονόμοι (heir)

2. Exodus 19.4–6; Revelation 1:5–6

Priests after Jesus

CRAFT US INTO PRIESTS after your own heart, Jesus. May we love this world and its peoples with the passionate, redeeming love that compelled you to the cross.

EXODUS 19:4–6

⁴אַתֶּם רְאִיתֶם אֲשֶׁר עָשִׂיתִי לְמִצְרָיִם וָאֶשָּׂא אֶתְכֶם עַל־כַּנְפֵי
נְשָׁרִים וָאָבִא אֶתְכֶם אֵלָי:
⁵וְעַתָּה אִם־שָׁמוֹעַ תִּשְׁמְעוּ בְּקֹלִי וּשְׁמַרְתֶּם אֶת־בְּרִיתִי
וִהְיִיתֶם לִי סְגֻלָּה מִכָּל־הָעַמִּים כִּי־לִי כָּל־הָאָרֶץ:
⁶וְאַתֶּם תִּהְיוּ־לִי מַמְלֶכֶת כֹּהֲנִים וְגוֹי קָדוֹשׁ אֵלֶּה הַדְּבָרִים
אֲשֶׁר תְּדַבֵּר אֶל־בְּנֵי יִשְׂרָאֵל:

רְאִיתֶם v.2.m.p.pf.Q. [ראה]; עָשִׂיתִי v.1.com.s.pf.Q. [עשה]; וָאֶשָּׂא v.c. + v.1.com.s.impf.Q. [נשא]; נְשָׁרִים (eagle); וָאָבִא v.c. + v.1.com.s.impf.H.defective [בוא]; וִהְיִיתֶם v.c. + v.2.m.p.pf.Q. [היה]; סְגֻלָּה (possession); תִּהְיוּ v.2.m.p.impf.Q. [היה]

REVELATION 1:5–6

⁵καὶ ἀπὸ Ἰησοῦ Χριστοῦ, ὁ μάρτυς, ὁ πιστός, ὁ πρωτότοκος τῶν νεκρῶν καὶ ὁ ἄρχων τῶν βασιλέων τῆς γῆς. Τῷ ἀγαπῶντι ἡμᾶς καὶ λύσαντι ἡμᾶς ἐκ τῶν ἁμαρτιῶν ἡμῶν ἐν τῷ αἵματι αὐτοῦ, ⁶καὶ ἐποίησεν ἡμᾶς βασιλείαν, ἱερεῖς τῷ θεῷ καὶ πατρὶ αὐτοῦ, αὐτῷ ἡ δόξα καὶ τὸ κράτος εἰς τοὺς αἰῶνας [τῶν αἰώνων]· ἀμήν.

μάρτυς (witness); πρωτότοκος (firstborn); ἄρχων (ruler); λύσαντι (loose); ἱερεῖς (priest); κράτος (power)

3. Isaiah 61:5–7; 1 Peter 2:4–5

Come and Be Built

WHAT IS THE SECRET OF REACHING OTHERS for Christ? We ourselves must come to him. We must come and keep on coming with our sinfulness, our brokenness, our need. We must come and keep on coming until his transforming love builds us into people whose very presence makes others hungry for God.

ISAIAH 61:5–7

⁵וְעָמְדוּ זָרִים וְרָעוּ צֹאנְכֶם וּבְנֵי נֵכָר אִכָּרֵיכֶם וְכֹרְמֵיכֶם:
⁶וְאַתֶּם כֹּהֲנֵי יְהוָה תִּקָּרֵאוּ מְשָׁרְתֵי אֱלֹהֵינוּ יֵאָמֵר לָכֶם חֵיל
גּוֹיִם תֹּאכֵלוּ וּבִכְבוֹדָם תִּתְיַמָּרוּ:
⁷תַּחַת בָּשְׁתְּכֶם מִשְׁנֶה וּכְלִמָּה יָרֹנּוּ חֶלְקָם לָכֵן בְּאַרְצָם מִשְׁנֶה
יִירָשׁוּ שִׂמְחַת עוֹלָם תִּהְיֶה לָהֶם:

זָרִים (stranger); וְרָעוּ v.c. + v.3.c.p.pf.Q. [רעה]; נֵכָר (foreigner); אִכָּרֵיכֶם (farmer); וְכֹרְמֵיכֶם (vinedresser); תִּתְיַמָּרוּ v.2.m.p.impf.Ht.pause [ימר / אמר]; בָּשְׁתְּכֶם (shame); מִשְׁנֶה (double); וּכְלִמָּה (insult); יָרֹנּוּ v.3.m.p.impf.Q. [רנן]; יִירָשׁוּ v.3.m.p.impf.Q.pause [ירשׁ]

1 PETER 2:4–5

⁴πρὸς ὃν προσερχόμενοι λίθον ζῶντα ὑπὸ ἀνθρώπων μὲν ἀποδεδοκιμασμένον παρὰ δὲ θεῷ ἐκλεκτὸν ἔντιμον, ⁵καὶ αὐτοὶ ὡς λίθοι ζῶντες οἰκοδομεῖσθε οἶκος πνευματικὸς εἰς ἱεράτευμα ἅγιον ἀνενέγκαι πνευματικὰς θυσίας εὐπροσδέκτους [τῷ] θεῷ διὰ Ἰησοῦ Χριστοῦ.

ἀποδεδοκιμασμένον v.m.s.acc.pf.pass.ptc. [ἀποδοκιμάζω] (reject); ἐκλεκτὸν (chosen); ἔντιμον (precious); οἰκοδομεῖσθε (build); πνευματικὸς (spiritual); ἱεράτευμα (priesthood); ἀνενέγκαι v.aor.act.in. [ἀναφέρω]; θυσίας (sacrifice); εὐπροσδέκτους (acceptable)

4. Numbers 15:25–26; 1 John 2:1–2

Atonement in All Things

AT-ONE-MENT IS THE AIM OF THE PRIEST. For us, then, who are called by God to be priests for the whole world, every act, every word, every choice holds the potential of expressing God's redeeming love.

NUMBERS 15:25–26

²⁵וְכִפֶּר הַכֹּהֵן עַל־כָּל־עֲדַת בְּנֵי יִשְׂרָאֵל וְנִסְלַח לָהֶם כִּי־
שְׁגָגָה הִוא וְהֵם הֵבִיאוּ אֶת־קָרְבָּנָם אִשֶּׁה לַיהוָה וְחַטָּאתָם לִפְנֵי
יְהוָה עַל־שִׁגְגָתָם:
²⁶וְנִסְלַח לְכָל־עֲדַת בְּנֵי יִשְׂרָאֵל וְלַגֵּר הַגָּר בְּתוֹכָם כִּי
לְכָל־הָעָם בִּשְׁגָגָה:

וְנִסְלַח (forgive); שְׁגָגָה (sin of error); הֵבִיאוּ v.3.m.p.pf.H. [בוא]; הַגָּר d.a. +
v.m.s.ptc.Q. [גור]

1 JOHN 2:1–2

¹Τεκνία μου, ταῦτα γράφω ὑμῖν ἵνα μὴ ἁμάρτητε. καὶ ἐάν τις
ἁμάρτῃ, παράκλητον ἔχομεν πρὸς τὸν πατέρα Ἰησοῦν
Χριστὸν δίκαιον· ²καὶ αὐτὸς ἱλασμός ἐστιν περὶ τῶν ἁμαρτιῶν
ἡμῶν, οὐ περὶ τῶν ἡμετέρων δὲ μόνον ἀλλὰ καὶ περὶ ὅλου τοῦ
κόσμου.

Τεκνία (little child); ἁμάρτητε (sin); παράκλητον (intercessor); ἱλασμός (expiation, propitiation); ἐστιν v.3.s.pres.ind. [εἰμί]; ἡμετέρων (our)

177

5. Isaiah 66:18–19a; Matthew 25:44–45

Banquets of Mercy

PRIESTHOOD IS ABOUT MERCY. The mercy that we receive from God is like the young lad's bread and fish. It is meant to become a banquet table for the nourishment of countless other hungry souls. But we can only give away that which we have received. Our task behind the task, then, is to receive mercy, much-needed mercy, first for our own sin, then for the sin of others.

ISAIAH 66:18–19A

¹⁸וְאָנֹכִי מַעֲשֵׂיהֶם וּמַחְשְׁבֹתֵיהֶם בָּאָה לְקַבֵּץ אֶת־כָּל־הַגּוֹיִם
וְהַלְּשֹׁנוֹת וּבָאוּ וְרָאוּ אֶת־כְּבוֹדִי:
¹⁹וְשַׂמְתִּי בָהֶם אוֹת וְשִׁלַּחְתִּי מֵהֶם פְּלֵיטִים אֶל־הַגּוֹיִם

בָּאָה v.f.s.ptc.Q. [בוא]; וּבָאוּ v.c. + v.3.c.p.pf.Q. [בוא]; וְרָאוּ v.c. + v.3.c.p.pf.Q. [ראה]; וְשַׂמְתִּי v.c. + v.1.com.s.pf.Q. [שׂים]; פְּלֵיטִים (fugitive)

MATTHEW 25:44–45

⁴⁴τότε ἀποκριθήσονται καὶ αὐτοὶ λέγοντες, Κύριε, πότε σε εἴδομεν πεινῶντα ἢ διψῶντα ἢ ξένον ἢ γυμνὸν ἢ ἀσθενῆ ἢ ἐν φυλακῇ καὶ οὐ διηκονήσαμέν σοι; ⁴⁵τότε ἀποκριθήσεται αὐτοῖς λέγων, Ἀμὴν λέγω ὑμῖν, ἐφ᾽ ὅσον οὐκ ἐποιήσατε ἑνὶ τούτων τῶν ἐλαχίστων, οὐδὲ ἐμοὶ ἐποιήσατε.

τότε (how long); εἴδομεν v.1.p.aor.act.ind. [ὁράω]; πεινῶντα (hunger); διψῶντα (thirst); ξένον (stranger); γυμνὸν (naked); ἀσθενῆ (sick); φυλακῇ (prison); ἐφ᾽ ὅσον prep. + cor.pr.nt.s.acc. (in view of the fact); ἐλαχίστων (least)

0. Deuteronomy 10:12–13; Colossians 3:23–24

Love in All Labor

GRANT US WILLING HEARTS, O God, so that whether our labor for the day is to sweep the floor or to preach to thousands, we do it all for you, from love. Amen.

DEUTERONOMY 10:12–13

¹²וְעַתָּה יִשְׂרָאֵל מָה יְהוָה אֱלֹהֶיךָ שֹׁאֵל מֵעִמָּךְ כִּי אִם־לְיִרְאָה
אֶת־יְהוָה אֱלֹהֶיךָ לָלֶכֶת בְּכָל־דְּרָכָיו וּלְאַהֲבָה אֹתוֹ וְלַעֲבֹד
אֶת־יְהוָה אֱלֹהֶיךָ בְּכָל־לְבָבְךָ וּבְכָל־נַפְשֶׁךָ:
¹³לִשְׁמֹר אֶת־מִצְוֹת יְהוָה וְאֶת־חֻקֹּתָיו אֲשֶׁר אָנֹכִי מְצַוְּךָ הַיּוֹם
לְטוֹב לָךְ:

לָלֶכֶת prep. + v.in.cs.Q. [הלך]; מְצַוְּךָ v.m.s.act.ptc.P. [צוה] + 2.m.s.pr.sf.

COLOSSIANS 3:23–24

²³ὃ ἐὰν ποιῆτε, ἐκ ψυχῆς ἐργάζεσθε ὡς τῷ κυρίῳ καὶ οὐκ ἀνθρώποις, ²⁴εἰδότες ὅτι ἀπὸ κυρίου ἀπολήμψεσθε τὴν ἀνταπόδοσιν τῆς κληρονομίας. τῷ κυρίῳ Χριστῷ δουλεύετε·

ἐργάζεσθε (work); εἰδότες v.m.p.nom.pf.act.ptc. [οἶδα]; ἀπολήμψεσθε v.2.p.fut.mid.ind. [ἀπολαμβάνω] (receive); ἀνταπόδοσιν (reward); κληρονομίας (inheritance); δουλεύετε (serve)

7. 1 Samuel 12:24; Romans 12:1

Sacrificial Joy

IT IS NOT SO MUCH THE "WHAT" as it is the "why" and the "how" that matter in sacrificial living. For the heart that is deeply in love, all sacrifice for the beloved is sheer joy.

1 SAMUEL 12:24

²⁴אַ֣ךְ ׀ יְר֣אוּ אֶת־יְהוָ֗ה וַעֲבַדְתֶּ֥ם אֹת֛וֹ בֶּאֱמֶ֖ת בְּכָל־לְבַבְכֶ֑ם כִּ֣י רְא֔וּ אֵ֥ת אֲשֶׁר־הִגְדִּ֖ל עִמָּכֶֽם׃

[ראה] ‎יְראוּ v.2.m.p.impv.Q. [‎ירא]; יְראוּ v.2.m.p.impv.Q.

ROMANS 12:1

¹Παρακαλῶ οὖν ὑμᾶς, ἀδελφοί, διὰ τῶν οἰκτιρμῶν τοῦ θεοῦ παραστῆσαι τὰ σώματα ὑμῶν θυσίαν ζῶσαν ἁγίαν εὐάρεστον τῷ θεῷ, τὴν λογικὴν λατρείαν ὑμῶν·

οἰκτιρμῶν (mercy); παραστῆσαι v.aor.act.in. [παρίστημι] (offering); θυσίαν (sacrifice); εὐάρεστον (acceptable); λογικὴν (spiritual, rational); λατρείαν (service, worship)

Sabbath

1. Genesis 2:1–9; Mark 2:27–28

A Celebration of Being

THE CAPSTONE OF CREATION was God speaking into existence a holy rest, a celebration of *being*. We have tried to make the Sabbath into drudgery ever since.

GENESIS 2:1–3

¹וַיְכֻלּ֛וּ הַשָּׁמַ֥יִם וְהָאָ֖רֶץ וְכָל־צְבָאָֽם׃
²וַיְכַ֤ל אֱלֹהִים֙ בַּיּ֣וֹם הַשְּׁבִיעִ֔י מְלַאכְתּ֖וֹ אֲשֶׁ֣ר עָשָׂ֑ה וַיִּשְׁבֹּת֙
בַּיּ֣וֹם הַשְּׁבִיעִ֔י מִכָּל־מְלַאכְתּ֖וֹ אֲשֶׁ֥ר עָשָֽׂה׃
³וַיְבָ֤רֶךְ אֱלֹהִים֙ אֶת־י֣וֹם הַשְּׁבִיעִ֔י וַיְקַדֵּ֖שׁ אֹת֑וֹ כִּ֣י ב֤וֹ שָׁבַת֙
מִכָּל־מְלַאכְתּ֔וֹ אֲשֶׁר־בָּרָ֥א אֱלֹהִ֖ים לַעֲשֽׂוֹת׃

וַיְכֻלּוּ v.c. + v.3.m.p.impf.Pu. [כלה]; וַיְכַל v.c. + v.3.m.s.impf.P. [כלה]; לַעֲשׂוֹת prep. + v.in.cs.Q. [עשׂה]

MARK 2:27–28

²⁷καὶ ἔλεγεν αὐτοῖς, Τὸ σάββατον διὰ τὸν ἄνθρωπον ἐγένετο καὶ οὐχ ὁ ἄνθρωπος διὰ τὸ σάββατον· ²⁸ὥστε κύριος ἐστιν ὁ υἱὸς τοῦ ἀνθρώπου καὶ τοῦ σαββάτου.

ἐγένετο v.3.s.aor.mid.ind. [γίνομαι]; ἐστιν v.3.s.pres.ind. [εἰμί]

2. Exodus 31:13–14, 16; Luke 13:14–16

Day of Healing, Day of Joy

MAYBE, JUST MAYBE, we have it all wrong about the Sabbath. What if instead of it being a day of limitation and forced piety it is really to be a day of healing and liberation and joy?

EXODUS 31:13–14, 16

¹³וְאַתָּה דַּבֵּר אֶל־בְּנֵי יִשְׂרָאֵל לֵאמֹר אַךְ אֶת־שַׁבְּתֹתַי תִּשְׁמֹרוּ
כִּי אוֹת הִוא בֵּינִי וּבֵינֵיכֶם לְדֹרֹתֵיכֶם לָדַעַת כִּי אֲנִי יְהוָה מְקַדִּשְׁכֶם:
¹⁴וּשְׁמַרְתֶּם אֶת־הַשַּׁבָּת כִּי קֹדֶשׁ הִוא לָכֶם מְחַלְלֶיהָ מוֹת יוּמָת
כִּי כָּל־הָעֹשֶׂה בָהּ מְלָאכָה וְנִכְרְתָה הַנֶּפֶשׁ הַהִוא מִקֶּרֶב עַמֶּיהָ:
¹⁶וְשָׁמְרוּ בְנֵי־יִשְׂרָאֵל אֶת־הַשַּׁבָּת לַעֲשׂוֹת אֶת־הַשַּׁבָּת
לְדֹרֹתָם בְּרִית עוֹלָם:

שַׁבְּתֹתַי n.m./f.p. + 1.com.s.pr.sf.; לָדַעַת prep. + v.in.cs.Q. [ידע]; יוּמָת v.3.m.s.impf.Ho. [מות]; לַעֲשׂוֹת prep. + v.in.cs.Q. [עשה]; יוּמָת v.3.m.s.impf.Ho. [מות]

LUKE 13:14–16

¹⁴ἀποκριθεὶς δὲ ὁ ἀρχισυνάγωγος, ἀγανακτῶν ὅτι τῷ σαββάτῳ ἐθεράπευσεν ὁ Ἰησοῦς, ἔλεγεν τῷ ὄχλῳ ὅτι Ἓξ ἡμέραι εἰσὶν ἐν αἷς δεῖ ἐργάζεσθαι· ἐν αὐταῖς οὖν ἐρχόμενοι θεραπεύεσθε καὶ μὴ τῇ ἡμέρᾳ τοῦ σαββάτου. ¹⁵ἀπεκρίθη δὲ αὐτῷ ὁ κύριος καὶ εἶπεν, Ὑποκριταί, ἕκαστος ὑμῶν τῷ σαββάτῳ οὐ λύει τὸν βοῦν αὐτοῦ ἢ τὸν ὄνον ἀπὸ τῆς φάτνης καὶ ἀπαγαγὼν ποτίζει; ¹⁶ταύτην δὲ θυγατέρα Ἀβραὰμ οὖσαν, ἣν ἔδησεν ὁ Σατανᾶς ἰδοὺ δέκα καὶ ὀκτὼ ἔτη, οὐκ ἔδει λυθῆναι ἀπὸ τοῦ δεσμοῦ τούτου τῇ ἡμέρᾳ τοῦ σαββάτου;

ἀρχισυνάγωγος (synagogue leader); ἀγανακτῶν (be angry); ἐθεράπευσεν (heal); Ἓξ (six); ἐργάζεσθαι (work); εἶπεν v.3.s.aor.act.ind. [λέγω]; Ὑποκριταί (hyprocrite); λύει (loose); βοῦν (ox); ὄνον (donkey); φάτνης (manger); ἀπαγαγὼν (bring to); ποτίζει (water); θυγατέρα (daughter); ἔδησεν (bind); Σατανᾶς (Satan); ὀκτὼ (eight); δεσμοῦ (bond)

3. Exodus 31:15, 17; Hebrews 4:1–3

Sabbath Love

YOU ARE MY REST, JESUS. You are the open arms that welcome me, the voice that bids me cease from endless and restless toil. You are my Sabbath, now and forever. Amen.

EXODUS 31:15, 17

¹⁵שֵׁשֶׁת יָמִים יֵעָשֶׂה מְלָאכָה וּבַיּוֹם הַשְּׁבִיעִי שַׁבַּת שַׁבָּתוֹן
קֹדֶשׁ לַיהוָה כָּל־הָעֹשֶׂה מְלָאכָה בְּיוֹם הַשַּׁבָּת מוֹת יוּמָת:
¹⁷בֵּינִי וּבֵין בְּנֵי יִשְׂרָאֵל אוֹת הִוא לְעֹלָם כִּי־שֵׁשֶׁת יָמִים עָשָׂה
יְהוָה אֶת־הַשָּׁמַיִם וְאֶת־הָאָרֶץ וּבַיּוֹם הַשְּׁבִיעִי שָׁבַת וַיִּנָּפַשׁ:

יֵעָשֶׂה v.3.m.s.impf.N. [עשׂה]; יוּמָת v.3.m.s.impf.Ho. [מות]; וַיִּנָּפַשׁ (be refreshed)

HEBREWS 4:1–3

¹φοβηθῶμεν οὖν, μήποτε καταλειπομένης ἐπαγγελίας εἰσελθεῖν εἰς τὴν κατάπαυσιν αὐτοῦ δοκῇ τις ἐξ ὑμῶν ὑστερηκέναι. ²καὶ γὰρ ἐσμεν εὐηγγελισμένοι καθάπερ κἀκεῖνοι· ἀλλ᾽ οὐκ ὠφέλησεν ὁ λόγος τῆς ἀκοῆς ἐκείνους μὴ συγκεκερασμένους τῇ πίστει τοῖς ἀκούσασιν. ³εἰσερχόμεθα γὰρ εἰς [τὴν] κατάπαυσιν οἱ πιστεύσαντες, καθὼς εἴρηκεν,

Ὡς ὤμοσα ἐν τῇ ὀργῇ μου,
Εἰ εἰσελεύσονται εἰς τὴν κατάπαυσίν μου,
Καίτοι τῶν ἔργων ἀπὸ καταβολῆς κόσμου γενηθέντων.

μήποτε (lest); καταλειπομένης (leave behind); εἰσελθεῖν v.aor.act.in. [εἰσέρχομαι]; κατάπαυσιν (rest); ὑστερηκέναι v.pf.act.ind. [ὑστερέω] (lack); καθάπερ (just as); κἀκεῖνοι (even those); ὠφέλησεν (help); ἀκοῆς (preaching); συγκεκερασμένους v.m.p.acc.pf.pass.ptc. [συγκεράννυμι] (mix together); ὤμοσα v.1.s.aor.act.ind. [ὀμνύω] (swear); ὀργῇ (anger); εἰσελεύσονται v.1.s.fut.mid.ind. [εἰσέρχομαι] (enter); καίτοι (although); καταβολῆς (foundation); γενηθέντων v.nt.p.gen.aor.pass.ptc. [γίνομαι]

4. Psalm 92:2–4 [1–3]; Revelation 4:8–11

Sabbath Music

WITH MUCH GLAD MUSIC, memories of past goodness, and joyful expectation of your future faithfulness, I will join the saints and angels in happy Sabbath praise. For you deserve it, my God, you are worthy of it all.

PSALM 92:2–4 [1–3]

²טוֹב לְהֹדוֹת לַיהוָה וּלְזַמֵּר לְשִׁמְךָ עֶלְיוֹן:
³לְהַגִּיד בַּבֹּקֶר חַסְדֶּךָ וֶאֱמוּנָתְךָ בַּלֵּילוֹת:
⁴עֲלֵי־עָשׂוֹר וַעֲלֵי־נָבֶל עֲלֵי הִגָּיוֹן בְּכִנּוֹר:

לְהֹדוֹת prep. + v.in.cs.H. [ידה]; וּלְזַמֵּר (sing); לְהַגִּיד prep. + v.in.cs.H. [נגד]; וֶאֱמוּנָתְךָ (faithfulness); עֲלֵי prep.; עָשׂוֹר (ten); נָבֶל (harp); הִגָּיוֹן (melody); בְּכִנּוֹר (harp)

REVELATION 4:8–11

⁸καὶ τὰ τέσσαρα ζῷα, ἓν καθ᾽ ἓν αὐτῶν ἔχων ἀνὰ πτέρυγας ἕξ, κυκλόθεν καὶ ἔσωθεν γέμουσιν ὀφθαλμῶν, καὶ ἀνάπαυσιν οὐκ ἔχουσιν ἡμέρας καὶ νυκτὸς λέγοντες,
  Ἅγιος ἅγιος ἅγιος
  κύριος ὁ θεὸς ὁ παντοκράτωρ,
    ὁ ἦν καὶ ὁ ὢν καὶ ὁ ἐρχόμενος.
⁹καὶ ὅταν δώσουσιν τὰ ζῷα δόξαν καὶ τιμὴν καὶ εὐχαριστίαν τῷ καθημένῳ ἐπὶ τῷ θρόνῳ τῷ ζῶντι εἰς τοὺς αἰῶνας τῶν αἰώνων, ¹⁰πεσοῦνται οἱ εἴκοσι τέσσαρες πρεσβύτεροι ἐνώπιον τοῦ καθημένου ἐπὶ τοῦ θρόνου καὶ προσκυνήσουσιν τῷ ζῶντι εἰς τοὺς αἰῶνας τῶν αἰώνων καὶ βαλοῦσιν τοὺς στεφάνους αὐτῶν ἐνώπιον τοῦ θρόνου λέγοντες,
  ¹¹Ἄξιος εἶ, ὁ κύριος καὶ ὁ θεὸς ἡμῶν,
    λαβεῖν τὴν δόξαν καὶ τὴν τιμὴν καὶ τὴν δύναμιν,
    ὅτι σὺ ἔκτισας τὰ πάντα
    καὶ διὰ τὸ θέλημά σου ἦσαν καὶ ἐκτίσθησαν.

τέσσαρα (four); ἓν καθ᾽ ἕν (each one); ἀνὰ (each); πτέρυγας (wing); κυκλόθεν (all around); ἔσωθεν (within); ἀνάπαυσιν (rest); παντοκράτωρ (Almighty); τιμὴν (honor); εὐχαριστίαν (thanksgiving); ζῶντι (living creature); πεσοῦνται v.3.p.fut.mid.ind. [πίπτω]; ἐνώπιον (before); στεφάνους (crown); ἔκτισας (create)

5. Isaiah 58:13–14; Luke 12:29–31

Sabbath Arms

How WEARY I AM, JESUS. Deliver me from the anxious preoc-
cupations and fearful self-sufficiency that blind me to you. Pick
me up in tender arms. Carry your little child in arms of Sabbath rest.

ISAIAH 58:13–14

¹³אִם־תָּשִׁיב מִשַּׁבָּת רַגְלֶךָ עֲשׂוֹת חֲפָצֶיךָ בְּיוֹם קָדְשִׁי וְקָרָאתָ
לַשַּׁבָּת עֹנֶג לִקְדוֹשׁ יְהוָה מְכֻבָּד וְכִבַּדְתּוֹ מֵעֲשׂוֹת דְּרָכֶיךָ
מִמְּצוֹא חֶפְצְךָ וְדַבֵּר דָּבָר:
¹⁴אָז תִּתְעַנַּג עַל־יְהוָה וְהִרְכַּבְתִּיךָ עַל־בָּמֳתֵי אָרֶץ וְהַאֲכַלְתִּיךָ
נַחֲלַת יַעֲקֹב אָבִיךָ כִּי פִּי יְהוָה דִּבֵּר:

תָּשִׁיב v.2.m.s.impf.H. [שׁוב]; עֲשׂוֹת v.in.cs.Q. [עשׂה]; חֲפָצֶיךָ (delight); עֹנֶג
(delight); וְכִבַּדְתּוֹ cj. + v.2.m.s.pf.P. [כבד] + 3.m.s.pr.sf.; מֵעֲשׂוֹת prep. +
v.in.cs.Q. [עשׂה]; מִמְּצוֹא prep. + v.in.cs.Q. [מצא]; תִּתְעַנַּג v.2.m.s.impf.Ht. [ענג]
(delight); וְהִרְכַּבְתִּיךָ v.c. + v.1.com.s.pf.H. [רכב] + 2.m.s.pr.sf.; וְהַאֲכַלְתִּיךָ v.c.
+ v.1.com.s.pf.H. [אכל] + 2.m.s.pr.sf.

LUKE 12:29–31

²⁹καὶ ὑμεῖς μὴ ζητεῖτε τί φάγητε καὶ τί πίητε καὶ μὴ
μετεωρίζεσθε· ³⁰ταῦτα γὰρ πάντα τὰ ἔθνη τοῦ κόσμου
ἐπιζητοῦσιν, ὑμῶν δὲ ὁ πατὴρ οἶδεν ὅτι χρῄζετε τούτων. ³¹πλὴν
ζητεῖτε τὴν βασιλείαν αὐτοῦ, καὶ ταῦτα προστεθήσεται ὑμῖν.

μετεωρίζεσθε (worry); ἐπιζητοῦσιν (seek); οἶδεν v.3.s.pf.act.ind. [οἶδα];
χρῄζετε (needy); προστεθήσεται v.3.s.fut.pass.ind. [προστίθημι] (add to)

6. 1 Kings 8:56–57; Hebrews 4:9–10

The Certainty of It All

YOUR REST IS AS CERTAIN as the tree outside my window or my cat who purrs gently in my lap even now. For it was by your word that these things were created, and the same word called forth Sabbath rest. And nothing in creation is more certain or more reliable than your word.

1 KINGS 8:56–57

⁵⁶בָּרוּךְ יְהוָה אֲשֶׁר נָתַן מְנוּחָה לְעַמּוֹ יִשְׂרָאֵל כְּכֹל אֲשֶׁר דִּבֵּר
לֹא־נָפַל דָּבָר אֶחָד מִכֹּל דְּבָרוֹ הַטּוֹב אֲשֶׁר דִּבֶּר בְּיַד מֹשֶׁה
עַבְדּוֹ:
⁵⁷יְהִי יְהוָה אֱלֹהֵינוּ עִמָּנוּ כַּאֲשֶׁר הָיָה עִם־אֲבֹתֵינוּ אַל־יַעַזְבֵנוּ
וְאַל־יִטְּשֵׁנוּ:

+ [עזב] .v.3.m.s.jus.Q יַעַזְבֵנוּ ;[היה] .v.3.m.s.jus.Q יְהִי ;(rest) מְנוּחָה
1.com.p.pr.sf.; יִטְּשֵׁנוּ v.3.m.s.jus.Q. [נטשׁ] (abandon) + 1.com.p.pr.sf.

HEBREWS 4:9–10

⁹ἄρα ἀπολείπεται σαββατισμὸς τῷ λαῷ τοῦ θεοῦ. ¹⁰ὁ γὰρ
εἰσελθὼν εἰς τὴν κατάπαυσιν αὐτοῦ καὶ αὐτὸς κατέπαυσεν
ἀπὸ τῶν ἔργων αὐτοῦ ὥσπερ ἀπὸ τῶν ἰδίων ὁ θεός.

ἄρα (then); ἀπολείπεται (remain); σαββατισμὸς (Sabbath rest);
εἰσελθὼν v.m.s.nom.aor.act.ptc. [εἰσέρχομαι]; κατάπαυσιν (give rest);
κατέπαυσεν (rest); ὥσπερ (as)

7. Isaiah 30:15–16; 2 Thessalonians 3:11–13

Returning and Rest

RETURNING AND REST . . . quietness and strength . . . such healing words for care-worn servants, those of us who forgot somehow that it is your will and your strength, Lord, that bring about all good.

ISAIAH 30:15–16

¹⁵כִּי כֹה־אָמַר אֲדֹנָי יְהוִה קְדוֹשׁ יִשְׂרָאֵל בְּשׁוּבָה וָנַחַת תִּוָּשֵׁעוּן
בְּהַשְׁקֵט וּבְבִטְחָה תִּהְיֶה גְּבוּרַתְכֶם וְלֹא אֲבִיתֶם:
¹⁶וַתֹּאמְרוּ לֹא־כִי עַל־סוּס נָנוּס עַל־כֵּן תְּנוּסוּן וְעַל־קַל נִרְכָּב
עַל־כֵּן יֵקַלּוּ רֹדְפֵיכֶם:

בְּשׁוּבָה (repentance); וָנַחַת (rest); תִּוָּשֵׁעוּן v.2.m.p.impf.N. [ישׁע] + para.;
בְּהַשְׁקֵט prep. + v.in.cs.H. [שׁקט] (be quiet); אֲבִיתֶם v.2.m.p.pf.Q. [אבה]; תְּנוּסוּן
v.2.m.p.impf.N. [נוס] + para.; יֵקַלּוּ v.3.m.p.impf.N. [קלל]

2 THESSALONIANS 3:11–13

¹¹ἀκούομεν γὰρ τινας περιπατοῦντας ἐν ὑμῖν ἀτάκτως μηδὲν
ἐργαζομένους ἀλλὰ περιεργαζομένους· ¹²τοῖς δὲ τοιούτοις
παραγγέλλομεν καὶ παρακαλοῦμεν ἐν κυρίῳ Ἰησοῦ Χριστῷ,
ἵνα μετὰ ἡσυχίας ἐργαζόμενοι τὸν ἑαυτῶν ἄρτον ἐσθίωσιν.
¹³ Ὑμεῖς δέ, ἀδελφοί, μὴ ἐγκακήσητε καλοποιοῦντες.

ἀτάκτως (in idleness); περιεργαζομένους (be a busybody); παραγγέλλομεν (command); ἡσυχίας (quiet); ἐργαζόμενοι (work); ἐγκακήσητε
v.2.p.aor.act.sub. [ἐγκακέω] (become weary); καλοποιοῦντες (do good)

Week 26

Fear

1. Deuteronomy 10:20; Acts 9:31

Love That Fears

THE FEAR OF THE LORD felt by the saint is not a sick, cringing fear of punishment. It is, rather, the kind of confidence a young child has in her father. She is convinced that his power is much greater than anything that might harm her, and equally convinced that he will use his strength on her behalf. Thus she loves him deeply, "fears" him the most, and all the while rests in his care.

DEUTERONOMY 10:20

²⁰אֶת־יְהוָה אֱלֹהֶיךָ תִּירָא אֹתוֹ תַעֲבֹד וּבוֹ תִדְבָּק וּבִשְׁמוֹ תִּשָּׁבֵעַ׃

ACTS 9:31

³¹Ἡ μὲν οὖν ἐκκλησία καθ᾽ ὅλης τῆς Ἰουδαίας καὶ Γαλιλαίας καὶ Σαμαρείας εἶχεν εἰρήνην οἰκοδομουμένη καὶ πορευομένη τῷ φόβῳ τοῦ κυρίου καὶ τῇ παρακλήσει τοῦ ἁγίου πνεύματος ἐπληθύνετο.

Ἡ μὲν οὖν d.a.f.s.nom. + pt. + cj. (then in fact); οἰκοδομουμένη (build); φόβῳ (fear); παρακλήσει (comfort); ἐπληθύνετο (increase)

2. Psalm 27:1; Romans 8:38–39

Not Even Family Life
Will Separate You . . .

It's odd, Jesus, how I believe your love will sustain me through all sorts of terrible catastrophes (and indeed it has), yet I fight almost daily to believe your love is enough to preserve me in the mundane struggles of family life. Lord, help my unbelief.

Psalm 27:1

¹לְדָוִד יְהוָה אוֹרִי וְיִשְׁעִי מִמִּי אִירָא יְהוָה מָעוֹז־חַיַּי מִמִּי אֶפְחָד׃

וְיִשְׁעִי (help); אִירָא v.1.com.s.impf.Q. [ירא]; מָעוֹז (strength); אֶפְחָד (fear)

Romans 8:38–39

³⁸πέπεισμαι γὰρ ὅτι οὔτε θάνατος οὔτε ζωὴ οὔτε ἄγγελοι οὔτε ἀρχαὶ οὔτε ἐνεστῶτα οὔτε μέλλοντα οὔτε δυνάμεις ³⁹οὔτε ὕψωμα οὔτε βάθος οὔτε τις κτίσις ἑτέρα δυνήσεται ἡμᾶς χωρίσαι ἀπὸ τῆς ἀγάπης τοῦ θεοῦ τῆς ἐν Χριστῷ Ἰησοῦ τῷ κυρίῳ ἡμῶν.

πέπεισμαι v.1.s.pf.pass.ind. [πείθω] (persuade); ἐνεστῶτα v.nt.p.nom.pf.act.ptc. [ἐνίστημι]; ὕψωμα (height); βάθος (depth); κτίσις (creature); χωρίσαι (separate)

3. Psalm 73:26; Philippians 2:13

What Makes for Wisdom

THE BIBLE SAYS THE FEAR OF THE LORD is the beginning of wisdom. It seems to me a fear of my own propensity for foolishness comes next, for only God can give me the capacity both to want and to do his will.

PSALM 73:26

²⁶כָּלָה שְׁאֵרִי וּלְבָבִי צוּר־לְבָבִי וְחֶלְקִי אֱלֹהִים לְעוֹלָם׃

שְׁאֵרִי (flesh)

PHILIPPIANS 2:13

¹³θεὸς γάρ ἐστιν ὁ ἐνεργῶν ἐν ὑμῖν καὶ τὸ θέλειν καὶ τὸ ἐνεργεῖν ὑπὲρ τῆς εὐδοκίας.

ἐστιν v.3.s.pres.ind. [εἰμί]; ἐνεργῶν (be at work); εὐδοκίας (favor)

1. Psalm 73.21-23, Hebrews 2.14-15

Not a Spirit of Fear

COME, SPIRIT OF THE LIVING GOD! Come into my dark and trembling fear. Let your fierce and tender love restore my soul to its rightful place of rest in you.

PSALM 73:21–23

²¹כִּי יִתְחַמֵּץ לְבָבִי וְכִלְיוֹתַי אֶשְׁתּוֹנָן:

²²וַאֲנִי־בַעַר וְלֹא אֵדָע בְּהֵמוֹת הָיִיתִי עִמָּךְ:

²³וַאֲנִי תָמִיד עִמָּךְ אָחַזְתָּ בְּיַד־יְמִינִי:

יִתְחַמֵּץ (be bitter); וְכִלְיוֹתַי (kidney); אֶשְׁתּוֹנָן v.1.com.s.impf.Htpl. with metathesis [שׁנן] (sharpen); בַעַר (brute); אֵדָע v.1.com.s.impf.Q. [ידע]; הָיִיתִי v.1.com.s.pf.Q. [היה]

HEBREWS 2:14–15

¹⁴ἐπεὶ οὖν τὰ παιδία κεκοινώνηκεν αἵματος καὶ σαρκός, καὶ αὐτὸς παραπλησίως μετέσχεν τῶν αὐτῶν, ἵνα διὰ τοῦ θανάτου καταργήσῃ τὸν τὸ κράτος ἔχοντα τοῦ θανάτου, τοῦτ᾽ ἔστιν τὸν διάβολον, ¹⁵καὶ ἀπαλλάξῃ τούτους, ὅσοι φόβῳ θανάτου διὰ παντὸς τοῦ ζῆν ἔνοχοι ἦσαν δουλείας.

ἐπεὶ (because); κεκοινώνηκεν v.3.s.pf.act.ind. [κοινωνέω] (share); παραπλησίως (likewise); μετέσχεν (share); καταργήσῃ (destroy); κράτος (power); ἔστιν v.3.s.pres.ind. [εἰμί]; διάβολον (devil); ἀπαλλάξῃ (deliver); φόβῳ (fear); ἔνοχοι (subjected to); ἦσαν v.3.p.impf.ind. [εἰμί]; δουλείας (bondage)

5. Psalm 57:2–3 [1–2]; John 16:33

Good Cheer? Ridiculous!

NO GREATER MIRACLE has ever come to pass than that I should
be of good cheer in the midst of a destructive storm.

PSALM 57:2–3 [1–2]

¹לַמְנַצֵּחַ אַל־תַּשְׁחֵת לְדָוִד מִכְתָּם בְּבָרְחוֹ מִפְּנֵי־שָׁאוּל
בַּמְּעָרָה:
²חָנֵּנִי אֱלֹהִים חָנֵּנִי כִּי בְךָ חָסָיָה נַפְשִׁי וּבְצֵל־כְּנָפֶיךָ אֶחְסֶה
עַד יַעֲבֹר הַוּוֹת:
³אֶקְרָא לֵאלֹהִים עֶלְיוֹן לָאֵל גֹּמֵר עָלָי:

חָנֵּנִי v.2.m.s.impv.Q. [חנן] + 1.com.s.pr.sf.; חָסָיָה v.3.f.s.pf.Q. [חסה] (seek);
הַוּוֹת n.f.p. (destruction); גֹּמֵר (complete)

JOHN 16:33

³³ταῦτα λελάληκα ὑμῖν ἵνα ἐν ἐμοὶ εἰρήνην ἔχητε· ἐν τῷ
κόσμῳ θλῖψιν ἔχετε· ἀλλὰ θαρσεῖτε, ἐγὼ νενίκηκα τὸν
κόσμον.

θλῖψιν (affliction); θαρσεῖτε (buck up); νενίκηκα (conquer)

6. Psalm 94:18–19; 2 Corinthians 4:7

Stainless Steel Saints

FOR A HARDCORE PERFECTIONIST these are not easy words, Lord. I'd much rather be a stainless steel bowl than a fragile clay jar. But you are wise. The more I see my limitations, the more I understand grace. And the more I love my Lord. That, after all, is what the spiritual life is all about.

PSALM 94:18–19

18 אִם־אָמַרְתִּי מָטָה רַגְלִי חַסְדְּךָ יְהוָה יִסְעָדֵנִי׃
19בְּרֹב שַׂרְעַפַּי בְּקִרְבִּי תַּנְחוּמֶיךָ יְשַׁעַשְׁעוּ נַפְשִׁי׃

מָטָה (totter); יִסְעָדֵנִי v.3.m.s.impf.Q. [סעד] (sustain) + 1.com.s.pr.sf.; שַׂרְעַפַּי (doubt); תַּנְחוּמֶיךָ (consolation); יְשַׁעַשְׁעוּ v.3.m.p.impf.Plpl. [שׁעע] (delight)

2 CORINTHIANS 4:7

7Ἔχομεν δὲ τὸν θησαυρὸν τοῦτον ἐν ὀστρακίνοις σκεύεσιν, ἵνα ἡ ὑπερβολὴ τῆς δυνάμεως ᾖ τοῦ θεοῦ καὶ μὴ ἐξ ἡμῶν·

θησαυρὸν (treasure); ὀστρακίνοις (clay); σκεύεσιν (vessel); ὑπερβολὴ (extraordinary)

7. Psalm 116:3–4; 1 Corinthians 15:56–57

The Final Victory

UNDERGIRD US, O GOD, as we face the final battleground of death. Even there let us know the truth, that perfect love casts out fear.

PSALM 116:3–4

³אֲפָפוּנִי חֶבְלֵי־מָוֶת וּמְצָרֵי שְׁאוֹל מְצָאוּנִי צָרָה וְיָגוֹן אֶמְצָא:
⁴וּבְשֵׁם־יְהוָה אֶקְרָא אָנָּה יְהוָה מַלְּטָה נַפְשִׁי:

אֲפָפוּנִי v.3.m.p.pf.Q. [אפף] (surround) + 1.com.s.pr.sf.; וּמְצָרֵי (strait); וְיָגוֹן (grief); אָנָּה (where)

1 CORINTHIANS 15:56–57

⁵⁶τὸ δὲ κέντρον τοῦ θανάτου ἡ ἁμαρτία, ἡ δὲ δύναμις τῆς ἁμαρτίας ὁ νόμος· ⁵⁷τῷ δὲ θεῷ χάρις τῷ διδόντι ἡμῖν τὸ νῖκος διὰ τοῦ κυρίου ἡμῶν Ἰησοῦ Χριστοῦ.

κέντρον (sting); νῖκος (victory)

Love

1. Zephaniah 3:17; 1 John 3:1–2

Being Your Beloved

TO BE YOUR BELOVED, MY GOD, is the thing I long for the most. Could there be anything at all more wonderful, or necessary, or true? And yet how often I struggle to believe it. The more I know and believe I am your beloved, the more I am healed of all my fears.

ZEPHANIAH 3:17

יְהוָה אֱלֹהַיִךְ בְּקִרְבֵּךְ גִּבּוֹר יוֹשִׁיעַ יָשִׂישׂ עָלַיִךְ בְּשִׂמְחָה¹⁷
יַחֲרִישׁ בְּאַהֲבָתוֹ יָגִיל עָלַיִךְ בְּרִנָּה׃

יוֹשִׁיעַ v.3.m.s.impf.H. [יָשַׁע]; יָשִׂישׂ (rejoice); יַחֲרִישׁ (be silent); יָגִיל (exult); בְּרִנָּה (cry of joy)

1 JOHN 3:1–2

¹Ἴδετε ποταπὴν ἀγάπην δέδωκεν ἡμῖν ὁ πατὴρ, ἵνα τέκνα θεοῦ κληθῶμεν, καὶ ἐσμέν. διὰ τοῦτο ὁ κόσμος οὐ γινώσκει ἡμᾶς, ὅτι οὐκ ἔγνω αὐτόν. ²Ἀγαπητοί, νῦν τέκνα θεοῦ ἐσμεν, καὶ οὔπω ἐφανερώθη τί ἐσόμεθα. οἴδαμεν ὅτι ἐὰν φανερωθῇ, ὅμοιοι αὐτῷ ἐσόμεθα, ὅτι ὀψόμεθα αὐτὸν καθώς ἐστιν.

ἴδετε v.2.p.aor.act.impv. [ὁράω]; ποταπὴν (what kind); τέκνα (little child); νῦν (now); οὔπω (not yet); ἐσόμεθα v.1.p.fut.act.ind. [εἰμί]; ὅμοιοι (similar); ὀψόμεθα v.1.p.fut.mid.ind. [ὁράω]; ἐστιν v.3.s.pres.ind. [εἰμί]

2. Psalm 103:1–2; Mark 12:30–31

Love in Two Directions

GENUINE LOVE FOR GOD cannot help but fill our mouths with praise and gratitude toward God, and our hands and hearts with blessing—for others.

PSALM 103:1–2

¹לְדָוִד בָּרֲכִי נַפְשִׁי אֶת־יְהוָה וְכָל־קְרָבַי אֶת־שֵׁם קָדְשׁוֹ׃
²בָּרֲכִי נַפְשִׁי אֶת־יְהוָה וְאַל־תִּשְׁכְּחִי כָּל־גְּמוּלָיו׃

גְּמוּלָיו (benefit)

MARK 12:30–31

³⁰καὶ ἀγαπήσεις κύριον τὸν θεόν σου ἐξ ὅλης τῆς καρδίας σου καὶ ἐξ ὅλης τῆς ψυχῆς σου καὶ ἐξ ὅλης τῆς διανοίας σου καὶ ἐξ ὅλης τῆς ἰσχύος σου. ³¹δευτέρα αὕτη, ἀγαπήσεις τὸν πλησίον σου ὡς σεαυτόν. μείζων τούτων ἄλλη ἐντολὴ οὐκ ἔστιν.

διανοίας (mind); ἰσχύος (strength); δευτέρα (second); πλησίον (neighbor); μείζων (greater); ἔστιν v.3.s.pres.ind. [εἰμί]

3. Genesis 2.23–24, 1 Peter 1:22

A Mighty Hint of the Divine

Faulty as it is, there is no greater proof of God's existence or of his goodness, than healthy, mutual love between a woman and a man. Fragile as human love can sometimes be, there is nothing stronger in all the world, save the love of God.

Genesis 2:23–24

²³וַיֹּאמֶר הָאָדָם זֹאת הַפַּעַם עֶצֶם מֵעֲצָמַי וּבָשָׂר מִבְּשָׂרִי לְזֹאת יִקָּרֵא אִשָּׁה כִּי מֵאִישׁ לֻקֳחָה־זֹּאת:
²⁴עַל־כֵּן יַעֲזָב־אִישׁ אֶת־אָבִיו וְאֶת־אִמּוֹ וְדָבַק בְּאִשְׁתּוֹ וְהָיוּ לְבָשָׂר אֶחָד:

לֻקֳחָה v.3.f.s.pf.Pu. [לקח]; וְהָיוּ v.c. + v.3.c.p.pf.Q. [היה]

1 Peter 1:22

²²Τὰς ψυχὰς ὑμῶν ἡγνικότες ἐν τῇ ὑπακοῇ τῆς ἀληθείας εἰς φιλαδελφίαν ἀνυπόκριτον, ἐκ [καθαρᾶς] καρδίας ἀλλήλους ἀγαπήσατε ἐκτενῶς

ἡγνικότες v.m.p.nom.pf.act.ptc. [ἁγνίζω] (purify); ὑπακοῇ (obedience); φιλαδελφίαν (brother love); ἀνυπόκριτον (sincere); ἐκτενῶς (deeply)

4. Genesis 1:27, 31a; Matthew 19:19b

Learning to Love the Me I Am

WHAT DOES THIS MEAN, God who made me? What does it mean to love myself as you love me? How can I look at myself and know that, despite my weakness and lack, I am your beloved? Maybe I can begin by looking into Jesus' eyes, and seeing my own reflection looking back.

GENESIS 1:27, 31A

27וַיִּבְרָא אֱלֹהִים אֶת־הָאָדָם בְּצַלְמוֹ בְּצֶלֶם אֱלֹהִים בָּרָא אֹתוֹ
זָכָר וּנְקֵבָה בָּרָא אֹתָם:
31וַיַּרְא אֱלֹהִים אֶת־כָּל־אֲשֶׁר עָשָׂה וְהִנֵּה־טוֹב מְאֹד:

בְּצֶלֶם (image); וּנְקֵבָה (female); וַיַּרְא v.c. + v.3.m.s.impf.Q. [ראה]

MATTHEW 19:19B

19καί, Ἀγαπήσεις τὸν πλησίον σου ὡς σεαυτόν.

5. Jonah 4:10–11; Matthew 25:40

The King in Disguise

MY PRAYER TODAY IS VERY SIMPLE, JESUS. When I see those who are small and weak today, may I truly see and honor and care for you in them. Amen.

JONAH 4:10–11

10וַיֹּאמֶר יְהוָה אַתָּה חַסְתָּ עַל־הַקִּיקָיוֹן אֲשֶׁר לֹא־עָמַלְתָּ בּוֹ
וְלֹא גִדַּלְתּוֹ שֶׁבִּן־לַיְלָה הָיָה וּבִן־לַיְלָה אָבָד:
11וַאֲנִי לֹא אָחוּס עַל־נִינְוֵה הָעִיר הַגְּדוֹלָה אֲשֶׁר יֶשׁ־בָּהּ הַרְבֵּה
מִשְׁתֵּים־עֶשְׂרֵה רִבּוֹ אָדָם אֲשֶׁר לֹא־יָדַע בֵּין־יְמִינוֹ לִשְׂמֹאלוֹ
וּבְהֵמָה רַבָּה:

חַסְתָּ v.2.m.s.pf.Q. [חוס] (pity); הַקִּיקָיוֹן (gourd); עָמַלְתָּ (labor); גִדַּלְתּוֹ v.2.m.s.pf.P. [גדל] + 3.m.s.pr.sf.; שֶׁבִּן rel.pr. + n.m.s.cs.; אָחוּס v.1.com.s.impf.Q. [חוס]; רִבּוֹ (ten thousand)

MATTHEW 25:40

40καὶ ἀποκριθεὶς ὁ βασιλεὺς ἐρεῖ αὐτοῖς, Ἀμὴν λέγω ὑμῖν, ἐφ' ὅσον ἐποιήσατε ἑνὶ τούτων τῶν ἀδελφῶν μου τῶν ἐλαχίστων, ἐμοὶ ἐποιήσατε.

ἐφ' ὅσον prep. (for ἐπί) + cor.pr.nt.s.acc. (because as much as); ἐλαχίστων (least)

6. Leviticus 19:33–34; Matthew 5:43–45

Loving "Others"

THE LIST FORMS IN MY HEART almost against my will . . . a list of "other" people, people who didn't make it onto my prayer list, people I avoid, people whose needs and well-being, frankly, never cross my mind. Now what?

LEVITICUS 19:33–34

³³וְכִי־יָגוּר אִתְּךָ גֵּר בְּאַרְצְכֶם לֹא תוֹנוּ אֹתוֹ:
³⁴כְּאֶזְרָח מִכֶּם יִהְיֶה לָכֶם הַגֵּר הַגָּר אִתְּכֶם וְאָהַבְתָּ לוֹ כָּמוֹךָ
כִּי־גֵרִים הֱיִיתֶם בְּאֶרֶץ מִצְרָיִם אֲנִי יְהוָה אֱלֹהֵיכֶם:

תוֹנוּ v.2.m.p.impf.H. [ינה] (oppress); כְּאֶזְרָח (inhabitant); הַגֵּר d.a. +
v.m.s.ptc.Q. [גור]; הֱיִיתֶם v.2.m.p.pf.Q. [היה]

MATTHEW 5:43–45

⁴³Ἠκούσατε ὅτι ἐρρέθη, Ἀγαπήσεις τὸν πλησίον σου καὶ μισήσεις τὸν ἐχθρόν σου. ⁴⁴ἐγὼ δὲ λέγω ὑμῖν, ἀγαπᾶτε τοὺς ἐχθροὺς ὑμῶν καὶ προσεύχεσθε ὑπὲρ τῶν διωκόντων ὑμᾶς, ⁴⁵ὅπως γένησθε υἱοὶ τοῦ πατρὸς ὑμῶν τοῦ ἐν οὐρανοῖς, ὅτι τὸν ἥλιον αὐτοῦ ἀνατέλλει ἐπὶ πονηροὺς καὶ ἀγαθοὺς καὶ βρέχει ἐπὶ δικαίους καὶ ἀδίκους.

ἐρρέθη v.3.s.aor.pass.ind. [ῥέω] (command); πλησίον (neighbor); μισή-σεις (hate); ἐχθρόν (enemy); διωκόντων (persecute); ἥλιον (sun); ἀνατέλλει (cause to rise); βρέχει (send rain)

7. Song of Solomon 8:6–7; 1 Corinthians 13:13

Tucked into Love

I HIDE MYSELF IN YOUR STRONG LOVE, God of my life. And with me, tucked into my heart, I hide all those whom I love. Love us into wholeness. Love us into life. Love us with forever love. In Jesus' name.

SONG OF SOLOMON 8:6–7

⁶שִׂימֵנִי כַחוֹתָם עַל־לִבֶּךָ כַּחוֹתָם עַל־זְרוֹעֶךָ כִּי־עַזָּה כַמָּוֶת אַהֲבָה קָשָׁה כִשְׁאוֹל קִנְאָה רְשָׁפֶיהָ רִשְׁפֵּי אֵשׁ שַׁלְהֶבֶתְיָה:
⁷מַיִם רַבִּים לֹא יוּכְלוּ לְכַבּוֹת אֶת־הָאַהֲבָה וּנְהָרוֹת לֹא יִשְׁטְפוּהָ אִם־יִתֵּן אִישׁ אֶת־כָּל־הוֹן בֵּיתוֹ בָּאַהֲבָה בּוֹז יָבוּזוּ לוֹ:

שִׂימֵנִי v.2.m.s.impv.Q. [שׂים] + 1.com.s.pr.sf.; כַחוֹתָם prep. + d.a. + n.m.s. (seal); עַזָּה (strong); קִנְאָה (jealousy); רְשָׁפֶיהָ (flame); שַׁלְהֶבֶתְיָה n.f.s. (flame) + PN. abbreviated [יהוה]; יוּכְלוּ v.3.m.p.impf.Q. [יכל]; לְכַבּוֹת prep. + v.in.cs.P. [כבה]; יִשְׁטְפוּהָ v.3.m.p.impf.Q. [שׁטף] (overflow) + 3.f.s.pr.sf.; יִתֵּן v.3.m.s.impf.Q. [נתן]; הוֹן (wealth); בּוֹז (despise)

1 CORINTHIANS 13:13

¹³νυνὶ δὲ μένει πίστις, ἐλπίς, ἀγάπη, τὰ τρία ταῦτα· μείζων δὲ τούτων ἡ ἀγάπη.

νυνὶ (now); μείζων (better)

Week 28

Peace

1. Ezekiel 34:25–26; John 14:27

Make Way for the Prince!

MAKE WAY FOR THE PRINCE OF PEACE! He comes with his treaty, with promises of secure love, of beast-banishing power, of certain hope. Make way for the One who comes in gentleness and joy!

EZEKIEL 34:25–26

²⁵וְכָרַתִּי לָהֶם בְּרִית שָׁלוֹם וְהִשְׁבַּתִּי חַיָּה־רָעָה מִן־הָאָרֶץ
וְיָשְׁבוּ בַמִּדְבָּר לָבֶטַח וְיָשְׁנוּ בַּיְּעָרִים:
²⁶וְנָתַתִּי אוֹתָם וּסְבִיבוֹת גִּבְעָתִי בְּרָכָה וְהוֹרַדְתִּי הַגֶּשֶׁם
בְּעִתּוֹ גִּשְׁמֵי בְרָכָה יִהְיוּ:

לָבֶטַח [שבת]; וְהִשְׁבַּתִּי .v.c. + v.1.com.s.pf.H [כרת]; v.1.com.s.pf.Q. וְכָרַתִּי
(security); וְיָשְׁנוּ (sleep); וְנָתַתִּי .v.c. + v.1.com.s.pf.Q [נתן]; וְהוֹרַדְתִּי .v.c. +
v.1.com.s.pf.H. [ירד]; יִהְיוּ v.3.m.p.impf.Q. [היה]; הַגֶּשֶׁם (rain)

JOHN 14:27

²⁷Εἰρήνην ἀφίημι ὑμῖν, εἰρήνην τὴν ἐμὴν δίδωμι ὑμῖν· οὐ
καθὼς ὁ κόσμος δίδωσιν ἐγὼ δίδωμι ὑμῖν. μὴ ταρασσέσθω
ὑμῶν ἡ καρδία μηδὲ δειλιάτω.

ταρασσέσθω v.3.s.pres.pass.impv. [ταράσσω] (trouble); δειλιάτω (be fearful)

2. Isaiah 48:18; Philippians 4:9

Steps to Peace

To LISTEN TO GOD, to say "yes," to be obedient in the small thing at hand—these are the steps to peace. Not the kind of peace that ebbs and flows with circumstantial tides. No, this peace is the incarnate steadiness of Christ himself, gracing us with unhindered and quiet joy.

ISAIAH 48:18

18לוּא הִקְשַׁבְתָּ לְמִצְוֹתָי וַיְהִי כַנָּהָר שְׁלוֹמֶךָ וְצִדְקָתְךָ
כְּגַלֵּי הַיָּם:

כְּגַלֵּי; [היה] .v.c. + v.3.m.s.impf.Q וַיְהִי ;(pay attention) הִקְשַׁבְתָּ ;(if only) לוּא
(wave)

PHILIPPIANS 4:9

9ἃ καὶ ἐμάθετε καὶ παρελάβετε καὶ ἠκούσατε καὶ εἴδετε ἐν
ἐμοί, ταῦτα πράσσετε· καὶ ὁ θεὸς τῆς εἰρήνης ἔσται μεθ᾽ ὑμῶν.

εἴδετε v.2.p.aor.act.ind. [ὁράω]; ἐμάθετε v.2.p.aor.act.ind. [μανθάνω]
(learn); παρελάβετε v.2.p.aor.act.ind. [παραλαμβάνω] (receive); πράσ-
σετε (accomplish); ἔσται v.3.s.fut.ind. [εἰμί]

3. 1 Chronicles 22:18; Ephesians 2:13–14

Blankets and Bandages

YOU ARE OUR PEACE, O CHRIST. We come to you with broken hearts, bruised relationships, lacerated souls. We come grieving and lost and sad. Wrap us in blankets and bandages of peace. Wrap us in you. For you are our peace. Amen.

1 CHRONICLES 22:18

18הֲלֹא יְהוָה אֱלֹהֵיכֶם עִמָּכֶם וְהֵנִיחַ לָכֶם מִסָּבִיב כִּי נָתַן
בְּיָדִי אֵת יֹשְׁבֵי הָאָרֶץ וְנִכְבְּשָׁה הָאָרֶץ לִפְנֵי יְהוָה וְלִפְנֵי עַמּוֹ:

וְהֵנִיחַ v.c. + v.3.m.s.pf.H. [נוח]; וְנִכְבְּשָׁה (subdue)

EPHESIANS 2:13–14

13νυνὶ δὲ ἐν Χριστῷ Ἰησοῦ ὑμεῖς οἵ ποτε ὄντες μακρὰν ἐγενήθητε ἐγγὺς ἐν τῷ αἵματι τοῦ Χριστοῦ. 14Αὐτὸς γάρ ἐστιν ἡ εἰρήνη ἡμῶν, ὁ ποιήσας τὰ ἀμφότερα ἓν καὶ τὸ μεσότοιχον τοῦ φραγμοῦ λύσας, τὴν ἔχθραν ἐν τῇ σαρκὶ αὐτοῦ,

νυνὶ (now); ὄντες v.m.p.nom.pr.ptc. [εἰμί]; μακρὰν (distant); ἐγενήθητε v.2.p.aor.pass.ind. [γίνομαι]; ἐγγὺς (near); ἐστιν v.3.s.pres.ind. [εἰμί]; ἀμφότερα (both); μεσότοιχον (dividing wall); φραγμοῦ (fence); λύσας (destroy); ἔχθραν (hostility)

4. Proverbs 20:22; Romans 12:17–18

Not Enough Room

GOD HAS SO CONSTITUTED THE HUMAN HEART that there simply isn't room in it for both peace that passes understanding *and* vindictiveness. One or the other has to go.

PROVERBS 20:22

²²אַל־תֹּאמַר אֲשַׁלְּמָה־רָע קַוֵּה לַיהוָה וְיֹשַׁע לָךְ׃

אֲשַׁלְּמָה v.1.com.s.coh.P. [שלם]; קַוֵּה (wait); וְיֹשַׁע cj. + v.3.m.s.impf.H. [ישע]

ROMANS 12:17–18

¹⁷μηδενὶ κακὸν ἀντὶ κακοῦ ἀποδιδόντες, προνοούμενοι καλὰ ἐνώπιον πάντων ἀνθρώπων· ¹⁸εἰ δυνατὸν τὸ ἐξ ὑμῶν, μετὰ πάντων ἀνθρώπων εἰρηνεύοντες·

ἀντι (for); ἀποδιδόντες (repay); προνοούμενοι v.m.p.nom.pres.mid.part. [προνοέω] (be careful); ἐνώπιον (before); δυνατὸν (able); εἰρηνεύοντες (be at peace)

5. Psalm 16:8–9; Philippians 4:4–7

The Secret of Peace

WHAT WE NEED EVEN MORE THAN DELIVERANCE from trouble is the sure knowledge that God is with us in the midst of trouble. That is the secret of peace. Emmanuel. God *with* us.

PSALM 16:8–9

‎⁸שִׁוִּיתִי יְהוָה לְנֶגְדִּי תָמִיד כִּי מִימִינִי בַּל־אֶמּוֹט׃
‎⁹לָכֵן שָׂמַח לִבִּי וַיָּגֶל כְּבוֹדִי אַף־בְּשָׂרִי יִשְׁכֹּן לָבֶטַח׃

שִׁוִּיתִי v.1.com.s.pf.P. [שׁוה] (put); מִימִינִי prep. + n.m.s. + 1.com.s.pr.sf.; אֶמּוֹט v.1.com.s.impf.N. [מוט] (totter); וַיָּגֶל v.c. + v.3.m.s.impf.Q. [גיל] (rejoice); לָבֶטַח (security)

PHILIPPIANS 4:4–7

⁴Χαίρετε ἐν κυρίῳ πάντοτε· πάλιν ἐρῶ, χαίρετε. ⁵τὸ ἐπιεικὲς ὑμῶν γνωσθήτω πᾶσιν ἀνθρώποις. ὁ κύριος ἐγγύς. ⁶μηδὲν μεριμνᾶτε, ἀλλ᾽ ἐν παντὶ τῇ προσευχῇ καὶ τῇ δεήσει μετὰ εὐχαριστίας τὰ αἰτήματα ὑμῶν γνωριζέσθω πρὸς τὸν θεόν. ⁷καὶ ἡ εἰρήνη τοῦ θεοῦ ἡ ὑπερέχουσα πάντα νοῦν φρουρήσει τὰς καρδίας ὑμῶν καὶ τὰ νοήματα ὑμῶν ἐν Χριστῷ Ἰησοῦ.

πάντοτε (always); ἐρῶ v.1.s.fut.act.ind. [λέγω]; ἐπιεικὲς (gentle); ἐγγύς (near); μεριμνᾶτε (be concerned); προσευχῇ (prayer); δεήσει (petition); εὐχαριστίας (thanksgiving); αἰτήματα (request); ὑπερέχουσα (excel); νοῦν (comprehension); φρουρήσει (keep); νοήματα (mind)

6. Zechariah 8.16–17; Matthew 5:9

Peacemakers after the Order of Christ

PEACEMAKERS AFTER THE ORDER OF CHRIST are an entirely different breed than those who, to avoid displeasing significant others, will do anything to "keep the peace." Witness the scourging of the temple, or the faces of enraged religious leaders after the Prince of Peace called them dead men's bones. Peacemakers after the order of Christ have reconciliation in their souls—the holy drive to bring back to oneness, to bring to peace, everything that sin has broken. In doing this they face the same consequences faced by our Lord.

ZECHARIAH 8:16–17

¹⁶אֵלֶּה הַדְּבָרִים אֲשֶׁר תַּעֲשׂוּ דַּבְּרוּ אֱמֶת אִישׁ אֶת־רֵעֵהוּ אֱמֶת
וּמִשְׁפַּט שָׁלוֹם שִׁפְטוּ בְּשַׁעֲרֵיכֶם׃
¹⁷וְאִישׁ אֶת־רָעַת רֵעֵהוּ אַל־תַּחְשְׁבוּ בִּלְבַבְכֶם וּשְׁבֻעַת שֶׁקֶר
אַל־תֶּאֱהָבוּ כִּי אֶת־כָּל־אֵלֶּה אֲשֶׁר שָׂנֵאתִי נְאֻם־יְהוָה׃

תַּעֲשׂוּ v.2.m.p.impf.Q. [עשׂה]; וּשְׁבֻעַת (oath)

MATTHEW 5:9

⁹μακάριοι οἱ εἰρηνοποιοί,
ὅτι αὐτοὶ υἱοὶ θεοῦ κληθήσονται.

εἰρηνοποιοί (make peace)

7. Numbers 6:24–26; 2 Thessalonians 3:16

Let Me Be Peace

TODAY, GOD, MAY I BE ONE whose presence brings to others a peace that remains long after I am gone. In Jesus' name, amen.

NUMBERS 6:24–26

²⁴יְבָרֶכְךָ יְהוָה וְיִשְׁמְרֶךָ:

²⁵יָאֵר יְהוָה פָּנָיו אֵלֶיךָ וִיחֻנֶּךָּ

²⁶יִשָּׂא יְהוָה פָּנָיו אֵלֶיךָ וְיָשֵׂם לְךָ שָׁלוֹם:

[שמר] v.3.m.s.impf.Q. וְיִשְׁמְרֶךָ; + 2.m.s.pr.sf.; [ברך] v.3.m.s.impf.P. יְבָרֶכְךָ + 2.m.s.pr.sf.; יָאֵר v.3.m.s.impf.apocopated [אור] (shine); וִיחֻנֶּךָּ cj. + v.3.m.s.impf.Q. [חנן] + 2.m.s.pr.sf.pause; יִשָּׂא v.3.m.s.impf.Q. [נשא]; וְיָשֵׂם v.c. + v.3.m.s.impf.Q. [שים]

2 THESSALONIANS 3:16

¹⁶Αὐτὸς δὲ ὁ κύριος τῆς εἰρήνης δῴη ὑμῖν τὴν εἰρήνην διὰ παντὸς ἐν παντὶ τρόπῳ. ὁ κύριος μετὰ πάντων ὑμῶν.

δῴη v.3.s.aor.act.sub. [δίδωμι]; τρόπῳ (way)

Friendship

1. Psalm 25:14–15; James 4:4

Waltzing with God

WE ARE DANCING, GOD AND I, the holy dance of friendship, stepping out our parts, circling 'round the sanctuary deep within the soul. We go rhythmically and steadily. We waltz ourselves to oneness, God and I.

PSALM 25:14–15

סוֹד יְהוָה לִירֵאָיו וּבְרִיתוֹ לְהוֹדִיעָם: ¹⁴

עֵינַי תָּמִיד אֶל־יְהוָה כִּי הוּא־יוֹצִיא מֵרֶשֶׁת רַגְלָי: ¹⁵

סוֹד (council); לִירֵאָיו prep. + n.m.p. + 3.m.s.pr.sf.; לְהוֹדִיעָם prep. + v.in.cs.H. [ידע] + 3.m.p.pr.sf.; יוֹצִיא v.3.m.s.impf.H. [יצא]; מֵרֶשֶׁת (net)

JAMES 4:4

⁴μοιχαλίδες, οὐκ οἴδατε ὅτι ἡ φιλία τοῦ κόσμου ἔχθρα τοῦ θεοῦ ἐστιν; ὃς ἐὰν οὖν βουληθῇ φίλος εἶναι τοῦ κόσμου, ἐχθρὸς τοῦ θεοῦ καθίσταται.

μοιχαλίδες (adultress); φιλία (love); ἔχθρα (enmity); ἐστιν v.3.s.pres.ind. [εἰμί]; βουληθῇ (desire); φίλος (friend); εἶναι v.pres.in. [εἰμί]; ἐχθρὸς (enemy); καθίσταται (make)

2. Proverbs 18:24; Mark 3:32–35

Closer Than a Brother

JESUS KNOWS THE PAIN OF FAMILY REJECTION. His response to it gives us a model for healing our own familial pain. Friends! Spiritual friends. Friends that stick closer than a brother. Friends that enflesh the very heart of God. We've heard that blood is thicker than water. But the Spirit is thicker than blood. Nothing heals family wounds more effectively than the love of spiritual friends.

PROVERBS 18:24

‫²⁴אִישׁ רֵעִים לְהִתְרֹעֵעַ וְיֵשׁ אֹהֵב דָּבֵק מֵאָח:‬

‫לְהִתְרֹעֵעַ‬ prep. + v.in.cs.Ht. [‫רעע‬] (associate with)

MARK 3:32–35

³²καὶ ἐκάθητο περὶ αὐτὸν ὄχλος, καὶ λέγουσιν αὐτῷ, Ἰδοὺ ἡ μήτηρ σου καὶ οἱ ἀδελφοί σου [καὶ αἱ ἀδελφαί σου] ἔξω ζητοῦσιν σε. ³³καὶ ἀποκριθεὶς αὐτοῖς λέγει, Τίς ἐστιν ἡ μήτηρ μου καὶ οἱ ἀδελφοί [μου]; ³⁴καὶ περιβλεψάμενος τοὺς περὶ αὐτὸν κύκλῳ καθημένους λέγει, Ἴδε ἡ μήτηρ μου καὶ οἱ ἀδελφοί μου. ³⁵ὃς [γὰρ] ἂν ποιήσῃ τὸ θέλημα τοῦ θεοῦ, οὗτος ἀδελφός μου καὶ ἀδελφὴ καὶ μήτηρ ἐστίν.

ἐκάθητο (sit); ἐστιν v.3.s.pres.ind. [εἰμί]; περιβλεψάμενος (look around); κύκλῳ (all around)

3. Psalm 101:6; Philippians 2:25

Being Epaphroditus

EVERYONE NEEDS AN EPAPHRODITUS. Everyone needs to be an Epaphroditus too.

PSALM 101:6

⁶עֵינַי בְּנֶאֶמְנֵי־אֶרֶץ לָשֶׁבֶת עִמָּדִי הֹלֵךְ בְּדֶרֶךְ תָּמִים הוּא יְשָׁרְתֵנִי׃

בְּנֶאֶמְנֵי prep. + v.m.p.cs.ptc.N. [אמן]; לָשֶׁבֶת prep. + v.in.cs.Q. [ישב]; יְשָׁרְתֵנִי
v.3.m.s.impf.P. [שרת] + 1.com.s.pr.sf.

PHILIPPIANS 2:25

²⁵Ἀναγκαῖον δὲ ἡγησάμην Ἐπαφρόδιτον τὸν ἀδελφὸν καὶ συνεργὸν καὶ συστρατιώτην μου, ὑμῶν δὲ ἀπόστολον καὶ λειτουργὸν τῆς χρείας μου, πέμψαι πρὸς ὑμᾶς,

Ἀναγκαῖον (necessary); ἡγησάμην v.1.s.aor.mid.ind. [ἡγέομαι]; συνεργὸν (fellow worker); συστρατιώτην (fellow elder); χρείας (need)

211

4. Psalm 22:26 [25]; 2 Timothy 4:11, 16–17

Forging the Way

IT HAS OFTEN BEEN THE CASE that God's choice servants must walk in loneliness, through cold and friendless wastelands. God gives us the record of their wanderings so we can find safe passage through deserts of our own.

PSALM 22:26 [25]

²⁶מֵאִתְּךָ תְהִלָּתִי בְּקָהָל רָב נְדָרַי אֲשַׁלֵּם נֶגֶד יְרֵאָיו׃

2 TIMOTHY 4:11, 16–17

¹¹Λουκᾶς ἐστιν μόνος μετ᾽ ἐμοῦ. Μᾶρκον ἀναλαβὼν ἄγε μετὰ σεαυτοῦ, ἔστιν γάρ μοι εὔχρηστος εἰς διακονίαν. ¹⁶Ἐν τῇ πρώτῃ μου ἀπολογίᾳ οὐδείς μοι παρεγένετο, ἀλλὰ πάντες με ἐγκατέλιπον· μὴ αὐτοῖς λογισθείη· ¹⁷ὁ δὲ κύριος μοι παρέστη καὶ ἐνεδυνάμωσεν με, ἵνα δι᾽ ἐμοῦ τὸ κήρυγμα πληροφορηθῇ καὶ ἀκούσωσιν πάντα τὰ ἔθνη, καὶ ἐρρύσθην ἐκ στόματος λέοντος.

ἔστιν v.3.s.pres.ind. [εἰμί]; ἀναλαβὼν (take along); εὔχρηστος (useful); διακονίαν (ministry); ἀπολογίᾳ (defense); παρεγένετο (stand by); ἐγκατέλιπον (abandon); λογισθείη (reckon); παρέστη (stand by); ἐνεδυνάμωσεν (strengthen); κήρυγμα (preaching); πληροφορηθῇ (fulfill); ἐρρύσθην (delivery); λέοντος (lion)

5. Ecclesiastes 4:9–10; Acts 16:23–25

True Friendship

A COMMON GODLY VISION, shared work, mutual encouragement, mutual safety, mutual staying power—a threefold mutuality between two people and God—this is friendship.

ECCLESIASTES 4:9–10

⁹טוֹבִים הַשְּׁנַיִם מִן־הָאֶחָד אֲשֶׁר יֵשׁ־לָהֶם שָׂכָר טוֹב בַּעֲמָלָם:
¹⁰כִּי אִם־יִפֹּלוּ הָאֶחָד יָקִים אֶת־חֲבֵרוֹ וְאִילוֹ הָאֶחָד שֶׁיִּפּוֹל
וְאֵין שֵׁנִי לַהֲקִימוֹ:

שָׂכָר (wages); בַּעֲמָלָם prep. + n.m./f.s. + 3.m.p.p.pr.sf.; יִפֹּלוּ v.3.m.p.impf.Q.pause [נפל]; יָקִים v.3.m.p.impf.H. [קום]; חֲבֵרוֹ (companion); וְאִילוֹ cj. + pt. + 3.m.s.pr.sf. (alas for him); שֶׁיִּפּוֹל rel.pr. + v.3.m.s.impf.Q.plene [נפל]; לַהֲקִימוֹ prep. + v.in.cst.H. [קום] + 3.m.s.pr.sf.

ACTS 16:23–25

²³πολλάς τε ἐπιθέντες αὐτοῖς πληγὰς ἔβαλον εἰς φυλακὴν παραγγείλαντες τῷ δεσμοφύλακι ἀσφαλῶς τηρεῖν αὐτούς. ²⁴ὃς παραγγελίαν τοιαύτην λαβὼν ἔβαλεν αὐτοὺς εἰς τὴν ἐσωτέραν φυλακὴν καὶ τοὺς πόδας ἠσφαλίσατο αὐτῶν εἰς τὸ ξύλον. ²⁵Κατὰ δὲ τὸ μεσονύκτιον Παῦλος καὶ Σιλᾶς προσευχόμενοι ὕμνουν τὸν θεόν, ἐπηκροῶντο δὲ αὐτῶν οἱ δέσμιοι.

ἐπιθέντες v.m.p.nom.aor.act.ptc. [ἐπιτίθημι] (give); πληγὰς (blow); φυλακὴν (prison); παραγγείλαντες (command); δεσμοφύλακι (jailer); ἀσφαλῶς (securely); ἐσωτέραν (inner); ἠσφαλίσατο v.3.s.aor.mid.ind. [ἀσφαλίζω] (fasten); ξύλον (stocks); μεσονύκτιον (midnight); ὕμνουν (sing hymns); ἐπηκροῶντο (listen); δέσμιοι (prisoner)

6. Proverbs 27:6; Mark 8:33

A Difficult Word

THE GIVING AND RECEIVING OF CORRECTION is nothing for friends to undertake lightly. Yet how authentic can the friendship be if there is no room for a difficult, albeit loving word?

PROVERBS 27:6

‎נֶאֱמָנִים פִּצְעֵי אוֹהֵב וְנַעְתָּרוֹת נְשִׁיקוֹת שׂוֹנֵא:⁶

‎פִּצְעֵי (wounds); ‎וְנַעְתָּרוֹת cj. + v.f.p.ptc.N. [עתר] (abundant); ‎נְשִׁיקוֹת (kiss)

MARK 8:33

³³ὁ δὲ ἐπιστραφεὶς καὶ ἰδὼν τοὺς μαθητὰς αὐτοῦ ἐπετίμησεν Πέτρῳ καὶ λέγει, Ὕπαγε ὀπίσω μου, Σατανᾶ, ὅτι οὐ φρονεῖς τὰ τοῦ θεοῦ ἀλλὰ τὰ τῶν ἀνθρώπων.

ἐπιστραφεὶς (turn); ἰδὼν v.m.s.nom.aor.act.ptc. [ὁράω]; ἐπετίμησεν (rebuke); ὀπίσω (behind); Σατανᾶ (Satan); φρονεῖς (think)

7. Proverbs 17.9, John 15.12–19

Laying Down My Life

THE CALL TO LOVE AS JESUS LOVES is the call to be a friend, to habitually lay down my life for others. This is not the self-chosen and self-aggrandizing martyrdom that has innoculated who knows how many hearts against God. No, it is the pouring out of one's Christ-life. Such an outpouring is made possible only by the continuous bubbling up of more Christ-life within.

PROVERBS 17:9

⁹מְכַסֶּה־פֶּשַׁע מְבַקֵּשׁ אַהֲבָה וְשֹׁנֶה בְדָבָר מַפְרִיד אַלּוּף׃

מַפְרִיד (separate)

JOHN 15:12–13

¹²αὕτη ἐστὶν ἡ ἐντολὴ ἡ ἐμή, ἵνα ἀγαπᾶτε ἀλλήλους καθὼς ἠγάπησα ὑμᾶς. ¹³μείζονα ταύτης ἀγάπην οὐδεὶς ἔχει, ἵνα τις τὴν ψυχὴν αὐτοῦ θῇ ὑπὲρ τῶν φίλων αὐτοῦ.

ἐστὶν v.3.s.pres.ind. [εἰμί]; μείζονα (greatly); θῇ v.3.s.aor.act.sub. [τίθημι]

Week 30

Mutuality

1. Leviticus 19:17–18; Ephesians 5:21

"A Change of Habit"

WHICH EVIL HABIT IS HARDER TO GIVE UP, lording over or groveling? Give them up we must, though, if we are to reverence Christ. For mutual submission cannot coexist with either.

LEVITICUS 19:17–18

¹⁷לֹא־תִשְׂנָא אֶת־אָחִיךָ בִּלְבָבֶךָ הוֹכֵחַ תּוֹכִיחַ אֶת־עֲמִיתֶךָ וְלֹא־
תִשָּׂא עָלָיו חֵטְא׃
¹⁸לֹא־תִקֹּם וְלֹא־תִטֹּר אֶת־בְּנֵי עַמֶּךָ וְאָהַבְתָּ לְרֵעֲךָ כָּמוֹךָ
אֲנִי יְהוָה׃

הוֹכֵחַ v.in.ab.H. [יכח]; תּוֹכִיחַ v.2.m.s.impf.H. [יקח]; עֲמִיתֶךָ (fellow); תִשָּׂא v.2.m.s.impf.Q. [נשא]; תִקֹּם v.2.m.s.impf.Q. [נקם] (avenge); תִטֹּר v.2.m.s.impf.Q. [נטר] (harbor a grudge); כָּמוֹךָ prep. + 2.m.s.pr.sf.

EPHESIANS 5:21

²¹ Ὑποτασσόμενοι ἀλλήλοις ἐν φόβῳ Χριστοῦ,

ʽ Ὑποτασσόμενοι (subject); φόβῳ (fear)

2. Exodus 35:20 21; 1 Corinthians 12:12–14

"Freedom in Limitation"

HUMILITY BRINGS GREAT LIBERTY because when we no longer have to know it all, do it all, or be it all, we are freed to enjoy those things that we and others can know, do, and be.

EXODUS 35:20–21

²⁰וַיֵּצְאוּ כָּל־עֲדַת בְּנֵי־יִשְׂרָאֵל מִלִּפְנֵי מֹשֶׁה:
²¹וַיָּבֹאוּ כָּל־אִישׁ אֲשֶׁר־נְשָׂאוֹ לִבּוֹ וְכֹל אֲשֶׁר נָדְבָה רוּחוֹ אֹתוֹ
הֵבִיאוּ אֶת־תְּרוּמַת יְהוָה לִמְלֶאכֶת אֹהֶל מוֹעֵד וּלְכָל־עֲבֹדָתוֹ
וּלְבִגְדֵי הַקֹּדֶשׁ:

וַיֵּצְאוּ v.c. + v.3.m.p.impf.Q. [יצא]; וַיָּבֹאוּ v.c. + v.3.m.p.impf.Q. [בוא]; נָדְבָה
(free will); הֵבִיאוּ v.c. + v.3.m.p.pf.H. [בוא]

1 CORINTHIANS 12:12–14

¹²Καθάπερ γὰρ τὸ σῶμα ἕν ἐστιν καὶ μέλη πολλὰ ἔχει, πάντα δὲ τὰ μέλη τοῦ σώματος πολλὰ ὄντα ἕν ἐστιν σῶμα, οὕτως καὶ ὁ Χριστός· ¹³καὶ γὰρ ἐν ἑνὶ πνεύματι ἡμεῖς πάντες εἰς ἓν σῶμα ἐβαπτίσθημεν, εἴτε Ἰουδαῖοι εἴτε Ἕλληνες εἴτε δοῦλοι εἴτε ἐλεύθεροι, καὶ πάντες ἓν πνεῦμα ἐποτίσθημεν. ¹⁴καὶ γὰρ τὸ σῶμα οὐκ ἔστιν ἓν μέλος ἀλλὰ πολλά.

Καθάπερ (just as); ἐστιν v.3.s.pres.ind. [εἰμί]; μέλη (part); ἐλεύθεροι (free); ἐποτίσθημεν v.1.p.aor.pass.ind. [ποτίζω] (cause to drink)

3. Nehemiah 2:17–18; Philippians 4:2–3

True Yoke-Partners

LORD, HOW WE LONG TO LABOR TOGETHER in your work as those
who are true yoke-partners. We would so much like to pull in
the same direction, to stop questioning the wisdom of the One
who yokes us in teams, to find joy in the task to which we're
called. May your Spirit bring us along until we do.

NEHEMIAH 2:17–18

17וָאוֹמַ֣ר אֲלֵהֶ֗ם אַתֶּ֤ם רֹאִים֙ הָרָעָה֙ אֲשֶׁ֣ר אֲנַ֣חְנוּ בָ֔הּ אֲשֶׁ֤ר יְרוּשָׁלִַ֙ם֙
חֲרֵבָ֔ה וּשְׁעָרֶ֖יהָ נִצְּת֣וּ בָאֵ֑שׁ לְכ֗וּ וְנִבְנֶה֙ אֶת־חוֹמַ֣ת יְרוּשָׁלִַ֔ם
וְלֹא־נִהְיֶ֥ה ע֖וֹד חֶרְפָּֽה:
18וָאַגִּ֨יד לָהֶ֜ם אֶת־יַ֣ד אֱלֹהַ֗י אֲשֶׁר־הִיא֙ טוֹבָ֣ה עָלַ֔י וְאַף־דִּבְרֵ֣י
הַמֶּ֔לֶךְ אֲשֶׁ֖ר אָֽמַר־לִ֑י וַיֹּֽאמְרוּ֙ נָק֣וּם וּבָנִ֔ינוּ וַיְחַזְּק֥וּ יְדֵיהֶ֖ם
לַטּוֹבָֽה:

וָאוֹמַ֣ר v.c. + v.1.com.s.impf.Q. [אמר]; רֹאִים֙ v.m.p.ptc.Q. [ראה]; נִצְּת֣וּ
v.3.c.p.pf.N. [יצת] (burn); לְכ֗וּ v.2.m.p.impv.Q. [הלך]; וָאַגִּ֨יד v.c. +
v.1.com.s.impf.H. [נגד]; וּבָנִ֔ינוּ v.c. + v.1.com.s.pf.Q. [בנה]

PHILIPPIANS 4:2–3

2Ευοδίαν παρακαλῶ καὶ Συντύχην παρακαλῶ τὸ αὐτὸ
φρονεῖν ἐν κυρίῳ. 3ναὶ ἐρωτῶ καὶ σέ, γνήσιε σύζυγε,
συλλαμβάνου αὐταῖς, αἵτινες ἐν τῷ εὐαγγελίῳ συνήθλησάν
μοι μετὰ καὶ Κλήμεντος καὶ τῶν λοιπῶν συνεργῶν μου, ὧν
τὰ ὀνόματα ἐν βίβλῳ ζωῆς.

φρονεῖν (think); ναὶ (indeed); γνήσιε (true); σύζυγε (comrade); συλλαμβάνου (help); συνήθλησάν v.3.p.aor.act.ind. [συναθλέω] (struggle
together); συνεργῶν (fellow worker); βίβλῳ (book)

4. Judges 4:4–6; Philemon 15–17

"Humbled and Honored, All at Once"

WHEN WE FINALLY REALIZE that our only true authority is Christ we are both humbled and honored. Humbled because the honor goes to Christ. Honored because Christ has chosen to reveal himself to others even through us. Why is this such a difficult gift to accept?

JUDGES 4:4–6

⁴וּדְבוֹרָה אִשָּׁה נְבִיאָה אֵשֶׁת לַפִּידוֹת הִיא שֹׁפְטָה אֶת־יִשְׂרָאֵל
בָּעֵת הַהִיא:
⁵וְהִיא יוֹשֶׁבֶת תַּחַת־תֹּמֶר דְּבוֹרָה בֵּין הָרָמָה וּבֵין בֵּית־אֵל
בְּהַר אֶפְרָיִם וַיַּעֲלוּ אֵלֶיהָ בְּנֵי יִשְׂרָאֵל לַמִּשְׁפָּט:
⁶וַתִּשְׁלַח וַתִּקְרָא לְבָרָק בֶּן־אֲבִינֹעַם מִקֶּדֶשׁ נַפְתָּלִי וַתֹּאמֶר
אֵלָיו הֲלֹא צִוָּה יְהוָה אֱלֹהֵי־יִשְׂרָאֵל לֵךְ וּמָשַׁכְתָּ בְּהַר תָּבוֹר
וְלָקַחְתָּ עִמְּךָ עֲשֶׂרֶת אֲלָפִים אִישׁ מִבְּנֵי נַפְתָּלִי וּמִבְּנֵי זְבֻלוּן:

תֹּמֶר (date palm); וַיַּעֲלוּ [עלה] v.c. + v.3.m.p.impf.Q. לֵךְ v.2.m.s.impv.Q.
[הלך]; וּמָשַׁכְתָּ (draw)

PHILEMON 15–17

¹⁵τάχα γὰρ διὰ τοῦτο ἐχωρίσθη πρὸς ὥραν, ἵνα αἰώνιον αὐτὸν ἀπέχῃς, ¹⁶οὐκέτι ὡς δοῦλον ἀλλ᾽ ὑπὲρ δοῦλον, ἀδελφὸν ἀγαπητόν, μάλιστα ἐμοί, πόσῳ δὲ μᾶλλον σοὶ καὶ ἐν σαρκὶ καὶ ἐν κυρίῳ. ¹⁷εἰ οὖν με ἔχεις κοινωνόν, προσλαβοῦ αὐτὸν ὡς ἐμέ.

τάχα (perhaps); ἐχωρίσθη (be separated); ἀπέχῃς (receive completely); οὐκέτι (no longer); μάλιστα (especially); πόσῳ (how much); κοινωνόν (partner); προσλαβοῦ (receive into one's circle)

219

5. Job 1:1, 5; Romans 8:33–34

"Bearing One Another's Burdens"

AT THE VERY HEART OF INTERCESSION is loving others as we love ourselves. To intercede is to carry someone else's pain, someone else's life as it is—to wrap and bathe them in the healing love of God with the same thorough attention we would wish for ourselves. It is God's will for us, his children, to tenderly minister to one another in this way and so fulfill the law of Christ.

JOB 1:1, 5

¹אִישׁ הָיָה בְאֶרֶץ־עוּץ אִיּוֹב שְׁמוֹ וְהָיָה הָאִישׁ הַהוּא תָּם וְיָשָׁר
וִירֵא אֱלֹהִים וְסָר מֵרָע:
⁵וַיְהִי כִּי הִקִּיפוּ יְמֵי הַמִּשְׁתֶּה וַיִּשְׁלַח אִיּוֹב וַיְקַדְּשֵׁם
וְהִשְׁכִּים בַּבֹּקֶר וְהֶעֱלָה עֹלוֹת מִסְפַּר כֻּלָּם כִּי אָמַר אִיּוֹב אוּלַי
חָטְאוּ בָנַי וּבֵרֲכוּ אֱלֹהִים בִּלְבָבָם כָּכָה יַעֲשֶׂה אִיּוֹב כָּל־
הַיָּמִים:

וַיְהִי v.c. [סור]; v.m.s.ptc.Q. + v.c. וְסָר ;.adj.m.s.cs. + .cj וִירֵא ;(complete) תָּם
.H וַיְהִי v.c. וַיְקַדְּשֵׁם ;(banquet) הַמִּשְׁתֶּה ;[נקף].v.3.c.p.pf.H הִקִּיפוּ ;[היה].v.3.m.s.impf.Q+
v.c. + v.3.m.s.impf.P. [קדשׁ] + 3.m.p.pr.sf.; אוּלַי (perhaps)

ROMANS 8:33–34

³³τίς ἐγκαλέσει κατὰ ἐκλεκτῶν θεοῦ; θεὸς ὁ δικαιῶν· ³⁴τίς ὁ κατακρινῶν; Χριστὸς [Ἰησοῦς] ὁ ἀποθανών, μᾶλλον δὲ ἐγερθείς, ὃς καί ἐστιν ἐν δεξιᾷ τοῦ θεοῦ, ὃς καὶ ἐντυγχάνει ὑπὲρ ἡμῶν.

ἐγκαλέσει (accuse); ἐκλεκτῶν (chosen); κατακρινῶν (condemn); ἀπο-θανών v.m.s.nom.aor.act.ptc. [ἀποθνήσκω]; ἐστιν v.3.s.pres.ind. [εἰμί]; ἐν-τυγχάνει (intercede)

6. Jeremiah 8.21–22; 1 Corinthians 12:26–27

"Bearing Another's Joy"

HERE AGAIN, INTERCESSION REVEALS ITSELF as the sharing of another's soul condition, only in this case the sharing is of the other's joy. This is a kind of reverse intercession whereby the incarnate joy of another soul becomes medicine for our own sad hearts. This transfusion of joy is a very real form of mutual burden-bearing that we are called to share.

JEREMIAH 8:21–22

²¹עַל־שֶׁבֶר בַּת־עַמִּי הָשְׁבָּרְתִּי קָדַרְתִּי שַׁמָּה הֶחֱזִקָתְנִי׃
²²הַצְרִי אֵין בְּגִלְעָד אִם־רֹפֵא אֵין שָׁם כִּי מַדּוּעַ לֹא עָלְתָה אֲרֻכַת
בַּת־עַמִּי׃

שֶׁבֶר (destruction); קָדַרְתִּי (be in mourning); שַׁמָּה (waste); הֶחֱזִקָתְנִי v.3.f.s.pf.H. [חזק] + 1.com.s.pr.sf.pause; הַצְרִי (balsam); עָלְתָה v.3.f.s.pf.Q. [עלה]; אֲרֻכַת (healing)

1 CORINTHIANS 12:26–27

²⁶καὶ εἴτε πάσχει ἓν μέλος, συμπάσχει πάντα τὰ μέλη· εἴτε δοξάζεται [ἓν] μέλος, συγχαίρει πάντα τὰ μέλη. ²⁷Ὑμεῖς δέ ἐστε σῶμα Χριστοῦ καὶ μέλη ἐκ μέρους.

πάσχει (suffer); συμπάσχει (suffer together); μέλη (member); συγ-χαίρει (rejoice together); μέρους (part)

7. Malachi 3:16; Romans 1:11–12

"Friends"

HOW PRECIOUS THE GIFT OF SPIRITUAL FRIENDS who build us up
in faith, hope, and love! How I long to be such a friend to others, and to always have such friends in my life! But even when
through providence we experience relational drought God
supplies us through the saints that have gone before. In their
lives and writing we may be thoroughly refreshed. There are
times, too, when we are a friend to someone else without even
knowing it, unselfconsciously carrying the fragrance of life
that we ourselves have received.

MALACHI 3:16

¹⁶אָז נִדְבְּרוּ יִרְאֵי יְהוָה אִישׁ אֶת־רֵעֵהוּ וַיַּקְשֵׁב יְהוָה וַיִּשְׁמָע
וַיִּכָּתֵב סֵפֶר זִכָּרוֹן לְפָנָיו לְיִרְאֵי יְהוָה וּלְחֹשְׁבֵי שְׁמוֹ:

וַיַּקְשֵׁב (pay attention); זִכָּרוֹן (memorial)

ROMANS 1:11–12

¹¹ἐπιποθῶ γὰρ ἰδεῖν ὑμᾶς, ἵνα τι μεταδῶ χάρισμα ὑμῖν
πνευματικὸν εἰς τὸ στηριχθῆναι ὑμᾶς, ¹²τοῦτο δέ ἐστιν
συμπαρακληθῆναι ἐν ὑμῖν διὰ τῆς ἐν ἀλλήλοις πίστεως ὑμῶν
τε καὶ ἐμοῦ.

ἐπιποθῶ (long for); ἰδεῖν v.aor.act.in. [ὁράω]; μεταδῶ v.1.s.aor.act.sub.
[μεταδίδωμι] (impart); πνευματικὸν (spiritual); στηριχθῆναι (strengthen);
ἐστιν v.3.s.pres.ind. [εἰμί]; συμπαρακληθῆναι (receive encouragement
together)

Suffering

1. Genesis 6:11–12; Luke 13:1–3

The Beginning and the End

YES, THERE IS VIOLENCE and yes, the righteous suffer. But it did not begin with us. From before the dawn of creation God suffered. In his "eternal now," outside of time, affliction crushed the heart of God. He was the Lamb slain before the foundation of the world. We need to know this and know it well. Before we ever suffered, God suffered for us. This is the mystery of suffering—that in God's suffering we find our own. And it is in God's suffering that all suffering will end.

GENESIS 6:11–12

¹¹וַתִּשָּׁחֵת הָאָרֶץ לִפְנֵי הָאֱלֹהִים וַתִּמָּלֵא הָאָרֶץ חָמָס:
¹²וַיַּרְא אֱלֹהִים אֶת־הָאָרֶץ וְהִנֵּה נִשְׁחָתָה כִּי־הִשְׁחִית כָּל־בָּשָׂר
אֶת־דַּרְכּוֹ עַל־הָאָרֶץ:

וַיַּרְא v.c. + v.3.m.s.impf.Q. [ראה]

LUKE 13:1–3

¹Παρῆσαν δέ τινες ἐν αὐτῷ τῷ καιρῷ ἀπαγγέλλοντες αὐτῷ περὶ τῶν Γαλιλαίων ὧν τὸ αἷμα Πιλᾶτος ἔμιξεν μετὰ τῶν θυσιῶν αὐτῶν. ²καὶ ἀποκριθεὶς εἶπεν αὐτοῖς, Δοκεῖτε ὅτι οἱ Γαλιλαῖοι οὗτοι ἁμαρτωλοὶ παρὰ πάντας τοὺς Γαλιλαίους ἐγένοντο, ὅτι ταῦτα πεπόνθασιν; ³οὐχί, λέγω ὑμῖν, ἀλλ᾽ ἐὰν μὴ μετανοῆτε πάντες ὁμοίως ἀπολεῖσθε.

Παρῆσαν (be present); ἀπαγγέλλοντες (proclaim); ἔμιξεν v.3.s.aor.act.ind. [μίγνυμι] (mix); θυσιῶν (sacrifice); εἶπεν v.3.s.aor.act.ind. [λέγω]; ἁμαρτωλοὶ (sinner); πεπόνθασιν v.3.p.2.pf.act.ind. [πάσχω] (suffer); μετανοῆτε (report); ὁμοίως (similarly)

2. Jeremiah 12:1–2; Hebrews 11:37–38

Why Not Me?

WHY, GOD? WHY CANCER, WAR, DIVORCE, ABUSE, FAMINE? Why must the righteous suffer while the guilty go scott-free? Are you capricious, God, doling out miracles here and there when you're in the mood, some of them grossly unfair? Sometimes it seems that way. Then I remember the words of my friend dying from cancer: "Why not me? Why should I be spared any of the suffering the rest of the world feels, just because I'm a Christian?" He uttered the very heart of God. Why not me?

JEREMIAH 12:1–2

¹צַדִּיק אַתָּה יְהוָה כִּי אָרִיב אֵלֶיךָ אַךְ מִשְׁפָּטִים אֲדַבֵּר אוֹתָךְ מַדּוּעַ
דֶּרֶךְ רְשָׁעִים צָלֵחָה שָׁלוּ כָּל־בֹּגְדֵי בָגֶד:
²נְטַעְתָּם גַּם־שֹׁרָשׁוּ יֵלְכוּ גַּם־עָשׂוּ פֶרִי קָרוֹב אַתָּה בְּפִיהֶם
וְרָחוֹק מִכִּלְיוֹתֵיהֶם:

צָלֵחָה v.3.f.s.pf.Q.pause [צלח]; שָׁלוּ v.3.m.p.pf.Q. [שלה] (be at ease); בָגֶד (treachery); נְטַעְתָּם v.2.m.s.pf.Q. [נטע] + 3.m.p.pr.sf.; שֹׁרָשׁוּ (take root); יֵלְכוּ v.3.m.p.impf.Q. [הלך]; עָשׂוּ v.3.m.p.pf.Q. [עשׂה]; מִכִּלְיוֹתֵיהֶם (kidney)

HEBREWS 11:37–38

³⁷ἐλιθάσθησαν, ἐπρίσθησαν, ἐν φόνῳ μαχαίρης ἀπέθανον, περιῆλθον ἐν μηλωταῖς, ἐν αἰγείοις δέρμασιν, ὑστερούμενοι, θλιβόμενοι, κακουχούμενοι, ³⁸ὧν οὐκ ἦν ἄξιος ὁ κόσμος, ἐπὶ ἐρημίαις πλανώμενοι καὶ ὄρεσιν καὶ σπηλαίοις καὶ ταῖς ὀπαῖς τῆς γῆς.

ἐλιθάσθησαν v.3.p.aor.pass.ind. [λιθάζω] (stone); ἐπρίσθησαν (saw); φόνῳ (killing); μαχαίρης (sword); περιῆλθον v.1.s.aor.act.ind. [περιέρχο-μαι] (go around); μηλωταῖς (sheepskin); αἰγείοις (goat); δέρμασιν (skin); ὑστερούμενοι (be lacking); θλιβόμενοι (afflict); κακουχούμενοι (torment); ἦν v.3.s.impf.ind. [εἰμί]; ἄξιος (worthy); ἐρημίαις (desert); πλανώμενοι (wander); σπηλαίοις (cave); ὀπαῖς (hole)

3. 1 Samuel 15:23; 1 Timothy 6:10

Hidden Cause

I READ SOMEWHERE that 80 percent of all physical illness is caused by repressed negative emotions. Eighty percent of our ailments, in other words, might be prevented if we took care of our inner world. In the same way, I believe, at least 80 percent of our spiritual ills are the self-inflicted result of repressed but cherished idolatry.

1 SAMUEL 15:23

²³כִּי חַטַּאת־קֶסֶם מֶרִי וְאָוֶן וּתְרָפִים הַפְצַר יַעַן מָאַסְתָּ אֶת־דְּבַר
יְהוָה וַיִּמְאָסְךָ מִמֶּלֶךְ:

קֶסֶם (divination); מֶרִי (rebellion); וּתְרָפִים (idols); הַפְצַר v.in.ab.H. [פצר] (push); וַיִּמְאָסְךָ v.c. + v. 3.m.s.impf.Q. [מאס] + 2.m.s.pr.sf.

1 TIMOTHY 6:10

¹⁰ῥίζα γὰρ πάντων τῶν κακῶν ἐστιν ἡ φιλαργυρία, ἧς τινες ὀρεγόμενοι ἀπεπλανήθησαν ἀπὸ τῆς πίστεως καὶ ἑαυτοὺς περιέπειραν ὀδύναις πολλαῖς.

ῥίζα (root); ἐστιν v.3.s.pres.ind. [εἰμί]; φιλαργυρία (money love); ὀρε-γόμενοι (eager for); ἀπεπλανήθησαν v.3.p.aor.pass.ind. [ἀποπλανάω] (wander); περιέπειραν (pierce); ὀδύναις (pain)

4. Leviticus 23:22; James 1:27

Among the Little Ones

JESUS MAKES HIS HOME among the little ones of this world. True
worshipers always seek him and find him and love him there.

LEVITICUS 23:22

²²וּֽבְקֻצְרְכֶם אֶת־קְצִיר אַרְצְכֶם לֹֽא־תְכַלֶּה פְּאַת שָֽׂדְךָ בְּקֻצְרֶךָ
וְלֶקֶט קְצִירְךָ לֹא תְלַקֵּט לֶֽעָנִי וְלַגֵּר תַּעֲזֹב אֹתָם אֲנִי יְהוָה
אֱלֹהֵיכֶֽם׃

וּֽבְקֻצְרְכֶם cj. + v.in.cs.Q. [קצר] (reap) + 2.m.p.pr.sf.; קָצִיר (harvest);
בְּקֻצְרֶךָ cj. + v.in.cs.Q. [קצר] + 2.m.s.pr.sf.; וְלֶקֶט (gleaning); תְלַקֵּט (glean)

JAMES 1:27

²⁷θρησκεία καθαρὰ καὶ ἀμίαντος παρὰ τῷ θεῷ καὶ πατρὶ αὕτη
ἐστίν, ἐπισκέπτεσθαι ὀρφανοὺς καὶ χήρας ἐν τῇ θλίψει αὐτῶν,
ἄσπιλον ἑαυτὸν τηρεῖν ἀπὸ τοῦ κόσμου.

θρησκεία (religion); καθαρὰ (pure); ἀμίαντος (undefiled); ἐπισκέπτεσθαι
v.mid.in. [ἐπισκέπτομαι] (care for); ὀρφανοὺς (orphan); χήρας (widow);
θλίψει (affliction); ἄσπιλον (unblemished)

5. Isaiah 50:5–7; Hebrews 12:1–2

Jesus, Keep Me True!

JESUS, KEEP ME TRUE! Keep my eyes on you even as saints and angels urge me on in the race. Suffering is part of the course, a mystery, to be sure, but a necessary part. It was for you, so it is for me. Jesus, keep me true!

ISAIAH 50:5–7

⁵אֲדֹנָי יְהוִה פָּתַח־לִי אֹזֶן וְאָנֹכִי לֹא מָרִיתִי אָחוֹר לֹא נְסוּגֹתִי׃

⁶גֵּוִי נָתַתִּי לְמַכִּים וּלְחָיַי לְמֹרְטִים פָּנַי לֹא הִסְתַּרְתִּי מִכְּלִמּוֹת וָרֹק׃

⁷וַאדֹנָי יְהוִה יַעֲזָר־לִי עַל־כֵּן לֹא נִכְלָמְתִּי עַל־כֵּן שַׂמְתִּי פָנַי כַּחַלָּמִישׁ וָאֵדַע כִּי־לֹא אֵבוֹשׁ׃

מָרִיתִי v.1.com.s.pf.Q. [מרה] (rebel); אָחוֹר (behind); נְסוּגֹתִי v.1.com.s.pf.N. [סוג] (backslide); גֵּוִי (back); נָתַתִּי v.1.com.s.pf.Q. [נתן]; לְמַכִּים prep. + v.m.p.act.ptc.H. [נכה]; וּלְחָיַי (jaw); לְמֹרְטִים (pluck); מִכְּלִמּוֹת (insult); וָרֹק (spit); נִכְלָמְתִּי (be humiliated); שַׂמְתִּי v.1.com.s.pf.Q. [שים]; כַּחַלָּמִישׁ (flint); וָאֵדַע v.1.com.s.impf.Q. [ידע]

HEBREWS 12:1–2

¹Τοιγαροῦν καὶ ἡμεῖς τοσοῦτον ἔχοντες περικείμενον ἡμῖν νέφος μαρτύρων, ὄγκον ἀποθέμενοι πάντα καὶ τὴν εὐπερίστατον ἁμαρτίαν, δι᾽ ὑπομονῆς τρέχωμεν τὸν προκείμενον ἡμῖν ἀγῶνα ²ἀφορῶντες εἰς τὸν τῆς πίστεως ἀρχηγὸν καὶ τελειωτὴν Ἰησοῦν, ὃς ἀντὶ τῆς προκειμένης αὐτῷ χαρᾶς ὑπέμεινεν σταυρὸν αἰσχύνης καταφρονήσας ἐν δεξιᾷ τε τοῦ θρόνου τοῦ θεοῦ κεκάθικεν.

Τοιγαροῦν (therefore); τοσοῦτον (so great); περικείμενον (be surrounded by); νέφος (cloud); μαρτύρων (witness); ὄγκον (weight); ἀποθέμενοι (relinquish); εὐπερίστατον (easily distracting); ὑπομονῆς (patience); τρέχωμεν (run); προκείμενον (be present); ἀγῶνα (race); ἀφορῶντες (fix eyes); ἀρχηγὸν (leader); τελειωτὴν (perfecter); ἀντὶ (for); ὑπέμεινεν (bear); σταυρὸν (cross); αἰσχύνης (shame); καταφρονήσας (despise); κεκάθικεν v.3.s.pf.act.ind. [καθίζω] (sit)

6. Jeremiah 4:18–19; Colossians 1:24–26

Filling Up That Which Is Lacking

IT IS POSSIBLE FOR THE CHILD OF GOD to offer all his or her sufferings up as a kind of intercession, a means of experiencing, with Christ, a portion of this world's pain. This "filling up that which is lacking" is not always a verbalized prayer: "I offer this pain to you, Lord, as a kind of intercession." Rather it is the Godward suffering, the experience of suffering even as one experiences union with Christ.

JEREMIAH 4:18–19

¹⁸דַּרְכֵּךְ וּמַעֲלָלַיִךְ עָשׂוֹ אֵלֶּה לָךְ זֹאת רָעָתֵךְ כִּי מָר כִּי נָגַע
עַד־לִבֵּךְ:

¹⁹מֵעַי מֵעַי אוֹחִילָה קִירוֹת לִבִּי הֹמֶה־לִּי לִבִּי לֹא אַחֲרִישׁ כִּי
קוֹל שׁוֹפָר שָׁמַעַתְּ נַפְשִׁי תְּרוּעַת מִלְחָמָה:

וּמַעֲלָלַיִךְ (practices); עָשׂוֹ v.3.c.p.pf.Q. [עשׂה]; מָר (bitter); מֵעַי (bowels);
אוֹחִילָה v.1.com.s.coh.H.Qe. [יחל] (tarry); הֹמֶה (pound); אַחֲרִישׁ (be silent);
תְּרוּעַת (shout)

COLOSSIANS 1:24–26

²⁴Νῦν χαίρω ἐν τοῖς παθήμασιν ὑπὲρ ὑμῶν καὶ ἀνταναπληρῶ
τὰ ὑστερήματα τῶν θλίψεων τοῦ Χριστοῦ ἐν τῇ σαρκί μου
ὑπὲρ τοῦ σώματος αὐτοῦ, ὅ ἐστιν ἡ ἐκκλησία, ²⁵ἧς ἐγενόμην
ἐγὼ διάκονος κατὰ τὴν οἰκονομίαν τοῦ θεοῦ τὴν δοθεῖσαν
μοι εἰς ὑμᾶς πληρῶσαι τὸν λόγον τοῦ θεοῦ, ²⁶τὸ μυστήριον
τὸ ἀποκεκρυμμένον ἀπὸ τῶν αἰώνων καὶ ἀπὸ τῶν γενεῶν—
νῦν δὲ ἐφανερώθη τοῖς ἁγίοις αὐτοῦ,

Νῦν (now); παθήμασιν (suffering); ἀνταναπληρῶ (completely fill); ὑστερήματα (lack); θλίψεων (affliction); ἐστιν v.3.s.pres.ind. [εἰμί]; διάκονος (servant); οἰκονομίαν (stewardship); δοθεῖσαν v.f.s.acc.aor.pass.ptc. [δίδωμι]; ἀποκεκρυμμένον v.nt.s.acc.pf.pass.ptc. [ἀποκρύπτω] (hide away); γενεῶν (generation); ἐφανερώθη (reveal)

7. Ezekiel 47:12; Revelation 22:1–3

The Final Word

THIS IS GOD'S SOLEMN PROMISE TO US. Life, not death, will have the final word. As surely as the water flows and the trees bear their fruit, suffering will shed its mystery in the transforming light of day. And all will be well.

EZEKIEL 47:12

וְעַל־הַנַּחַל יַעֲלֶה עַל־שְׂפָתוֹ מִזֶּה וּמִזֶּה כָּל־עֵץ־מַאֲכָל [superscript 12]
לֹא־יִבּוֹל עָלֵהוּ וְלֹא־יִתֹּם פִּרְיוֹ לָחֳדָשָׁיו יְבַכֵּר כִּי מֵימָיו
מִן־הַמִּקְדָּשׁ הֵמָּה יוֹצְאִים וְהָיָה פִרְיוֹ לְמַאֲכָל וְעָלֵהוּ
לִתְרוּפָה:

מַאֲכָל (food); יִבּוֹל v.3.m.s.impf.Q. [נבל] (wither); עָלֵהוּ (leaf); יִתֹּם v.3.m.s.impf.Q. [תמם]; יְבַכֵּר (bear new fruit); לִתְרוּפָה (healing)

REVELATION 22:1–3

¹Καὶ ἔδειξεν μοι ποταμὸν ὕδατος ζωῆς λαμπρὸν ὡς κρύσταλλον, ἐκπορευόμενον ἐκ τοῦ θρόνου τοῦ θεοῦ καὶ τοῦ ἀρνίου. ²ἐν μέσῳ τῆς πλατείας αὐτῆς καὶ τοῦ ποταμοῦ ἐντεῦθεν καὶ ἐκεῖθεν ξύλον ζωῆς ποιοῦν καρποὺς δώδεκα, κατὰ μῆνα ἕκαστον ἀποδιδοῦν τὸν καρπὸν αὐτοῦ, καὶ τὰ φύλλα τοῦ ξύλου εἰς θεραπείαν τῶν ἐθνῶν. ³καὶ πᾶν κατάθεμα οὐκ ἔσται ἔτι. καὶ ὁ θρόνος τοῦ θεοῦ καὶ τοῦ ἀρνίου ἐν αὐτῇ ἔσται, καὶ οἱ δοῦλοι αὐτοῦ λατρεύσουσιν αὐτω,

ἔδειξεν v.3.s.aor.act.ind. [δείκνυμι] (show); ποταμὸν (river); λαμπρὸν (radiant); κρύσταλλον (crystal); ἐκπορευόμενον (go out); ἀρνίου (lamb); πλατείας (street); ἐντεῦθεν (from here); ἐκεῖθεν (from there); ξύλον (tree); μῆνα (month); ἀποδιδοῦν (yield); φύλλα (leaf); θεραπείαν (healing); κατάθεμα (curse); ἔσται v.3.s.fut.ind. [εἰμί]; λατρεύσουσιν (serve)

Week 32

The Journey

1. Psalm 39:12; 1 Peter 2:11–12

The Gift of Loneliness

IS NOT THIS THE GREATEST GIFT of our fundamental loneliness—the reminder that our true state in this world is one of sojourner, not citizen?

PSALM 39:12

¹²בְּתוֹכָחוֹת עַל־עָוֹן יִסַּרְתָּ אִישׁ וַתֶּמֶס כָּעָשׁ חֲמוּדוֹ אַךְ הֶבֶל
כָּל־אָדָם סֶלָה:

בְּתוֹכָחוֹת (reproof); יִסַּרְתָּ (correct); וַתֶּמֶס v.c. + v.2.m.s.impf.H.apocopated
[מסה] (melt); כָּעָשׁ (moth); חֲמוּדוֹ (desire)

1 PETER 2:11–12

¹¹Ἀγαπητοί, παρακαλῶ ὡς παροίκους καὶ παρεπιδήμους
ἀπέχεσθαι τῶν σαρκικῶν ἐπιθυμιῶν αἵτινες στρατεύονται
κατὰ τῆς ψυχῆς· ¹²τὴν ἀναστροφὴν ὑμῶν ἐν τοῖς ἔθνεσιν
ἔχοντες καλήν, ἵνα, ἐν ᾧ καταλαλοῦσιν ὑμῶν ὡς κακοποιῶν
ἐκ τῶν καλῶν ἔργων ἐποπτεύοντες δοξάσωσιν τὸν θεὸν ἐν
ἡμέρᾳ ἐπισκοπῆς.

παροίκους (stranger); παρεπιδήμους (sojourner); ἀπέχεσθαι (abstain);
σαρκικῶν (fleshly); ἐπιθυμιῶν (desire); στρατεύονται (war); ἀναστροφὴν
(behavior); καταλαλοῦσιν (malign); κακοποιῶν (criminal); ἐποπτεύοντες (see); ἐπισκοπῆς (visitation)

2. Psalm 84:5–7; 2 Corinthians 3:18

The Process Is the Point

MANY OF US GO THROUGH OUR WHOLE LIFE JOURNEY never realizing that in God's sight the process is the point.

PSALM 84:5–7

⁵אַשְׁרֵי יוֹשְׁבֵי בֵיתֶךָ עוֹד יְהַלְלוּךָ סֶּלָה׃
⁶אַשְׁרֵי אָדָם עוֹז־לוֹ בָךְ מְסִלּוֹת בִּלְבָבָם׃
⁷עֹבְרֵי בְּעֵמֶק הַבָּכָא מַעְיָן יְשִׁיתוּהוּ גַּם־בְּרָכוֹת יַעְטֶה מוֹרֶה׃

אַשְׁרֵי (blessing); יְהַלְלוּךָ v.3.m.p.impf.P. [הלל] + 2.m.s.pr.sf.; מְסִלּוֹת (highway); מַעְיָן (spring); יְשִׁיתוּהוּ v.3.m.p.impf.H. [שׁית] + 3.m.s.pr.sf.; בְּרָכוֹת (pool); יַעְטֶה (cover); מוֹרֶה (early rain)

2 CORINTHIANS 3:18

¹⁸ἡμεῖς δὲ πάντες ἀνακεκαλυμμένῳ προσώπῳ τὴν δόξαν κυρίου κατοπτριζόμενοι τὴν αὐτὴν εἰκόνα μεταμορφούμεθα ἀπὸ δόξης εἰς δόξαν καθάπερ ἀπὸ κυρίου πνεύματος.

ἀνακεκαλυμμένῳ v.nt.s.dat.pf.pass.ptc. [ἀνακαλύπτω] (uncover); κατοπτριζόμενοι (contemplate); εἰκόνα (image); μεταμορφούμεθα (transform); καθάπερ (just as)

3. Isaiah 42:16; Luke 1:78–79

The Way We Have Not Known

IN ALL DARKNESS, BLINDNESS, AND IGNORANCE God comes to make a way. This way is not one that we have known, for all our ways are dark, blind, and ignorant. The way of God may be known, and is known even as we know Christ. He is the way.

ISAIAH 42:16

וְהוֹלַכְתִּי עִוְרִים בְּדֶרֶךְ לֹא יָדָעוּ בִּנְתִיבוֹת לֹא־יָדְעוּ אַדְרִיכֵם¹⁶
אָשִׂים מַחְשָׁךְ לִפְנֵיהֶם לָאוֹר וּמַעֲקַשִּׁים לְמִישׁוֹר אֵלֶּה הַדְּבָרִים
עֲשִׂיתִם וְלֹא עֲזַבְתִּים:

מַחְשָׁךְ ;v.c. + v.1.com.s.pf.H. [הלך] וְהוֹלַכְתִּי ;עִוְרִים (blind); בִּנְתִיבוֹת (way)
(dark place); וּמַעֲקַשִּׁים (crooked place); לְמִישׁוֹר (plain); עֲשִׂיתִם v.1.com.s.pf.Q.
[עשה] + 3.m.p.pr.sf.; עֲזַבְתִּים v.1.com.s.pf.Q. [עזב] + 3.m.p.pr.sf.

LUKE 1:78–79

⁷⁸διὰ σπλάγχνα ἐλέους θεοῦ ἡμῶν,
    ἐν οἷς ἐπισκέψεται ἡμᾶς ἀνατολὴ ἐξ ὕψους,
⁷⁹ἐπιφᾶναι τοῖς ἐν σκότει καὶ σκιᾷ θανάτου
    καθημένοις,
    τοῦ κατευθῦναι τοὺς πόδας ἡμῶν εἰς ὁδὸν εἰρήνης.

σπλάγχνα (inner parts); ἐλέους (mercy); ἐν οἷς prep. + rel.pr.m.p.dat. (through which); ἐπισκέψεται v.3.s.f.mid.ind. [ἐπισκέπτομαι] (visit); ἀνα- τολὴ (rising sun); ὕψους (height); ἐπιφᾶναι (appear); σκότει (darkness); σκιᾷ (shadow); καθημένοις (sit); κατευθῦναι (make straight)

1. Psalm 18:31–33; Hebrews 12:12–13

Overcoming

GOD NEVER PROMISED AN EASY WAY. He promised an overcoming way—strength for the journey, steady feet for rocky paths, armor for the battle, the capacity for choice. Let us choose, then, to be sojourners until our journey takes us home.

PSALM 18:31–33

³¹הָאֵל תָּמִים דַּרְכּוֹ אִמְרַת־יְהוָה צְרוּפָה מָגֵן הוּא לְכֹל הַחֹסִים בּוֹ:

³²כִּי מִי אֱלוֹהַּ מִבַּלְעֲדֵי יְהוָה וּמִי צוּר זוּלָתִי אֱלֹהֵינוּ:

³³הָאֵל הַמְאַזְּרֵנִי חָיִל וַיִּתֵּן תָּמִים דַּרְכִּי:

אִמְרַת (saying); צְרוּפָה (refine); הַחֹסִים d.a. + v.m.s.ptc.Q. [חוס] (pity); מִבַּלְעֲדֵי prep. + adv. (besides); זוּלָתִי prep./cj.cs. (except) + 1.com.s.pr.sf.; הַמְאַזְּרֵנִי d.a. + v.m.s.act.ptc.P. [אזר] (put on) + 1.com.s.pr.sf.; וַיִּתֵּן v.c. + 3.m.s.impf.Q. [נתן]

HEBREWS 12:12–13

¹²Διὸ τὰς παρειμένας χεῖρας καὶ τὰ παραλελυμένα γόνατα ἀνορθώσατε, ¹³καὶ τροχιὰς ὀρθὰς ποιεῖτε τοῖς ποσὶν ὑμῶν, ἵνα μὴ τὸ χωλὸν ἐκτραπῇ, ἰαθῇ δὲ μᾶλλον.

παρειμένας (weakened); παραλελυμένα (disable); γόνατα (knee); ἀνορθώσατε (straighten); τροχιὰς (path); ὀρθὰς (straight); χωλὸν (lame); ἐκτραπῇ (twist); ἰαθῇ v.3.s.aor.pass.sub. [ἰάομαι] (heal)

5. Psalm 139:9–12; 1 Corinthians 13:12

Traveling in the Dark

VERY OFTEN WE MUST TRAVEL IN THE DARK. But we need not fear when we do, because God is all Light. And our journey is in him. So when the darkness comes we can know that we are safe. Nestled in the dark softness of his garments, journeying along, we may be sure that he strides us homeward in the light.

PSALM 139:9–12

⁹אֶשָּׂא כַנְפֵי־שָׁחַר אֶשְׁכְּנָה בְּאַחֲרִית יָם:

¹⁰גַּם־שָׁם יָדְךָ תַנְחֵנִי וְתֹאחֲזֵנִי יְמִינֶךָ:

¹¹וָאֹמַר אַךְ־חֹשֶׁךְ יְשׁוּפֵנִי וְלַיְלָה אוֹר בַּעֲדֵנִי:

¹²גַּם־חֹשֶׁךְ לֹא־יַחְשִׁיךְ מִמֶּךָ וְלַיְלָה כַּיּוֹם יָאִיר כַּחֲשֵׁיכָה כָּאוֹרָה:

אֶשָּׂא v.1.com.s.impf.Q. [נשא]; שָׁחַר (dawn); אֶשְׁכְּנָה v.1.com.s.coh.Q. [שכן]; תַנְחֵנִי v.3.f.s.impf.H. [נחה] + 1.com.s.pr.sf.; וְתֹאחֲזֵנִי cj. + v.3.f.s.impf.Q. [אחז] + 1.com.s.pr.sf.; וָאֹמַר v.c. + v.1.com.s.impf.Q. [אמר]; יְשׁוּפֵנִי v.3.m.s.impf.Q. [שוף] (cover) + 1.com.s.pr.sf.; בַּעֲדֵנִי prep. + 1.com.s.pr.sf.; יַחְשִׁיךְ (grow dark); יָאִיר v.3.m.s.impf.H. [אור] (be light); כַּחֲשֵׁיכָה (darkness)

1 CORINTHIANS 13:12

¹²βλέπομεν γὰρ ἄρτι δι᾽ ἐσόπτρου ἐν αἰνίγματι, τότε δὲ πρόσωπον πρὸς πρόσωπον· ἄρτι γινώσκω ἐκ μέρους, τότε δὲ ἐπιγνώσομαι καθὼς καὶ ἐπεγνώσθην.

ἄρτι (now); ἐσόπτρου (mirror); ἐν αἰνίγματι (indistinctly); μέρους (part); ἐπιγνώσομαι (know)

6. Numbers 14:6–9; 2 Corinthians 5:6–9

Following the Guide

THE EYES OF FAITH MUST BE FIXED on the One who guides us home. Whether conditions seem favorable for the journey or not, when God says, "Arise and go," we are fools to do otherwise. And when God says, "Rest here," woe to us if we insist on pressing on. Oh, he will not abandon us if we make the wrong choice. But much of our hardship along the way is altogether of our own doing.

NUMBERS 14:6–9

⁶וִיהוֹשֻׁעַ בִּן־נוּן וְכָלֵב בֶּן־יְפֻנֶּה מִן־הַתָּרִים אֶת־הָאָרֶץ קָרְעוּ
בִּגְדֵיהֶם:
⁷וַיֹּאמְרוּ אֶל־כָּל־עֲדַת בְּנֵי־יִשְׂרָאֵל לֵאמֹר הָאָרֶץ אֲשֶׁר עָבַרְנוּ
בָהּ לָתוּר אֹתָהּ טוֹבָה הָאָרֶץ מְאֹד מְאֹד:
⁸אִם־חָפֵץ בָּנוּ יְהוָה וְהֵבִיא אֹתָנוּ אֶל־הָאָרֶץ הַזֹּאת וּנְתָנָהּ לָנוּ
אֶרֶץ אֲשֶׁר־הִוא זָבַת חָלָב וּדְבָשׁ:
⁹אַךְ בַּיהוָה אַל־תִּמְרֹדוּ וְאַתֶּם אַל־תִּירְאוּ אֶת־עַם הָאָרֶץ כִּי
לַחְמֵנוּ הֵם סָר צִלָּם מֵעֲלֵיהֶם וַיהוָה אִתָּנוּ אַל־תִּירָאֻם:

הַתָּרִים d.a. + v.m.p.act.ptc.Q. [תּוּר] (explore); וְהֵבִיא v.c. + v.3.m.s.pf.H. [בוא]; זָבַת v.f.s.ptc.cs.Q. [זוּב] (flow); חָלָב (milk); תִּמְרֹדוּ (rebel); סָר v.3.m.s.pf.Q. [סוּר]; צִלָּם (shadow); תִּירָאֻם v.2.m.p.jus.Q.pause [ירא] + 3.m.p.pr.sf.

2 CORINTHIANS 5:6–9

⁶Θαρροῦντες οὖν πάντοτε καὶ εἰδότες ὅτι ἐνδημοῦντες ἐν τῷ σώματι ἐκδημοῦμεν ἀπὸ τοῦ κυρίου· ⁷διὰ πίστεως γὰρ περιπατοῦμεν, οὐ διὰ εἴδους· ⁸θαρροῦμεν δὲ καὶ εὐδοκοῦμεν μᾶλλον ἐκδημῆσαι ἐκ τοῦ σώματος καὶ ἐνδημῆσαι πρὸς τὸν κύριον. ⁹διὸ καὶ φιλοτιμούμεθα, εἴτε ἐνδημοῦντες εἴτε ἐκδημοῦντες, εὐάρεστοι αὐτῷ εἶναι.

Θαρροῦντες (be courageous); πάντοτε (always); εἰδότες v.m.p.nom.pf.act.ptc. [οἶδα]; ἐνδημοῦντες (be at home); ἐκδημοῦμεν (be away); εἴδους (form); εὐδοκοῦμεν (resolve); φιλοτιμούμεθα (aspire); εὐάρεστοι (pleasing); εἶναι v.pres.in. [εἰμί]

7. Psalm 27:4; Philippians 1:6

Journey of Transformation

AS SURELY AS THE SHRIVELLED, SMALL BROWN BULB grows into a fragrant lily, we Christians with all our rough edges and snaggly points will one day grow to our full stature, transformed into the image of Christ. God's word, his incorruptible seed, will bring it all to pass.

PSALM 27:4

⁴אַחַת שָׁאַלְתִּי מֵאֵת־יְהוָה אוֹתָהּ אֲבַקֵּשׁ שִׁבְתִּי בְּבֵית־יְהוָה כָּל־
יְמֵי חַיַּי לַחֲזוֹת בְּנֹעַם־יְהוָה וּלְבַקֵּר בְּהֵיכָלוֹ׃

שִׁבְתִּי v.in.cs.Q. [ישׁב] + 1.com.s.pr.sf.; לַחֲזוֹת prep. + v.in.cs.Q. [חזה]; בְּנֹעַם (pleasantness); וּלְבַקֵּר (attend)

PHILIPPIANS 1:6

⁶πεποιθὼς αὐτὸ τοῦτο, ὅτι ὁ ἐναρξάμενος ἐν ὑμῖν ἔργον ἀγαθὸν ἐπιτελέσει ἄχρι ἡμέρας Χριστοῦ Ἰησοῦ·

πεποιθὼς v.m.s.nom.pf.act.ptc. [πείθω]; ἐναρξάμενος (begin); ἐπιτελέσει (finish); ἄχρι (until)

How Long?

1. Habakkuk 1:2–4; Matthew 24:21–22

How Long until There Is Peace?

NO MATTER HOW SHORT THE DURATION OF SUFFERING, it always seems too long. Is there ever a war or an illness that is the right length of time? My God, bring an end to the violence! Begin with the mayhem in my heart.

HABAKKUK 1:2–4

²עַד־אָנָה יְהוָה שִׁוַּעְתִּי וְלֹא תִשְׁמָע אֶזְעַק אֵלֶיךָ חָמָס וְלֹא תוֹשִׁיעַ:
³לָמָּה תַרְאֵנִי אָוֶן וְעָמָל תַּבִּיט וְשֹׁד וְחָמָס לְנֶגְדִּי וַיְהִי
רִיב וּמָדוֹן יִשָּׂא:
⁴עַל־כֵּן תָּפוּג תּוֹרָה וְלֹא־יֵצֵא לָנֶצַח מִשְׁפָּט כִּי רָשָׁע מַכְתִּיר
אֶת־הַצַּדִּיק עַל־כֵּן יֵצֵא מִשְׁפָּט מְעֻקָּל:

אָנָה (where); שִׁוַּעְתִּי (cry for help); תּוֹשִׁיעַ v.2.m.s.impf.H. [ישע];
תַרְאֵנִי v.2.m.s.impf.H. [ראה] + 1.c.s.pr.sf.; תַּבִּיט v.2.m.s.impf.H. [נבט]; וְשֹׁד (violence); וַיְהִי v.c. + v.3.m.s.impf.Q. [היה]; וּמָדוֹן (strife); יִשָּׂא v.3.m.s.impf.Q. [נשא]; תָּפוּג (be paralyzed); יֵצֵא v.3.m.s.impf.Q. [יצא]; לָנֶצַח (forever); מַכְתִּיר (surround); מְעֻקָּל (twisted)

MATTHEW 24:21–22

²¹ἔσται γὰρ τότε θλῖψις μεγάλη οἵα οὐ γέγονεν ἀπ᾽ ἀρχῆς κόσμου ἕως τοῦ νῦν οὐδ᾽ οὐ μὴ γένηται. ²²καὶ εἰ μὴ ἐκολοβώθησαν αἱ ἡμέραι ἐκεῖναι, οὐκ ἂν ἐσώθη πᾶσα σάρξ· διὰ δὲ τοὺς ἐκλεκτοὺς κολοβωθήσονται αἱ ἡμέραι ἐκεῖναι.

ἔσται v.3.s.fut.ind. [εἰμί]; θλῖψις (affliction); οἵα (such that); γέγονεν v.3.s.aor.act.ind. [γίνομαι]; νῦν (now); γένηται v.3.s.aor.mid.sub. [γίνομαι]; ἐκολοβώθησαν (shorten); ἐκλεκτοὺς (chosen)

2. Psalm 74:10–11; Romans 8:35–37

Your Love Is Longer Than My Trouble

THOUGH I CANNOT UNDERSTAND the "how long" or the "why" of these hardships, I can believe your promise, Lord, that I am not alone in them. You are with me because you love me! And even if things get so bad that I cannot believe that anymore, you will still be there and you will carry me through. Because you love me.

PSALM 74:10–11

10 עַד־מָתַי אֱלֹהִים יְחָרֶף צָר יְנָאֵץ אוֹיֵב שִׁמְךָ לָנֶצַח:
11 לָמָּה תָשִׁיב יָדְךָ וִימִינֶךָ מִקֶּרֶב חֵוקְךָ כַלֵּה:

יְחָרֶף (taunt); יְנָאֵץ (despise); לָנֶצַח (forever); תָשִׁיב v.2.m.s.impf.H. [שׁוב];
חֵוקְךָ (bosom); כַלֵּה (keep)

ROMANS 8:35–37

35τίς ἡμᾶς χωρίσει ἀπὸ τῆς ἀγάπης τοῦ Χριστοῦ; θλῖψις ἢ στενοχωρία ἢ διωγμὸς ἢ λιμὸς ἢ γυμνότης ἢ κίνδυνος ἢ μάχαιρα; 36καθὼς γέγραπται ὅτι

Ἕνεκεν σοῦ θανατούμεθα ὅλην τὴν ἡμέραν,
ἐλογίσθημεν ὡς πρόβατα σφαγῆς.
37ἀλλ᾽ ἐν τούτοις πᾶσιν ὑπερνικῶμεν διὰ τοῦ ἀγαπήσαντος ἡμᾶς.

χωρίσει (separate); θλῖψις (affliction); στενοχωρία (distress); διωγμὸς (persecution); λιμὸς (famine); γυμνότης (nakedness); κίνδυνος (peril); μάχαιρα (sword); Ἕνεκεν (because of); θανατούμεθα (kill); ἐλογίσθημεν (consider); πρόβατα (sheep); σφαγῆς (slaughter); ὑπερνικῶμεν (gain victory)

3. Esther 3:5–6; Revelation 6:9–10

The Answer

IN THE HEART OF HEAVEN ITSELF burns the unanswered, anguished prayer: "How long?" The answer will surely come.

ESTHER 3:5–6

⁵וַיַּרְא הָמָן כִּי־אֵין מָרְדֳּכַי כֹּרֵעַ וּמִשְׁתַּחֲוֶה לוֹ וַיִּמָּלֵא
הָמָן חֵמָה:
⁶וַיִּבֶז בְּעֵינָיו לִשְׁלֹחַ יָד בְּמָרְדֳּכַי לְבַדּוֹ כִּי־הִגִּידוּ לוֹ
אֶת־עַם מָרְדֳּכָי וַיְבַקֵּשׁ הָמָן לְהַשְׁמִיד אֶת־כָּל־הַיְּהוּדִים אֲשֶׁר
בְּכָל־מַלְכוּת אֲחַשְׁוֵרוֹשׁ עַם מָרְדֳּכָי:

וַיַּרְא v.c. + v.3.m.s.impf.Q. [ראה]; כֹּרֵעַ (bow); וּמִשְׁתַּחֲוֶה cj. + v.m.s.ptc.act.Hisht. [חוה]; וַיִּבֶז v.c. + v.3.m.s.impf.Q. [בזה] (despise); הִגִּידוּ v.3.m.p.impf.H. [נגד]

REVELATION 6:9–10

⁹Καὶ ὅτε ἤνοιξεν τὴν πέμπτην σφραγῖδα, εἶδον ὑποκάτω τοῦ
θυσιαστηρίου τὰς ψυχὰς τῶν ἐσφαγμένων διὰ τὸν λόγον τοῦ
θεοῦ καὶ διὰ τὴν μαρτυρίαν ἣν εἶχον. ¹⁰καὶ ἔκραξαν φωνῇ
μεγάλῃ λέγοντες, Ἕως πότε, ὁ δεσπότης ὁ ἅγιος καὶ ἀληθινός,
οὐ κρίνεις καὶ ἐκδικεῖς τὸ αἷμα ἡμῶν ἐκ τῶν κατοικούντων
ἐπὶ τῆς γῆς;

ἤνοιξεν v.3.s.aor.act.ind. [ἀνοίγω]; πέμπτην (fifth); σφραγῖδα (seal);
εἶδον v.1.s.aor.act.ind. [ὁράω]; ὑποκάτω (under); θυσιαστηρίου (altar);
ἐσφαγμένων (slay); μαρτυρίαν (testimony); εἶχον v.3.p.impf.act.ind. [ἔχω];
πότε (how long); δεσπότης (master); ἀληθινός (true); ἐκδικεῖς (avenger);
κατοικούντων (live)

239

4. Judges 11:30–31, 34, 39a; Matthew 14:5–8

Jephthah's Daughter

I WEEP FOR YOU, JEPHTHAH'S DAUGHTER. Did they write "Jeph-thah's daughter" on your tombstone? Or did your father's vio-lence even take away your name? I weep, poor lost child, for you and for us, for violence undeserved, for the Jephthahs that we are. *How long until we learn the way of love?*

JUDGES 11:30–31, 34, 39A

³⁰וַיִּדַּר יִפְתָּח נֶדֶר לַיהוָה וַיֹּאמַר אִם־נָתוֹן תִּתֵּן אֶת־בְּנֵי
עַמּוֹן בְּיָדִי: ³¹ וְהָיָה הַיּוֹצֵא אֲשֶׁר יֵצֵא מִדַּלְתֵי בֵיתִי
לִקְרָאתִי בְּשׁוּבִי בְשָׁלוֹם מִבְּנֵי עַמּוֹן וְהָיָה לַיהוָה וְהַעֲלִיתִהוּ עוֹלָה:
³⁴וַיָּבֹא יִפְתָּח הַמִּצְפָּה אֶל־בֵּיתוֹ וְהִנֵּה בִתּוֹ יֹצֵאת לִקְרָאתוֹ
בְתֻפִּים וּבִמְחֹלוֹת וְרַק הִיא יְחִידָה אֵין־לוֹ מִמֶּנּוּ בֵּן אוֹ־בַת:
³⁹וַיְהִי מִקֵּץ שְׁנַיִם חֳדָשִׁים וַתָּשָׁב אֶל־אָבִיהָ וַיַּעַשׂ לָהּ אֶת־
נִדְרוֹ אֲשֶׁר נָדָר וְהִיא לֹא־יָדְעָה אִישׁ:

וַיִּדַּר v.c. + v.3.m.s.impf.Q. [נדר] (vow); תִּתֵּן v.2.m.s.impf.Q. [נתן]; יֵצֵא v.3.m.s.impf.Q. [יצא]; לִקְרָאתִי prep. + n.f.s.cs. [as prep.] + 1.com.s.pr.sf.; וְהַעֲלִיתִהוּ v.c. + v.1.com.s.pf.H. [עלה] + 3.m.s.pr.sf.; וַיָּבֹא v.c. + v.3.m.s.impf.Q. [בוא]; בְתֻפִּים (tambourine); וּבִמְחֹלוֹת (dance); יְחִידָה (alone); וַיְהִי v.c. + v.3.m.s.impf.Q. [היה]; וַתָּשָׁב v.c. + v.3.f.s.impf.Q. [שוב]; וַיַּעַשׂ v.c. + v.3.m.s.impf.Q. [עשה]

MATTHEW 14:5–8

⁵καὶ θέλων αὐτὸν ἀποκτεῖναι ἐφοβήθη τὸν ὄχλον, ὅτι ὡς προφήτην αὐτὸν εἶχον. ⁶γενεσίοις δὲ γενομένοις τοῦ Ἡρῴδου ὠρχήσατο ἡ θυγάτηρ τῆς Ἡρῳδιάδος ἐν τῷ μέσῳ καὶ ἤρεσεν τῷ Ἡρῴδῃ, ⁷ὅθεν μεθ' ὅρκου ὡμολόγησεν αὐτῇ δοῦναι ὃ ἐὰν αἰτήσηται. ⁸ἡ δὲ προβιβασθεῖσα ὑπὸ τῆς μητρὸς αὐτῆς, Δός μοι, φησίν, ὧδε ἐπὶ πίνακι τὴν κεφαλὴν Ἰωάννου τοῦ βαπτιστοῦ.

γενεσίοις (birthday party); ὠρχήσατο v.3.s.aor.mid.ind. [ὀρχέομαι] (dance); ἤρεσεν v.3.s.aor.act.ind. [ἀρέσκω] (please); ὅθεν (therefore); ὅρκου (oath); ὡμολόγησεν (promise); προβιβασθεῖσα (bring forward); φησίν v.3.s.pres.act.ind. [φημί]; πίνακι (dish)

5. Psalm 88:8–9; 2 Corinthians 4:16, 18

Renewal Will Come

MAY I SEE MY LIFE, not with these physical eyes, but with the unseen eyes of trust in God, who brings all things to completion and will make all things well. Troubled days are certain but God's renewal is even more certain. So I cast myself on him again, even as my flesh cries: "How long?"

PSALM 88:8–9

⁸עָלַי סָמְכָה חֲמָתֶךָ וְכָל־מִשְׁבָּרֶיךָ עִנִּיתָ סֶּלָה׃
⁹הִרְחַקְתָּ מְיֻדָּעַי מִמֶּנִּי שַׁתַּנִי תוֹעֵבוֹת לָמוֹ כָּלֻא וְלֹא אֵצֵא׃

עָלַי prep. + 1.com.s.pr.sf; סָמְכָה (support); מִשְׁבָּרֶיךָ (wave); עִנִּיתָ
v.2.m.s.pf.P. [ענה]; מְיֻדָּעַי v.m.p.ptc.Pu. [ידע] + 1.com.s.pr.sf.; מִמֶּנִּי prep. +
1.com.s.pr.sf.; שַׁתַּנִי v.2.m.s.pf.Q. [שית] + 1.com.s.pr.sf.; כָּלֻא (restrain); אֵצֵא
v.1.com.s.impf.Q. [יצא]

2 CORINTHIANS 4:16, 18

¹⁶Διὸ οὐκ ἐγκακοῦμεν, ἀλλ᾽ εἰ καὶ ὁ ἔξω ἡμῶν ἄνθρωπος διαφθείρεται, ἀλλ᾽ ὁ ἔσω ἡμῶν ἀνακαινοῦται ἡμέρᾳ καὶ ἡμέρᾳ. ¹⁸μὴ σκοπούντων ἡμῶν τὰ βλεπόμενα ἀλλὰ τὰ μὴ βλεπόμενα· τὰ γὰρ βλεπόμενα πρόσκαιρα, τὰ δὲ μὴ βλεπόμενα αἰώνια.

ἐγκακοῦμεν (despair); διαφθείρεται (destroy); ἔσω (inner); ἀνακαιν-οῦται (renew); σκοπούντων (notice); πρόσκαιρα (temporary)

6. Lamentations 3:32–33; 1 Peter 1:6–7

Solid Gold

As I LOOK BACK OVER THE YEARS I see the truth of God's word—
that my faith has never been purified or deepened by pros-
perity, but only through tough times. So even though I struggle with my own desire for comfort and ease, at a deeper level
I know that this trial, too, is Christ-life in the making.

LAMENTATIONS 3:32–33

כִּי אִם־הוֹגָה וְרִחַם כְּרֹב חֲסָדָיו׃ ³²
כִּי לֹא עִנָּה מִלִּבּוֹ וַיַּגֶּה בְּנֵי־אִישׁ׃ ³³

הוֹגָה v.3.m.s.pf.H. [יגה] (vex); וַיַּגֶּה v.c. + v.3.m.s.impf.P. [יגה]

1 PETER 1:6–7

⁶ἐν ᾧ ἀγαλλιᾶσθε, ὀλίγον ἄρτι εἰ δέον [ἐστὶν] λυπηθέντες ἐν
ποικίλοις πειρασμοῖς, ἵνα τὸ δοκίμιον ὑμῶν τῆς πίστεως
πολυτιμότερον χρυσίου τοῦ ἀπολλυμένου διὰ πυρὸς δὲ
δοκιμαζομένου, εὑρεθῇ εἰς ἔπαινον καὶ δόξαν καὶ τιμὴν ἐν
ἀποκαλύψει Ἰησοῦ Χριστοῦ·

ἀγαλλιᾶσθε (be glad); ὀλίγον (little); ἄρτι (now); ἐστὶν v.3.s.pres.ind.
[εἰμί]; λυπηθέντες v.m.p.nom.aor.pass.ptc. [λυπέω] (grieve); ποικίλοις
(various); πειρασμοῖς (trial); δοκίμιον (testing); πολυτιμότερον (valuable);
χρυσίου (gold); δοκιμαζομένου (test); εὑρεθῇ v.3.s.aor.pass.sub. [εὑρίσκω];
ἔπαινον (praise); τιμὴν (honor); ἀποκαλύψει (revelation)

7. Isaiah 49:13–15; Matthew 24:3–4, 36, 44a

Watching for Jesus

WHEN I WAS A CHILD I sometimes rushed out into the yard for a quick check of the clouds, looking for the return of the flannelgraph Jesus they told me about in Sunday school. He was supposed to come in a flash and absolutely surprise everyone. But I thought I just might be able to catch him. Now I watch for his return from a different point of view, anticipating his coming the way a child anticipates her mother's return from an out-of-town trip.

ISAIAH 49:13–15

רָנּוּ¹³
שָׁמַיִם וְגִילִי אָרֶץ יִפְצְחוּ הָרִים רִנָּה כִּי־נִחַם יְהוָה עַמּוֹ וַעֲנִיָּו יְרַחֵם:
¹⁴וַתֹּאמֶר צִיּוֹן עֲזָבַנִי יְהוָה וַאדֹנָי שְׁכֵחָנִי:
הֲתִשְׁכַּח¹⁵
אִשָּׁה עוּלָהּ מֵרַחֵם בֶּן־בִּטְנָהּ גַּם־אֵלֶּה תִּשְׁכַּחְנָה וְאָנֹכִי לֹא אֶשְׁכָּחֵךְ:

יִפְצְחוּ v.2.m.p.impv.Q. [רנן]; וְגִילִי v.c. + v.2.f.s.impv.Q. [גיל] (rejoice); יִפְצְחוּ (break forth); רִנָּה (rejoicing); עֲזָבַנִי v.3.m.s.pf.Q. [עזב] + 1.com.s.pr.sf.; שְׁכֵחָנִי v.3.m.s.pf.Q. [שכח] + 1.com.s.pr.sf.; הֲתִשְׁכַּח int.pt. + 3.f.s.impf.Q. [שכח]; עוּלָהּ (suckling child); אֶשְׁכָּחֵךְ v.1.com.s.impf.Q. [שכח] + 2.f.s.pr.sf.

MATTHEW 24:3–4, 36, 44a

³Καθημένου δὲ αὐτοῦ ἐπὶ τοῦ Ὄρους τῶν Ἐλαιῶν προσῆλθον αὐτῷ οἱ μαθηταὶ κατ᾽ ἰδίαν λέγοντες, Εἰπὲ ἡμῖν, πότε ταῦτα ἔσται καὶ τί τὸ σημεῖον τῆς σῆς παρουσίας καὶ συντελείας τοῦ αἰῶνος; ⁴καὶ ἀποκριθεὶς ὁ Ἰησοῦς εἶπεν αὐτοῖς, βλέπετε μή τις ὑμᾶς πλανήσῃ. ³⁶Περὶ δὲ τῆς ἡμέρας ἐκείνης καὶ ὥρας οὐδεὶς οἶδεν, οὐδὲ οἱ ἄγγελοι τῶν οὐρανῶν οὐδὲ ὁ υἱός, εἰ μὴ ὁ πατὴρ μόνος. ⁴⁴διὰ τοῦτο καὶ ὑμεῖς γίνεσθε ἕτοιμοι,

Καθημένου (sit); Ἐλαιῶν (olive tree); προσῆλθον v.1.s.aor.act.ind [προσέρχομαι]; Εἰπὲ v.2.s.aor.act.impv. [λέγω]; πότε (how long); ἔσται v.3.s.fut.ind. [εἰμί]; σῆς (your); παρουσίας (coming); συντελείας (completion); εἶπεν v.3.s.aor.act.ind. [λέγω]; πλανήσῃ (decree); οἶδεν v.3.s.pf.act.ind. [οἶδα]; ἕτοιμοι (ready)

Week 34

Temptation

1. Genesis 3:6; Matthew 4:1–3

Tempted by the Good

FOR THOSE WHO BELONG UTTERLY TO GOD the temptation always comes through something that is good or even necessary. Saying "no" at such times is irrational to the natural mind.

GENESIS 3:6

⁶וַתֵּרֶא הָאִשָּׁה כִּי טוֹב הָעֵץ לְמַאֲכָל וְכִי תַאֲוָה־הוּא לָעֵינַיִם
וְנֶחְמָד הָעֵץ לְהַשְׂכִּיל וַתִּקַּח מִפִּרְיוֹ וַתֹּאכַל וַתִּתֵּן גַּם־
לְאִישָׁהּ עִמָּהּ וַיֹּאכַל׃

וַתֵּרֶא v.c. + v.3.f.s.impf.Q. [רֹאה]; לְמַאֲכָל (food); תַאֲוָה (desire); וְנֶחְמָד (desire); וַתִּקַּח v.c. + v.3.f.s.impf.Q. [לקח]; וַתִּתֵּן v.c. + v.3.f.s.impf.Q. [נתן]

MATTHEW 4:1–3

¹Τότε ὁ Ἰησοῦς ἀνήχθη εἰς τὴν ἔρημον ὑπὸ τοῦ πνεύματος πειρασθῆναι ὑπὸ τοῦ διαβόλου. ²καὶ νηστεύσας ἡμέρας τεσσεράκοντα καὶ νύκτας τεσσεράκοντα, ὕστερον ἐπείνασεν. ³Καὶ προσελθὼν ὁ πειράζων εἶπεν αὐτῷ, Εἰ υἱὸς εἶ τοῦ θεοῦ, εἰπὲ ἵνα οἱ λίθοι οὗτοι ἄρτοι γένωνται.

ἀνήχθη v.3.s.aor.pass.ind. [ἀνάγω] (bring up); πειρασθῆναι (tempt); διαβόλου (devil); νηστεύσας (fast); τεσσεράκοντα (forty); ὕστερον (later); ἐπείνασεν (be hungry); προσελθὼν v.m.s.nom.aor.act.ptc. [προσέρχομαι]; εἶπεν v.3.s.aor.act.ind. [λέγω]; εἰπὲ v.2.s.aor.act.impv. [λέγω]

2. 1 Samuel 8.4–5; 1 John 2:15–17

Transformed Desire

GOD, HELP ME SEE the "this-worldness" of my own heart. Breathe your will into my will so that I do not will anything but your will. Transform my desires until they burn only the flame of Christ. Amen.

1 SAMUEL 8:4–5

⁴וַיִּתְקַבְּצוּ כֹּל זִקְנֵי יִשְׂרָאֵל וַיָּבֹאוּ אֶל־שְׁמוּאֵל הָרָמָתָה׃
⁵וַיֹּאמְרוּ אֵלָיו הִנֵּה אַתָּה זָקַנְתָּ וּבָנֶיךָ לֹא הָלְכוּ בִּדְרָכֶיךָ
עַתָּה שִׂימָה־לָּנוּ מֶלֶךְ לְשָׁפְטֵנוּ כְּכָל־הַגּוֹיִם׃

וַיָּבֹאוּ v.c. + v.3.m.p.impf.Q. [בוא]; שִׂימָה v.2.m.s.impv.Q.para. [שׂים]; לְשָׁפְטֵנוּ prep. + v.in.cs.Q. [שׁפט] + 1.com.p.pr.sf.

1 JOHN 2:15–17

¹⁵Μὴ ἀγαπᾶτε τὸν κόσμον μηδὲ τὰ ἐν τῷ κόσμῳ. ἐάν τις ἀγαπᾷ τὸν κόσμον, οὐκ ἔστιν ἡ ἀγάπη τοῦ πατρὸς ἐν αὐτῷ· ¹⁶ὅτι πᾶν τὸ ἐν τῷ κόσμῳ, ἡ ἐπιθυμία τῆς σαρκὸς καὶ ἡ ἐπιθυμία τῶν ὀφθαλμῶν καὶ ἡ ἀλαζονεία τοῦ βίου, οὐκ ἔστιν ἐκ τοῦ πατρὸς ἀλλ᾽ ἐκ τοῦ κόσμου ἐστίν. ¹⁷καὶ ὁ κόσμος παράγεται καὶ ἡ ἐπιθυμία αὐτοῦ, ὁ δὲ ποιῶν τὸ θέλημα τοῦ θεοῦ μένει εἰς τὸν αἰῶνα.

ἔστιν v.3.s.pres.ind. [εἰμί]; ἐπιθυμία (desire); ἀλαζονεία (pride); βίου (life); παράγεται (pass away)

3. Genesis 4:6–7; James 1:12–13

Crouching Outside the Door?

LET'S FACE IT—we have a choice in all of this. From sin's first malignant twinge to the final ugly act, we have a choice. The easiest time to say "no" is when sin is still outside the door. Keep the door closed. It's that simple.

GENESIS 4:6–7

⁶וַיֹּאמֶר יְהוָה אֶל־קָיִן לָמָּה חָרָה לָךְ וְלָמָּה נָפְלוּ פָנֶיךָ׃
⁷הֲלוֹא אִם־תֵּיטִיב שְׂאֵת וְאִם לֹא תֵיטִיב לַפֶּתַח חַטָּאת רֹבֵץ וְאֵלֶיךָ
תְּשׁוּקָתוֹ וְאַתָּה תִּמְשָׁל־בּוֹ׃

שְׂאֵת v.in.cst.Q. [נשׂא]; רֹבֵץ (crouch); תְּשׁוּקָתוֹ (desire)

JAMES 1:12–13

¹²Μακάριος ἀνὴρ ὃς ὑπομένει πειρασμόν, ὅτι δόκιμος γενόμενος λήμψεται τὸν στέφανον τῆς ζωῆς ὃν ἐπηγγείλατο τοῖς ἀγαπῶσιν αὐτόν. ¹³μηδεὶς πειραζόμενος λεγέτω ὅτι Ἀπὸ θεοῦ πειράζομαι· ὁ γὰρ θεὸς ἀπείραστός ἐστιν κακῶν, πειράζει δὲ αὐτὸς οὐδένα.

ὑπομένει (endure); πειρασμόν (temptation); δόκιμος (genuine); γενόμενος v.m.s.nom.aor.mid.ptc. [γίνομαι]; λήμψεται v.3.s.fut.mid.ind. [λαμβάνω]; στέφανον (crown); ἐπηγγείλατο (promise); πειραζόμενος (tempt); ἀπείραστος (without temptation)

4. Job 1:6–7; Luke 4:13–14a

The Real Target

WE CAN BE SURE THE DEVIL IS ROAMING and just as sure that he knows where we live. Remember, all the warnings about the devil are given to Christians. If the devil could find opportune times to attack the Son of God, the devil will surely attack us. But here's the part the devil never seems to get: every time we resist him we are filled anew with the power of the Spirit, the kind of power that gives God a good reputation wherever we go. So it is that the devourer devours himself.

JOB 1:6–7

וַיְהִי הַיּוֹם וַיָּבֹאוּ בְּנֵי הָאֱלֹהִים לְהִתְיַצֵּב עַל־יְהֹוָה ⁶
וַיָּבוֹא גַם־הַשָּׂטָן בְּתוֹכָם:
וַיֹּאמֶר יְהֹוָה אֶל־הַשָּׂטָן מֵאַיִן תָּבֹא וַיַּעַן הַשָּׂטָן אֶת־יְהֹוָה ⁷
וַיֹּאמַר מִשּׁוּט בָּאָרֶץ וּמֵהִתְהַלֵּךְ בָּהּ:

לְהִתְיַצֵּב וַיְהִי v.c. + 3.m.s.impf.Q. [הָיָה]; וַיָּבֹאוּ v.c. + 3.m.p.impf.Q. [בּוֹא] (stand firm); הַשָּׂטָן (adversary); תָּבֹא v.c. + 2.m.s.impf.Q. [בּוֹא]; וַיַּעַן v.c. + 3.m.s.impf.Q. [עָנָה]; מִשּׁוּט prep. + v.in.cs.Q. [שׁוּט] (wander about); וּמֵהִתְהַלֵּךְ cj. + prep. + v.in.cs.Ht. [הָלַךְ]

LUKE 4:13–14A

¹³Καὶ συντελέσας πάντα πειρασμὸν ὁ διάβολος ἀπέστη ἀπ᾽ αὐτοῦ ἄχρι καιροῦ. ¹⁴Καὶ ὑπέστρεψεν ὁ Ἰησοῦς ἐν τῇ δυνάμει τοῦ πνεύματος εἰς τὴν Γαλιλαίαν.

συντελέσας (finish); πειρασμὸν (trial); διάβολος (devil); ἀπέστη v.3.s.aor.act.ind. [ἀφίστημι] (withdraw); ἄχρι (until); ὑπέστρεψεν (return)

5. Proverbs 4:26–27; Mark 9:43

Hell-Bent Limbs

I THINK THE MOST BASIC ELEMENT in resisting temptation has to do with gut-level honesty, with knowing my own hell-bent limbs. How can I name them and cut them off if I've convinced myself that I'm lily white?

PROVERBS 4:26–27

²⁶פַּלֵּס מַעְגַּל רַגְלֶךָ וְכָל־דְּרָכֶיךָ יִכֹּנוּ׃
²⁷אַל־תֵּט־יָמִין וּשְׂמֹאול הָסֵר רַגְלְךָ מֵרָע׃

פַּלֵּס (level); מַעְגַּל (course); יִכֹּנוּ v.3.m.p.impf.N. [כון]; תֵּט v.2.m.s.jus.Q. [נטה]; הָסֵר v.2.m.s.impv.H. [סור]

MARK 9:43

⁴³Καὶ ἐὰν σκανδαλίζῃ σε ἡ χείρ σου, ἀπόκοψον αὐτήν· καλόν ἐστίν σε κυλλὸν εἰσελθεῖν εἰς τὴν ζωὴν ἢ τὰς δύο χεῖρας ἔχοντα ἀπελθεῖν εἰς τὴν γέενναν, εἰς τὸ πῦρ τὸ ἄσβεστον.

σκανδαλίζῃ (cause to sin); ἀπόκοψον v.2.s.aor.act.impv. [ἀποκόπτω] (cut off); κυλλὸν (cripple); εἰσελθεῖν v.aor.act.in. [εἰσέρχομαι]; ἀπελθεῖν v.aor.act.in. [ἀπέρχομαι]; γέενναν (hell); ἄσβεστον (inextinguishable)

6. Psalm 91.14–15, Hebrews 2:18

Our Defender

THANK GOD THERE IS MORE than me to rely on when the test comes! How could I deliver myself when I got myself in trouble to begin with? In the time of testing, when my flesh is weak and my spirit is confused, Christ comes to my defense, ready to protect and deliver. *Christus victor!* Christ is my victory!

PSALM 91:14–15

‫¹⁴כִּי בִי חָשַׁק וַאֲפַלְּטֵהוּ אֲשַׂגְּבֵהוּ כִּי־יָדַע שְׁמִי׃‬
‫¹⁵יִקְרָאֵנִי וְאֶעֱנֵהוּ עִמּוֹ־אָנֹכִי בְצָרָה אֲחַלְּצֵהוּ וַאֲכַבְּדֵהוּ׃‬

חָשַׁק (love); וַאֲפַלְּטֵהוּ cj. + v.1.com.s.impf.P. [פלט] (escape) + 3.m.s.pr.sf.; אֲשַׂגְּבֵהוּ v.1.com.s.impf.P. [שׂגב] (be inaccessible) + 3.m.s.pr.sf.; יִקְרָאֵנִי v.3.m.s.impf.Q. [קרא] + 1.com.s.pr.sf.; וְאֶעֱנֵהוּ cj. + v.1.com.s.impf.Q. [ענה] + 3.m.s.pr.sf.; אֲחַלְּצֵהוּ v.1.com.s.impf.P. [חלץ] (rescue) + 3.m.s.pr.sf.; וַאֲכַבְּדֵהוּ cj. + v.1.com.s.impf.P. [כבד] + 3.m.s.pr.sf.

HEBREWS 2:18

¹⁸ἐν ᾧ γὰρ πέπονθεν αὐτὸς πειρασθείς, δύναται τοῖς πειραζομένοις βοηθῆσαι.

πέπονθεν v.3.s.aor.pf.act.ind. [πάσχω] (suffer); πειρασθείς (tempt); βοηθῆσαι (help)

7. Psalm 37:23–24; Hebrews 4:15–16

The Pretender

I COME TO YOU, JESUS, Incarnate Light, One who dissolves death into light. Here with me is dark temptation—starved beast howling, nagging, whining for flesh. Here it is, in all its ugliness and terror, in all its dark attraction. There is more. Here is my heart, my naked self, all my neediness, insecurity, desire. You are the true answer to all that I need. I give up this pretender to your place, this object of temptation. And I open myself fully to you. Amen.

PSALM 37:23–24

²³מֵיְהוָה מִצְעֲדֵי־גֶבֶר כּוֹנָנוּ וְדַרְכּוֹ יֶחְפָּץ׃
²⁴כִּי־יִפֹּל לֹא־יוּטָל כִּי־יְהוָה סוֹמֵךְ יָדוֹ׃

מִצְעֲדֵי (step); כּוֹנָנוּ v.3.m.p.pf.Pulal [כון]; יִפֹּל v.3.m.s.impf.Q. [נפל]; יוּטָל v.3.m.s.impf.Ho. [טול] (cast out); סוֹמֵךְ (support)

HEBREWS 4:15–16

¹⁵οὐ γὰρ ἔχομεν ἀρχιερέα μὴ δυνάμενον συμπαθῆσαι ταῖς ἀσθενείαις ἡμῶν, πεπειρασμένον δὲ κατὰ πάντα καθ᾽ ὁμοιότητα χωρὶς ἁμαρτίας. ¹⁶προσερχώμεθα οὖν μετὰ παρρησίας τῷ θρόνῳ τῆς χάριτος, ἵνα λάβωμεν ἔλεος καὶ χάριν εὕρωμεν εἰς εὔκαιρον βοήθειαν.

συμπαθῆσαι (sympathize with); ἀσθενείαις (weakness); πεπειρασμένον (tempt); ὁμοιότητα (similarity); χωρὶς (without); παρρησίας (boldness); λάβωμεν v.1.p.aor.act.sub. [λαμβάνω]; ἔλεος (mercy); εὔκαιρον (timely); βοήθειαν (help)

Completion

1. Zechariah 3:1; Revelation 12:10–11

The Accuser, Thrown Down

WE ARE ABLE TO CLING TO LIFE even in the face of death when we know that Satan, the accuser, will be overcome once and for all. The authority of God's word is bringing it about even now, yes, even in my heart. For the Lamb is Victor and I belong to the Lamb. Amen and amen.

ZECHARIAH 3:1

¹וַיַּרְאֵנִי אֶת־יְהוֹשֻׁעַ הַכֹּהֵן הַגָּדוֹל עֹמֵד לִפְנֵי מַלְאַךְ יְהוָה וְהַשָּׂטָן עֹמֵד עַל־יְמִינוֹ לְשִׂטְנוֹ:

וַיַּרְאֵנִי v.c. + v.3.m.s.impf.H. [רָאָה] + 1.com.s.pr.sf.; וְהַשָּׂטָן (accuser); לְשִׂטְנוֹ prep. + v.in.cs.Q. [שָׂטַן] (oppose) + 3.m.s.pr.sf.

REVELATION 12:10–11

¹⁰καὶ ἤκουσα φωνὴν μεγάλην ἐν τῷ οὐρανῷ λέγουσαν,
    Ἄρτι ἐγένετο ἡ σωτηρία καὶ ἡ δύναμις
      καὶ ἡ βασιλεία τοῦ θεοῦ ἡμῶν
      καὶ ἡ ἐξουσία τοῦ χριστοῦ αὐτοῦ,
    ὅτι ἐβλήθη ὁ κατήγωρ τῶν ἀδελφῶν ἡμῶν,
      ὁ κατηγορῶν αὐτοὺς ἐνώπιον τοῦ θεοῦ ἡμῶν
      ἡμέρας καὶ νυκτός.
¹¹καὶ αὐτοὶ ἐνίκησαν αὐτὸν διὰ τὸ αἷμα τοῦ ἀρνίου
      καὶ διὰ τὸν λόγον τῆς μαρτυρίας αὐτῶν
    καὶ οὐκ ἠγάπησαν τὴν ψυχὴν αὐτῶν ἄχρι θανάτου.

Ἄρτι (now); ἐγένετο v.3.s.aor.mid.ind. [γίνομαι]; σωτηρία (salvation); ἐβλήθη v.3.s.aor.pass.ind. [βάλλω]; κατήγωρ (accuser); ἐνώπιον (before); ἐνίκησαν (conquer); ἀρνίου (lamb); μαρτυρίας (witness); ἄχρι (until)

2. Daniel 12:2–3; Revelation 22:12

Desires Fulfilled

VINDICATION BELONGS TO GOD. And his vindication will be such that we will all be astounded. We do not realize now the wisdom of some of those who will "shine like the brightness of the sky," nor are we sufficiently aware that attitudes of shame and contempt toward God that we choose for ourselves now will be magnified toward God in eternity, when all veils of flesh have been removed. Whatever we truly long for now, we will receive a thousandfold then. This is what God's vindication is about. Giving us what we really wanted all along.

DANIEL 12:2–3

²וְרַבִּים מִיְּשֵׁנֵי אַדְמַת־עָפָר יָקִיצוּ אֵלֶּה לְחַיֵּי עוֹלָם וְאֵלֶּה
לַחֲרָפוֹת לְדִרְאוֹן עוֹלָם:
³וְהַמַּשְׂכִּלִים יַזְהִרוּ כְּזֹהַר הָרָקִיעַ וּמַצְדִּיקֵי הָרַבִּים
כַּכּוֹכָבִים לְעוֹלָם וָעֶד:

מִיְּשֵׁנֵי prep. + n.m.p.cs. (sleeper); יָקִיצוּ (awake); לְדִרְאוֹן (content); יַזְהִרוּ v.3.m.p.impf.H.defective [זהר] (be careful); כְּזֹהַר (brightness); הָרָקִיעַ (expanse); כַּכּוֹכָבִים (star)

REVELATION 22:12

¹²Ἰδοὺ ἔρχομαι ταχύ, καὶ ὁ μισθός μου μετ᾽ ἐμοῦ ἀποδοῦναι ἑκάστῳ ὡς τὸ ἔργον ἐστὶν αὐτοῦ.

ταχύ (quickly); μισθός (wages); ἀποδοῦναι v.aor.act.in. [ἀποδίδωμι] (give); ἐστὶν v.3.s.pres.ind. [εἰμί]

3. Jeremiah 31.33–34; John 17:20–22

Oneness

ONENESS WITH GOD, oneness with each other, the final healing of spiritual and relational fragmentation—this is salvation fulfilled. How dimly we understand the singular desire of God! His desire is, quite simply, oneness.

JEREMIAH 31:33–34

³³כִּי זֹאת הַבְּרִית אֲשֶׁר אֶכְרֹת אֶת־בֵּית יִשְׂרָאֵל אַחֲרֵי הַיָּמִים
הָהֵם נְאֻם־יְהוָה נָתַתִּי אֶת־תּוֹרָתִי בְּקִרְבָּם וְעַל־לִבָּם אֶכְתֲּבֶנָּה
וְהָיִיתִי לָהֶם לֵאלֹהִים וְהֵמָּה יִהְיוּ־לִי לְעָם:
³⁴וְלֹא יְלַמְּדוּ עוֹד אִישׁ אֶת־רֵעֵהוּ וְאִישׁ אֶת־אָחִיו לֵאמֹר דְּעוּ
אֶת־יְהוָה כִּי־כוּלָּם יֵדְעוּ אוֹתִי לְמִקְטַנָּם וְעַד־גְּדוֹלָם נְאֻם־
יְהוָה כִּי אֶסְלַח לַעֲוֹנָם וּלְחַטָּאתָם לֹא אֶזְכָּר־עוֹד:

נָתַתִּי v.1.com.s.pf.Q. [נתן]; אֶכְתֲּבֶנָּה v.1.com.s.impf.Q. [כתב] + en. + 3.f.s.pr.sf.; וְהָיִיתִי v.c. + v.1.com.s.pf.Q. [היה]; יִהְיוּ v.3.m.s.impf.Q. [היה]; דְּעוּ v.2.m.p.impv.Q. [ידע]; יֵדְעוּ v.3.m.s.impf.Q. [ידע]; לְמִקְטַנָּם prep. + prep. + adj.m.s. + 3.m.p.pr.sf.; אֶסְלַח (forgive)

JOHN 17:20–22

²⁰Οὐ περὶ τούτων δὲ ἐρωτῶ μόνον, ἀλλὰ καὶ περὶ τῶν πιστευόντων διὰ τοῦ λόγου αὐτῶν εἰς ἐμέ, ²¹ἵνα πάντες ἓν ὦσιν, καθὼς σύ, πάτερ, ἐν ἐμοὶ καγὼ ἐν σοί, ἵνα καὶ αὐτοὶ ἐν ἡμῖν ὦσιν, ἵνα ὁ κόσμος πιστεύῃ ὅτι σύ με ἀπέστειλας. ²²καγὼ τὴν δόξαν ἣν δέδωκας μοι δέδωκάς αὐτοῖς, ἵνα ὦσιν ἓν καθὼς ἡμεῖς ἕν·

ὦσιν v.3.p.pres.act.sub. [εἰμί]; δέδωκάς v.2.s.pf.act.ind. [δίδωμι]

4. Isaiah 60:18–19; Revelation 20:10, 14

Holy Fire

SOMEHOW THE SAME SPIRIT-FIRE that ignites holiness in the saint will be the ultimate fire of damnation to evil. *How* the flame burns and what its end result is depends on the direction one faces. Holy fire is home, hearth, gladness, life, light, peace, joy, the Spirit of Christ to all that proceeds from and returns to God. The same fire is fear, damnation, hell to all that does not.

ISAIAH 60:18–19

¹⁸לֹא־יִשָּׁמַע עוֹד חָמָס בְּאַרְצֵךְ שֹׁד וָשֶׁבֶר בִּגְבוּלָיִךְ וְקָרָאת
יְשׁוּעָה חוֹמֹתַיִךְ וּשְׁעָרַיִךְ תְּהִלָּה׃
¹⁹לֹא־יִהְיֶה־לָּךְ עוֹד הַשֶּׁמֶשׁ לְאוֹר יוֹמָם וּלְנֹגַהּ הַיָּרֵחַ לֹא־
יָאִיר לָךְ וְהָיָה־לָךְ יְהוָה לְאוֹר עוֹלָם וֵאלֹהַיִךְ לְתִפְאַרְתֵּךְ׃

שֹׁד (bribe); וָשֶׁבֶר (destruction); יוֹמָם (by day); וּלְנֹגַהּ (brightness); הַיָּרֵחַ (moon); יָאִיר v.3.m.s.impf.H. [אוֹר] (shine); לְתִפְאַרְתֵּךְ (glory)

REVELATION 20:10, 14

¹⁰καὶ ὁ διάβολος ὁ πλανῶν αὐτοὺς ἐβλήθη εἰς τὴν λίμνην τοῦ πυρὸς καὶ θείου ὅπου καὶ τὸ θηρίον καὶ ὁ ψευδοπροφήτης, καὶ βασανισθήσονται ἡμέρας καὶ νυκτὸς εἰς τοὺς αἰῶνας τῶν αἰώνων. ¹⁴καὶ ὁ θάνατος καὶ ὁ ᾅδης ἐβλήθησαν εἰς τὴν λίμνην τοῦ πυρός. οὗτος ὁ θάνατος ὁ δεύτερός ἐστιν, ἡ λίμνη τοῦ πυρός.

διάβολος (devil); πλανῶν (deceive); ἐβλήθη v.3.s.aor.pass.ind. [βάλλω]; λίμνην (lake); θείου (sulphur); θηρίον (beast); ψευδοπροφήτης (false prophet); βασανισθήσονται (torment); ᾅδης (hell)

5. Isaiah 52:10; Colossians 3.1–4

The Revelation of God's Children

IN THE FINAL BARING OF HIS HOLY ARM to all nations, God will finally reveal us as we really are—glorious and beautiful, radiant with Christ, victors over sin and death. All entities, whether human or angelic, will see the revelation and fall mute before the majesty of God.

ISAIAH 52:10

חָשַׂף יְהוָה אֶת־זְרוֹעַ קָדְשׁוֹ לְעֵינֵי כָּל־הַגּוֹיִם וְרָאוּ כָּל־ ¹⁰
אַפְסֵי־אָרֶץ אֵת יְשׁוּעַת אֱלֹהֵינוּ:

חָשַׂף (lay bare); וְרָאוּ v.c. + v.3.c.p.pf.Q. [רָאה]; אַפְסֵי (end)

COLOSSIANS 3:1–4

¹Εἰ οὖν συνηγέρθητε τῷ Χριστῷ, τὰ ἄνω ζητεῖτε, οὗ ὁ Χριστός ἐστιν ἐν δεξιᾷ τοῦ θεοῦ καθήμενος· ²τὰ ἄνω φρονεῖτε, μὴ τὰ ἐπὶ τῆς γῆς. ³ἀπεθάνετε γὰρ καὶ ἡ ζωὴ ὑμῶν κέκρυπται σὺν τῷ Χριστῷ ἐν τῷ θεῷ. ⁴ὅταν ὁ Χριστὸς φανερωθῇ, ἡ ζωὴ ὑμῶν, τότε καὶ ὑμεῖς σὺν αὐτῷ φανερωθήσεσθε ἐν δόξῃ.

συνηγέρθητε v.2.p.aor.pass.ind. [συνεγείρω] (raise together); ἄνω (above); φρονεῖτε (think of); ἀπεθάνετε v.2.p.aor.act.ind. [αποθνήσκω]; κέκρυπται (hide); φανερωθῇ (reveal)

6. Isaiah 52:14–15; Philippians 2:10–11

Twofold Glory

JESUS CHRIST WILL BE KNOWN as he is, unveiled, in all his humility and all his majesty and every soul who ever lived will be speechless at the revelation. For the glory of the Lord is twofold—his weakness and his strength. We will be astonished because we see him as one or the other, depending on what we want him to be.

ISAIAH 52:14–15

14כַּאֲשֶׁר שָׁמְמוּ עָלֶיךָ רַבִּים כֵּן־מִשְׁחַת מֵאִישׁ מַרְאֵהוּ וְתֹאֲרוֹ
מִבְּנֵי אָדָם:
15כֵּן יַזֶּה גּוֹיִם רַבִּים עָלָיו יִקְפְּצוּ מְלָכִים פִּיהֶם כִּי אֲשֶׁר לֹא־
סֻפַּר לָהֶם רָאוּ וַאֲשֶׁר לֹא־שָׁמְעוּ הִתְבּוֹנָנוּ:

מִשְׁחַת (disfigurement); וְתֹאֲרוֹ (form); יַזֶּה v.3.m.s.impf.H. [נזה] (sprinkle); יִקְפְּצוּ (shut); רָאוּ v.3.c.p.pf.Q. [ראה]; הִתְבּוֹנָנוּ v.3.c.p.pf.Htpl. [בין]

PHILIPPIANS 2:10–11

10ἵνα ἐν τῷ ὀνόματι Ἰησοῦ πᾶν γόνυ κάμψῃ ἐπουρανίων καὶ ἐπιγείων καὶ καταχθονίων 11καὶ πᾶσα γλῶσσα ἐξομολογήσηται ὅτι κύριος Ἰησοῦς Χριστὸς εἰς δόξαν θεοῦ πατρός.

γόνυ (knee); κάμψῃ v.3.s.aor.act.sub. [κάμπτω] (bow); ἐπουρανίων (heavenly being); ἐπιγείων (earthly being); καταχθονίων (underwordly being); ἐξομολογήσηται v.3.s.aor.mid.sub. [ἐξομολογέω] (confess)

7. Isaiah 65:17; Revelation 21.1–2

When Memories Are Healed

WHAT A COMFORT, MY CREATOR, to know that you will heal memories in the new creation, that all that is in us that is of death, loss, emptiness, sorrow, and pain will be forgotten. I hold this promise close to my heart, cherishing the seed-life in your words. The promise itself begins to heal the pain.

ISAIAH 65:17

¹⁷כִּי־הִנְנִי בוֹרֵא שָׁמַיִם חֲדָשִׁים וָאָרֶץ חֲדָשָׁה וְלֹא תִזָּכַרְנָה
הָרִאשֹׁנוֹת וְלֹא תַעֲלֶינָה עַל־לֵב:

תַעֲלֶינָה v.3.f.p.impf.Q. [עלה]

REVELATION 21:1–2

¹Καὶ εἶδον οὐρανὸν καινὸν καὶ γῆν καινήν. ὁ γὰρ πρῶτος
οὐρανὸς καὶ ἡ πρώτη γῆ ἀπῆλθαν καὶ ἡ θάλασσα οὐκ ἔστιν
ἔτι. ²καὶ τὴν πόλιν τὴν ἁγίαν Ἰερουσαλὴμ καινὴν εἶδον
καταβαίνουσαν ἐκ τοῦ οὐρανοῦ ἀπὸ τοῦ θεοῦ ἡτοιμασμένην
ὡς νύμφην κεκοσμημένην τῷ ἀνδρὶ αὐτῆς.

εἶδον v.1.s.aor.act.ind. [ὁράω]; καινήν (new); ἀπῆλθαν v.3.p.aor.act.ind. [ἀπέρχομαι]; ἔστιν v.3.s.pres.ind. [εἰμί]; καινὴν (new); ἡτοιμασμένην v.f.s.acc.pf.pass.ptc. [ἑτοιμάζω] (prepare); νύμφην (bride); κεκοσμημένην v.f.s.acc.pf.pass.ptc. [κοσμέω] (adorn)

Week 36

Prayer

1. 2 Chronicles 5:13–14; Luke 10:21–22

Prayer of Worship

"GOD IS GREAT; GOD IS GOOD." When our hearts know and our mouths speak and we live these words, we are praying the prayer of worship.

2 CHRONICLES 5:13–14

¹³וַיְהִ֣י כְאֶחָ֡ד לַמְחַצְּצרִ֣ים וְלַמְשֹׁרֲרִים֩ לְהַשְׁמִ֨יעַ קֹול־אֶחָ֜ד
לְהַלֵּ֣ל וּלְהֹדֹ֣ות לַיהוָה֒ וּכְהָרִ֣ים קֹ֗ול בַּחֲצֹצְרֹ֤ות וּבִמְצִלְתַּ֙יִם֙
וּבִכְלֵ֣י הַשִּׁ֔יר וּבְהַלֵּ֤ל לַֽיהוָה֙ כִּ֣י טֹ֔וב כִּ֥י לְעֹולָ֖ם חַסְדֹּ֑ו
וְהַבַּ֛יִת מָלֵ֥א עָנָ֖ן בֵּ֥ית יְהוָֽה׃
¹⁴וְלֹא־יָכְל֧וּ הַכֹּהֲנִ֛ים לַעֲמֹ֥ד לְשָׁרֵ֖ת מִפְּנֵ֣י הֶעָנָ֑ן כִּי־מָלֵ֥א
כְבֹוד־יְהוָ֖ה אֶת־בֵּ֥ית הָאֱלֹהִֽים׃

וַיְהִ֣י v.3.m.s.impf.Q. [היה]; לַמְחַצְּצרִ֣ים (trumpeter); וְלַמְשֹׁרֲרִים cj. + prep. + d.s. + v.m.p.ptc.Po. [שׁיר]; וּלְהֹדֹ֣ות cj. + prep. + v.in.cs.H.defective [ידה]; וּכְהָרִ֣ים cj. + prep. + v.in.cs.H. [רום]; בַּחֲצֹצְרֹ֤ות (trumpet); וּבִמְצִלְתַּ֙יִם֙ (cymbals)

LUKE 10:21–22

²¹Ἐν αὐτῇ τῇ ὥρᾳ ἠγαλλιάσατο [ἐν] τῷ πνεύματι τῷ ἁγίῳ καὶ εἶπεν, Ἐξομολογοῦμαί σοι, πάτερ, κύριε τοῦ οὐρανοῦ καὶ τῆς γῆς, ὅτι ἀπέκρυψας ταῦτα ἀπὸ σοφῶν καὶ συνετῶν καὶ ἀπεκάλυψας αὐτὰ νηπίοις· ναὶ ὁ πατήρ, ὅτι οὕτως εὐδοκία ἐγένετο ἔμπροσθέν σου. ²²Πάντα μοι παρεδόθη ὑπὸ τοῦ πατρός μου, καὶ οὐδεὶς γινώσκει τίς ἐστιν ὁ υἱὸς εἰ μὴ ὁ πατήρ, καὶ τίς ἐστιν ὁ πατὴρ εἰ μὴ ὁ υἱὸς καὶ ᾧ ἐὰν βούληται ὁ υἱὸς ἀποκαλύψαι.

ἠγαλλιάσατο (be glad); εἶπεν v.3.s.aor.act.ind. [λέγω]; Ἐξομολογοῦμαι (admit); ἀπέκρυψας (hide); σοφῶν (wise); συνετῶν (learned); ἀπεκάλυψας (reveal); νηπίοις (infant); ναὶ (indeed); εὐδοκία (good pleasure); ἐγένετο v.3.s.aor.mid.ind. [γίνομαι]; ἔμπροσθέν (before); παρεδόθη v.3.s.aor.pass.ind. [παραδίδωμι]; βούληται (desire)

2. Psalm 126:5–6; Hebrews 5:7

Prayer of Tears

PRAYER OF TEARS. Altar tears, tears of trembling, wordless words, rain of heaven, molten love. Grief and joy, myrrh and honey, freely flowing, running down.

PSALM 126:5–6

‏⁵הַזֹּרְעִים בְּדִמְעָה בְּרִנָּה יִקְצֹרוּ׃
‏⁶הָלוֹךְ יֵלֵךְ וּבָכֹה נֹשֵׂא מֶשֶׁךְ־הַזָּרַע בֹּא־יָבוֹא בְרִנָּה נֹשֵׂא
אֲלֻמֹּתָיו׃

‏בְּדִמְעָה (tear); ‏בְּרִנָּה (cry of joy); ‏יִקְצֹרוּ (reap); ‏יֵלֵךְ v.3.m.s.impf.Q. [‏הלך]; ‏מֶשֶׁךְ (trail); ‏בֹּא v.in.ab.Q. [‏בוא]; ‏אֲלֻמֹּתָיו (sheaf)

HEBREWS 5:7

⁷ὃς ἐν ταῖς ἡμέραις τῆς σαρκὸς αὐτοῦ δεήσεις τε καὶ ἱκετηρίας πρὸς τὸν δυνάμενον σῴζειν αὐτὸν ἐκ θανάτου μετὰ κραυγῆς ἰσχυρᾶς καὶ δακρύων προσενέγκας καὶ εἰσακουσθεὶς ἀπὸ τῆς εὐλαβείας,

δεήσεις (prayer); ἱκετηρίας (request); κραυγῆς (crying); ἰσχυρᾶς (loud); δακρύων (tear); εἰσακουσθεὶς (obey); εὐλαβείας (reverence)

3. Job 42:8; Luke 22:31–32

Intercession

WHICH IS THE GREATER CHALLENGE—to intercede for the one who has hurt me or to require the intercession of one whom I have hurt? It is a trick question, of course. The two are one and the same, for all intercession proceeds from Christ, whose scarred hands hold mine and from whose pierced side flows soul blood for all the world. Whether I intercede or am the object of intercession, it all comes from Christ and cost the agony of his soul.

JOB 42:8

⁸וְעַתָּה קְחוּ־לָכֶם שִׁבְעָה־פָרִים וְשִׁבְעָה אֵילִים וּלְכוּ אֶל־עַבְדִּי
אִיּוֹב וְהַעֲלִיתֶם עוֹלָה בַּעַדְכֶם וְאִיּוֹב עַבְדִּי יִתְפַּלֵּל עֲלֵיכֶם
כִּי אִם־פָּנָיו אֶשָּׂא לְבִלְתִּי עֲשׂוֹת עִמָּכֶם נְבָלָה כִּי לֹא דִבַּרְתֶּם
אֵלַי נְכוֹנָה כְּעַבְדִּי אִיּוֹב׃

וְהַעֲלִיתֶם v.c. + v.2.m.p.pf.H. [עלה]; וְלְכוּ v.2.m.p.impv.Q. [הלך]; וּלְכוּ cj. + v.2.m.p.impv.Q. [הלך]; וְהַעֲלִיתֶם v.c. + v.2.m.p.pf.H. [עלה]; אֶשָּׂא v.1.com.s.impf.Q. [נשא]; עֲשׂוֹת v.in.cs.Q. [עשׂה]; נְבָלָה (folly); נְכוֹנָה v.f.s.ptc.N. [כון]

LUKE 22:31–32

³¹Σίμων Σίμων, ἰδοὺ ὁ Σατανᾶς ἐξῃτήσατο ὑμᾶς τοῦ σινιάσαι ὡς τὸν σῖτον· ³²ἐγὼ δὲ ἐδεήθην περὶ σοῦ ἵνα μὴ ἐκλίπῃ ἡ πίστις σου· καὶ σύ ποτε ἐπιστρέψας στήρισον τοὺς ἀδελφούς σου.

Σατανᾶς (Satan); ἐξῃτήσατο v.3.s.aor.mid.ind. [ἐξαιτέω] (demand); σινιάσαι (sift); σῖτον (wheat); ἐδεήθην v.1.s.aor.pass.ind. [δέομαι] (beg); ἐκλίπῃ (fail); ποτε (once); ἐπιστρέψας (return); στήρισον (strengthen)

4. 2 Kings 4:32–33; Matthew 6:5–6

Secret Prayer

JUST AS LOVERS REQUIRE PRIVACY—time and space to be alone together—the soul requires solitude for true prayer. The reward God gives to those who go into their room and shut the door is something akin to the reward lovers have for their love.

2 KINGS 4:32–33

‏³²וַיָּבֹא אֱלִישָׁע הַבָּיְתָה וְהִנֵּה הַנַּעַר מֵת מֻשְׁכָּב עַל־מִטָּתוֹ:
‏³³וַיָּבֹא וַיִּסְגֹּר הַדֶּלֶת בְּעַד שְׁנֵיהֶם וַיִּתְפַּלֵּל אֶל־יְהוָה:

וַיָּבֹא v.c. + v.3.m.s.impf.Q. [בוא]; מֵת v.m.s.ptc.Q. [מות]; מִטָּתוֹ (bed)

MATTHEW 6:5–6

⁵Καὶ ὅταν προσεύχησθε, οὐκ ἔσεσθε ὡς οἱ ὑποκριταί, ὅτι φιλοῦσιν ἐν ταῖς συναγωγαῖς καὶ ἐν ταῖς γωνίαις τῶν πλατειῶν ἑστῶτες προσεύχεσθαι, ὅπως φανῶσιν τοῖς ἀνθρώποις· ἀμὴν λέγω ὑμῖν, ἀπέχουσιν τὸν μισθὸν αὐτῶν. ⁶σὺ δὲ ὅταν προσεύχῃ, εἴσελθε εἰς τὸ ταμεῖόν σου καὶ κλείσας τὴν θύραν σου πρόσευξαι τῷ πατρί σου τῷ ἐν τῷ κρυπτῷ· καὶ ὁ πατήρ σου ὁ βλέπων ἐν τῷ κρυπτῷ ἀποδώσει σοι.

ἔσεσθε v.2.p.fut.ind. [εἰμί]; ὑποκριταί (hypocrite); φιλοῦσιν (love); γωνίαις (corner); πλατειῶν (street); ἑστῶτες v.m.p.nom.pf.act.ptc. [ἵστημι]; φανῶσιν (be visible); ἀπέχουσιν (receive in full); μισθὸν (reward); εἴσελθε v.2.s.aor.act.impv. [εἰσέρχομαι]; ταμεῖον (closet); κλείσας (lock); θύραν (door); κρυπτῷ (secret)

261

5. 1 Samuel 1:12–14; Romans 8:26–27

Too Deep for Words

THE SIGHS, GROANS, AND SEARCHINGS OF THE SPIRIT are behind all true prayer, whether verbalized or not. How weak we are, how blind and foolish in our dictations to God! How much better, then, to cease from our anxious pleas and instead, listen to the sighs too deep for words and let *them* form our prayer.

1 SAMUEL 1:12–14

¹²וְהָיָה כִּי הִרְבְּתָה לְהִתְפַּלֵּל לִפְנֵי יְהוָה וְעֵלִי שֹׁמֵר אֶת־פִּיהָ:

¹³וְחַנָּה הִיא מְדַבֶּרֶת עַל־לִבָּהּ רַק שְׂפָתֶיהָ נָּעוֹת וְקוֹלָהּ לֹא יִשָּׁמֵעַ וַיַּחְשְׁבֶהָ עֵלִי לְשִׁכֹּרָה:

¹⁴וַיֹּאמֶר אֵלֶיהָ עֵלִי עַד־מָתַי תִּשְׁתַּכָּרִין הָסִירִי אֶת־יֵינֵךְ מֵעָלָיִךְ:

הִרְבְּתָה v.3.f.s.pf.H. [רבה]; נָּעוֹת v.f.p.ptc.Q. [נוע] (move); וַיַּחְשְׁבֶהָ v.c. + v.3.m.s.impf.Q. [חשב] + 3.f.s.pr.sf.; לְשִׁכֹּרָה (drunkard); תִּשְׁתַּכָּרִין v.2.f.s.impf.Ht. [שכר] (be drunk) + para.; הָסִירִי v.2.f.s.impv.H. [סור]

ROMANS 8:26–27

²⁶Ὡσαύτως δὲ καὶ τὸ πνεῦμα συναντιλαμβάνεται τῇ ἀσθενείᾳ ἡμῶν· τὸ γὰρ τί προσευξώμεθα καθὸ δεῖ οὐκ οἴδαμεν, ἀλλὰ αὐτὸ τὸ πνεῦμα ὑπερεντυγχάνει στεναγμοῖς ἀλαλήτοις· ²⁷ὁ δὲ ἐραυνῶν τὰς καρδίας οἶδεν τί τὸ φρόνημα τοῦ πνεύματος, ὅτι κατὰ θεὸν ἐντυγχάνει ὑπὲρ ἁγίων.

Ὡσαύτως (likewise); συναντιλαμβάνεται (help); ἀσθενείᾳ (weakness); καθὸ δεῖ adv. (κατα + ο) + v.3.s.pres.ind.impersonal [δέω] (inasmuch as necessary); ὑπερεντυγχάνει (intercede); στεναγμοῖς (groan); ἀλαλήτοις (wordless); ἐραυνῶν (search); οἶδεν v.3.s.pf.act.ind. [οἶδα]; φρόνημα (set one's mind on); ἐντυγχάνει (approach)

6. Psalm 150:1 2, 6; Ephesians 5.18–20

Waves of Worship

LORD, HOW I YEARN FOR CORPORATE PRAYER that is a mighty chorus of heartfelt praise, an intoxicating fullness of spiritual songs and hymns, hell-shattering waves of sheer worship! May I help to bring it about by living that prayer myself, day by day.

PSALM 150:1–2, 6

¹הַלְלוּ יָהּ הַלְלוּ־אֵל בְּקָדְשׁוֹ הַלְלוּהוּ בִּרְקִיעַ עֻזּוֹ:
²הַלְלוּהוּ בִגְבוּרֹתָיו הַלְלוּהוּ כְּרֹב גֻּדְלוֹ:
⁶כֹּל הַנְּשָׁמָה תְּהַלֵּל יָהּ הַלְלוּ־יָהּ:

הַלְלוּהוּ v.2.m.p.impv.P. [הלל] + 3.m.s.pr.sf.; בִּרְקִיעַ (firmament); גֻּדְלוֹ (greatness); הַנְּשָׁמָה (breath)

EPHESIANS 5:18–20

¹⁸καὶ μὴ μεθύσκεσθε οἴνῳ, ἐν ᾧ ἐστιν ἀσωτία, ἀλλὰ πληροῦσθε ἐν πνεύματι, ¹⁹λαλοῦντες ἑαυτοῖς [ἐν] ψαλμοῖς καὶ ὕμνοις καὶ ᾠδαῖς πνευματικαῖς, ᾄδοντες καὶ ψάλλοντες τῇ καρδίᾳ ὑμῶν τῷ κυρίῳ, ²⁰εὐχαριστοῦντες πάντοτε ὑπὲρ πάντων ἐν ὀνόματι τοῦ κυρίου ἡμῶν Ἰησοῦ Χριστοῦ τῷ θεῷ καὶ πατρί.

μεθύσκεσθε (be intoxicated); οἴνῳ (wine); ἀσωτία (debauchery); ψαλμοῖς (psalm); ὕμνοις (hymn); ᾠδαῖς (song); πνευματικαῖς (spiritual); ᾄδοντες v.m.p.nom.pres.act.ptc. [ᾄδω] (sing); ψάλλοντες (sing praise); εὐχαριστοῦντες (give thanks); πάντοτε (always)

7. Daniel 6:10; Ephesians 6:18

The Heart of the Matter

PRAYER IS THE HEART OF THE MATTER. It is the core of the spiritual life, the oxygen for the saint, the force that overthrows evil and sets us free. So, then, let us follow the apostle's admonition, and keep alert, all times, everywhere. Let us be people of prayer.

DANIEL 6:10 (A.)

$$^{10}\text{כָּל־קֳבֵל דְּנָה מַלְכָּא דָּרְיָוֶשׁ רְשַׁם כְּתָבָא וֶאֱסָרָא׃}$$

EPHESIANS 6:18

^{18}Διὰ πάσης προσευχῆς καὶ δεήσεως προσευχόμενοι ἐν παντὶ καιρῷ ἐν πνεύματι, καὶ εἰς αὐτὸ ἀγρυπνοῦντες ἐν πάσῃ προσκαρτερήσει καὶ δεήσει περὶ πάντων τῶν ἁγίων

προσευχῆς (prayer); δεήσεως (petition); ἀγρυπνοῦντες v.m.p.nom.pers.act.ptc. [ἀγρυπνέω] (be alert); προσκαρτερήσει (patience)

Faith

1. Amos 5:22–24; James 2:14–17

True Faith, True Work

THE TEST OF MY FAITH is always my relationship with those around me, particularly those who are at a disadvantage compared to me. Spirituality is intensely practical. The greatest saints get that way not by running away from the world and its horrendous need, but by staying firmly in touch, by mediating Christ to the world exactly where the world is.

AMOS 5:22–24

²²כִּי אִם־תַּעֲלוּ־לִי עֹלוֹת וּמִנְחֹתֵיכֶם לֹא אֶרְצֶה וְשֶׁלֶם מְרִיאֵיכֶם לֹא אַבִּיט׃

²³הָסֵר מֵעָלַי הֲמוֹן שִׁרֶיךָ וְזִמְרַת נְבָלֶיךָ לֹא אֶשְׁמָע׃

²⁴וְיִגַּל כַּמַּיִם מִשְׁפָּט וּצְדָקָה כְּנַחַל אֵיתָן׃

תַּעֲלוּ v.2.m.p.impf.H. [עלה]; וְשֶׁלֶם (peace offering); מְרִיאֵיכֶם (fatling); אַבִּיט v.1.com.s.impf.H. [נבט]; הָסֵר v.2.m.s.impv.H. [סור]; וְזִמְרַת (melody); נְבָלֶיךָ (harp); וְיִגַּל cj. + v.3.m.s.impf.N. [גלל] (roll); אֵיתָן (lasting)

JAMES 2:14–17

¹⁴Τί τὸ ὄφελος, ἀδελφοί μου, ἐὰν πίστιν λέγῃ τις ἔχειν ἔργα δὲ μὴ ἔχῃ; μὴ δύναται ἡ πίστις σῶσαι αὐτόν; ¹⁵ἐὰν ἀδελφὸς ἢ ἀδελφὴ γυμνοὶ ὑπάρχωσιν καὶ λειπόμενοι τῆς ἐφημέρου τροφῆς ¹⁶εἴπῃ δέ τις αὐτοῖς ἐξ ὑμῶν· ὑπάγετε ἐν εἰρήνῃ, θερμαίνεσθε καὶ χορτάζεσθε, μὴ δῶτε δὲ αὐτοῖς τὰ ἐπιτήδεια τοῦ σώματος, τί τὸ ὄφελος; ¹⁷οὕτως καὶ ἡ πίστις, ἐὰν μὴ ἔχῃ ἔργα, νεκρά ἐστιν καθ' ἑαυτήν.

ὄφελος (benefit); γυμνοὶ (naked); ὑπάρχωσιν v.3.p.pres.act.sub. [ὑπάρχω]; λειπόμενοι (lack); ἐφημέρου (daily); τροφῆς (food); εἴπῃ v.3.s.aor.act.sub. [λέγω]; θερμαίνεσθε (warm self); χορτάζεσθε (feed); ἐπιτήδεια (necessary)

2. Micah 7:7–8; Luke 2:25–26

Persevering Faith

FAITH MEANS PERSEVERANCE, not to see a particular work accomplished or a goal reached, but to see the Lord. The Lord himself is the object of our faith. If we can remember that, we can endure the dark night. We can overcome.

MICAH 7:7–8

7 וַאֲנִי בַּיהוָה אֲצַפֶּה אוֹחִילָה לֵאלֹהֵי יִשְׁעִי יִשְׁמָעֵנִי אֱלֹהָי׃
8 אַל־תִּשְׂמְחִי אֹיַבְתִּי לִי כִּי נָפַלְתִּי קָמְתִּי כִּי־אֵשֵׁב בַּחֹשֶׁךְ
יְהוָה אוֹר לִי׃

אוֹחִילָה v.1.com.s.coh.H. [יחל] (tarry); יִשְׁמָעֵנִי v.3.m.s.impf.Q. [שמע] + 1.com.s.pr.sf.; אֹיַבְתִּי v.1.com.s.pf.Q. [איב]; קָמְתִּי v.1.com.s.pf.Q. [קום]; אֵשֵׁב v.1.c.s.impf.Q. [ישב]

LUKE 2:25–26

²⁵Καὶ ἰδοὺ ἄνθρωπος ἦν ἐν Ἰερουσαλὴμ ᾧ ὄνομα Συμεὼν καὶ ὁ ἄνθρωπος οὗτος δίκαιος καὶ εὐλαβὴς προσδεχόμενος παράκλησιν τοῦ Ἰσραήλ, καὶ πνεῦμα ἦν ἅγιον ἐπ᾽ αὐτόν· ²⁶καὶ ἦν αὐτῷ κεχρηματισμένον ὑπὸ τοῦ πνεύματος τοῦ ἁγίου μὴ ἰδεῖν θάνατον πρὶν [ἢ] ἂν ἴδῃ τὸν Χριστὸν κυρίου.

ἦν v.3.s.impf.ind. [εἰμί]; εὐλαβὴς (pious); προσδεχόμενος (await); παράκλησιν (comfort); κεχρηματισμένον v.nt.s.nom.pf.pass.ptc. [χρηματίζω] (reveal); ἰδεῖν v.aor.act.in. [ὁράω]; πρὶν (before); ἴδῃ v.3.s.aor.act.sub. [ὁράω]

9. Psalm 4:3; Matthew 21:21–22

Set Apart for Himself

THE KEY IN ALL THIS, of course, is the little phrase "set apart for himself." Faith is knowing that every molecule of my being is set apart for God, and that all my willing is for his will. When I live this way, think this way, and pray this way, I become the means for Jesus to walk this earth again. My God! How could such incredible power be poured into the world through me? Yet this is your will for all your children! This is your will for me.

PSALM 4:3

³בְּנֵי אִישׁ עַד־מֶה כְבוֹדִי לִכְלִמָּה תֶּאֱהָבוּן רִיק תְּבַקְשׁוּ כָזָב סֶלָה׃

לִכְלִמָּה (insult); תֶּאֱהָבוּן v.2.m.p.impf.Q.pause [אהב] + para.; רִיק (worth-less); כָזָב (lie)

MATTHEW 21:21–22

²¹ἀποκριθεὶς δὲ ὁ Ἰησοῦς εἶπεν αὐτοῖς, Ἀμὴν λέγω ὑμῖν, ἐὰν ἔχητε πίστιν καὶ μὴ διακριθῆτε, οὐ μόνον τὸ τῆς συκῆς ποιήσετε, ἀλλὰ κἂν τῷ ὄρει τούτῳ εἴπητε, Ἄρθητι καὶ βλήθητι εἰς τὴν θάλασσαν, γενήσεται· ²²καὶ πάντα ὅσα ἂν αἰτήσητε ἐν τῇ προσευχῇ πιστεύοντες λήμψεσθε.

εἶπεν v.3.s.aor.act.ind. [λέγω]; διακριθῆτε (doubt); συκῆς (fig tree); Ἄρθητι v.2.s.aor.pass.impv. [αἴρω]; βλήθητι v.2.s.aor.pass.impv. [βάλλω]; προσευχῇ (prayer); λήμψεσθε v.2.p.fut.mid.ind. [λαμβάνω]

4. 2 Chronicles 32:7–8; Acts 23:10–11

Faith or Fear?

FAITH OR FEAR—that is the choice we face with every confrontation against evil. Fear is the cold water the enemy throws on our spiritual flame. Faith is the arm that raises the shield of Christ. The good news is that even faith is a gift! Let us take hold of faith!

2 CHRONICLES 32:7–8

חִזְקוּ וְאִמְצוּ אַל־תִּירְאוּ וְאַל־תֵּחַתּוּ מִפְּנֵי מֶלֶךְ אַשּׁוּר ⁷
וּמִלִּפְנֵי כָּל־הֶהָמוֹן אֲשֶׁר־עִמּוֹ כִּי־עִמָּנוּ רַב מֵעִמּוֹ:
עִמּוֹ זְרוֹעַ בָּשָׂר וְעִמָּנוּ יְהוָה אֱלֹהֵינוּ לְעָזְרֵנוּ וּלְהִלָּחֵם ⁸
מִלְחֲמֹתֵנוּ וַיִּסָּמְכוּ הָעָם עַל־דִּבְרֵי יְחִזְקִיָּהוּ מֶלֶךְ־יְהוּדָה:

וְאִמְצוּ (be strong); תֵּחַתּוּ v.2.m.p.impf.Q. [חתת]; לְעָזְרֵנוּ prep. + v.in.cs.Q.
[עזר] + 1.com.p.pr.sf.; וַיִּסָּמְכוּ (support)

ACTS 23:10–11

¹⁰Πολλῆς δὲ γινομένης στάσεως φοβηθεὶς ὁ χιλίαρχος μὴ διασπασθῇ ὁ Παῦλος ὑπ᾽ αὐτῶν ἐκέλευσεν τὸ στράτευμα καταβὰν ἁρπάσαι αὐτὸν ἐκ μέσου αὐτῶν ἄγειν τε εἰς τὴν παρεμβολήν. ¹¹Τῇ δὲ ἐπιούσῃ νυκτὶ ἐπιστὰς αὐτῷ ὁ κύριος εἶπεν, θάρσει· ὡς γὰρ διεμαρτύρω τὰ περὶ ἐμοῦ εἰς Ἰερουσαλήμ, οὕτω σε δεῖ καὶ εἰς Ῥώμην μαρτυρῆσαι.

στάσεως (strife); χιλίαρχος (commander); διασπασθῇ (tear apart); ἐκέλευσεν (command); στράτευμα (army); ἁρπάσαι (seize); παρεμβολήν (barracks); ἐπιούσῃ (next); ἐπιστὰς v.m.s.nom.aor.act.ptc. [ἐφίστημι] (stand near); εἶπεν v.3.s.aor.act.ind. [λέγω]; θάρσει (be courageous); διεμαρτύρω (testify)

5. Judges 0:25, 27; 2 Corinthians 3:4–6

Faith in God's Vision for Me

FAITH MEANS OBEDIENCE to the vision God has for me. It means walking, no *marching*, face-first into my worst fears and slaying them with the breath of God. Faith without obedience is not faith at all.

JUDGES 6:25, 27

²⁵וַיְהִי בַּלַּיְלָה הַהוּא וַיֹּאמֶר לוֹ יְהוָה קַח אֶת־פַּר־הַשּׁוֹר אֲשֶׁר
לְאָבִיךָ וּפַר הַשֵּׁנִי שֶׁבַע שָׁנִים וְהָרַסְתָּ אֶת־מִזְבַּח הַבַּעַל
אֲשֶׁר לְאָבִיךָ וְאֶת־הָאֲשֵׁרָה אֲשֶׁר־עָלָיו תִּכְרֹת:
²⁷וַיִּקַּח גִּדְעוֹן עֲשָׂרָה אֲנָשִׁים מֵעֲבָדָיו וַיַּעַשׂ כַּאֲשֶׁר דִּבֶּר
אֵלָיו יְהוָה וַיְהִי כַּאֲשֶׁר יָרֵא אֶת־בֵּית אָבִיו וְאֶת־אַנְשֵׁי הָעִיר
מֵעֲשׂוֹת יוֹמָם וַיַּעַשׂ לָיְלָה:

וַיְהִי v.3.m.s.impf.Q. [הִיה]; קַח v.2.m.s.impv.Q. [לקח]; וְהָרַסְתָּ (destroy);
הָאֲשֵׁרָה (sacred pole); וַיִּקַּח v.3.m.s.impf.Q. [לקח]; וַיַּעַשׂ v.3.m.s.impf.Q. [עשה];
מֵעֲשׂוֹת prep. + v.in.cs.Q. [עשה]

2 CORINTHIANS 3:4–6

⁴Πεποίθησιν δὲ τοιαύτην ἔχομεν διὰ τοῦ Χριστοῦ πρὸς τὸν θεόν. ⁵οὐχ ὅτι ἀφ᾽ ἑαυτῶν ἱκανοί ἐσμεν λογίσασθαί τι ὡς ἐξ ἑαυτῶν, ἀλλ᾽ ἡ ἱκανότης ἡμῶν ἐκ τοῦ θεοῦ, ⁶ὃς καὶ ἱκάνωσεν ἡμᾶς διακόνους καινῆς διαθήκης, οὐ γράμματος ἀλλὰ πνεύματος· τὸ γὰρ γράμμα ἀποκτέννει, τὸ δὲ πνεῦμα ζῳοποιεῖ.

Πεποίθησιν (trust); ἱκανοί (fit); ἱκανότης (fitness); ἱκάνωσεν (qualify); καινῆς (new); διαθήκης (covenant); γράμματος (letter); ζῳοποιεῖ (enliven)

269

6. Exodus 4:1; Mark 9:21–24

Ambivalence

HERE'S THE REAL CLENCHER. Even in our unbelief we can exercise faith, for we can rely on the fact that we do know and do believe and have experienced. God honors this kind of faith, too!

EXODUS 4:1

וַיַּעַן מֹשֶׁה וַיֹּאמֶר וְהֵן לֹא־יַאֲמִינוּ לִי וְלֹא יִשְׁמְעוּ בְּקֹלִי¹
כִּי יֹאמְרוּ לֹא־נִרְאָה אֵלֶיךָ יְהוָה:

וַיַּעַן v.c. + v.3.m.s.impf.Q. [ענה]

MARK 9:21–24

²¹καὶ ἐπηρώτησεν τὸν πατέρα αὐτοῦ, Πόσος χρόνος ἐστὶν ὡς τοῦτο γέγονεν αὐτῷ; ὁ δὲ εἶπεν, Ἐκ παιδιόθεν· ²²καὶ πολλάκις καὶ εἰς πῦρ αὐτὸν ἔβαλεν καὶ εἰς ὕδατα ἵνα ἀπολέσῃ αὐτόν· ἀλλ' εἴ τι δύνῃ, βοήθησον ἡμῖν σπλαγχνισθεὶς ἐφ' ἡμᾶς. ²³ὁ δὲ Ἰησοῦς εἶπεν αὐτῷ, Τὸ Εἰ δύνῃ, πάντα δυνατὰ τῷ πιστεύοντι. ²⁴εὐθὺς κράξας ὁ πατὴρ τοῦ παιδίου ἔλεγεν, Πιστεύω· βοήθει μου τῇ ἀπιστίᾳ.

ἐστὶν v.3.s.pres.ind. [εἰμί]; εἶπεν v.3.s.aor.act.ind. [λέγω]; Ἐκ παιδιόθεν (from childhood); πολλάκις (frequently); ἀπολέσῃ v.3.s.aor.act.sub. [ἀπόλλυμι]; βοήθησον (help); σπλαγχνισθεὶς (sympathize); ἀπιστίᾳ (unbelief)

7. Numbers 11:26–29; 1 Corinthians 3:5–7, 9

Faith in Whom?

THE MOST SUBTLE ENEMY OF FAITH, perhaps, is the tendency to shift from faith in *God* to faith in God's *instruments*. This is especially true when God's instruments are people. We need to see the clay feet of our leaders, because it prevents the shift from becoming permanent and gets our faith back where it belongs.

NUMBERS 11:26–29

26וַיִּשָּׁאֲרוּ שְׁנֵי־אֲנָשִׁים בַּמַּחֲנֶה שֵׁם הָאֶחָד אֶלְדָּד וְשֵׁם
הַשֵּׁנִי מֵידָד וַתָּנַח עֲלֵיהֶם הָרוּחַ וְהֵמָּה בַּכְּתֻבִים וְלֹא יָצְאוּ
הָאֹהֱלָה וַיִּתְנַבְּאוּ בַּמַּחֲנֶה:
27וַיָּרָץ הַנַּעַר וַיַּגֵּד לְמֹשֶׁה וַיֹּאמַר אֶלְדָּד וּמֵידָד מִתְנַבְּאִים
בַּמַּחֲנֶה:
28וַיַּעַן יְהוֹשֻׁעַ בִּן־נוּן מְשָׁרֵת מֹשֶׁה מִבְּחֻרָיו וַיֹּאמַר אֲדֹנִי
מֹשֶׁה כְּלָאֵם:
29וַיֹּאמֶר לוֹ מֹשֶׁה הַמְקַנֵּא אַתָּה לִי וּמִי יִתֵּן כָּל־עַם יְהוָה נְבִיאִים
כִּי־יִתֵּן יְהוָה אֶת־רוּחוֹ עֲלֵיהֶם:

וַתָּנַח v.c. + v.3.f.s.impf.Q. [נוח]; וַיָּרָץ v.c. + v.3.m.s.impf.Q. [רוץ]; וַיַּגֵּד v.c.
+ v.3.m.s.impf.H. [נגד]; וַיַּעַן v.c. + v.3.m.s.impf.Q. [ענה]; כְּלָאֵם v.m.s.impv.Q.
[כלא] + 3.m.p.pr.sf.; הַמְקַנֵּא int.pt. + v.m.s.act.ptc.P. [קנא] (be jealous); יִתֵּן
v.c. + v.3.m.s.jus.Q. [נתן]

1 CORINTHIANS 3:5–7, 9

5τί οὖν ἐστιν Ἀπολλῶς; τί δέ ἐστιν Παῦλος; διάκονοι δι' ὧν
ἐπιστεύσατε, καὶ ἑκάστῳ ὡς ὁ κύριος ἔδωκεν. 6ἐγὼ ἐφύτευσα,
Ἀπολλῶς ἐπότισεν, ἀλλὰ ὁ θεὸς ηὔξανεν· 7ὥστε οὔτε ὁ
φυτεύων ἐστίν τι οὔτε ὁ ποτίζων ἀλλ᾽ ὁ αὐξάνων θεός. 9θεοῦ
γάρ ἐσμεν συνεργοί, θεοῦ γεώργιον, θεοῦ οἰκοδομή ἐστε.

διάκονοι (servant); ἔδωκεν v.3.s.aor.act.ind. [δίδωμι]; ἐφύτευσα (plant);
ἐπότισεν (water); ηὔξανεν v.3.s.impf.act.ind. [αὐξάνω] (grow); συνεργοί
(fellow worker); γεώργιον (field); οἰκοδομή (building)

Week 38

One Another

1. Genesis 37:19–20; Matthew 24:9–10

Fire from Heaven

WHILE WE SHOUT DOWN FIRE FROM HEAVEN to consume everyone who isn't like us, Jesus hastens to Jerusalem, to the cross, to the fire.

GENESIS 37:19–20

¹⁹וַיֹּאמְרוּ אִישׁ אֶל־אָחִיו הִנֵּה בַּעַל הַחֲלֹמוֹת הַלָּזֶה בָּא:
²⁰וְעַתָּה לְכוּ וְנַהַרְגֵהוּ וְנַשְׁלִכֵהוּ בְּאַחַד הַבֹּרוֹת וְאָמַרְנוּ
חַיָּה רָעָה אֲכָלָתְהוּ וְנִרְאֶה מַה־יִּהְיוּ חֲלֹמֹתָיו:

בָּא v.m.s.ptc.Q. [בוא]; לְכוּ v.2.m.p.impv.Q [הלך]; וְנַהַרְגֵהוּ cj. + v.1.com.p.impf.Q. [הרג] + 3.m.s.pr.sf.; וְנַשְׁלִכֵהוּ cj. + v.1.com.p.impf.H. [שלך] + 3.m.s.pr.sf.; אֲכָלָתְהוּ v.3.f.s.pf.Q. [אכל] + 3.m.s.pr.sf.; יִּהְיוּ v.3.m.p.impf.Q. [היה]

MATTHEW 24:9–10

⁹τότε παραδώσουσιν ὑμᾶς εἰς θλῖψιν καὶ ἀποκτενοῦσιν ὑμᾶς, καὶ ἔσεσθε μισούμενοι ὑπὸ πάντων τῶν ἐθνῶν διὰ τὸ ὄνομα μου. ¹⁰καὶ τότε σκανδαλισθήσονται πολλοὶ καὶ ἀλλήλους παραδώσουσιν καὶ μισήσουσιν ἀλλήλους·

παραδώσουσιν v.3.p.fut.act.ind. [παραδίδωμι]; θλῖψιν (affliction); ἔσεσθε v.2.p.fut.ind. [εἰμί]; μισούμενοι (hate); σκανδαλισθήσονται (fall away)

2. Deuteronomy 10:19; 1 John 4:11–12

Has Anything Really Changed?

MAY I NEVER FORGET the lash of the whip, the emptiness, the longing, the loss of self, the days of my captivity, O God my Savior. For if I forget how it was for me, how will I remember how it is for others? And if I forget how it is for others, how can I love them where they are? For if I cannot love them where they are, I am still in Egypt. Nothing has really changed.

DEUTERONOMY 10:19

19 וַאֲהַבְתֶּם אֶת־הַגֵּר כִּי־גֵרִים הֱיִיתֶם בְּאֶרֶץ מִצְרָיִם:

הֱיִיתֶם v.2.m.p.pf.Q. [היה]

1 JOHN 4:11–12

11Ἀγαπητοί, εἰ οὕτως ὁ θεὸς ἠγάπησεν ἡμᾶς, καὶ ἡμεῖς ὀφείλομεν ἀλλήλους ἀγαπᾶν. 12θεὸν οὐδεὶς πώποτε τεθέαται. ἐὰν ἀγαπῶμεν ἀλλήλους, ὁ θεὸς ἐν ἡμῖν μένει καὶ ἡ ἀγάπη αὐτοῦ ἐν ἡμῖν τετελειωμένη ἐστίν.

ὀφείλομεν (owe); πώποτε (at any time); τεθέαται v.3.s.pf.mid.ind. [θεάομαι] (see); τετελειωμένη (complete)

3. Exodus 18:19–20; Hebrews 3:12–13

Every Day, No Exceptions

WE ARE LIKE A.A. MEMBERS, working the program. Every day, without exception, we need an exhortation from someone else. Not from someone "up there" or "out there" who is above it all, but from one of us. We need some kind of message that turns us toward and not away from the living God, away from and not toward the deceitfulness of sin. Every single day. No exceptions.

EXODUS 18:19–20

19עַתָּה שְׁמַע בְּקֹלִי אִיעָצְךָ וִיהִי אֱלֹהִים עִמָּךְ הֱיֵה אַתָּה לָעָם
מוּל הָאֱלֹהִים וְהֵבֵאתָ אַתָּה אֶת־הַדְּבָרִים אֶל־הָאֱלֹהִים:
20וְהִזְהַרְתָּה אֶתְהֶם אֶת־הַחֻקִּים וְאֶת־הַתּוֹרֹת וְהוֹדַעְתָּ לָהֶם
אֶת־הַדֶּרֶךְ יֵלְכוּ בָהּ וְאֶת־הַמַּעֲשֶׂה אֲשֶׁר יַעֲשׂוּן:

אִיעָצְךָ v.1.com.s.impf.Q. [יעץ] + 2.m.s.pr.sf.; וִיהִי cj. + v.3.m.s.jus.Q. [היה]; הֱיֵה v.2.m.s.impv. Q. [היה]; מוּל (before); וְהֵבֵאתָ v.c. + v.2.m.s.impf. H. [בוא]; וְהִזְהַרְתָּה v.c. + v.2.m.s.pf.H.plene [זהר] (be mindful of); וְהוֹדַעְתָּ v.c. + v.2.m.s.pf.H. [ידע]; יֵלְכוּ v.3.m.p.impf.Q. [הלך]; יַעֲשׂוּן v.3.m.p.impf.Q. [עשׂה] + para.

HEBREWS 3:12–13

12Βλέπετε, ἀδελφοί, μήποτε ἔσται ἔν τινι ὑμῶν καρδία πονηρὰ ἀπιστίας ἐν τῷ ἀποστῆναι ἀπὸ θεοῦ ζῶντος, 13ἀλλὰ παρακαλεῖτε ἑαυτοὺς καθ᾽ ἑκάστην ἡμέραν, ἄχρις οὗ τὸ Σήμερον καλεῖται, ἵνα μὴ σκληρυνθῇ τις ἐξ ὑμῶν ἀπάτῃ τῆς ἁμαρτίας–

μήποτε (lest); ἔσται v.3.s.fut.ind. [εἰμί]; ἀπιστίας (unbelief); ἀποστῆναι v.aor.act.in. [ἀφίστημι] (become apostate); ἄχρις (while); Σήμερον (today); σκληρυνθῇ (harden); ἀπάτη (deception)

4. Genesis 50:17; Colossians 3:12–13

Bearing With

SOME KINDS OF "BEARING WITH" would not appear to be very difficult—nothing like the kind Joseph was required to give his elder brothers. Bearing with despite petty annoyances over this or that small habit, this or that preference in some inconsequential thing. Yet this is precisely the kind of "bearing with" that is most lacking in the church. So we have the phenomenon of churches splitting over the color of the carpet, or the use of a guitar to hymn the love of God.

GENESIS 50:17

¹⁷כֹּה־תֹאמְרוּ לְיוֹסֵף אָנָּא שָׂא נָא פֶּשַׁע אַחֶיךָ וְחַטָּאתָם כִּי־רָעָה
גְמָלוּךָ וְעַתָּה שָׂא נָא לְפֶשַׁע עַבְדֵי אֱלֹהֵי אָבִיךָ וַיֵּבְךְ יוֹסֵף
בְּדַבְּרָם אֵלָיו:

אָנָּא (where?); שָׂא v.2.m.s.impv.Q. [נשא]; גְמָלוּךָ v.3.c.p.pf.Q. [גמל] (do evil to) + 2.m.s.pr.sf.; וַיֵּבְךְ v.c. + v.3.m.s.impf.Q. [בכה]; בְּדַבְּרָם prep. + v.in.cst.P. [דבר] + 3.m.p.pr.sf.

COLOSSIANS 3:12–13

¹²Ἐνδύσασθε οὖν, ὡς ἐκλεκτοὶ τοῦ θεοῦ ἅγιοι καὶ ἠγαπημένοι, σπλάγχνα οἰκτιρμοῦ χρηστότητα ταπεινοφροσύνην πραΰτητα μακροθυμίαν, ¹³ἀνεχόμενοι ἀλλήλων καὶ χαριζόμενοι ἑαυτοῖς ἐάν τις πρός τινα ἔχῃ μομφήν· καθὼς καὶ ὁ κύριος ἐχαρίσατο ὑμῖν, οὕτως καὶ ὑμεῖς·

Ἐνδύσασθε (clothe); ἐκλεκτοὶ (chosen); σπλάγχνα (affection); οἰκτιρμοῦ (pity); χρηστότητα (generosity); ταπεινοφροσύνην (humility); πραΰτητα (gentleness); μακροθυμίαν (patience); ἀνεχόμενοι (endure); χαριζόμενοι (forgive); μομφήν (complaint)

275

5. 2 Chronicles 7:14; 1 Peter 5:5a

The River of God's Choosing

GOD, I HAVE A CONFESSION TO MAKE. A part of me wants to escape from the dust and drudge of life in the local church. A part of me scorns the church because of her petty conflicts, her lack of vision, her perennial preoccupation with everything but that which is most necessary. That part of me is pure and holy, I tell myself. But the truth is, that part of me is proud. The local church is like the River Jordan, the only place where Naaman could be healed. Teach me, O God, to let go of my grim-jawed pride, to dip, to swim, to joy in the river of your choosing. Then I will be healed.

2 CHRONICLES 7:14

‏ וְיִכָּנְע֨וּ עַמִּ֜י אֲשֶׁ֧ר נִקְרָא־שְׁמִ֣י עֲלֵיהֶ֗ם וְיִֽתְפַּֽלְל֞וּ וִיבַקְשׁ֤וּ ‏14
‏ פָנַי֙ וְיָשֻׁ֙בוּ֙ מִדַּרְכֵיהֶ֣ם הָרָעִ֔ים וַאֲנִי֙ אֶשְׁמַ֣ע מִן־הַשָּׁמַ֔יִם ‏
‏ וְאֶסְלַח֙ לְחַטָּאתָ֔ם וְאֶרְפָּ֖א אֶת־אַרְצָֽם׃ ‏

וְיִכָּנְעוּ (be humbled); וְיָשֻׁבוּ cj. + v.3.m.p.impf.Q. [שׁוב]

1 PETER 5:5A

⁵πάντες δὲ ἀλλήλοις τὴν ταπεινοφροσύνην ἐγκομβώσασθε, ὅτι
    [Ὁ] θεὸς ὑπερηφάνοις ἀντιτάσσεται,
    ταπεινοῖς δὲ δίδωσιν χάριν.

ταπεινοφροσύνην (humility); ἐγκομβώσασθε (clothe oneself); ὑπερ-ηφάνοις (proud); ἀντιτάσσεται (oppose); ταπεινοῖς (humble)

6. Exodus 23.5, Hebrews 10:24–25

No Distinctions

THIS IS THE PART OF THE GOSPEL that is so hard to accept. God makes no distinction between the one who hates me and the one who loves me. Both are fit subjects for my care.

EXODUS 23:5

⁵כִּי־תִרְאֶה חֲמוֹר שֹׂנַאֲךָ רֹבֵץ תַּחַת מַשָּׂאוֹ וְחָדַלְתָּ מֵעֲזֹב לוֹ עָזֹב תַּעֲזֹב עִמּוֹ׃ ס

שֹׂנַאֲךָ v.m.s.act.ptc. [שׂנא] + 2.m.s.pr.sf.; רֹבֵץ (lie down)

HEBREWS 10:24–25

²⁴καὶ κατανοῶμεν ἀλλήλους εἰς παροξυσμὸν ἀγάπης καὶ καλῶν ἔργων, ²⁵μὴ ἐγκαταλείποντες τὴν ἐπισυναγωγὴν ἑαυτῶν, καθὼς ἔθος τισίν, ἀλλὰ παρακαλοῦντες, καὶ τοσούτῳ μᾶλλον ὅσῳ βλέπετε ἐγγίζουσαν τὴν ἡμέραν.

κατανοῶμεν (consider); παροξυσμὸν (provoke); ἐγκαταλείποντες (abandon); ἐπισυναγωγὴν (assembling); ἔθος (custom); τοσούτῳ (so great); ἐγγίζουσαν (approach)

7. Leviticus 19:2, 13a; Ephesians 4:25

About Holiness . . .

ONE OF THE GREATEST FRAUDS the devil has perpetrated is the belief that holiness is some kind of pious removal from the world of actual people, some kind of halo-encrusted, filmy, impotent existence that any sane, healthy person would do well to avoid. Real sanctity is about integrity in places like the mouth and on the job and in the back yard with your neighbor. This is what God had in mind when he said, "Be holy as I am holy."

LEVITICUS 19:2, 13A

²דַּבֵּר אֶל־כָּל־עֲדַת בְּנֵי־יִשְׂרָאֵל וְאָמַרְתָּ אֲלֵהֶם קְדֹשִׁים תִּהְיוּ
כִּי קָדוֹשׁ אֲנִי יְהוָה אֱלֹהֵיכֶם:
¹³לֹא־תַעֲשֹׁק אֶת־רֵעֲךָ וְלֹא תִגְזֹל

תִּהְיוּ v.2.m.p.impf.Q. [הָיָה]; תַּעֲשֹׁק (oppress); תִגְזֹל (plunder)

EPHESIANS 4:25

²⁵Διὸ ἀποθέμενοι τὸ ψεῦδος λαλεῖτε ἀλήθειαν ἕκαστος μετὰ τοῦ πλησίον αὐτοῦ, ὅτι ἐσμὲν ἀλλήλων μέλη.

ἀποθέμενοι v.m.p.nom.aor.mid.part. [ἀποτίθημι] (lay aside); ψεῦδος (lie); πλησίον (neighbor); μέλη (member)

Anger

1. Ecclesiastes 7:9; Ephesians 4.26–27

Room for the Devil

THE HEART THAT MAKES ROOM for permanent anger makes room for the devil himself.

ECCLESIASTES 7:9

⁹אַל־תְּבַהֵל בְּרוּחֲךָ לִכְעוֹס כִּי כַעַס בְּחֵיק כְּסִילִים יָנוּחַ:

תְּבַהֵל (hasten); כַּעַס (anger); בְּחֵיק (bosom); כְּסִילִים (stupid one)

EPHESIANS 4:26–27

²⁶ὀργίζεσθε καὶ μὴ ἁμαρτάνετε· ὁ ἥλιος μὴ ἐπιδυέτω ἐπὶ [τῷ] παροργισμῷ ὑμῶν, ²⁷μηδὲ δίδοτε τόπον [τῷ] διαβόλῳ.

ὀργίζεσθε (be angry); ἁμαρτάνετε (sin); ἥλιος (sun); ἐπιδυέτω v.3.s.pres.act.impv. [ἐπιδύω] (set); παροργισμῷ (anger); διαβόλῳ (devil)

2. Proverbs 29:22; Colossians 3:8

Anger and the Tongue

BITTER TONGUES ARE RUSTY KNIVES that slash and poison souls, none more so than the soul of the one who speaks.

PROVERBS 29:22

²²אִישׁ־אַף יְגָרֶה מָדוֹן וּבַעַל חֵמָה רַב־פָּשַׁע:

יְגָרֶה v.3.m.s.impf.P. [גרה] (stir up); מָדוֹן (strife)

COLOSSIANS 3:8

⁸νυνὶ δὲ ἀπόθεσθε καὶ ὑμεῖς τὰ πάντα, ὀργήν, θυμόν, κακίαν, βλασφημίαν, αἰσχρολογίαν ἐκ τοῦ στόματος ὑμῶν·

νυνὶ (now); ἀπόθεσθε v.2.p.aor.mid.impv. [ἀποτίθημι] (lay aside); ὀργήν (anger); θυμόν (wrath); κακίαν (wickedness); βλασφημίαν (blasphemy); αἰσχρολογίαν (obscenity)

3. Isaiah 59:15b–17; John 2:14–16

The Real Christ, the Fury

THIS IS NOT A PALE, ETHEREAL JESUS staring vapidly from a musty old picture. This is the real Christ—wrapped in a cloak of fury over the injustice and oppression of the world, the greed and corruption in the very house of God. This is the real Christ, whose salvation and righteousness are inseparable from holy anger. This is the real Christ who feels and acts with passion. He is the God the world longs to know.

ISAIAH 59:15B–17

וַיַּרְא יְהוָה וַיֵּרַע בְּעֵינָיו כִּי־אֵין מִשְׁפָּט:¹⁵

וַיַּרְא כִּי־אֵין אִישׁ וַיִּשְׁתּוֹמֵם כִּי אֵין מַפְגִּיעַ וַתּוֹשַׁע לוֹ¹⁶
זְרֹעוֹ וְצִדְקָתוֹ הִיא סְמָכָתְהוּ:

וַיִּלְבַּשׁ צְדָקָה כַּשִּׁרְיָן וְכוֹבַע יְשׁוּעָה בְּרֹאשׁוֹ וַיִּלְבַּשׁ¹⁷
בִּגְדֵי נָקָם תִּלְבֹּשֶׁת וַיַּעַט כַּמְעִיל קִנְאָה:

וַיַּרְא v.3.m.s.impf.Q. [רֹאה]; וַיֵּרַע v.c. + v.3.m.s.impf.Q. [רֹעע]; וַיִּשְׁתּוֹמֵם v.c. + v.3.m.s.impf.Htpo. [שׁוֹם]; מַפְגִּיעַ (encounter); וַתּוֹשַׁע v.c. + v.3.f.s.impf.H. [יֹשׁע]; סְמָכָתְהוּ v.3.f.s.pf.Q. [סֹמך] (support) + 3.m.s.pr.sf.; כַּשִּׁרְיָן (armor); וְכוֹבַע (helmet); נָקָם (vengeance); תִּלְבֹּשֶׁת (garment); וַיַּעַט v.c. + v.3.m.s.impf.Q. [עֹטה] (wrap); כַּמְעִיל (robe); קִנְאָה (jealousy)

JOHN 2:14–16

¹⁴καὶ εὗρεν ἐν τῷ ἱερῷ τοὺς πωλοῦντας βόας καὶ πρόβατα καὶ περιστερὰς καὶ τοὺς κερματιστὰς καθημένους, ¹⁵καὶ ποιήσας φραγέλλιον ἐκ σχοινίων πάντας ἐξέβαλεν ἐκ τοῦ ἱεροῦ τά τε πρόβατα καὶ τοὺς βόας, καὶ τῶν κολλυβιστῶν ἐξέχεεν τὸ κέρμα καὶ τὰς τραπέζας ἀνέτρεψεν, ¹⁶καὶ τοῖς τὰς περιστερὰς πωλοῦσιν εἶπεν, Ἄρατε ταῦτα ἐντεῦθεν, μὴ ποιεῖτε τὸν οἶκον τοῦ πατρός μου οἶκον ἐμπορίου.

πωλοῦντας (sell); βόας (ox); πρόβατα (sheep); περιστερὰς (dove); κερματιστὰς (money-changer); φραγέλλιον (whip); σχοινίων (rope); κολλυβιστῶν (money-changer); ἐξέχεεν (pour out); κέρμα (coin); τραπέζας (table); ἀνέτρεψεν (overturn); εἶπεν v.3.s.aor.act.ind. [λέγω]; ἄρατε v.2.p.aor.act.impv. [αἴρω]; ἐντεῦθεν (from now on); ἐμπορίου (market)

4. Psalm 78:37–39; John 3:17

No Condemnation

WE DO NOT NEED CONDEMNATION from God. We have already con-
demned ourselves. God knows this much better than we do. We
religious people are the last ones to understand the grace of the
gospel. We really would prefer a God-damning religion.

PSALM 78:37–39

³⁷וְלִבָּם לֹא־נָכוֹן עִמּוֹ וְלֹא נֶאֶמְנוּ בִּבְרִיתוֹ:

³⁸וְהוּא רַחוּם יְכַפֵּר עָוֹן וְלֹא־יַשְׁחִית וְהִרְבָּה לְהָשִׁיב אַפּוֹ
וְלֹא־יָעִיר כָּל־חֲמָתוֹ:

³⁹וַיִּזְכֹּר כִּי־בָשָׂר הֵמָּה רוּחַ הוֹלֵךְ וְלֹא יָשׁוּב:

נָכוֹן v.m.s.ptc.N. [כון]; רַחוּם (compassionate); לְהָשִׁיב prep. + v.in.cs.H.
[שוב]; יָעִיר v.3.m.s.impf.H. [עור]; חֲמָתוֹ (anger)

JOHN 3:17

¹⁷οὐ γὰρ ἀπέστειλεν ὁ θεὸς τὸν υἱὸν εἰς τὸν κόσμον ἵνα κρίνῃ
τὸν κόσμον, ἀλλ᾽ ἵνα σωθῇ ὁ κόσμος δι᾽ αὐτοῦ.

5. Jonah 4:1–2; Acts 9:1–3

Life-Giving Anger

HERE IS THE PART OF GOD'S ANGER that is most astonishing. It is not essentially punitive, but life-giving. God's anger is against all that kills life. This is why God can be patient, merciful, and angry all at the same time.

JONAH 4:1–2

¹וַיֵּרַע אֶל־יוֹנָה רָעָה גְדוֹלָה וַיִּחַר לוֹ:
²וַיִּתְפַּלֵּל אֶל־יְהוָה וַיֹּאמַר אָנָּה יְהוָה הֲלוֹא־זֶה דְבָרִי עַד־
הֱיוֹתִי עַל־אַדְמָתִי עַל־כֵּן קִדַּמְתִּי לִבְרֹחַ תַּרְשִׁישָׁה כִּי יָדַעְתִּי
כִּי אַתָּה אֵל־חַנּוּן וְרַחוּם אֶרֶךְ אַפַּיִם וְרַב־חֶסֶד וְנִחָם עַל־
הָרָעָה:

וַיֵּרַע v.c. + v.3.m.s.impf.Q. [רעע]; וַיִּחַר v.c. + v.3.m.s.impf.Q. [חרה]; אָנָּה (where to?); הֱיוֹתִי v.in.cst.Q. [היה] + 1.com.s.pr.sf.; קִדַּמְתִּי (go before); חַנּוּן (gracious); וְרַחוּם (compassionate); וְנִחָם v.m.s.ptc.N. [נחם]

ACTS 9:1–3

¹Ὁ δὲ Σαῦλος ἔτι ἐμπνέων ἀπειλῆς καὶ φόνου εἰς τοὺς μαθητὰς τοῦ κυρίου, προσελθὼν τῷ ἀρχιερεῖ ²ἠτήσατο παρ' αὐτοῦ ἐπιστολὰς εἰς Δαμασκὸν πρὸς τὰς συναγωγάς, ὅπως ἐάν τινας εὕρῃ τῆς ὁδοῦ ὄντας, ἄνδρας τε καὶ γυναῖκας, δεδεμένους ἀγάγῃ εἰς Ἰερουσαλήμ. ³ἐν δὲ τῷ πορεύεσθαι ἐγένετο αὐτὸν ἐγγίζειν τῇ Δαμασκῷ, ἐξαίφνης τε αὐτὸν περιήστραψεν φῶς ἐκ τοῦ οὐρανοῦ

ἐμπνέων (breach); ἀπειλῆς (threat); φόνου (murder); προσελθὼν v.m.s.nom.aor.act.ptc. [προσέρχομαι]; ἠτήσατο v.3.s.aor.mid.ind. [αἰτέω]; ἐπιστολὰς (letter); εὕρῃ v.3.s.aor.act.sub. [εὑρίσκω]; ἀγάγῃ v.3.s.aor.act.sub. [ἄγω]; ἐγένετο v.3.s.aor.mid.ind. [γίνομαι]; ἐγγίζειν (approach); ἐξαίφνης (suddenly); περιήστραψεν (shine around)

6. Habakkuk 2:1; John 19:24–25

Transformation

WHAT DOES GOD DO when we are angry at him? Not what we expect. God listens. God absorbs. God receives our anger into himself and there, in the furnace of his own affliction, transforms it into something we never guessed—forgiveness. Reconciliation.

HABAKKUK 2:1

עַל־מִשְׁמַרְתִּי אֶעֱמֹדָה וְאֶתְיַצְּבָה עַל־מָצוֹר וַאֲצַפֶּה לִרְאוֹת מַה־
יְדַבֶּר־בִּי וּמָה אָשִׁיב עַל־תּוֹכַחְתִּי:

אֶעֱמֹדָה v.1.com.s.coh.Q. [עמד]; וְאֶתְיַצְּבָה cj. + v.1.com.s.coh.Ht. [יצב] (take a stand); מָצוֹר (station); וַאֲצַפֶּה (watch); לִרְאוֹת prep. + v.in.cs.Q. [ראה]; אָשִׁיב v.1.com.s.impf.H. [שוב]; תּוֹכַחְתִּי n.f.s. (reproof) + 1.com.s.pr.sf.

JOHN 19:24–25

²⁴εἶπαν οὖν πρὸς ἀλλήλους, Μὴ σχίσωμεν αὐτόν, ἀλλὰ λάχωμεν περὶ αὐτοῦ τίνος ἔσται· ἵνα ἡ γραφὴ πληρωθῇ [ἡ λέγουσα],

Διεμερίσαντο τὰ ἱμάτιά μου ἑαυτοῖς
καὶ ἐπὶ τὸν ἱματισμόν μου ἔβαλον κλῆρον.

Οἱ μὲν οὖν στρατιῶται ταῦτα ἐποίησαν. ²⁵ εἱστήκεισαν δὲ παρὰ τῷ σταυρῷ τοῦ Ἰησοῦ ἡ μήτηρ αὐτοῦ καὶ ἡ ἀδελφὴ τῆς μητρὸς αὐτοῦ, Μαρία ἡ τοῦ Κλωπᾶ καὶ Μαρία ἡ Μαγδαληνή.

εἶπαν v.3.p.aor.act.ind. [λέγω]; σχίσωμεν (split); λάχωμεν (cast lots); ἔσται v.3.s.fut.ind. [εἰμί]; Διεμερίσαντο v.3.p.aor.mid.ind. [διαμερίζω] (distribute); ἱματισμόν (clothing); κλῆρον (portion); στρατιῶται (soldier); εἱστήκεισαν v.3.p.plup.act.ind. [ἵστημι]; σταυρῷ (cross)

7. Deuteronomy 10:16–17; Mark 3:5–6

Healing Anger

"PURE" ANGER IS A GIFT FROM GOD, holding the power to heal, to cleanse, to make positive change, to give life. Anger can only do these things, though, when tempered with compassion and when rightly focused. This is the kind of anger that drove Jesus to heal on the Sabbath. It is not the kind of anger most of us entertain most of the time.

DEUTERONOMY 10:16–17

16וּמַלְתֶּם אֵת עָרְלַת לְבַבְכֶם וְעָרְפְּכֶם לֹא תַקְשׁוּ עוֹד׃

17כִּי יְהוָה אֱלֹהֵיכֶם הוּא אֱלֹהֵי הָאֱלֹהִים וַאֲדֹנֵי הָאֲדֹנִים הָאֵל הַגָּדֹל הַגִּבֹּר וְהַנּוֹרָא אֲשֶׁר לֹא־יִשָּׂא פָנִים וְלֹא יִקַּח שֹׁחַד׃

וּמַלְתֶּם v.c. + v.2.m.p.pf.Q. [מול] (circumcise); עָרְלַת (foreskin); וְעָרְפְּכֶם (neck); תַקְשׁוּ v.2.m.p.impf.H. [קשה] (be hard); וְהַנּוֹרָא cj. + d.a. + v.m.s.ptc.N. [ירא]; יִשָּׂא v.3.m.s.impf.Q. [נשא]; יִקַּח v.3.m.s.impf.Q. [לקח]; שֹׁחַד (bribe)

MARK 3:5–6

⁵καὶ περιβλεψάμενος αὐτοὺς μετ' ὀργῆς, συλλυπούμενος ἐπὶ τῇ πωρώσει τῆς καρδίας αὐτῶν λέγει τῷ ἀνθρώπῳ, Ἔκτεινον τὴν χεῖρα. καὶ ἐξέτεινεν καὶ ἀπεκατεστάθη ἡ χεὶρ αὐτοῦ. ⁶καὶ ἐξελθόντες οἱ Φαρισαῖοι εὐθὺς μετὰ τῶν Ἡρῳδιανῶν συμβούλιον ἐδίδουν κατ' αὐτοῦ ὅπως αὐτὸν ἀπολέσωσιν.

περιβλεψάμενος (look around); ὀργῆς (anger); συλλυπούμενος (feel sympathy); πωρώσει (stubborn); Ἔκτεινον (stretch out); ἐξέτεινεν v.3.s.aor.act.ind. [ἐκτείνω]; ἀπεκατεστάθη v.3.s.aor.pass.ind. [ἀποκαθίστημι] (restore); ἐξελθόντες v.m.p.nom.aor.act.ptc. [ἐξέρχομαι]; συμβούλιον (counsel)

Week 40

Pain

1. Jeremiah 8:18–19; Luke 22:41–42, 44

The Agony of Jesus

IN TINY INCREMENTS I COME to understand the agony of Jesus. At one time I thought it was the terror I would feel, facing my own execution. But the agony of Jesus is of a different order, wholly "other." It is the extinction of hope, the loss of promise, the dwelling place of souls who have said their final "NO!" to God.

JEREMIAH 8:18–19

¹⁸מַבְלִיגִיתִי עֲלֵי יָגוֹן עָלַי לִבִּי דַוָּי:
¹⁹הִנֵּה־קוֹל שַׁוְעַת בַּת־עַמִּי מֵאֶרֶץ מַרְחַקִּים הַיהוָה אֵין בְּצִיּוֹן אִם־מַלְכָּהּ אֵין בָּהּ מַדּוּעַ הִכְעִסוּנִי בִּפְסִלֵיהֶם בְּהַבְלֵי נֵכָר:

מַבְלִיגִיתִי n.f.s. (joy) + 1.com.s.pr.sf.; יָגוֹן (grief); דַוָּי (faint); שַׁוְעַת (cry for help); מַרְחַקִּים (distance); הִכְעִסוּנִי v.3.c.p.pf.H. [כעס] + 1.com.s.pr.sf.; בִּפְסִלֵיהֶם (idol); בְּהַבְלֵי (idol); נֵכָר (foreigner)

LUKE 22:41–42, 44

⁴¹καὶ αὐτὸς ἀπεσπάσθη ἀπ᾽ αὐτῶν ὡσεὶ λίθου βολὴν καὶ θεὶς τὰ γόνατα προσηύχετο ⁴²λέγων, Πάτερ, εἰ βούλει παρένεγκε τοῦτο τὸ ποτήριον ἀπ᾽ ἐμοῦ· πλὴν μὴ τὸ θέλημά μου ἀλλὰ τὸ σὸν γινέσθω. ⁴⁴καὶ γενόμενος ἐν ἀγωνίᾳ ἐκτενέστερον προσηύχετο· καὶ ἐγένετο ὁ ἱδρὼς αὐτοῦ ὡσεὶ θρόμβοι αἵματος καταβαίνοντες ἐπὶ τὴν γῆν.

ἀπεσπάσθη v.3.s.aor.pass.ind. [ἀποσπάω] (withdraw); βολὴν (throw); θεὶς v.m.s.nom.aor.act.ptc. [τίθημι]; γόνατα (knee); βούλει (want); παρένεγκε v.2.s.aor.act.impv. [παραφέρω]; ποτήριον (cup); πλὴν (but); σὸν (your); ἀγωνίᾳ (agony); ἐκτενέστερον (fervently); ἐγένετο v.3.s.aor.mid.ind. [γίνομαι]; ἱδρὼς (sweat); θρόμβοι (clot)

2. Jeremiah 17.14; Mark 5.22–24

Where Death and Life Comingle

THERE IS A FINAL NECESSITY to bringing one's pain to Jesus. Some of us never realize that all pain is Jesus' pain. To find hope in the midst of loss, our pain must go to its true home, in the pierced heart of Jesus, where death and life comingle and where the universe is healed.

JEREMIAH 17:14

^{14}רְפָאֵנִי יְהוָה וְאֵרָפֵא הוֹשִׁיעֵנִי וְאִוָּשֵׁעָה כִּי תְהִלָּתִי אָתָּה׃

רְפָאֵנִי v.2.m.s.impv.Q. [רפא] + 1.com.s.pr.sf.; הוֹשִׁיעֵנִי v.2.m.s.impv.H. [ישע] + 1.com.s.pr.sf.; וְאִוָּשֵׁעָה cj. + v.1.com.s.coh.N. [ישע]

MARK 5:22–24

^{22}καὶ ἔρχεται εἷς τῶν ἀρχισυναγώγων, ὀνόματι Ἰάϊρος, καὶ ἰδὼν αὐτὸν πίπτει πρὸς τοὺς πόδας αὐτοῦ ^{23}καὶ παρακαλεῖ αὐτὸν πολλὰ λέγων ὅτι Τὸ θυγάτριον μου ἐσχάτως ἔχει, ἵνα ἐλθὼν ἐπιθῇς τὰς χεῖρας αὐτῇ ἵνα σωθῇ καὶ ζήσῃ. ^{24}καὶ ἀπῆλθεν μετ' αὐτοῦ. Καὶ ἠκολούθει αὐτῷ ὄχλος πολὺς καὶ συνέθλιβον αὐτόν.

ἀρχισυναγώγων (synagogue leader); ἰδὼν v.m.s.nom.aor.act.ptc. [ὁράω]; θυγάτριον (little daughter); ἐσχάτως ἔχει adv. + v.3.s.pres.act.ind. [ἔχω] (she is at the point of death); ἐλθὼν v.m.s.nom.aor.act.ptc. [ἔρχομαι]; ἐπιθῇς v.2.s.aor.act.sub. [ἐπιτίθημι] (lay on); ἀπῆλθεν v.3.s.aor.act.ind. [ἀπέρχομαι]; συνέθλιβον v.3.p.impf.act.ind. [συνθλίβω] (press upon)

3. Psalm 88:14–15 [13–14]; John 20:13–15

Waiting in the Dark

JESUS STANDS BEHIND US, unperceived, precisely at the moment of our deepest grief. He stands in his resurrection, in fresh triumph over death. Yet although we neither see nor hear him, this does not offend Jesus. He simply comes closer, calls us by name, and waits with us until we can perceive him once again.

PSALM 88:14–15 [13–14]

¹⁴וַאֲנִי אֵלֶיךָ יְהוָה שִׁוַּעְתִּי וּבַבֹּקֶר תְּפִלָּתִי תְקַדְּמֶךָּ׃
¹⁵לָמָה יְהוָה תִּזְנַח נַפְשִׁי תַּסְתִּיר פָּנֶיךָ מִמֶּנִּי׃

שִׁוַּעְתִּי (cry for help); תְקַדְּמֶךָּ v.3.f.s.impf.P. [קדם] + en. + 2.m.s.pr.sf. (be before); תִּזְנַח (reject)

JOHN 20:13–15

¹³καὶ λέγουσιν αὐτῇ ἐκεῖνοι, Γύναι, τί κλαίεις; λέγει αὐτοῖς ὅτι Ἦραν τὸν κύριον μου, καὶ οὐκ οἶδα ποῦ ἔθηκαν αὐτόν. ¹⁴ταῦτα εἰποῦσα ἐστράφη εἰς τὰ ὀπίσω καὶ θεωρεῖ τὸν Ἰησοῦν ἐστῶτα καὶ οὐκ ᾔδει ὅτι Ἰησοῦς ἐστιν. ¹⁵λέγει αὐτῇ Ἰησοῦς, Γύναι, τί κλαίεις; τίνα ζητεῖς; ἐκείνη δοκοῦσα ὅτι ὁ κηπουρός ἐστιν λέγει αὐτῷ, Κύριε, εἰ σὺ ἐβάστασας αὐτόν, εἰπέ μοι ποῦ ἔθηκας αὐτόν, καγὼ αὐτὸν ἀρῶ.

κλαίεις (weep); ἔθηκαν v.3.p.aor.act.ind. [τίθημι]; εἰποῦσα v.f.s.nom.aor.act.ptc. [λέγω]; ὀπίσω (behind); θεωρεῖ (see); ᾔδει v.3.s.plup.act.ind. [οἶδα]; ἐστιν v.3.s.pres.ind. [εἰμί]; κηπουρός (gardner); ἐβάστασας (take); εἰπέ v.2.s.aor.act.impv. [λέγω]; ἀρῶ v.1.s.fut.act.ind. [αἴρω]

4. 1 Samuel 1:2, 8; Mark 3:19b–21

Families That Wound

ONE OF THE SHARPEST PAINS we can experience is persecution at the hands of our own family. Jesus knew this pain. Just as Jesus found his true family among spiritual kindred, so can we. That is how this kind of pain is healed.

1 SAMUEL 1:2, 8

²וְלוֹ שְׁתֵּי נָשִׁים שֵׁם אַחַת חַנָּה וְשֵׁם הַשֵּׁנִית פְּנִנָּה וַיְהִי
לִפְנִנָּה יְלָדִים וּלְחַנָּה אֵין יְלָדִים:
⁸וַיֹּאמֶר לָהּ אֶלְקָנָה אִישָׁהּ חַנָּה לָמֶה תִבְכִּי וְלָמֶה לֹא תֹאכְלִי
וְלָמֶה יֵרַע לְבָבֵךְ הֲלוֹא אָנֹכִי טוֹב לָךְ מֵעֲשָׂרָה בָּנִים:

וַיְהִי v.c. + v.3.m.s.impf.Q. [היה]; תִבְכִּי v.2.f.s.impf.Q. [בכה]; יֵרַע
v.3.m.s.impf.Q. [רעע]

MARK 3:19B–21

¹⁹ὃς καὶ παρέδωκεν αὐτόν. ²⁰Καὶ ἔρχεται εἰς οἶκον· καὶ
συνέρχεται πάλιν [ὁ] ὄχλος, ὥστε μὴ δύνασθαι αὐτοὺς μηδὲ
ἄρτον φαγεῖν. ²¹καὶ ἀκούσαντες οἱ παρ' αὐτοῦ ἐξῆλθον
κρατῆσαι αὐτόν· ἔλεγον γὰρ ὅτι ἐξέστη.

παρέδωκεν v.3.s.aor.act.ind. [παραδίδωμι]; συνέρχεται (assemble); ἐξῆλθον v.1.s.aor.act.ind. [ἐξέρχομαι]; κρατῆσαι (take hold); ἐξέστη
v.3.s.aor.act.ind. [ἐξίστημι] (lose one's mind)

5. Ruth 1:19–21; Luke 2:34–35

Bigger Than My Pain

"Why call me Pleasant when my real name is Bitter?" I have allowed myself to become my pain, to become my situation. O God, raise me up and give me life that is larger than my experience.

Ruth 1:19–21

19וַתֵּלַכְנָה שְׁתֵּיהֶם עַד־בֹּאָנָה בֵּית לָחֶם וַיְהִי כְּבֹאָנָה בֵּית לֶחֶם
וַתֵּהֹם כָּל־הָעִיר עֲלֵיהֶן וַתֹּאמַרְנָה הֲזֹאת נָעֳמִי:
20וַתֹּאמֶר אֲלֵיהֶן אַל־תִּקְרֶאנָה לִי נָעֳמִי קְרֶאןָ לִי מָרָא כִּי־הֵמַר
שַׁדַּי לִי מְאֹד:
21אֲנִי מְלֵאָה הָלַכְתִּי וְרֵיקָם הֱשִׁיבַנִי יְהוָה לָמָּה תִקְרֶאנָה לִי נָעֳמִי
וַיהוָה עָנָה בִי וְשַׁדַּי הֵרַע לִי:

וַיְהִי;.v.c. + v.3.f.p.impf.Q [הלך]; בֹּאָנָה v.in.cs.Q [בוא] + 3.f.p.pr.sf.; וַתֵּלַכְנָה
v.c. + v.3.m.s.impf.Q [היה]; וַתֵּהֹם v.c. + v.3.f.s.impf.N [הום] (be troubled);
מָרָא (bitter); הֵמַר v.3.m.s.pf.H [מרר] (be bitter); שַׁדַּי (Shaddai); וְרֵיקָם
(empty); הֱשִׁיבַנִי v.3.m.s.pf.H [שוב] + 1.com.s.pr.sf.; הֵרַע v.3.m.s.pf.H [רעע]

Luke 2:34–35

34καὶ εὐλόγησεν αὐτοὺς Συμεὼν καὶ εἶπεν πρὸς Μαριὰμ τὴν μητέρα αὐτοῦ, Ἰδοὺ οὗτος κεῖται εἰς πτῶσιν καὶ ἀνάστασιν πολλῶν ἐν τῷ Ἰσραὴλ καὶ εἰς σημεῖον ἀντιλεγόμενον 35– καὶ σοῦ [δὲ] αὐτῆς τὴν ψυχὴν διελεύσεται ῥομφαία–, ὅπως ἂν ἀποκαλυφθῶσιν ἐκ πολλῶν καρδιῶν διαλογισμοί.

εἶπεν v.3.s.aor.act.ind. [λέγω]; κεῖται v.3.s.pres.mid.ind. [κεῖμαι] (be destined); πτῶσιν (fall); ἀντιλεγόμενον (oppose); διελεύσεται v.3.s.fut.mid.ind. [διέρχομαι] (go about); ῥομφαία (sword); ἀποκαλυφθῶσιν (reveal); διαλογισμοί (thought)

6. Judges 19:24–26; Luke 22:63–65

Christ Outside the Door

EVERY TIME A WOMAN IS RAPED, a child is abused, Christ is raped. Christ is abused. Unless we work to eliminate the social structures that perpetuate such evil, we put Christ outside the door for the night. And blithely we sleep on.

JUDGES 19:24–26

²⁴הִנֵּה בִתִּי הַבְּתוּלָה וּפִילַגְשֵׁהוּ אוֹצִיאָה־נָּא אוֹתָם וְעַנּוּ אוֹתָם
וַעֲשׂוּ לָהֶם הַטּוֹב בְּעֵינֵיכֶם וְלָאִישׁ הַזֶּה לֹא תַעֲשׂוּ דְּבַר
הַנְּבָלָה הַזֹּאת:
²⁵וְלֹא־אָבוּ הָאֲנָשִׁים לִשְׁמֹעַ לוֹ וַיַּחֲזֵק הָאִישׁ בְּפִילַגְשׁוֹ
וַיֹּצֵא אֲלֵיהֶם הַחוּץ וַיֵּדְעוּ אוֹתָהּ וַיִּתְעַלְּלוּ־בָהּ כָּל־
הַלַּיְלָה עַד־הַבֹּקֶר וַיְשַׁלְּחוּהָ כַּעֲלוֹת הַשָּׁחַר:
²⁶וַתָּבֹא הָאִשָּׁה לִפְנוֹת הַבֹּקֶר וַתִּפֹּל פֶּתַח בֵּית־הָאִישׁ אֲשֶׁר־
אֲדוֹנֶיהָ שָׁם עַד־הָאוֹר:

וּפִילַגְשֵׁהוּ (concubine); אוֹצִיאָה v.1.com.s.coh.H. [יצא]; וְעַנּוּ cj. +
v.2.m.p.impv.P. [ענה]; וַעֲשׂוּ cj. + v.2.m.p.impv.Q. [עשה]; תַעֲשׂוּ v.2.m.p.impf.Q.
[עשה]; הַנְּבָלָה (folly); אָבוּ v.3.c.p.pf.Q. [אבה]; וַיֹּצֵא v.c. + v.3.m.s.impf.H. [יצא];
וַיֵּדְעוּ v.c. + v.3.m.p.impf.Q. [ידע]; וַיִּתְעַלְּלוּ (be ruthless); וַיְשַׁלְּחוּהָ v.c. +
v.3.m.p.impf.P. [שלח] + 3.f.s.pr.sf.; כַּעֲלוֹת prep. + v.in.cs.Q. [עלה]; הַשָּׁחַר
(dawn); וַתָּבֹא v.c. + v.3.f.s.impf.Q. [בוא]; לִפְנוֹת prep. + v.in.cs.Q. [פנה]; וַתִּפֹּל
v.c. + v.3.f.s.impf.Q. [נפל]

LUKE 22:63–65

⁶³Καὶ οἱ ἄνδρες οἱ συνέχοντες αὐτὸν ἐνέπαιζον αὐτῷ
δέροντες, ⁶⁴καὶ περικαλύψαντες αὐτὸν ἐπηρώτων λέγοντες,
Προφήτευσον, τίς ἐστιν ὁ παίσας σε; ⁶⁵καὶ ἕτερα πολλὰ
βλασφημοῦντες ἔλεγον εἰς αὐτόν.

συνέχοντες (seize); ἐνέπαιζον (mock); δέροντες (beat); περικαλύψαντες (cover up); Προφήτευσον (prophesy); ἐστιν v.3.s.pres.ind. [εἰμί]; παίσας
(hit); βλασφημοῦντες (blaspheme)

291

7. Psalm 4:2 [1]; Mark 5:30, 33–34

Room in Our Distress

MAY I BE LIKE GOD, a hospitable soul who gives others "room in their distress." May the space around me be a safe place where the virtue of Jesus can heal others' wounds.

PSALM 4:2 [1]

²בְּקָרְאִי עֲנֵנִי אֱלֹהֵי צִדְקִי בַּצָּר הִרְחַבְתָּ לִּי חָנֵּנִי וּשְׁמַע
תְּפִלָּתִי:

בְּקָרְאִי prep. + v.in.cs.Q. [קרא] + 1.com.s.pr.sf.; עֲנֵנִי v.2.m.s.impv.Q. [ענה] + 1.com.s.pr.sf.; בַּצָּר (distress); הִרְחַבְתָּ (enlarge); חָנֵּנִי v.2.m.s.impv.Q. [חנן] + 1.com.s.pr.sf.

MARK 5:30, 33–34

³⁰καὶ εὐθὺς ὁ Ἰησοῦς ἐπιγνοὺς ἐν ἑαυτῷ τὴν ἐξ αὐτοῦ δύναμιν ἐξελθοῦσαν ἐπιστραφεὶς ἐν τῷ ὄχλῳ ἔλεγεν, Τίς μου ἥψατο τῶν ἱματίων; ³³ἡ δὲ γυνὴ φοβηθεῖσα καὶ τρέμουσα, εἰδυῖα ὃ γέγονεν αὐτῇ, ἦλθεν καὶ προσέπεσεν αὐτῷ καὶ εἶπεν αὐτῷ πᾶσαν τὴν ἀλήθειαν. ³⁴ὁ δὲ εἶπεν αὐτῇ, θυγάτηρ, ἡ πίστις σου σέσωκεν σε· ὕπαγε εἰς εἰρήνην καὶ ἴσθι ὑγιὴς ἀπὸ τῆς μάστιγος σου.

ἐπιγνοὺς (know); ἐξελθοῦσαν v.f.s.acc.aor.act.ptc. [ἐξέρχομαι]; ἐπιστραφεὶς (turn around); ἥψατο v.3.s.aor.mid.ind. [ἅπτω] (touch); τρέμουσα (tremble); εἰδυῖα v.f.s.nom.pf.act.ptc. [οἶδα]; ἦλθεν v.3.s.aor.act.ind. [ἔρχομαι]; προσέπεσεν (fall upon); εἶπεν v.3.s.aor.act.ind. [λέγω]; Θυγάτηρ (daughter); ἴσθι v.2.s.pres.impv. [εἰμί]; ὑγιὴς (healthy); μάστιγος (suffering)

Day of Atonement

1. Exodus 20:19–20; Romans 6:12–13

The Fear of the Lord Brings Wholeness

THERE IS SOMETHING CRAZY about the way we are afraid of God,
the One who gives us life and wholeness, but we aren't afraid
of sin, the thing that kills us. To reverse that order is to rightly
fear the Lord.

EXODUS 20:19–20

¹⁹וַיֹּאמְרוּ אֶל־מֹשֶׁה דַּבֵּר־אַתָּה עִמָּנוּ וְנִשְׁמָעָה וְאַל־יְדַבֵּר עִמָּנוּ אֱלֹהִים
פֶּן־נָמוּת:²⁰ וַיֹּאמֶר מֹשֶׁה אֶל־הָעָם אַל־תִּירָאוּ כִּי לְבַעֲבוּר
נַסּוֹת
אֶתְכֶם בָּא הָאֱלֹהִים וּבַעֲבוּר תִּהְיֶה יִרְאָתוֹ עַל־פְּנֵיכֶם לְבִלְתִּי תֶחֱטָאוּ:

וְנִשְׁמָעָה cj. + v.1.com.p.coh.Q. [שׁמע]; לְבַעֲבוּר (in order to); תִּירָאוּ
v.2.m.p.impf.Q.pause [ירא]; נַסּוֹת v.in.cs.P. [נסה] (test); בָּא v.3.m.s.pf.Q.
[בוא]; תֶחֱטָאוּ v.2.m.p.impf.Q.pause [חטא]

ROMANS 6:12–13

¹²Μὴ οὖν βασιλευέτω ἡ ἁμαρτία ἐν τῷ θνητῷ ὑμῶν σώματι
εἰς τὸ ὑπακούειν ταῖς ἐπιθυμίαις αὐτοῦ, ¹³μηδὲ παριστάνετε
τὰ μέλη ὑμῶν ὅπλα ἀδικίας τῇ ἁμαρτίᾳ, ἀλλὰ παραστήσατε
ἑαυτοὺς τῷ θεῷ ὡσεὶ ἐκ νεκρῶν ζῶντας καὶ τὰ μέλη ὑμῶν
ὅπλα δικαιοσύνης τῷ θεῷ.

βασιλευέτω (reign); θνητῷ (mortal); ὑπακούειν (obey); ἐπιθυμίαις
(desire); παριστάνετε (offer); μέλη (member); ὅπλα (instrument); ἀδικίας (unrighteousness); παραστήσατε (present); ὡσεὶ (like)

2. Exodus 24:7–8; 1 Corinthians 11:25–26

The Cup of Obedience

YOUR CUP OF SUFFERING has become our cup of life, O Lord.
May it also be our cup of obedience.

EXODUS 24:7–8

⁷וַיִּקַּח סֵפֶר הַבְּרִית וַיִּקְרָא בְּאָזְנֵי הָעָם וַיֹּאמְרוּ כֹּל אֲשֶׁר־
דִּבֶּר יְהוָה נַעֲשֶׂה וְנִשְׁמָע:
⁸וַיִּקַּח מֹשֶׁה אֶת־הַדָּם וַיִּזְרֹק עַל־הָעָם וַיֹּאמֶר הִנֵּה דַם־
הַבְּרִית אֲשֶׁר כָּרַת יְהוָה עִמָּכֶם עַל כָּל־הַדְּבָרִים הָאֵלֶּה:

וַיִּקַּח v.c. + v.3.m.s.impf.Q. [לקח]

1 CORINTHIANS 11:25–26

²⁵ὡσαύτως καὶ τὸ ποτήριον μετὰ τὸ δειπνῆσαι λέγων, Τοῦτο
τὸ ποτήριον ἡ καινὴ διαθήκη ἐστὶν ἐν τῷ ἐμῷ αἵματι· τοῦτο
ποιεῖτε, ὁσάκις ἐὰν πίνητε, εἰς τὴν ἐμὴν ἀνάμνησιν. ²⁶ὁσάκις
γὰρ ἐὰν ἐσθίητε τὸν ἄρτον τοῦτον καὶ τὸ ποτήριον πίνητε,
τὸν θάνατον τοῦ κυρίου καταγγέλλετε ἄχρις οὗ ἔλθῃ.

ὡσαύτως (likewise); ποτήριον (cup); δειπνῆσαι (eat); καινὴ (new);
διαθήκη (covenant); ἐστὶν v.3.s.pres.ind. [εἰμί]; ὁσάκις (as far as);
ἀνάμνησιν (remembrance); καταγγέλλετε (proclaim); ἄχρις (until); ἔλθῃ
v.3.s.aor.act.sub. [ἔρχομαι]

3. Leviticus 26:3–5; Matthew 7.24–25

Your Purpose Is Our Shalom

WHAT YOU HAVE WANTED all along for us, through us, in us, is shalom. In the stormy chaos of life you call us to shalom. Will we say yes?

LEVITICUS 26:3–5

³אִם־בְּחֻקֹּתַי תֵּלֵכוּ וְאֶת־מִצְוֹתַי תִּשְׁמְרוּ וַעֲשִׂיתֶם אֹתָם:
⁴וְנָתַתִּי גִשְׁמֵיכֶם בְּעִתָּם וְנָתְנָה הָאָרֶץ יְבוּלָהּ וְעֵץ הַשָּׂדֶה יִתֵּן פִּרְיוֹ:
⁵וְהִשִּׂיג לָכֶם דַּיִשׁ אֶת־בָּצִיר וּבָצִיר יַשִּׂיג אֶת־זָרַע וַאֲכַלְתֶּם
לַחְמְכֶם לָשֹׂבַע וִישַׁבְתֶּם לָבֶטַח בְּאַרְצְכֶם:

תֵּלֵכוּ v.2.m.p.impf.Q.pause [הלך]; וַעֲשִׂיתֶם v.c. + v.2.m.p.pf.Q. [עשה]; וְנָתַתִּי v.c. + v.1.com.s.pf.Q. [נתן]; גִשְׁמֵיכֶם (rain); יְבוּלָהּ (produce); יִתֵּן v.3.m.s.impf.Q. [נתן]; וְהִשִּׂיג v.c. + v.3.m.s.pf.H. [נשג]; דַּיִשׁ (threshing); בָּצִיר (vintage); יַשִּׂיג v.c. + v.3.m.s.impf.H. [נשג]; לָבֶטַח (security)

MATTHEW 7:24–25

²⁴Πᾶς οὖν ὅστις ἀκούει μου τοὺς λόγους τούτους καὶ ποιεῖ αὐτούς, ὁμοιωθήσεται ἀνδρὶ φρονίμῳ, ὅστις ᾠκοδόμησεν αὐτοῦ τὴν οἰκίαν ἐπὶ τὴν πέτραν· ²⁵καὶ κατέβη ἡ βροχὴ καὶ ἦλθον οἱ ποταμοὶ καὶ ἔπνευσαν οἱ ἄνεμοι καὶ προσέπεσαν τῇ οἰκίᾳ ἐκείνῃ, καὶ οὐκ ἔπεσεν, τεθεμελίωτο γὰρ ἐπὶ τὴν πέτραν.

ὁμοιωθήσεται (be like); φρονίμῳ (wise); ᾠκοδόμησεν v.3.s.aor.act.ind. [οἰκοδομέω] (build); πέτραν (rock); κατέβη v.3.s.aor.act.ind. [καταβαίνω]; βροχὴ (rain); ἦλθον v.3.p.aor.act.ind. [ἔρχομαι]; ποταμοὶ (river); ἔπνευ-σαν (blow); ἄνεμοι (wind); προσέπεσαν v.3.s.aor.act.ind. [προσπίπτω] (beat upon); ἔπεσεν v.3.s.aor.act.ind. [πίπτω]; τεθεμελίωτο v.3.s.plup.pass.ind. [θεμελιόω] (be founded)

4. Jeremiah 17:9–10; Romans 5:12

Jacob Heart

THE HEART IS A JACOB, A DECEIVER. It tells us more or less than what is true, and always with a self-protective bent. From that first fatal bite it has been so.

JEREMIAH 17:9–10

⁹עָקֹב הַלֵּב מִכֹּל וְאָנֻשׁ הוּא מִי יֵדָעֶנּוּ׃

¹⁰אֲנִי יְהוָה חֹקֵר לֵב בֹּחֵן כְּלָיוֹת וְלָתֵת לְאִישׁ כִּדְרָכָיו כִּפְרִי מַעֲלָלָיו׃

עָקֹב (deceitful); וְאָנֻשׁ (sick); יֵדָעֶנּוּ v.3.m.s.impf.Q. [ידע] + para. + 3.m.s.pr.sf.; חֹקֵר (search); בֹּחֵן (examine); כְּלָיוֹת (kidney); וְלָתֵת cj. + prep. + v.in.cs.Q. [נתן]; מַעֲלָלָיו (deed)

ROMANS 5:12

¹²Διὰ τοῦτο ὥσπερ δι᾽ ἑνὸς ἀνθρώπου ἡ ἁμαρτία εἰς τὸν κόσμον εἰσῆλθεν καὶ διὰ τῆς ἁμαρτίας ὁ θάνατος, καὶ οὕτως εἰς πάντας ἀνθρώπους ὁ θάνατος διῆλθεν, ἐφ᾽ ᾧ πάντες ἥμαρτον·

ὥσπερ (just as); εἰσῆλθεν v.3.s.aor.act.ind. [εἰσέρχομαι]; διῆλθεν v.3.s.aor.act.ind. [διέρχομαι] (come); ἥμαρτον (sin)

5. Lamentations 3:22–23; Luke 1:50–53

New Mercies Every Day

EVERY MORNING IT IS THE SAME, God. You awaken me with whispered news—Good News—and mercies for the day. Humility and mercy. Exaltation and mercy. Fullness and mercy. Oh, that I would truly listen with my heart!

LAMENTATIONS 3:22–23

‏²²חַסְדֵי יְהוָה כִּי לֹא־תָמְנוּ כִּי לֹא־כָלוּ רַחֲמָיו׃
‏²³חֲדָשִׁים לַבְּקָרִים רַבָּה אֱמוּנָתֶךָ׃

תָמְנוּ v.1.com.p.pf.Q. [תמם]; כָלוּ v.3.c.p.Q. [כלה]; רַחֲמָיו (mercy)

LUKE 1:50–53

⁵⁰καὶ τὸ ἔλεος αὐτοῦ εἰς γενεὰς καὶ γενεὰς
    τοῖς φοβουμένοις αὐτόν.
⁵¹Ἐποίησεν κράτος ἐν βραχίονι αὐτοῦ,
    διεσκόρπισεν ὑπερηφάνους διανοίᾳ καρδίας
    αὐτῶν·
⁵²καθεῖλεν δυνάστας ἀπὸ θρόνων
    καὶ ὕψωσεν ταπεινούς,
⁵³πεινῶντας ἐνέπλησεν ἀγαθῶν
    καὶ πλουτοῦντας ἐξαπέστειλεν κενούς.

ἔλεος (mercy); γενεὰς (generation); κράτος (might); βραχίονι (arm); διεσκόρπισεν v.3.s.aor.act.ind. [διασκορπίζω] (scatter); ὑπερηφάνους (proud); διανοίᾳ (understanding); καθεῖλεν v.3.s.aor.act.ind. [καθαιρέω] (destroy); δυνάστας (ruler); ὕψωσεν (raise up); ταπεινούς (poor); πεινῶντας (hunger); ἐνέπλησεν v.3.s.aor.act.ind. [ἐμπλιμπλήμαι] (fill); πλουτοῦντας (be rich); ἐξαπέστειλεν (send away); κενούς (empty)

6. Numbers 15:28–30; 1 John 1:9–10

Not If But When

IT REALLY ISN'T A QUESTION OF *IF* WE SIN. It's a matter of *when.* "Don't kid yourself," said John. "It's going to happen." We need to be as honest as God is merciful concerning our sin.

NUMBERS 15:28–30

28וְכִפֶּר הַכֹּהֵן עַל־הַנֶּפֶשׁ הַשֹּׁגֶגֶת בְּחֶטְאָה בִשְׁגָגָה לִפְנֵי
יְהוָה לְכַפֵּר עָלָיו וְנִסְלַח לֹו:
29הָאֶזְרָח בִּבְנֵי יִשְׂרָאֵל וְלַגֵּר הַגָּר בְּתוֹכָם תּוֹרָה אַחַת יִהְיֶה
לָכֶם לָעֹשֶׂה בִּשְׁגָגָה:
30וְהַנֶּפֶשׁ אֲשֶׁר־תַּעֲשֶׂה בְּיָד רָמָה מִן־הָאֶזְרָח וּמִן־הַגֵּר
אֶת־יְהוָה הוּא מְגַדֵּף וְנִכְרְתָה הַנֶּפֶשׁ הַהִוא מִקֶּרֶב עַמָּהּ:

הַשֹּׁגֶגֶת (sin); בִשְׁגָגָה (inadvertence); וְנִסְלַח (forgive); הָאֶזְרָח (inhabitant); הַגָּר d.a. + v.m.s.ptc.Q. [גור]; מְגַדֵּף (blaspheme); וְנִכְרְתָה v.c. + v.3.f.s.pf.N. [כרת]

1 JOHN 1:9–10

⁹ἐὰν ὁμολογῶμεν τὰς ἁμαρτίας ἡμῶν, πιστός ἐστιν καὶ δίκαιος, ἵνα ἀφῇ ἡμῖν τὰς ἁμαρτίας καὶ καθαρίσῃ ἡμᾶς ἀπὸ πάσης ἀδικίας. ¹⁰ἐὰν εἴπωμεν ὅτι οὐχ ἡμαρτήκαμεν, ψεύστην ποιοῦμεν αὐτὸν καὶ ὁ λόγος αὐτοῦ οὐκ ἔστιν ἐν ἡμῖν.

ὁμολογῶμεν (confess); ἔστιν v.3.s.pres.ind. [εἰμί]; ἀφῇ v.3.s.aor.act.sub. [ἀφίημι]; καθαρίσῃ (clean); ἀδικίας (unrighteousness); εἴπωμεν v.1.p.aor.act.sub. [λέγω]; ψεύστην (liar)

7. Joel 2.13–14; Acts 8:21–22

Metanoia

REPENTANCE IS THE TURNING AROUND without looking back. It is deciding to go home.

JOEL 2:13–14

¹³וְקִרְעוּ לְבַבְכֶם וְאַל־בִּגְדֵיכֶם וְשׁוּבוּ אֶל־יְהוָה אֱלֹהֵיכֶם כִּי־
חַנּוּן וְרַחוּם הוּא אֶרֶךְ אַפַּיִם וְרַב־חֶסֶד וְנִחָם עַל־הָרָעָה:
¹⁴מִי יוֹדֵעַ יָשׁוּב וְנִחָם וְהִשְׁאִיר אַחֲרָיו בְּרָכָה מִנְחָה וָנֶסֶךְ
לַיהוָה אֱלֹהֵיכֶם:

וְשׁוּבוּ cj. + v.2.m.p.impv.Q. [שׁוב]; חַנּוּן (gracious); וְרַחוּם (compassionate); וְנִחָם v.c. + m.s.ptc.N. [נחם]

ACTS 8:21–22

²¹οὐκ ἔστιν σοι μερὶς οὐδὲ κλῆρος ἐν τῷ λόγῳ τούτῳ, ἡ γὰρ καρδία σου οὐκ ἔστιν εὐθεῖα ἔναντι τοῦ θεοῦ. ²²μετανόησον οὖν ἀπὸ τῆς κακίας σου ταύτης καὶ δεήθητι τοῦ κυρίου, εἰ ἄρα ἀφεθήσεταί σοι ἡ ἐπίνοια τῆς καρδίας σου,

ἔστιν v.3.s.pres.ind. [εἰμί]; μερὶς (part); κλῆρος (lot); εὐθεῖα (upright); ἔναντι (in the eyes of); μετανόησον (repent); κακίας (wickedness); δεήθητι v.2.s.aor.pass.impv. [δέομαι] (ask); εἰ ἄρα (whether); ἀφεθήσεταί v.3.s.fut.pass.ind. [ἀφίημι]; ἐπίνοια (intent)

Week 42

Succoth (God's Presence, Providence, and Protection)

1. Genesis 8:22–9:1; James 5:7–8

Living in the Now

THERE ARE SEASONS FOR ALL THINGS, for plowing, planting, and harvest. Our problem is that no matter which season we are in, we hanker for somewhere else. God grant us the grace to be here, and now. For you are here. And now.

GENESIS 8:22–9:1

²²עֹד כָּל־יְמֵי הָאָרֶץ זֶרַע וְקָצִיר וְקֹר וָחֹם וְקַיִץ וָחֹרֶף וְיוֹם
וָלַיְלָה לֹא יִשְׁבֹּתוּ׃
¹וַיְבָרֶךְ אֱלֹהִים אֶת־נֹחַ וְאֶת־בָּנָיו וַיֹּאמֶר לָהֶם פְּרוּ וּרְבוּ
וּמִלְאוּ אֶת־הָאָרֶץ׃

וְקֹר (cold); וָחֹם (heat); וְקַיִץ (summer); וָחֹרֶף (autumn); פְּרוּ
v.2.m.p.impv.Q. [פרה] (be fruitful); וּרְבוּ cj. + v.2.m.p.impv.Q. [רבה]

JAMES 5:7–8

⁷Μακροθυμήσατε οὖν, ἀδελφοί, ἕως τῆς παρουσίας τοῦ
κυρίου. ἰδοὺ ὁ γεωργὸς ἐκδέχεται τὸν τίμιον καρπὸν τῆς γῆς
μακροθυμῶν ἐπ᾽ αὐτῷ ἕως λάβῃ πρόϊμον καὶ ὄψιμον.
⁸μακροθυμήσατε καὶ ὑμεῖς, στηρίξατε τὰς καρδίας ὑμῶν, ὅτι
ἡ παρουσία τοῦ κυρίου ἤγγικεν.

Μακροθυμήσατε (be patient); παρουσίας (coming); γεωργὸς (farmer);
ἐκδέχεται (await); τίμιον (precious); λάβῃ v.3.s.aor.act.sub. [λαμβάνω];
πρόϊμον (early [rain]); ὄψιμον (late [rain]); στηρίξατε (strengthen);
ἤγγικεν v.3.s.pf.act.ind. [ἐγγίζω] (approach)

2. Exodus 22:29; Romans 8:22–23

Firstfruits of Life

IN GIVING GOD OUR FIRSTFRUITS we remember the original gift of life—*of God's own life*—for ours. In giving God our firstfruits we image the One who gave all.

EXODUS 22:29

²⁹כֵּן־תַּעֲשֶׂה לְשֹׁרְךָ לְצֹאנֶךָ שִׁבְעַת יָמִים יִהְיֶה עִם־אִמּוֹ בַּיּוֹם הַשְּׁמִינִי תִּתְּנוֹ־לִי:

תִּתְּנוֹ v.2.m.s.impf.Q. [נתן] + 3.m.s.pr.sf.

ROMANS 8:22–23

²²οἴδαμεν γὰρ ὅτι πᾶσα ἡ κτίσις συστενάζει καὶ συνωδίνει ἄχρι τοῦ νῦν· ²³οὐ μόνον δέ, ἀλλὰ καὶ αὐτοὶ τὴν ἀπαρχὴν τοῦ πνεύματος ἔχοντες, ἡμεῖς καὶ αὐτοὶ ἐν ἑαυτοῖς στενάζομεν υἱοθεσίαν ἀπεκδεχόμενοι, τὴν ἀπολύτρωσιν τοῦ σώματος ἡμῶν.

κτίσις (creation); συστενάζει (groan together); συνωδίνει (suffer together); ἄχρι (until); ἀπαρχὴν (firstfruit); στενάζομεν (groan); υἱοθεσίαν (adoption); ἀπεκδεχόμενοι (anticipate); ἀπολύτρωσιν (redemption)

3. Leviticus 19:9–10; Luke 4:18–19

Generous God!

O GOD OF THE POOR and the sojourners, the prisoners and the oppressed—would that we would be as eager to show generosity as we are to receive it!

LEVITICUS 19:9–10

⁹וּבְקֻצְרְכֶם אֶת־קְצִיר אַרְצְכֶם לֹא תְכַלֶּה פְּאַת שָׂדְךָ לִקְצֹר
וְלֶקֶט קְצִירְךָ לֹא תְלַקֵּט:
¹⁰וְכַרְמְךָ לֹא תְעוֹלֵל וּפֶרֶט כַּרְמְךָ לֹא תְלַקֵּט לֶעָנִי וְלַגֵּר תַּעֲזֹב
אֹתָם אֲנִי יְהוָה אֱלֹהֵיכֶם:

וְלֶקֶט (gleaning); תְלַקֵּט (glean); תְעוֹלֵל v.2.m.s.impf.Po. [עלל] (glean);
וּפֶרֶט (windfall)

LUKE 4:18–19

¹⁸Πνεῦμα κυρίου ἐπ᾽ ἐμὲ
οὗ εἵνεκεν ἔχρισεν με
εὐαγγελίσασθαι πτωχοῖς,
ἀπέσταλκεν με, κηρύξαι αἰχμαλώτοις ἄφεσιν
καὶ τυφλοῖς ἀνάβλεψιν,
ἀποστεῖλαι τεθραυσμένους ἐν ἀφέσει,
¹⁹κηρύξαι ἐνιαυτὸν κυρίου δεκτόν.

εἵνεκεν (because of); ἔχρισεν v.3.s.aor.act.ind. [χρίω] (anoint); πτωχοῖς
(poor); ἀπέσταλκεν v.3.s.pf.act.ind. [ἀποστέλλω]; αἰχμαλώτοις (captive);
ἄφεσιν (pardon); ἀνάβλεψιν (renewed sight); τεθραυσμένους
v.m.p.acc.pf.pass.ptc. [θραύω] (oppress); ἐνιαυτὸν (year); δεκτόν (acceptable)

4. Isaiah 9:3; John 16:24

Sowing and Reaping Joy

FOR SHEER JOY GOD gives the harvest. But some of us don't know it.

ISAIAH 9:3

³כִּי אֶת־עֹל סֻבֳּלוֹ וְאֵת מַטֵּה שִׁכְמוֹ שֵׁבֶט הַנֹּגֵשׂ בּוֹ הַחִתֹּתָ
כְּיוֹם מִדְיָן:

עֹל (yoke); סֻבֳּלוֹ (burden); שִׁכְמוֹ (shoulders); הַנֹּגֵשׂ (drive); הַחִתֹּתָ v.2.m.s.pf.H. [חתת]

JOHN 16:24

²⁴ἕως ἄρτι οὐκ ᾐτήσατε οὐδὲν ἐν τῷ ὀνόματί μου· αἰτεῖτε καὶ λήμψεσθε, ἵνα ἡ χαρὰ ὑμῶν ᾖ πεπληρωμένη.

ἄρτι (now); ᾐτήσατε v.2.p.aor.act.ind. [ἀιτέω]; λήμψεσθε v.2.p.fut.mid.ind. [λαμβάνω]

5. Ecclesiastes 3:11–13; Mark 7:37

Alive and Well and Whole

IT IS GOD'S WILL that we should be fully present to our work and to our pleasure, joying in creation, fully alive. It is also God's will that we bring his will to pass everywhere we go, not just for ourselves but for others.

ECCLESIASTES 3:11–13

¹¹אֶת־הַכֹּל עָשָׂה יָפֶה בְעִתּוֹ גַּם אֶת־הָעֹלָם נָתַן בְּלִבָּם מִבְּלִי
אֲשֶׁר לֹא־יִמְצָא הָאָדָם אֶת־הַמַּעֲשֶׂה אֲשֶׁר־עָשָׂה הָאֱלֹהִים מֵרֹאשׁ
וְעַד־סוֹף:
¹²יָדַעְתִּי כִּי אֵין טוֹב בָּם כִּי אִם־לִשְׂמוֹחַ וְלַעֲשׂוֹת טוֹב בְּחַיָּיו:
¹³וְגַם כָּל־הָאָדָם שֶׁיֹּאכַל וְשָׁתָה וְרָאָה טוֹב בְּכָל־עֲמָלוֹ מַתַּת
אֱלֹהִים הִיא:

יָפֶה (beautiful); סוֹף (end); וְלַעֲשׂוֹת cj. + prep. + v.in.cs.Q. [עשׂה]; שֶׁיֹּאכַל rel.pr. + v.3.m.s.impf.Q. [אכל]; מַתַּת (gift)

MARK 7:37

³⁷καὶ ὑπερπερισσῶς ἐξεπλήσσοντο λέγοντες, Καλῶς πάντα πεποίηκεν, καὶ τοὺς κωφοὺς ποιεῖ ἀκούειν καὶ [τοὺς] ἀλάλους λαλεῖν.

ὑπερπερισσῶς (beautiful); ἐξεπλήσσοντο v.3.p.impf.pass.ind. [ἐκπλήσσω] (amaze); κωφοὺς (deaf); ἀλάλους (dumb)

6. Ecclesiastes 5:18–20; Romans 5:1–2

The Reason for It All

HOW CAN WE HELP BUT REJOICE when we realize what God intends?

ECCLESIASTES 5:18–20

¹⁸גַּם כָּל־הָאָדָם אֲשֶׁר נָתַן־לוֹ הָאֱלֹהִים עֹשֶׁר וּנְכָסִים וְהִשְׁלִיטוֹ
לֶאֱכֹל מִמֶּנּוּ וְלָשֵׂאת אֶת־חֶלְקוֹ וְלִשְׂמֹחַ בַּעֲמָלוֹ זֹה מַתַּת
אֱלֹהִים הִיא:
¹⁹כִּי לֹא הַרְבֵּה יִזְכֹּר אֶת־יְמֵי חַיָּיו כִּי הָאֱלֹהִים מַעֲנֶה בְּשִׂמְחַת
לִבּוֹ:

עֹשֶׁר (wealth); וּנְכָסִים (riches); וְהִשְׁלִיטוֹ v.c. + v.3.m.s.pf.H. [שׁלט]
(empower) + 3.m.s.pr.sf.; וְלָשֵׂאת cj. + prep. + v.in.cst.Q. [נשׂא]; מַתַּת (gift)

ROMANS 5:1–2

¹Δικαιωθέντες οὖν ἐκ πίστεως εἰρήνην ἔχομεν πρὸς τὸν θεὸν
διὰ τοῦ κυρίου ἡμῶν Ἰησοῦ Χριστοῦ ²δι' οὗ καὶ τὴν
προσαγωγὴν ἐσχήκαμεν [τῇ πίστει] εἰς τὴν χάριν ταύτην ἐν
ᾗ ἑστήκαμεν καὶ καυχώμεθα ἐπ' ἐλπίδι τῆς δόξης τοῦ θεοῦ.

προσαγωγὴν (approach); ἐσχήκαμεν v.1.p.pf.act.ind. [ἔχω]; καυχώμεθα
(boast)

7. Leviticus 23:42–43; Luke 9:33–35

I'm Going to Build a Booth

TODAY IN THE FACE OF NEED, listening to the whine of unbelief, knowing the staggering odds, I'm building a booth. I'm making a tent, a shelter, a tabernacle of hope, and I'm going to remember who my God is. That will be my credo.

LEVITICUS 23:42–43

⁴²בַּסֻּכֹּת תֵּשְׁבוּ שִׁבְעַת יָמִים כָּל־הָאֶזְרָח בְּיִשְׂרָאֵל יֵשְׁבוּ
בַּסֻּכֹּת׃
⁴³לְמַעַן יֵדְעוּ דֹרֹתֵיכֶם כִּי בַסֻּכּוֹת הוֹשַׁבְתִּי אֶת־בְּנֵי יִשְׂרָאֵל
בְּהוֹצִיאִי אוֹתָם מֵאֶרֶץ מִצְרָיִם אֲנִי יְהוָה אֱלֹהֵיכֶם׃

בַּסֻּכֹּת (hut); תֵּשְׁבוּ v.2.m.p.impf.Q. [יָשַׁב]; הָאֶזְרָח (native); יֵשְׁבוּ v.3.m.p.impf.Q. [יָשַׁב]; יֵדְעוּ v.3.m.p.impf.Q. [יָדַע]; הוֹשַׁבְתִּי v.1.com.s.pf.H. [יָשַׁב]; בְּהוֹצִיאִי prep. + v.in.cs.H. [יָצָא] + 1.com.s.pr.sf.

LUKE 9:33–35

³³καὶ ἐγένετο ἐν τῷ διαχωρίζεσθαι αὐτοὺς ἀπ᾽ αὐτοῦ εἶπεν ὁ Πέτρος πρὸς τὸν Ἰησοῦν, Ἐπιστάτα, καλόν ἐστιν ἡμᾶς ὧδε εἶναι, καὶ ποιήσωμεν σκηνὰς τρεῖς, μίαν σοὶ καὶ μίαν Μωϋσεῖ καὶ μίαν Ἠλίᾳ, μὴ εἰδὼς ὃ λέγει. ³⁴ταῦτα δὲ αὐτοῦ λέγοντος ἐγένετο νεφέλη καὶ ἐπεσκίαζεν αὐτούς· ἐφοβήθησαν δὲ ἐν τῷ εἰσελθεῖν αὐτοὺς εἰς τὴν νεφέλην. ³⁵καὶ φωνὴ ἐγένετο ἐκ τῆς νεφέλης λέγουσα, Οὗτός ἐστιν ὁ υἱός μου ὁ ἐκλελεγμένος, αὐτοῦ ἀκούετε.

ἐγένετο v.3.s.aor.mid.ind. [γίνομαι]; διαχωρίζεσθαι (leave); εἶπεν v.3.s.aor.act.ind. [λέγω]; Ἐπιστάτα (master); ἐστιν v.3.s.pres.ind. [εἰμί]; εἶναι v.pres.in. [εἰμί]; σκηνὰς (tent); εἰδὼς v.m.s.nom.pf.act.ptc. [οἶδα]; νεφέλη (cloud); ἐπεσκίαζεν (cover); εἰσελθεῖν v.aor.act.in. [εἰσέρχομαι]; ἐκλελεγμένος (select)

Simhat Torah (Inherent Grace and Joy in the Giving of the Law)

1. Deuteronomy 33:3–4; 1 John 4:17–19

Blazing Love

IN LOVE GOD GAVE THE LAW so as to consecrate us for wholeness, right in the middle of a broken world. That Law was love,
hot and impassioned covenant. White-hot it came in Jesus, to
melt away our fear, new covenant of love. O Beloved, blaze
your love for this world into my soul.

DEUTERONOMY 33:3–4

³אַף חֹבֵב עַמִּים כָּל־קְדֹשָׁיו בְּיָדֶךָ וְהֵם תֻּכּוּ לְרַגְלֶךָ יִשָּׂא
מִדַּבְּרֹתֶיךָ:
⁴תּוֹרָה צִוָּה־לָנוּ מֹשֶׁה מוֹרָשָׁה קְהִלַּת יַעֲקֹב:

חֹבֵב (love); תֻּכּוּ v.3.c.p.pf.Pu. [תכה] (assemble); יִשָּׂא v.3.m.s.impf.Q. [נשא];
מִדַּבְּרֹתֶיךָ prep. + n.f.p. + 2.m.s.pr.sf.; מוֹרָשָׁה (possession); קְהִלַּת (congrega-
tion)

1 JOHN 4:17–19

¹⁷ἐν τούτῳ τετελείωται ἡ ἀγάπη μεθ᾽ ἡμῶν, ἵνα παρρησίαν
ἔχωμεν ἐν τῇ ἡμέρᾳ τῆς κρίσεως, ὅτι καθὼς ἐκεῖνος ἐστιν καὶ
ἡμεῖς ἐσμεν ἐν τῷ κόσμῳ τούτῳ. ¹⁸φόβος οὐκ ἔστιν ἐν τῇ ἀγάπῃ
ἀλλ᾽ ἡ τελεία ἀγάπη ἔξω βάλλει τὸν φόβον, ὅτι ὁ φόβος
κόλασιν ἔχει, ὁ δὲ φοβούμενος οὐ τετελείωται ἐν τῇ ἀγάπῃ.
¹⁹ἡμεῖς ἀγαπῶμεν, ὅτι αὐτὸς πρῶτος ἠγάπησεν ἡμᾶς.

τετελείωται (perfect); παρρησίαν (confidence); κρίσεως (judgment);
ἔστιν v.3.s.pres.ind. [εἰμί]; φόβος (fear); τελεία (perfect); κόλασιν (punishment); τετελείωται v.3.s.pf.pass.ind. [τελειόω]

2. 1 Kings 2:3–4; John 15:9–10

The Law Is Love Enfleshed

CAPTURE MY HEART, LORD, that from sheer love I might obey
the commandments you've given me. For what are they but
love enfleshed toward you and toward my neighbor?

1 KINGS 2:3–4

³וְשָׁמַרְתָּ אֶת־מִשְׁמֶרֶת יְהוָה אֱלֹהֶיךָ לָלֶכֶת בִּדְרָכָיו לִשְׁמֹר
חֻקֹּתָיו מִצְוֹתָיו וּמִשְׁפָּטָיו וְעֵדְוֹתָיו כַּכָּתוּב בְּתוֹרַת מֹשֶׁה
לְמַעַן תַּשְׂכִּיל אֵת כָּל־אֲשֶׁר תַּעֲשֶׂה וְאֵת כָּל־אֲשֶׁר תִּפְנֶה שָׁם:
⁴לְמַעַן יָקִים יְהוָה אֶת־דְּבָרוֹ אֲשֶׁר דִּבֶּר עָלַי לֵאמֹר אִם־יִשְׁמְרוּ
בָנֶיךָ אֶת־דַּרְכָּם לָלֶכֶת לְפָנַי בֶּאֱמֶת בְּכָל־לְבָבָם וּבְכָל־
נַפְשָׁם לֵאמֹר לֹא־יִכָּרֵת לְךָ אִישׁ מֵעַל כִּסֵּא יִשְׂרָאֵל:

לָלֶכֶת prep. + v.in.cs.Q. [הלך]; כַּכָּתוּב prep. + d.a. + v.m.s.pass.ptc. [כתב];
יָקִים v.3.m.s.impf.H. [קום]

JOHN 15:9–10

⁹καθὼς ἠγάπησεν με ὁ πατήρ, καγὼ ὑμᾶς ἠγάπησα· μείνατε
ἐν τῇ ἀγάπῃ τῇ ἐμῇ. ¹⁰ἐὰν τὰς ἐντολάς μου τηρήσητε, μενεῖτε
ἐν τῇ ἀγάπῃ μου, καθὼς ἐγὼ τὰς ἐντολὰς τοῦ πατρός μου
τετήρηκα καὶ μένω αὐτοῦ ἐν τῇ ἀγάπῃ.

μείνατε v.2.p.aor.act.impv. [μένω]

3. 1 Chronicles 16:8–14; Romans 11:33–35

Rules for Celebration

SEARCH! REJOICE! SING, SHOUT, AND REMEMBER! These are scarcely a set of thou-shalt-nots. They set my soul aflame with living fire! There is a rarified recklessness in following God.

1 CHRONICLES 16:8–14

הוֹדוּ לַיהוָה קִרְאוּ בִשְׁמוֹ הוֹדִיעוּ בָעַמִּים עֲלִילֹתָיו: ⁸
שִׁירוּ לוֹ זַמְּרוּ־לוֹ שִׂיחוּ בְּכָל־נִפְלְאֹתָיו: ⁹
הִתְהַלְלוּ בְּשֵׁם קָדְשׁוֹ יִשְׂמַח לֵב מְבַקְשֵׁי יְהוָה: ¹⁰
דִּרְשׁוּ יְהוָה וְעֻזּוֹ בַּקְּשׁוּ פָנָיו תָּמִיד: ¹¹
זִכְרוּ נִפְלְאֹתָיו אֲשֶׁר עָשָׂה מֹפְתָיו וּמִשְׁפְּטֵי־פִיהוּ: ¹²
זֶרַע יִשְׂרָאֵל עַבְדּוֹ בְּנֵי יַעֲקֹב בְּחִירָיו: ¹³
הוּא יְהוָה אֱלֹהֵינוּ בְּכָל־הָאָרֶץ מִשְׁפָּטָיו: ¹⁴

הוֹדוּ v.2.m.p.impv.H. [ידה]; הוֹדִיעוּ v.2.m.p.impv.H. [ידע]; עֲלִילֹתָיו (deed); שִׁירוּ v.2.m.p.impv.Q. [שיר]; זַמְּרוּ (sing); שִׂיחוּ v.2.m.p.impv.Q. [שיח] (consider); מֹפְתָיו (sign); בְּחִירָיו (chosen)

ROMANS 11:33–35

³³Ὦ βάθος πλούτου καὶ σοφίας καὶ γνώσεως θεοῦ· ὡς ἀνεξεραύνητα τὰ κρίματα αὐτοῦ καὶ ἀνεξιχνίαστοι αἱ ὁδοὶ αὐτοῦ.
³⁴Τίς γὰρ ἔγνω νοῦν κυρίου;
ἢ τίς σύμβουλος αὐτοῦ ἐγένετο;
³⁵ἢ τίς προέδωκεν αὐτῷ,
καὶ ἀνταποδοθήσεται αὐτῷ;

βάθος (depth); πλούτου (riches); γνώσεως (knowledge); ἀνεξεραύνητα (unsearchable); κρίματα (decision); ἀνεξιχνίαστοι (incomprehensible); νοῦν (mind); σύμβουλος (counselor); ἐγένετο v.3.s.aor.mid.ind. [γίνομαι]; προέδωκεν v.3.s.aor.act.ind. [προδίδωμι] (give); ἀνταποδοθήσεται (repay)

4. Psalm 119:75–77; Hebrews 8:10–12

Trusting Your Wisdom

WHETHER IT TASTES BITTER OR SWEET your cup is utterly good, dearest Lord. I drink it now in faith, this cup of my life. I drink it with thanksgiving and sober joy.

PSALM 119:75–77

יָדַעְתִּי יְהוָה כִּי־צֶדֶק מִשְׁפָּטֶיךָ וֶאֱמוּנָה עִנִּיתָנִי׃ 75

יְהִי־נָא חַסְדְּךָ לְנַחֲמֵנִי כְּאִמְרָתְךָ לְעַבְדֶּךָ׃ 76

יְבֹאוּנִי רַחֲמֶיךָ וְאֶחְיֶה כִּי־תוֹרָתְךָ שַׁעֲשֻׁעָי׃ 77

עִנִּיתָנִי v.2.m.s.pf.P. [ענה] + 1.com.s.pr.sf.; יְהִי v.3.m.s.jus.Q. [היה]; כְּאִמְרָתְךָ (saying); יְבֹאוּנִי v.3.m.p.impf.Q. [בוא] + 1.com.s.pr.sf.; רַחֲמֶיךָ (mercy); שַׁעֲשֻׁעָי (delight)

HEBREWS 8:10–12

¹⁰ὅτι αὕτη ἡ διαθήκη, ἥν διαθήσομαι τῷ οἴκῳ Ἰσραὴλ
μετὰ τὰς ἡμέρας ἐκείνας, λέγει κύριος·
διδοὺς νόμους μου εἰς τὴν διάνοιαν αὐτῶν
καὶ ἐπὶ καρδίας αὐτῶν ἐπιγράψω αὐτούς,
καὶ ἔσομαι αὐτοῖς εἰς θεόν,
καὶ αὐτοὶ ἔσονται μοι εἰς λαόν·
¹¹καὶ οὐ μὴ διδάξωσιν ἕκαστος τὸν πολίτην
αὐτοῦ
καὶ ἕκαστος τὸν ἀδελφὸν αὐτοῦ λέγων·
γνῶθι τὸν κύριον,
ὅτι πάντες εἰδήσουσιν με
ἀπὸ μικροῦ ἕως μεγάλου αὐτῶν,
¹²ὅτι ἵλεως ἔσομαι ταῖς ἀδικίαις αὐτῶν
καὶ τῶν ἁμαρτιῶν αὐτῶν οὐ μὴ μνησθῶ ἔτι.

διαθήκη (covenant); διαθήσομαι (make covenant); διάνοιαν (mind); ἐπιγράψω (inscribe); πολίτην (citizen); εἰδήσουσιν v.3.p.fut.act.ind. [οἶδα]; μικροῦ (little); ἵλεως (merciful); ἀδικίαις (unrighteousness); μνησθῶ v.1.s.aor.pass.sub. [μιμνήσκω] (remember)

5. Psalm 119:162, 164; Revelation 19:1–2

A Heart Like God's

MAY MY REJOICING OVER RIGHTEOUSNESS and my abhorring of the wrong be in keeping with my God. Even when the judgment rests on me.

PSALM 119:162, 164

162שָׂשׂ אָנֹכִי עַל־אִמְרָתֶךָ כְּמוֹצֵא שָׁלָל רָב:

164שֶׁבַע בַּיּוֹם הִלַּלְתִּיךָ עַל מִשְׁפְּטֵי צִדְקֶךָ:

שָׂשׂ v.m.s.ptc.Q. [שׂושׂ] (rejoice); אִמְרָתֶךָ (saying); כְּמוֹצֵא prep. + v.m.s.act.ptc.Q. [יצא]; הִלַּלְתִּיךָ v.1.com.s.pf.P. [הלל] + 2.m.s.pr.sf.

REVELATION 19:1–2

¹Μετὰ ταῦτα ἤκουσα ὡς φωνὴν μεγάλην ὄχλου πολλοῦ ἐν τῷ οὐρανῷ λεγόντων,
  Ἀλληλουϊά·
  ἡ σωτηρία καὶ ἡ δόξα καὶ ἡ δύναμις τοῦ θεοῦ ἡμῶν,
    ²ὅτι ἀληθιναὶ καὶ δίκαιαι αἱ κρίσεις αὐτοῦ·
  ὅτι ἔκρινεν τὴν πόρνην τὴν μεγάλην
    ἥτις ἔφθειρεν τὴν γῆν ἐν τῇ πορνείᾳ αὐτῆς,
  καὶ ἐξεδίκησεν τὸ αἷμα τῶν δούλων αὐτοῦ
    ἐκ χειρὸς αὐτῆς.

Ἀλληλουϊά (hallelujah); σωτηρία (salvation); ἀληθιναὶ (real); κρίσεις (judgment); πόρνην (whore); ἔφθειρεν (ruin); πορνείᾳ (immorality); ἐξεδίκησεν v.3.s.aor.act.ind. [ἐκδικέω] (avenge)

6. Deuteronomy 28:1–2; Luke 11:28

Obedience from Another Angle

OBEDIENCE IS A MATTER OF BEING all that God has created us to be—nothing more and nothing less.

DEUTERONOMY 28:1–2

¹וְהָיָה אִם־שָׁמוֹעַ תִּשְׁמַע בְּקוֹל יְהוָה אֱלֹהֶיךָ לִשְׁמֹר לַעֲשׂוֹת אֶת־
כָּל־מִצְוֹתָיו אֲשֶׁר אָנֹכִי מְצַוְּךָ הַיּוֹם וּנְתָנְךָ יְהוָה אֱלֹהֶיךָ עֶלְיוֹן
עַל כָּל־גּוֹיֵי הָאָרֶץ:
²וּבָאוּ עָלֶיךָ כָּל־הַבְּרָכוֹת הָאֵלֶּה וְהִשִּׂיגֻךָ כִּי תִשְׁמַע
בְּקוֹל יְהוָה אֱלֹהֶיךָ:

לַעֲשׂוֹת prep. + v.in.cs.Q. [עשה]; מְצַוְּךָ v.m.s.act.ptc.P. [צוה] + 2.m.s.pr.sf.; וּנְתָנְךָ v.c. + v.3.m.s.pf.Q. [נתן] + 2.m.s.pr.sf.; וּבָאוּ v.c. + v.3.c.p.pf.Q. [בוא]; וְהִשִּׂיגֻךָ v.c. + v.3.c.p.pf.H.defective [נשג] + 2.m.s.pr.sf.

LUKE 11:28

²⁸αὐτὸς δὲ εἶπεν, Μενοῦν μακάριοι οἱ ἀκούοντες τὸν λόγον τοῦ θεοῦ καὶ φυλάσσοντες.

εἶπεν v.3.s.aor.act.ind. [λέγω]; Μενοῦν (on the contrary); φυλάσσοντες (keep)

7. Deuteronomy 32:46–47; Hebrews 2:1–4

Drifting

HOW DECEPTIVELY EASY IT IS TO DRIFT AWAY from the Center, to let my moorings slip. Lord, Lord! Come after me! Get my attention! Grab me by the collar! Do whatever it takes! I must be yours and yours alone.

DEUTERONOMY 32:46–47

‎⁴⁶וַיֹּאמֶר אֲלֵהֶם שִׂימוּ לְבַבְכֶם לְכָל־הַדְּבָרִים אֲשֶׁר אָנֹכִי מֵעִיד
בָּכֶם הַיּוֹם אֲשֶׁר תְּצַוֻּם אֶת־בְּנֵיכֶם לִשְׁמֹר לַעֲשׂוֹת אֶת־כָּל־
דִּבְרֵי הַתּוֹרָה הַזֹּאת:
‎⁴⁷כִּי לֹא־דָבָר רֵק הוּא מִכֶּם כִּי־הוּא חַיֵּיכֶם וּבַדָּבָר הַזֶּה תַּאֲרִיכוּ
יָמִים עַל־הָאֲדָמָה אֲשֶׁר אַתֶּם עֹבְרִים אֶת־הַיַּרְדֵּן שָׁמָּה לְרִשְׁתָּהּ:

שִׂימוּ v.2.m.p.impv.Q. [שׂוּם]; מֵעִיד v.m.s.act.ptc.H. [עוד] (admonish); תְּצַוֻּם v.2.m.p.impf.P. [צוה] + 3.m.p.pr.sf.; לַעֲשׂוֹת prep. + v.in.cs.Q. [עשׂה]; רֵק (worthless); תַּאֲרִיכוּ (lengthen); לְרִשְׁתָּהּ prep. + v.in.cs.Q. [ירשׁ] + 3.f.s.pr.sf.

HEBREWS 2:1–4

¹Διὰ τοῦτο δεῖ περισσοτέρως προσέχειν ἡμᾶς τοῖς ἀκουσθεῖσιν, μήποτε παραρυῶμεν. ²εἰ γὰρ ὁ δι᾽ ἀγγέλων λαληθεὶς λόγος ἐγένετο βέβαιος καὶ πᾶσα παράβασις καὶ παρακοὴ ἔλαβεν ἔνδικον μισθαποδοσίαν, ³πῶς ἡμεῖς ἐκφευξόμεθα τηλικαύτης ἀμελήσαντες σωτηρίας, ἥτις ἀρχὴν λαβοῦσα λαλεῖσθαι διὰ τοῦ κυρίου ὑπὸ τῶν ἀκουσάντων εἰς ἡμᾶς ἐβεβαιώθη, ⁴συνεπιμαρτυροῦντος τοῦ θεοῦ σημείοις τε καὶ τέρασιν καὶ ποικίλαις δυνάμεσιν καὶ πνεύματος ἁγίου μερισμοῖς κατὰ τὴν αὐτοῦ θέλησιν;

περισσοτέρως (far more); προσέχειν (pay attention); μήποτε (lest); παραρυῶμεν v.1.p.aor.act.sub. [παραρρέω] (drift off); ἐγένετο v.3.s.aor.mid.ind. [γίνομαι]; βέβαιος (firm); παράβασις (transgression); παρακοή (disobedience); ἔνδικον (deserved); μισθαποδοσίαν (punishment); ἐκφευξόμεθα v.1.p.fut.mid.ind. [ἐκθεύγω] (escape); τηλικαύτης (so great); ἀμελήσαντες (neglect); σωτηρίας (salvation); ἐβεβαιώθη v.3.s.aor.pass.ind. [βεβαιόω] (confirm); συνεπιμαρτυροῦντος (testify); τέρασιν (omen); ποικίλαις (various); μερισμοῖς (distribution); θέλησιν (will)

Week 44

All Saints' Eve (Halloween)

1. Isaiah 14:13–14; 2 Thessalonians 2:3–4

Heavenly Mutterings

EVIL BEGAN WITH THE SMALL, BITTER WHISPERINGS in an angel's heart.
O Holy One, magnify my heart-ears so I stay attuned to the whispers inside myself. Let them become shouts of praise instead.

ISAIAH 14:13–14

¹³וְאַתָּה אָמַרְתָּ בִלְבָבְךָ הַשָּׁמַיִם אֶעֱלֶה מִמַּעַל לְכוֹכְבֵי־אֵל
אָרִים כִּסְאִי וְאֵשֵׁב בְּהַר־מוֹעֵד בְּיַרְכְּתֵי צָפוֹן׃
¹⁴אֶעֱלֶה עַל־בָּמֳתֵי עָב אֶדַּמֶּה לְעֶלְיוֹן׃

אֶעֱלֶה v.1.com.s.impf.Q. [עלה]; לְכוֹכְבֵי (star); אָרִים v.1.com.s.impf.H.
[רום]; וְאֵשֵׁב cj. + v.1.com.s.impf.Q. [ישׁב]; בְּיַרְכְּתֵי (farthest reaches); עָב
(cloud); אֶדַּמֶּה v.1.com.s.impf.Ht. [דמה] (resemble)

2 THESSALONIANS 2:3–4

³μή τις ὑμᾶς ἐξαπατήσῃ κατὰ μηδένα τρόπον. ὅτι ἐὰν μὴ ἔλθῃ
ἡ ἀποστασία πρῶτον καὶ ἀποκαλυφθῇ ὁ ἄνθρωπος τῆς ἀνομίας,
ὁ υἱὸς τῆς ἀπωλείας, ⁴ὁ ἀντικείμενος καὶ ὑπεραιρόμενος ἐπὶ
πάντα λεγόμενον θεὸν ἢ σέβασμα, ὥστε αὐτὸν εἰς τὸν ναὸν τοῦ
θεοῦ καθίσαι ἀποδεικνύντα ἑαυτὸν ὅτι ἔστιν θεός.

ἐξαπατήσῃ v.3.s.aor.act.sub. [ἐξαπατάω] (deceive); τρόπον (way); ἔλθῃ
v.3.s.aor.act.sub. [ἔρχομαι]; ἀποστασία (apostasy); ἀποκαλυφθῇ (reveal);
ἀνομίας (lawlessness); ἀπωλείας (destruction); ἀντικείμενος (oppose);
ὑπεραιρόμενος (exalt one's self); σέβασμα (sanctuary); ναὸν (temple);
καθίσαι (sit); ἀποδεικνύντα (proclaim); ἔστιν v.3.s.pres.ind. [εἰμί]

2. Psalm 2.1–2; 1 Peter 5:8–9

Corner the Cat

WHEN A WILD ANIMAL ESCAPES, the animal keepers surround the beast and close in for the capture. When the lion roars, Father, help me hold hands tightly with my fellow Christians, so we receive courage and strength to endure the hunt.

PSALM 2:1–2

¹לָמָּה רָגְשׁוּ גוֹיִם וּלְאֻמִּים יֶהְגּוּ־רִיק:
²יִתְיַצְּבוּ מַלְכֵי־אֶרֶץ וְרוֹזְנִים נוֹסְדוּ־יָחַד עַל־יְהוָה וְעַל־מְשִׁיחוֹ:

רָגְשׁוּ (be in commotion); וּלְאֻמִּים (nation); יֶהְגּוּ v.3.m.p.impf.Q. [הגה] (muse); רִיק (empty); יִתְיַצְּבוּ (stand firm); וְרוֹזְנִים (ruler); נוֹסְדוּ v.3.c.p.pf.N. [יסד] (establish)

1 PETER 5:8–9

⁸Νήψατε, γρηγορήσατε. ὁ ἀντίδικος ὑμῶν διάβολος ὡς λέων ὠρυόμενος περιπατεῖ ζητῶν [τινα] καταπιεῖν· ⁹ᾧ ἀντίστητε στερεοὶ τῇ πίστει εἰδότες τὰ αὐτὰ τῶν παθημάτων τῇ ἐν [τῷ] κόσμῳ ὑμῶν ἀδελφότητι ἐπιτελεῖσθαι.

Νήψατε v.2.p.aor.act.impv. [νήθω] (be sober); γρηγορήσατε (be watchful); ἀντίδικος (adversary); διάβολος (devil); λέων (lion); ὠρυόμενος (roar); καταπιεῖν (devour); ἀντίστητε (resist); στερεοὶ adj.f.p.nom. (firm); εἰδότες v.m.p.nom.pf.act.ptc. [οἶδα]; παθημάτων (suffering); ἀδελφότητι (brotherhood); ἐπιτελεῖσθαι (accomplish)

3. Job 2:2; Ephesians 6:12

Invisible Enemy

IT'S A LOT EASIER TO STAND UP to a foe I can see coming, than battle with an invisible adversary who can surround me like the air. Transform my fearful, unseeing eyes into discerning ones, Lord. Help me be watchful.

JOB 2:2

²וַיֹּאמֶר יְהוָה אֶל־הַשָּׂטָן אֵי מִזֶּה תָּבֹא וַיַּעַן הַשָּׂטָן אֶת־
יְהוָה וַיֹּאמַר מִשֻּׁט בָּאָרֶץ וּמֵהִתְהַלֵּךְ בָּהּ׃

הַשָּׂטָן (adversary/Satan); אֵי (where); תָּבֹא v.2.m.s.impf.Q. [בוא]; וַיַּעַן v.c.
+ v.3.m.s.impf.Q. [ענה]; מִשֻּׁט prep. + v.in.cs.Q.defective [שוט] (roam);
וּמֵהִתְהַלֵּךְ cj. + prep. + v.in.cs.Ht. [הלך]

EPHESIANS 6:12

¹²ὅτι οὐκ ἔστιν ἡμῖν ἡ πάλη πρὸς αἷμα καὶ σάρκα ἀλλὰ πρὸς τὰς ἀρχάς, πρὸς τὰς ἐξουσίας, πρὸς τοὺς κοσμοκράτορας τοῦ σκότους τούτου, πρὸς τὰ πνευματικὰ τῆς πονηρίας ἐν τοῖς ἐπουρανίοις.

ἔστιν v.3.s.pres.ind. [εἰμί]; πάλη (struggle); κοσμοκράτορας (world-ruler); σκότους (darkness); πνευματικὰ (spiritual); πονηρίας (wickedness); ἐπουρανίοις (heaven)

4. Psalm 68:19 [18]; Ephesians 4:8–9

Unfathomable Love

IT IS HARD FOR ME TO HUMANLY COMPREHEND, dear Lord, that you would go to the depths of hell in my place, so that I might never taste its horrors. Thank you.

PSALM 68:19 [18]

¹⁹עָלִיתָ לַמָּרוֹם שָׁבִיתָ שֶּׁבִי לָקַחְתָּ מַתָּנוֹת בָּאָדָם וְאַף סוֹרְרִים
לִשְׁכֹּן יָהּ אֱלֹהִים:

עָלִיתָ v.2.m.s.pf.Q. [עלה]; שָׁבִיתָ v.2.m.s.pf.Q. [שבה] (capture); מַתָּנוֹת (gift);
סוֹרְרִים (be rebellious)

EPHESIANS 4:8–9

⁸διὸ λέγει,

Ἀναβὰς εἰς ὕψος ἠχμαλώτευσεν αἰχμαλωσίαν,
ἔδωκεν δόματα τοῖς ἀνθρώποις.

⁹τὸ δὲ Ἀνέβη τί ἐστιν, εἰ μὴ ὅτι καὶ κατέβη εἰς τὰ κατώτερα [μέρη] τῆς γῆς;

Ἀναβὰς v.m.s.nom.aor.act.ptc. [ἀναβαίνω]; ὕψος (bright); ἠχμαλώτευσεν v.3.s.aor.act.ind. [αἰχμαλωτεύω] (lead captive); αἰχμαλωσίαν (captivity); ἔδωκεν v.3.s.aor.act.ind. [δίδωμι]; δόματα (gift); ἐστιν v.3.s.pres.ind.
[εἰμί]; κατέβη v.3.s.aor.act.ind. [καταβαίνω]; κατώτερα (lower); μέρη
(part)

5. 1 Kings 18:38–40; Colossians 2:13–15

More Than Conquerors

I SAW YOU ONCE IN A DREAM, there, on the cross. I was tucked into your side somehow, watching as if from behind and within. All evil, whether to body, mind, or spirit, gathered like a malignant cloud of bees. It swarmed and flew at you. I was terrified. You absorbed it, all of it. My God, my God! It was your will to do so! Then the storm was gone. Light streamed forth. That was the night my fear died.

1 KINGS 18:38–40

³⁸וַתִּפֹּל אֵשׁ־יְהוָה וַתֹּאכַל אֶת־הָעֹלָה וְאֶת־הָעֵצִים וְאֶת־
הָאֲבָנִים וְאֶת־הֶעָפָר וְאֶת־הַמַּיִם אֲשֶׁר־בַּתְּעָלָה לִחֵכָה:
³⁹וַיַּרְא כָּל־הָעָם וַיִּפְּלוּ עַל־פְּנֵיהֶם וַיֹּאמְרוּ יְהוָה הוּא
הָאֱלֹהִים יְהוָה הוּא הָאֱלֹהִים:
⁴⁰וַיֹּאמֶר אֵלִיָּהוּ לָהֶם תִּפְשׂוּ אֶת־נְבִיאֵי הַבַּעַל אִישׁ אַל־יִמָּלֵט
מֵהֶם וַיִּתְפְּשׂוּם וַיּוֹרִדֵם אֵלִיָּהוּ אֶל־נַחַל קִישׁוֹן וַיִּשְׁחָטֵם
שָׁם:

[לחך] v.3.f.s.pf.P. לִחֵכָה] (trough); בַּתְּעָלָה] v.c. + v.3.f.p.impf.Q. [נפל]; וַתִּפֹּל
(lick up); [נפל] v.c. + v.3.m.p.impf.Q. וַיִּפְּלוּ]; [ראה] v.c. + v.3.m.s.impf.Q. וַיַּרְא
v.c. + v.3.m.s.impf.H. וַיּוֹרִדֵם + 3.m.p.pr.sf.; [תפש] v.c. + v.3.m.p.impf.Q. וַיִּתְפְּשׂוּם
[ירד] + 3.m.p.pr.sf.; [שחט] v.c. + v.3.m.s.impf.Q. וַיִּשְׁחָטֵם + 3.m.p.pr.sf.

COLOSSIANS 2:13–15

¹³καὶ ὑμᾶς νεκροὺς ὄντας [ἐν] τοῖς παραπτώμασιν καὶ τῇ ἀκροβυστίᾳ τῆς σαρκὸς ὑμῶν, συνεζωοποίησεν ὑμᾶς σὺν αὐτῷ, χαρισάμενος ἡμῖν πάντα τὰ παραπτώματα. ¹⁴ἐξαλείψας τὸ καθ' ἡμῶν χειρόγραφον τοῖς δόγμασιν ὃ ἦν ὑπεναντίον ἡμῖν, καὶ αὐτὸ ἦρκεν ἐκ τοῦ μέσου προσηλώσας αὐτὸ τῷ σταυρῷ ¹⁵ἀπεκδυσάμενος τὰς ἀρχὰς καὶ τὰς ἐξουσίας ἐδειγμάτισεν ἐν παρρησίᾳ, θριαμβεύσας αὐτοὺς ἐν αὐτῷ.

παραπτώμασιν (transgression); ἀκροβυστίᾳ (uncircumcision); συνε-ζωοποίησεν v.3.s.aor.act.ind. [συζωοποιέω] (make live together); χαρισά-μενος (forgive); ἐξαλείψας (wipe away); χειρόγραφον (debt note); δόγμασιν (decree); ἦν v.3.s.impf.ind. [εἰμί]; ὑπεναντίον adj.nt.s.nom. (opposite); ἦρκεν v.3.s.pf.act.ind. [αἴρω]; προσηλώσας (nail to); σταυρῷ (cross); ἀπεκδυσάμενος (disarm); ἐδειγμάτισεν v.3.s.aor.act.ind. [δειγματίζω] (make an example); ἐν παρρησίᾳ (publicly); θριαμβεύσας (triumph over)

6. Isaiah 14:15, 19; Revelation 19:20–21

To Hell with Death

WE CAN BE SURE THE DAY WILL COME, the day when God says, "To hell with death!" With unwincing fury the Holy One will bring it to completion. Then with angels and saints and Dame Julian we will sing of Sabbath rest, for truly "all manner of things shall be well."

ISAIAH 14:15, 19

15אַךְ אֶל־שְׁאוֹל תּוּרָד אֶל־יַרְכְּתֵי־בוֹר:
19וְאַתָּה הָשְׁלַכְתָּ מִקִּבְרְךָ כְּנֵצֶר נִתְעָב לְבוּשׁ הֲרֻגִים מְטֹעֲנֵי חָרֶב יוֹרְדֵי אֶל־אַבְנֵי־בוֹר כְּפֶגֶר מוּבָס:

תּוּרָד v.2.m.s.impf.Ho. [ירד]; יַרְכְּתֵי (farthest depth); נֵצֶר (shoot); נִתְעָב (abhor); מְטֹעֲנֵי v.m.p.cs.ptc.Hof. [טען] (pierce); כְּפֶגֶר (corpse); מוּבָס v.m.s.ptc.Ho. [בוס] (tread down)

REVELATION 19:20–21

20καὶ ἐπιάσθη τὸ θηρίον καὶ μετ᾽ αὐτοῦ ὁ ψευδοπροφήτης ὁ ποιήσας τὰ σημεῖα ἐνώπιον αὐτοῦ, ἐν οἷς ἐπλάνησεν τοὺς λαβόντας τὸ χάραγμα τοῦ θηρίου καὶ τοὺς προσκυνοῦντας τῇ εἰκόνι αὐτοῦ· ζῶντες ἐβλήθησαν οἱ δύο εἰς τὴν λίμνην τοῦ πυρὸς τῆς καιομένης ἐν θείῳ. 21καὶ οἱ λοιποὶ ἀπεκτάνθησαν ἐν τῇ ῥομφαίᾳ τοῦ καθημένου ἐπὶ τοῦ ἵππου τῇ ἐξελθούσῃ ἐκ τοῦ στόματος αὐτοῦ, καὶ πάντα τὰ ὄρνεα ἐχορτάσθησαν ἐκ τῶν σαρκῶν αὐτῶν.

ἐπιάσθη (seize); θηρίον (beast); ψευδοπροφήτης (false prophet); ἐνώπιον (before); ἐπλάνησεν (deceive); χάραγμα (mark); ἐβλήθησαν v.3.p.aor.pass.ind. [βάλλω]; λίμνην (lake); ῥομφαίᾳ (sword); ἵππου (horse); ἐξελθούσῃ v.f.s.dat.aor.act.ptc. [ἐξέρχομαι]; ὄρνεα (bird); ἐχορτάσθησαν (feed)

319

7. Isaiah 55:11–12; 2 Thessalonians 3:1–3

Holy Purpose

WHY SHOULD WE EVER FEAR AGAIN, Reliable One? You have purposed, with a holy purpose, that good shall triumph, that evil
shall not, and that when the final curtain falls there shall be joy.
Though now the way is hard, it shall not always be so. Help us,
then, to celebrate today, knowing the good that is to come. For
you are reliable, our good God. Your word is as good as done.

ISAIAH 55:11–12

‏¹¹ כֵּן יִהְיֶה דְבָרִי אֲשֶׁר יֵצֵא מִפִּי לֹא־יָשׁוּב אֵלַי רֵיקָם כִּי אִם־
עָשָׂה אֶת־אֲשֶׁר חָפַצְתִּי וְהִצְלִיחַ אֲשֶׁר שְׁלַחְתִּיו:
¹² כִּי־בְשִׂמְחָה תֵצֵאוּ וּבְשָׁלוֹם תּוּבָלוּן הֶהָרִים וְהַגְּבָעוֹת יִפְצְחוּ
לִפְנֵיכֶם רִנָּה וְכָל־עֲצֵי הַשָּׂדֶה יִמְחֲאוּ־כָף:‏

אֵצֵא v.3.m.s.impf.Q. [יצא]; יָשׁוּב v.3.m.s.impf.Q. [שוב]; רֵיקָם (without success); שְׁלַחְתִּיו v.1.com.s.pf.Q. [שלח] + 3.m.s.pr.sf.; תֵצֵאוּ v.2.m.p.impf.Q.pause
[יצא]; תּוּבָלוּן v.2.m.p.impf.Ho. + para. [יבל] (bring); יִפְצְחוּ (burst forth);
רִנָּה (cry of joy); יִמְחֲאוּ (clap)

2 THESSALONIANS 3:1–3

¹Τὸ λοιπὸν προσεύχεσθε, ἀδελφοί, περὶ ἡμῶν, ἵνα ὁ λόγος τοῦ
κυρίου τρέχῃ καὶ δοξάζηται καθὼς καὶ πρὸς ὑμᾶς, ²καὶ ἵνα
ῥυσθῶμεν ἀπὸ τῶν ἀτόπων καὶ πονηρῶν ἀνθρώπων· οὐ γὰρ
πάντων ἡ πίστις. ³πιστὸς δέ ἐστιν ὁ κύριος, ὃς στηρίξει ὑμᾶς
καὶ φυλάξει ἀπὸ τοῦ πονηροῦ.

τρέχῃ (run); ῥυσθῶμεν v.1.p.aor.pass.subj. [ῥύομαι] (deliver); ἀτόπων
(wrong); ἐστιν v.3.s.pres.ind. [εἰμί]; στηρίξει (strengthen); φυλάξει (guard)

Week 45

All Saints' (Spiritual Forebears)

1. Genesis 15:5–6; Hebrews 11:1–2

Reckless, Riotous Faith

RECKLESS, RIOTOUS FAITH—faith of Abraham and Deborah and
Daniel—that's what I want! I want wild, passionate belief that
shakes its fist at fear and takes risks and pierces through the
sin-filled gloom of this world. I want God-aliveness in me just
like it was in them. This is my prayer today, God of my life.

GENESIS 15:5–6

⁵וַיּוֹצֵא אֹתוֹ הַחוּצָה וַיֹּאמֶר הַבֶּט־נָא הַשָּׁמַיְמָה וּסְפֹר הַכּוֹכָבִים
אִם־תּוּכַל לִסְפֹּר אֹתָם וַיֹּאמֶר לוֹ כֹּה יִהְיֶה זַרְעֶךָ׃
⁶וְהֶאֱמִן בַּיהוָה וַיַּחְשְׁבֶהָ לּוֹ צְדָקָה׃

וַיּוֹצֵא v.c. + v.3.m.s.impf.H. [יצא]; הַבֶּט v.2.m.s.impv.H. [נבט]; תּוּכַל
v.2.m.s.impf.Q. [יכל]; וַיַּחְשְׁבֶהָ v.c. + v.3.m.s.impf.Q. [חשב] + 3.f.s.pr.sf.

HEBREWS 11:1–2

¹Ἔστιν δὲ πίστις ἐλπιζομένων ὑπόστασις, πραγμάτων ἔλεγχος
οὐ βλεπομένων. ²ἐν ταύτῃ γὰρ ἐμαρτυρήθησαν οἱ πρεσβύτεροι.

ἐλπιζομένων (hope); ὑπόστασις (assurance); πραγμάτων (thing); ἔλεγχος (proof)

2. Amos 1:1; Acts 16:13–14

Unexpected Revolutionaries

THIS IS ONE OF THE THINGS about God that I love the most. He picks farmers or women who work at the fabric shop to revolutionize the world. They don't know what's going to happen, of course, when he calls them. They just say "yes" to the small thing at hand, day by day. A few words spoken in obedience here, a few acts of mercy there. Then one day it happens. The gates of hell give way.

AMOS 1:1

דִּבְרֵי עָמוֹס אֲשֶׁר־הָיָה בַנֹּקְדִים מִתְּקוֹעַ אֲשֶׁר חָזָה עַל־יִשְׂרָאֵל בִּימֵי עֻזִּיָּה מֶלֶךְ־יְהוּדָה וּבִימֵי יָרָבְעָם בֶּן־יוֹאָשׁ מֶלֶךְ יִשְׂרָאֵל שְׁנָתַיִם לִפְנֵי הָרָעַשׁ:

בַנֹּקְדִים (shepherd); הָרָעַשׁ (earthquake)

ACTS 16:13–14

¹³τῇ τε ἡμέρᾳ τῶν σαββάτων ἐξήλθομεν ἔξω τῆς πύλης παρὰ ποταμὸν οὗ ἐνομίζομεν προσευχὴν εἶναι, καὶ καθίσαντες ἐλαλοῦμεν ταῖς συνελθούσαις γυναιξίν. ¹⁴καί τις γυνὴ ὀνόματι Λυδία, πορφυρόπωλις πόλεως Θυατείρων σεβομένη τὸν θεόν, ἤκουεν, ἧς ὁ κύριος διήνοιξεν τὴν καρδίαν προσέχειν τοῖς λαλουμένοις ὑπὸ τοῦ Παύλου.

ἐξήλθομεν v.1.p.aor.act.ind. [ἐξέρχομαι]; πύλης (gate); ποταμὸν (river); προσευχὴν (prayer); εἶναι v.pres.in. [εἰμί]; καθίσαντες (sit); συνελθού-σαις v.f.p.dat.aor.act.ptc. [συνέρχομαι] (assemble); πορφυρόπωλις (purple cloth dealer); σεβομένη (worship); διήνοιξεν (open)

3. 1 Kings 19:2–4; Acts 15:37–39

Terrors to the Devil

A REAL SAINT IS SOMEONE WHO GETS SCARED, angry, confused, foolish and all those other unsaintly things and yet somehow loves God all the more—which, by the way, is an absolute terror to the devil.

1 KINGS 19:2–4

²וַתִּשְׁלַח אִיזֶבֶל מַלְאָךְ אֶל־אֵלִיָּהוּ לֵאמֹר כֹּה־יַעֲשׂוּן אֱלֹהִים
וְכֹה יוֹסִפוּן כִּי־כָעֵת מָחָר אָשִׂים אֶת־נַפְשְׁךָ כְּנֶפֶשׁ אַחַד מֵהֶם:
³וַיַּרְא וַיָּקָם וַיֵּלֶךְ אֶל־נַפְשׁוֹ וַיָּבֹא בְּאֵר שֶׁבַע אֲשֶׁר לִיהוּדָה
וַיַּנַּח אֶת־נַעֲרוֹ שָׁם:
⁴וְהוּא־הָלַךְ בַּמִּדְבָּר דֶּרֶךְ יוֹם וַיָּבֹא וַיֵּשֶׁב תַּחַת רֹתֶם אֶחָד
וַיִּשְׁאַל אֶת־נַפְשׁוֹ לָמוּת וַיֹּאמֶר רַב עַתָּה יְהוָה קַח נַפְשִׁי
כִּי־לֹא־טוֹב אָנֹכִי מֵאֲבֹתָי:

יַעֲשׂוּן v.3.m.p.impf.Q. [עשׂה] + para.; יוֹסִפוּן v.3.m.p.impf.H. [יסף] + para.;
וַיַּרְא v.c. + v.3.m.s.impf.Q. [ראה]; וַיָּקָם v.c. + v.3.m.s.impf.Q. [קום]; וַיֵּלֶךְ v.c.
+ v.3.m.s.impf.Q. [הלך]; וַיָּבֹא v.c. + v.3.m.s.impf.Q. [בוא]; וַיַּנַּח v.c. +
v.3.m.s.impf.H. [נוח]; וַיֵּשֶׁב v.c. + v.3.m.s.impf.Q. [ישׁב]; קַח v.2.m.s.impv.Q.
[לקח]; מֵאֲבֹתָי prep. + n.m.p. + 1.com.s.pr.sf.pause

ACTS 15:37–39

³⁷Βαρναβᾶς δὲ ἐβούλετο συμπαραλαβεῖν καὶ τὸν Ἰωάννην τὸν
καλούμενον Μᾶρκον· ³⁸Παῦλος δὲ ἠξίου, τὸν ἀποστάντα ἀπ᾽
αὐτῶν ἀπὸ Παμφυλίας καὶ μὴ συνελθόντα αὐτοῖς εἰς τὸ ἔργον
μὴ συμπαραλαμβάνειν τοῦτον. ³⁹ἐγένετο δὲ παροξυσμὸς ὥστε
ἀποχωρισθῆναι αὐτοὺς ἀπ᾽ ἀλλήλων, τόν τε Βαρναβᾶν
παραλαβόντα τὸν Μᾶρκον ἐκπλεῦσαι εἰς Κύπρον,

συμπαραλαβεῖν (take with); ἠξίου v.3.s.impf.act.ind. [ἀξιόω] (request);
ἀποστάντα v.m.s.acc.aor.act.ptc. [ἀφίστημι] (depart); συνελθόντα
v.m.s.aor.act.ptc. [συνέρχομαι]; ἐγένετο v.3.s.aor.mid.ind. [γίνομαι]; παροξυσμὸς (disagreement); ἀποχωρισθῆναι (separate); ἐκπλεῦσαι (sail away)

4. Jeremiah 1:6–8; Matthew 8:5–8

Giants of Faith

GOD IS ESPECIALLY PLEASED with the Jeremiahs and housewives and other "unworthies" he calls because they know without question that if God is going to accomplish anything through them, it will have to be God who does it. These are the giants of our faith.

JEREMIAH 1:6–8

⁶וָאֹמַר אֲהָהּ אֲדֹנָי יְהוִה הִנֵּה לֹא־יָדַעְתִּי דַּבֵּר כִּי־נַעַר אָנֹכִי׃

⁷וַיֹּאמֶר יְהוָה אֵלַי אַל־תֹּאמַר נַעַר אָנֹכִי כִּי עַל־כָּל־אֲשֶׁר אֶשְׁלָחֲךָ תֵּלֵךְ וְאֵת כָּל־אֲשֶׁר אֲצַוְּךָ תְּדַבֵּר׃

⁸אַל־תִּירָא מִפְּנֵיהֶם כִּי־אִתְּךָ אֲנִי לְהַצִּלֶךָ נְאֻם־יְהוָה׃

וָאֹמַר v.c. + v.1.com.s.impf.Q. [אמר]; אֲהָהּ (Oh!); אֶשְׁלָחֲךָ v.1.com.s.impf.Q. [שלח] + 2.m.s.pr.sf.; תֵּלֵךְ v.2.m.s.impf.Q. [הלך]; אֲצַוְּךָ v.1.com.s.impf.P. [צוה] + 2.m.s.pr.sf.; תִּירָא v.2.m.s.impf.Q. [ירא]; לְהַצִּלֶךָ prep. + v.in.cs.H. [נצל] + 2.m.s.pr.sf.

MATTHEW 8:5–8

⁵Εἰσελθόντος δὲ αὐτοῦ εἰς Καφαρναοὺμ προσῆλθεν αὐτῷ ἑκατόνταρχος παρακαλῶν αὐτὸν ⁶καὶ λέγων, Κύριε, ὁ παῖς μου βέβληται ἐν τῇ οἰκίᾳ παραλυτικός, δεινῶς βασανιζόμενος. ⁷καὶ λέγει αὐτῷ, Ἐγὼ ἐλθὼν θεραπεύσω αὐτόν. ⁸καὶ ἀποκριθεὶς ὁ ἑκατόνταρχος ἔφη, Κύριε, οὐκ εἰμὶ ἱκανὸς ἵνα μου ὑπὸ τὴν στέγην εἰσέλθῃς, ἀλλὰ μόνον εἰπὲ λόγῳ, καὶ ἰαθήσεται ὁ παῖς μου.

Εἰσελθόντος v.m.s.gen.aor.act.ptc. [εἰσέρχομαι]; προσῆλθεν v.3.s.aor.act.ind. [προσέρχομαι]; ἑκατόνταρχος (centurion); βέβληται v.3.s.pf.pass.ind. [βάλλω]; παραλυτικός (lame person); δεινῶς (terribly); Βασανιζόμενος (torment); ἐλθὼν v.m.s.nom.aor.act.ptc. [ἔρχομαι]; θεραπεύσω (heal); ἱκανὸς (worthy); στέγην (root); εἰσέλθῃς v.2.s.aor.act.sub. [εἰσέρχομαι]; εἰπὲ v.2.s.aor.act.impv. [λέγω]; ἰαθήσεται (heal)

5. Hosea 1:2–3; Matthew 1:19, 24

Breaking the Taboos

NOW, HOW MANY OF US ARE WILLING to break a taboo, a marital or family taboo among upright religious folk, if that's what God calls us to do? How many of us are willing to bear the humiliation, the scorn, the contempt of the religious community, day in and day out? How many of us are willing to belong to God that much?

HOSEA 1:2–3

²תְּחִלַּת דִּבֶּר־יְהוָה בְּהוֹשֵׁעַ וַיֹּאמֶר יְהוָה אֶל־הוֹשֵׁעַ לֵךְ
קַח־לְךָ אֵשֶׁת זְנוּנִים וְיַלְדֵי זְנוּנִים כִּי־זָנֹה תִזְנֶה הָאָרֶץ
מֵאַחֲרֵי יְהוָה:
³וַיֵּלֶךְ וַיִּקַּח אֶת־גֹּמֶר בַּת־דִּבְלָיִם וַתַּהַר וַתֵּלֶד־לוֹ בֵּן:

תְּחִלַּת (beginning); לֵךְ v.2.m.s.impv.Q. [הלך]; קַח v.2.m.s.impv.Q. [לקח];
זְנוּנִים (fornication); וַיֵּלֶךְ v.c. + v.3.f.s.impf.Q. [הלך]; וַיִּקַּח v.c. + v.3.f.s.impf.Q.
[לקח]; וַתַּהַר v.c. + v.3.f.s.impf.Q. [הרה] (become pregnant); וַתֵּלֶד v.c. +
v.3.f.s.impf.Q. [ילד]

MATTHEW 1:19, 24

¹⁹Ἰωσὴφ δὲ ὁ ἀνὴρ αὐτῆς, δίκαιος ὢν καὶ μὴ θέλων αὐτὴν δειγματίσαι, ἐβουλήθη λάθρα ἀπολῦσαι αὐτήν. ²⁴ἐγερθεὶς δὲ ὁ Ἰωσὴφ ἀπὸ τοῦ ὕπνου ἐποίησεν ὡς προσέταξεν αὐτῷ ὁ ἄγγελος κυρίου καὶ παρέλαβεν τὴν γυναῖκα αὐτοῦ,

δειγματίσαι (make an example); ἐβουλήθη (wish); λάθρα adv. (secretly); ὕπνου (sleep); προσέταξεν (order)

6. Esther 4:16; Acts 7:54–57

No Price Too High

TO A TRUE SAINT THERE IS NO PRICE that is too high to pay in order to be true to God. All of life and all of death are exclusively devoted to God. What else is there to be said?

ESTHER 4:16

16 לֵךְ כְּנוֹס אֶת־כָּל־הַיְּהוּדִים הַנִּמְצְאִים בְּשׁוּשָׁן וְצוּמוּ עָלַי
וְאַל־תֹּאכְלוּ וְאַל־תִּשְׁתּוּ שְׁלֹשֶׁת יָמִים לַיְלָה וָיוֹם גַּם־אֲנִי
וְנַעֲרֹתַי אָצוּם כֵּן וּבְכֵן אָבוֹא אֶל־הַמֶּלֶךְ אֲשֶׁר לֹא־כַדָּת
וְכַאֲשֶׁר אָבַדְתִּי אָבָדְתִּי:

לֵךְ v.2.m.s.impv.Q. [הלך]; כְּנוֹס (gather); וְצוּמוּ cj. + v.2.m.p.impv.Q. [צום] (fast); תִּשְׁתּוּ v.2.m.p.impf. [שתה]; כַדָּת (order)

ACTS 7:54–57

⁵⁴Ἀκούοντες δὲ ταῦτα διεπρίοντο ταῖς καρδίαις αὐτῶν καὶ ἔβρυχον τοὺς ὀδόντας ἐπ᾽ αὐτόν. ⁵⁵ὑπάρχων δὲ πλήρης πνεύματος ἁγίου ἀτενίσας εἰς τὸν οὐρανὸν εἶδεν δόξαν θεοῦ καὶ Ἰησοῦν ἑστῶτα ἐκ δεξιῶν τοῦ θεοῦ ⁵⁶καὶ εἶπεν, Ἰδοὺ θεωρῶ τοὺς οὐρανοὺς διηνοιγμένους καὶ τὸν υἱὸν τοῦ ἀνθρώπου ἐκ δεξιῶν ἑστῶτα τοῦ θεοῦ. ⁵⁷κράξαντες δὲ φωνῇ μεγάλῃ συνέσχον τὰ ὦτα αὐτῶν καὶ ὥρμησαν ὁμοθυμαδὸν ἐπ᾽ αὐτὸν

διεπρίοντο v.3.p.impf.pass.ind. [διαπρίω] (be furious); ἔβρυχον (gnash); ὀδόντας (tooth); πλήρης (full); ἀτενίσας (look intently); εἶδεν v.3.s.aor.act.ind. [ὁράω]; ἑστῶτα v.m.s.acc.pf.act.ptc. [ἵστημι]; εἶπεν v.3.s.aor.act.ind. [λέγω]; διηνοιγμένους (open); συνέσχον (shut); ὦτα (ear); ὥρμησαν v.3.p.aor.act.ind. [ὁρμάω] (rush out); ὁμοθυμαδὸν (unanimously)

7. Jeremiah 1:4–5; Luke 1:26–28

The One Who Calls Is Faithful

THIS IS THE THING WE NEED to keep in the forefront when our call seems impossible. God knows us long before we can know him. He consecrates us long before we can say yes or no to that call. And it is his faithfulness that will bring to pass all that he has purposed for us. We must remember this and rest in him.

JEREMIAH 1:4–5

⁴וַיְהִי דְבַר־יְהוָה אֵלַי לֵאמֹר׃

⁵בְּטֶרֶם אֶצּוֹרְךָ בַבֶּטֶן יְדַעְתִּיךָ וּבְטֶרֶם תֵּצֵא מֵרֶחֶם הִקְדַּשְׁתִּיךָ
נָבִיא לַגּוֹיִם נְתַתִּיךָ׃

וַיְהִי v.c. + v.3.m.s.impf.Q. [הֵיה]; אֶצּוֹרְךָ v.1.com.s.impf.Q. [נצר] + 2.m.s.pr.sf.Qe.; יְדַעְתִּיךָ v.1.com.s.pf.Q. [ידע] + 2.m.s.pr.sf.; תֵּצֵא v.2.m.s.impf.Q. [יצא]; מֵרֶחֶם (womb); הִקְדַּשְׁתִּיךָ v.1.com.s.pf.H. [קדש] + 2.m.s.pr.sf.; נְתַתִּיךָ v.1.com.s.pf.Q. [נתן] + 2.m.s.pr.sf.

LUKE 1:26–28

²⁶Ἐν δὲ τῷ μηνὶ τῷ ἕκτῳ ἀπεστάλη ὁ ἄγγελος Γαβριὴλ ἀπὸ τοῦ θεοῦ εἰς πόλιν τῆς Γαλιλαίας ᾗ ὄνομα Ναζαρὲθ ²⁷πρὸς παρθένον ἐμνηστευμένην ἀνδρὶ ᾧ ὄνομα Ἰωσὴφ ἐξ οἴκου Δαυὶδ καὶ τὸ ὄνομα τῆς παρθένου Μαριάμ. ²⁸καὶ εἰσελθὼν πρὸς αὐτὴν εἶπεν, Χαῖρε, κεχαριτωμένη, ὁ κύριος μετὰ σοῦ.

μηνὶ (month); ἕκτῳ (sixth); παρθένον (virgin); ἐμνηστευμένην (engaged); εἰσελθὼν v.m.s.nom.aor.act.ptc. [εἰσέρχομαι]; εἶπεν v.3.s.aor.act.ind. [λέγω]; Χαῖρε (hail!); κεχαριτωμένη (show favor)

Week 46

Worship (1)

1. Psalm 95:6–7; Ephesians 3:14–15

What I Need to Know

THIS IS WHAT IT MEANS TO WORSHIP: to know that my name comes from God, to know that I am his, to know that I belong to God's flock, to know that he is speaking to me in such a way that I can hear and I can follow. Worship means to know these things, not in my head, but the way lovers know each other.

PSALM 95:6–7

⁶בֹּאוּ נִשְׁתַּחֲוֶה וְנִכְרָעָה נִבְרְכָה לִפְנֵי־יְהוָה עֹשֵׂנוּ׃
⁷כִּי הוּא אֱלֹהֵינוּ וַאֲנַחְנוּ עַם מַרְעִיתוֹ וְצֹאן יָדוֹ הַיּוֹם אִם־
בְּקֹלוֹ תִשְׁמָעוּ׃

בֹּאוּ v.2.m.p.impv.Q. [בוא]; נִשְׁתַּחֲוֶה v.1.com.p.impf.Hisht. [חוה]; וְנִכְרָעָה cj. + v.1.com.p.coh.Q.pause [כרע] (bow down); עֹשֵׂנוּ v.m.s.ptc.Q. [עשׂה] + 1.com.p.pr.sf.; מַרְעִיתוֹ (pasturing)

EPHESIANS 3:14–15

¹⁴Τούτου χάριν κάμπτω τὰ γόνατα μου πρὸς τὸν πατέρα, ¹⁵ἐξ οὗ πᾶσα πατριὰ ἐν οὐρανοῖς καὶ ἐπὶ γῆς ὀνομάζεται,

Τούτου (because of); κάμπτω (bend); γόνατα (knee); πατριὰ (family); ὀνομάζεται (name)

2. Psalm 122:1; Hebrews 12:28–29

Burn in Me

COME, MY FIERY LOVE, burn all the stubble and chaff, all the dead and lifeless wood that I call "me" but is not me at all. Burn in me until nothing else is left but you.

PSALM 122:1

¹שָׂמַחְתִּי בְּאֹמְרִים לִי בֵּית יְהוָה נֵלֵךְ:

נֵלֵךְ v.1.com.p.impf./coh.Q. [הלך]

HEBREWS 12:28–29

²⁸Διὸ βασιλείαν ἀσάλευτον παραλαμβάνοντες ἔχωμεν χάριν, δι᾽ ἧς λατρεύωμεν εὐαρέστως τῷ θεῷ μετὰ εὐλαβείας καὶ δέους· ²⁹καὶ γὰρ ὁ θεὸς ἡμῶν πῦρ καταναλίσκον.

ἀσάλευτον (unshakable); παραλαμβάνοντες (receive); λατρεύωμεν (serve); εὐαρέστως (acceptably); εὐλαβείας (reverence); δέους (awe); καταναλίσκον (consume)

3. Psalm 24:3–4; 1 Timothy 2:8

The Shell of Worship

IT IS NEVER THE OUTWARD SHELL of our worship that matters to God. The thing that matters is what is in our hearts. So we must not get sidetracked with foolish arguments over whether organs or tambourines are more holy, whether God is more pleased with Handel's "Hallelujah Chorus" or with an "Alleluia" chorus, or whether God cares if we are sitting on red or blue pew cushions to express our common thanks. God encounters what is in the depths of our heart when we come to worship. The outwardness is but a shell.

PSALM 24:3–4

³מִי־יַעֲלֶה בְהַר־יְהוָה וּמִי־יָקוּם בִּמְקוֹם קָדְשׁוֹ:
⁴נְקִי כַפַּיִם וּבַר־לֵבָב אֲשֶׁר לֹא־נָשָׂא לַשָּׁוְא נַפְשִׁי וְלֹא נִשְׁבַּע
לְמִרְמָה:

נְקִי (clean); וּבַר (pure); לְמִרְמָה (deceit)

1 TIMOTHY 2:8

⁸Βούλομαι οὖν προσεύχεσθαι τοὺς ἄνδρας ἐν παντὶ τόπῳ ἐπαίροντας ὁσίους χεῖρας χωρὶς ὀργῆς καὶ διαλογισμοῦ.

Βούλομαι (want); ἐπαίροντας (lift up); ὁσίους (holy); χωρὶς (without); ὀργῆς (wrath); διαλογισμοῦ (argument)

4. 2 Chronicles 31:20–21; Colossians 3:17

Life, Exactly as It Is

WORSHIP IS THE WHOLEHEARTED, Godward living of my life as it actually is. Worship is not a weekly escape from life, but a moment by moment embrace of life exactly as it is, knowing that in my life exactly as it is, I am moment by moment embraced in the arms of God.

2 CHRONICLES 31:20–21

²⁰וַיַּעַשׂ כָּזֹאת יְחִזְקִיָּהוּ בְּכָל־יְהוּדָה וַיַּעַשׂ הַטּוֹב וְהַיָּשָׁר
וְהָאֱמֶת לִפְנֵי יְהוָה אֱלֹהָיו:
²¹וּבְכָל־מַעֲשֶׂה אֲשֶׁר־הֵחֵל בַּעֲבוֹדַת בֵּית־הָאֱלֹהִים וּבַתּוֹרָה
וּבַמִּצְוָה לִדְרֹשׁ לֵאלֹהָיו בְּכָל־לְבָבוֹ עָשָׂה וְהִצְלִיחַ:

[חלל] הֵחֵל v.3.m.s.pf.H.; [עשׂה] וַיַּעַשׂ v.c. + v.3.m.s.Q.

COLOSSIANS 3:17

¹⁷καὶ πᾶν ὅ τι ἐὰν ποιῆτε ἐν λόγῳ ἢ ἐν ἔργῳ, πάντα ἐν ὀνόματι κυρίου Ἰησοῦ, εὐχαριστοῦντες τῷ θεῷ πατρὶ δι' αὐτοῦ.

εὐχαριστοῦντες (give thanks)

5. Psalm 150:3–5; Acts 2:42–43

Authentic Worship

WE PASTORS SPEND COUNTLESS HOURS and dollars trying to find
the secret to church growth, trying to find a method to get our
churches out of their abominable ruts. This is not a bad thing.
In the end, though, we must realize that the answer is not a
technique. The answer is an organic experience of the Holy
Spirit alive and well in our midst, so that our worship is powerful and systemic and centered on Christ. The overflow of
such worship is signs and wonders, which pour Christ into the
world. The only way out of the abominable rut is true worship.

PSALM 150:3–5

³הַלְלוּהוּ בְתֵקַע שׁוֹפָר הַלְלוּהוּ בְּנֵבֶל וְכִנּוֹר׃
⁴הַלְלוּהוּ בְתֹף וּמָחוֹל הַלְלוּהוּ בְּמִנִּים וְעוּגָב׃
⁵הַלְלוּהוּ בְצִלְצְלֵי־שָׁמַע הַלְלוּהוּ בְּצִלְצְלֵי תְרוּעָה׃

הַלְלוּהוּ v.2.m.p.impv.P. [הלל] + 3.m.s.pr.sf.; בְתֵקַע (blowing); בְּנֵבֶל (harp);
וְכִנּוֹר (lyre); בְתֹף (tambourine); וּמָחוֹל (dance); בְּמִנִּים (string); וְעוּגָב (pipe);
בְצִלְצְלֵי (cymbals); תְרוּעָה (shout)

ACTS 2:42–43

⁴²ἦσαν δὲ προσκαρτεροῦντες τῇ διδαχῇ τῶν ἀποστόλων καὶ τῇ
κοινωνίᾳ τῇ κλάσει τοῦ ἄρτου καὶ ταῖς προσευχαῖς. ⁴³Ἐγίνετο
δὲ πάσῃ ψυχῇ φόβος, πολλά τε τέρατα καὶ σημεῖα διὰ τῶν
ἀποστόλων ἐγίνετο.

προσκαρτεροῦντες (be faithful in); διδαχῇ (teaching); κοινωνίᾳ (fellowship); κλάσει (breaking); προσευχαῖς (prayer); φόβος (fear); τέρατα
(wonder)

6. Exodus 24:4–6; 1 Corinthians 14:26

Obedience as Worship

GOD'S INSTRUCTIONS TO MOSES concerning worship were highly specific. I have noticed that God's word to me is very specific when I want it to be general, and general when I want it to be specific. I ask for rules and God gives me freedom. I want no boundaries and God gives me rules. Part of my growth in worship has to do with obedience to God's word as it actually comes to me. It takes a long time for my soul to be convinced that God is actually setting me free through my obedience.

EXODUS 24:4–6

⁴וַיִּכְתֹּב מֹשֶׁה אֵת כָּל־דִּבְרֵי יְהוָה וַיַּשְׁכֵּם בַּבֹּקֶר וַיִּבֶן
מִזְבֵּחַ תַּחַת הָהָר וּשְׁתֵּים עֶשְׂרֵה מַצֵּבָה לִשְׁנֵים עָשָׂר שִׁבְטֵי
יִשְׂרָאֵל:
⁵וַיִּשְׁלַח אֶת־נַעֲרֵי בְּנֵי יִשְׂרָאֵל וַיַּעֲלוּ עֹלֹת וַיִּזְבְּחוּ זְבָחִים
שְׁלָמִים לַיהוָה פָּרִים:
⁶וַיִּקַּח מֹשֶׁה חֲצִי הַדָּם וַיָּשֶׂם בָּאַגָּנֹת וַחֲצִי הַדָּם זָרַק
עַל־הַמִּזְבֵּחַ:

וַיִּבֶן v.c. + v.3.m.s.impf.Q. [בנה]; מַצֵּבָה (pillar); וַיַּעֲלוּ v.c. + v.3.m.p.impf.H. [עלה]; וַיִּקַּח v.c. + v.3.m.s.impf.Q. [לקח]; וַיָּשֶׂם v.c. + v.3.m.s.impf.Q. [שים]; בָּאַגָּנֹת (basin); זָרַק (sprinkle)

1 CORINTHIANS 14:26

²⁶Τί οὖν ἐστιν, ἀδελφοί; ὅταν συνέρχησθε, ἕκαστος ψαλμὸν ἔχει, διδαχὴν ἔχει, ἀποκάλυψιν ἔχει, γλῶσσαν ἔχει, ἑρμηνείαν ἔχει· πάντα πρὸς οἰκοδομὴν γινέσθω.

ἐστιν v.3.s.pres.ind. [εἰμί]; ψαλμὸν (psalm); διδαχὴν (teaching); ἀποκάλυψιν (revelation); ἑρμηνείαν (interpretation); οἰκοδομὴν (edification)

7. Nehemiah 8:17–18; Acts 2:37–38

Immersion

REPENTANCE IS INCOMPLETE without immersion in the Spirit.
The same is true of worship.

NEHEMIAH 8:17–18

¹⁷וַיַּעֲשׂוּ כָל־הַקָּהָל הַשָּׁבִים מִן־הַשְּׁבִי סֻכּוֹת וַיֵּשְׁבוּ
בַסֻּכּוֹת כִּי לֹא־עָשׂוּ מִימֵי יֵשׁוּעַ בִּן־נוּן כֵּן בְּנֵי יִשְׂרָאֵל עַד
הַיּוֹם הַהוּא וַתְּהִי שִׂמְחָה גְּדוֹלָה מְאֹד:
¹⁸וַיִּקְרָא בְּסֵפֶר תּוֹרַת הָאֱלֹהִים יוֹם בְּיוֹם מִן־הַיּוֹם הָרִאשׁוֹן
עַד הַיּוֹם הָאַחֲרוֹן וַיַּעֲשׂוּ־חָג שִׁבְעַת יָמִים וּבַיּוֹם הַשְּׁמִינִי
עֲצֶרֶת כַּמִּשְׁפָּט:

סֻכּוֹת [שׁוּב]; .Q.v.c. + v.3.m.p.impf וַיַּעֲשׂוּ; הַשָּׁבִים d.a. + v.m.p.ptc.Q. [עשׂה]
(hut); וַיֵּשְׁבוּ v.c. + v.3.m.p.impf.Q. [ישׁב]; עָשׂוּ v.3.c.p.pf.Q. [ישׁב]; וַתְּהִי v.c. +
v.3.f.s.impf.Q. [היה]; הַשְּׁמִינִי (eighth); עֲצֶרֶת (festival)

ACTS 2:37–38

³⁷Ἀκούσαντες δὲ κατενύγησαν τὴν καρδίαν εἶπον τε πρὸς τὸν
Πέτρον καὶ τοὺς λοιποὺς ἀποστόλους, Τί ποιήσωμεν, ἄνδρες
ἀδελφοί; ³⁸Πέτρος δὲ πρὸς αὐτούς, Μετανοήσατε, [φησίν,] καὶ
βαπτισθήτω ἕκαστος ὑμῶν ἐπὶ τῷ ὀνόματι Ἰησοῦ Χριστοῦ
εἰς ἄφεσιν τῶν ἁμαρτιῶν ὑμῶν καὶ λήμψεσθε τὴν δωρεὰν τοῦ
ἁγίου πνεύματος.

κατενύγησαν v.3.p.aor.pass.ind. [κατανύσσω] (be pierced); εἶπον
v.3.p.aor.act.ind. [λέγω]; Μετανοήσατε (repent); ἄφεσιν (forgiveness);
δωρεὰν (gift)

Worship (2)

1. Isaiah 6:1–3; Revelation 1:8

Awesome Worship

HOLY ONE; LORD GOD; Yahweh; the Beginning and the End. Fall on your face in wonder before him! Adore him and marvel, that he knows you by name and loves you as his precious child.

ISAIAH 6:1–3

¹בִּשְׁנַת־מוֹת הַמֶּלֶךְ עֻזִּיָּהוּ וָאֶרְאֶה אֶת־אֲדֹנָי יֹשֵׁב עַל־כִּסֵּא
רָם וְנִשָּׂא וְשׁוּלָיו מְלֵאִים אֶת־הַהֵיכָל׃
²שְׂרָפִים עֹמְדִים מִמַּעַל לוֹ שֵׁשׁ כְּנָפַיִם שֵׁשׁ כְּנָפַיִם לְאֶחָד
בִּשְׁתַּיִם יְכַסֶּה פָנָיו וּבִשְׁתַּיִם יְכַסֶּה רַגְלָיו וּבִשְׁתַּיִם יְעוֹפֵף׃
³וְקָרָא זֶה אֶל־זֶה וְאָמַר קָדוֹשׁ קָדוֹשׁ
קָדוֹשׁ יְהוָה צְבָאוֹת מְלֹא כָל־הָאָרֶץ כְּבוֹדוֹ׃

רָם v.m.s.ptc.Q. [רום]; וְנִשָּׂא v.m.s.ptc.N. [נשא]; וְשׁוּלָיו (skirt); שְׂרָפִים (angel); יְעוֹפֵף v.3.m.s.impf.Po. [עוף]

REVELATION 1:8

⁸Ἐγώ εἰμι τὸ Ἄλφα καὶ τὸ Ὦ, λέγει κύριος ὁ θεός, ὁ ὢν καὶ ὁ ἦν καὶ ὁ ἐρχόμενος, ὁ παντοκράτωρ.

ἦν v.3.s.impf.ind. [εἰμί]; παντοκράτωρ (Almighty)

335

2. Isaiah 6:5; Luke 5:8

Worship When It Hurts

THERE ARE DAYS when everything has gone wrong. We feel battered, angry, frustrated, and very helpless. The last thing we feel worthy of is being called into the presence of the King. But, if we are obedient, our merciful King reaches out his hand and gives us healing for our brokenness, and the power to do miracles in his name. Awesome!

ISAIAH 6:5

⁵וָאֹמַר אוֹי־לִי כִי־נִדְמֵיתִי כִּי אִישׁ טְמֵא־שְׂפָתַיִם אָנֹכִי
וּבְתוֹךְ עַם־טְמֵא שְׂפָתַיִם אָנֹכִי יוֹשֵׁב כִּי אֶת־הַמֶּלֶךְ יְהוָה צְבָאוֹת
רָאוּ עֵינָי:

וָאֹמַר v.c. + v.1.com.s.impf.Q. [אמר]; אוֹי (woe); נִדְמֵיתִי v.1.com.s.pf.N.
[דמה] (silence); רָאוּ v.3.c.p.pf.Q. [ראה]

LUKE 5:8

⁸ἰδὼν δὲ Σίμων Πέτρος προσέπεσεν τοῖς γόνασιν Ἰησοῦ
λέγων, Ἔξελθε ἀπ' ἐμοῦ, ὅτι ἀνὴρ ἁμαρτωλός εἰμι, κύριε.

ἰδὼν v.m.s.nom.aor.act.ptc. [ὁράω]; προσέπεσεν (fall upon); γόνασιν
(knee); Ἔξελθε v.2.s.aor.act.impv. [ἐξέρχομαι]

3. Psalm 100:1–2; Luke 19:37–38

Joy of Worship

IMAGINE GETTING A MESSAGE that Jesus is going to arrive at your house in an hour! What a thrill to think you will see him, hear his voice, and touch him. You'd call family and friends over to await his arrival, and bring out the best in your larder to share. Well, our Lord is here today, and is already present at your table. He has given us the Holy Spirit to be our constant companion. Celebrate, and pass the cake!

PSALM 100:1–2

¹מִזְמוֹר לְתוֹדָה הָרִיעוּ לַיהוָה כָּל־הָאָרֶץ׃

²עִבְדוּ אֶת־יהוָה בְּשִׂמְחָה בֹּאוּ לְפָנָיו בִּרְנָנָה׃

לְתוֹדָה (thanksgiving); הָרִיעוּ v.2.m.p.impv.H. [רוע] (shout); בֹּאוּ v.2.m.p.impv.Q. [בוא]; בִּרְנָנָה (joyful shout)

LUKE 19:37–38

³⁷Ἐγγίζοντος δὲ αὐτοῦ ἤδη πρὸς τῇ καταβάσει τοῦ Ὄρους τῶν Ἐλαιῶν ἤρξαντο ἅπαν τὸ πλῆθος τῶν μαθητῶν χαίροντες αἰνεῖν τὸν θεὸν φωνῇ μεγάλῃ περὶ πασῶν ὧν εἶδον δυνάμεων, ³⁸λέγοντες,

Εὐλογημένος ὁ ἐρχόμενος,
   ὁ βασιλεὺς ἐν ὀνόματι κυρίου·
ἐν οὐρανῷ εἰρήνη
   καὶ δόξα ἐν ὑψίστοις.

Ἐγγίζοντος (approach); καταβάσει (descent); Ἐλαιῶν (olive tree); ἤρξαντο 3.p.aor.mid.ind. [ἄρχω]; πλῆθος (multitude); αἰνεῖν (praise); εἶδον v.1.s.aor.act.ind. [ὁράω]; ὑψίστοις (exalted)

4. Psalm 22:4–5 [3–4]; Luke 22:19–20

Faithful Worship

TRUST—THE FOUNDATION OF EVERY RELATIONSHIP. Are you trust-
worthy? The Lord believes you are. He's asked you to commit
to memory his perfect love and sacrifice, and to speak of it
over and over again to others, so that they can share it also.
Could you be called faithful to the task he has left you to do?

PSALM 22:4–5 [3–4]

⁴וְאַתָּה קָדוֹשׁ יוֹשֵׁב תְּהִלּוֹת יִשְׂרָאֵל׃
⁵בְּךָ בָּטְחוּ אֲבֹתֵינוּ בָּטְחוּ וַתְּפַלְּטֵמוֹ׃

וַתְּפַלְּטֵמוֹ v.c. + v.2.m.s.impf.P. [פלט] (rescue) + 3.m.p.pr.sf.

LUKE 22:19–20

¹⁹καὶ λαβὼν ἄρτον εὐχαριστήσας ἔκλασεν καὶ ἔδωκεν αὐτοῖς
λέγων, Τοῦτο ἐστιν τὸ σῶμα μου τὸ ὑπὲρ ὑμῶν διδόμενον·
τοῦτο ποιεῖτε εἰς τὴν ἐμὴν ἀνάμνησιν. ²⁰καὶ τὸ ποτήριον
ὡσαύτως μετὰ τὸ δειπνῆσαι, λέγων, Τοῦτο τὸ ποτήριον ἡ
καινὴ διαθήκη ἐν τῷ αἵματι μου τὸ ὑπὲρ ὑμῶν ἐκχυννόμενον.

εὐχαριστήσας (give thanks); ἔκλασεν (break); ἔδωκεν v.3.s.aor.act.ind.
[δίδωμι]; ἐστιν v.3.s.pres.ind. [εἰμί]; ἀνάμνησιν (remembrance); ποτήριον
(cup); ὡσαύτως (likewise); δειπνῆσαι (eat); καινὴ (new); διαθήκη
(covenant); ἐκχυννόμενον v.nt.s.nom.pres.pass.ptc. [ἐκχύννω] (shed)

5. Isaiah 6:7–8; Acts 26:16–18

Worship of the Chosen

HAVE YOU EVER JUMPED at the chance to be chosen for something special? Or are you the more cautious type, who needs to weigh the pros and cons first? Whether a risk taker or not, you've been called, as Paul before you, to "get up." Love is an action word. The Commander has called your name. Stand up, step forward, and share in the victory.

ISAIAH 6:7–8

⁷וַיַּגַּע עַל־פִּי וַיֹּאמֶר הִנֵּה נָגַע זֶה עַל־שְׂפָתֶיךָ וְסָר עֲוֹנֶךָ
וְחַטָּאתְךָ תְּכֻפָּר:
⁸וָאֶשְׁמַע אֶת־קוֹל אֲדֹנָי אֹמֵר אֶת־מִי אֶשְׁלַח וּמִי יֵלֶךְ־לָנוּ
וָאֹמַר הִנְנִי שְׁלָחֵנִי:

וַיַּגַּע [נגע] v.c. + v.3.m.s.impf.H.; וְסָר [סור] v.c. + v.3.m.s.pf.Q.; יֵלֶךְ
v.3.m.s.impf.Q. [הלך]; אֹמֵר [רְ v.c.] + v.1.com.s.impf.Q. [אמר]; שְׁלָחֵנִי
v.3.m.s.Q. [שלח] + 1.com.s.pr.sf.

ACTS 26:16–18

¹⁶ἀλλὰ ἀνάστηθι καὶ στῆθι ἐπὶ τοὺς πόδας σου· εἰς τοῦτο γὰρ ὤφθην σοι, προχειρίσασθαι σε ὑπηρέτην καὶ μάρτυρα ὧν τε εἶδες [με] ὧν τε ὀφθήσομαι σοι, ¹⁷ἐξαιρούμενός σε ἐκ τοῦ λαοῦ καὶ ἐκ τῶν ἐθνῶν εἰς οὓς ἐγὼ ἀποστέλλω σε ¹⁸ἀνοῖξαι ὀφθαλμοὺς αὐτῶν, τοῦ ἐπιστρέψαι ἀπὸ σκότους εἰς φῶς καὶ τῆς ἐξουσίας τοῦ Σατανᾶ ἐπὶ τὸν θεόν, τοῦ λαβεῖν αὐτοὺς ἄφεσιν ἁμαρτιῶν καὶ κλῆρον ἐν τοῖς ἡγιασμένοις πίστει τῇ εἰς ἐμέ.

ὤφθην v.1.s.aor.pass.ind. [ὁράω]; προχειρίσασθαι v.aor.mid.in. [προχειρίζομαι] (select); ὑπηρέτην (helper); μάρτυρα (witness); ἐξαιρούμενος (deliver); ἐπιστρέψαι (return); σκότους (darkness); Σατανᾶ (Satan); ἄφεσιν (forgiveness); κλῆρον (share); ἡγιασμένοις (sanctify)

6. 2 Chronicles 29:31; Hebrews 13:15–16

The Commitment of Worship

COMMITMENT MEANS HANGING IN THERE, even when it feels like things could not be worse. That's what a relationship is all about—trusting in one another and remaining loyal and true, in the good times and the bad. Trusting in the Lord's loving commitment to us and praising him *always,* no matter what. Always trusting he knows best. "It's amazing what praising can do." Our Lord is faithful.

2 CHRONICLES 29:31

³¹וַיַּעַן יְחִזְקִיָּהוּ וַיֹּאמֶר עַתָּה מִלֵּאתֶם יֶדְכֶם לַיהוָה גֹּשׁוּ
וְהָבִיאוּ זְבָחִים וְתוֹדוֹת לְבֵית יְהוָה וַיָּבִיאוּ הַקָּהָל זְבָחִים
וְתוֹדוֹת וְכָל־נְדִיב לֵב עֹלוֹת׃

וַיַּעַן v.c. + v.3.m.s.impf.Q. [עַנה]; גֹּשׁוּ v.2.m.p.impv.Q. [נגשׁ]; וְהָבִיאוּ v.c. +
v.2.m.p.impv.H. [בוא]; וְתוֹדוֹת (thanksgiving); וַיָּבִיאוּ v.c. + v.3.m.p.impf.Q.
[בוא]; נְדִיב (freewill offering)

HEBREWS 13:15–16

¹⁵δι' αὐτοῦ⁰ [οὖν] ἀναφέρωμεν θυσίαν αἰνέσεως διὰ παντὸς τῷ θεῷ, τοῦτ' ἔστιν καρπὸν χειλέων ὁμολογούντων τῷ ὀνόματι αὐτοῦ. ¹⁶τῆς δὲ εὐποιΐας καὶ κοινωνίας μὴ ἐπιλανθάνεσθε· τοιαύταις γὰρ θυσίαις εὐαρεστεῖται ὁ θεός.

ἀναφέρωμεν (offer); θυσίαν (sacrifice); αἰνέσεως (praise); διὰ παντὸς prep. + adj.nt.s.gen. (continually); χειλέων (lip); ἔστιν v.3.s.pres.ind. [εἰμί]; ὁμολογούντων (confess); εὐποιΐας (doing good); κοινωνίας (communion); ἐπιλανθάνεσθε (forget); εὐαρεστεῖται (be pleased)

7. 2 Chronicles 20:13; Acts 4:31

Worshiping Community

THIS WILL BE DIFFICULT, but imagine a place where gender, age, intelligence, or skin color is never an issue; a place where everyone receives equal status, equal respect, and equal love. Well, according to the teachings of Jesus, until we get to heaven, that place is supposed to be the place where Christians gather—your home and your church! How do yours rate? Ask God for a "heavenly heart" and start to make changes, one person at a time.

2 CHRONICLES 20:13

¹³וְכָל־יְהוּדָה עֹמְדִים לִפְנֵי יְהוָה גַּם־טַפָּם נְשֵׁיהֶם וּבְנֵיהֶם׃

טַפָּם (little child)

ACTS 4:31

³¹καὶ δεηθέντων αὐτῶν ἐσαλεύθη ὁ τόπος ἐν ᾧ ἦσαν συνηγμένοι, καὶ ἐπλήσθησαν ἅπαντες τοῦ ἁγίου πνεύματος καὶ ἐλάλουν τὸν λόγον τοῦ θεοῦ μετὰ παρρησίας.

δεηθέντων v.m.p.gen.aor.pass.ptc. [δέομαι] (ask); ἐσαλεύθη (shake); ἐπλήσθησαν v.3.p.aor.act.ind. [πιμπλήμι] (fall); παρρησίας (boldness)

Week 48

Thanksgiving

1. Genesis 27:28–29; Acts 14:16–17

Thanks for Abundance

How lavish you are, Creator! Music, color, dancing hearts, seasons and stars, verdant fields. May our lives hymn thanksgiving to you, today and evermore.

Genesis 27:28–29

²⁸וְיִתֶּן־לְךָ הָאֱלֹהִים מִטַּל הַשָּׁמַיִם וּמִשְׁמַנֵּי הָאָרֶץ וְרֹב דָּגָן וְתִירֹשׁ׃
²⁹יַעַבְדוּךָ עַמִּים וְיִשְׁתַּחֲווּ לְךָ לְאֻמִּים הֱוֵה גְבִיר לְאַחֶיךָ וְיִשְׁתַּחֲווּ לְךָ
בְּנֵי אִמֶּךָ אֹרְרֶיךָ אָרוּר וּמְבָרֲכֶיךָ בָּרוּךְ׃

וְיִתֶּן cj. + v.3.m.s.impf.Q.without accent [נתן]; מִטַּל (dew); דָּגָן (corn); וְתִירֹשׁ (new wine); יַעַבְדוּךָ v.3.m.p.impf.Q. [עבד] + 2.m.s.pr.sf.; וְיִשְׁתַּחֲווּ cj. + v.3.m.p.impf.Hisht.K. [חוה]; לְאֻמִּים (nation); הֱוֵה v.2.m.s.impv.Q. [הוה]; גְבִיר (master); וּמְבָרֲכֶיךָ cj. + v.m.p.pass.ptc.P. [ברך] + 2.m.s.pr.sf.

Acts 14:16–17

¹⁶ὃς ἐν ταῖς παρῳχημέναις γενεαῖς εἴασεν πάντα τὰ ἔθνη πορεύεσθαι ταῖς ὁδοῖς αὐτῶν· ¹⁷καίτοι οὐκ ἀμάρτυρον αὐτὸν ἀφῆκεν ἀγαθουργῶν, οὐρανόθεν ὑμῖν ὑετοὺς διδοὺς καὶ καιροὺς καρποφόρους, ἐμπιπλῶν τροφῆς καὶ εὐφροσύνης τὰς καρδίας ὑμῶν.

παρῳχημέναις v.f.p.dat.pf.pass.part. [παροίχομαι] (be gone); γενεαῖς (generation); εἴασεν v.3.s.aor.ind. [ἐάω] (allow); καίτοι (and yet); ἀμάρτυρον (without witness); ἀφῆκεν v.3.s.aor.act.ind. [ἀφίημι]; ἀγαθουργῶν (do good); οὐρανόθεν (from heaven); ὑετοὺς (rain); καρποφόρους (fruitful); ἐμπιπλῶν (fill); τροφῆς (food); εὐφροσύνης (joy)

2. Genesis 50:19–21; Romans 8:28–29

Evil Turned Upside Down

IT IS VERY HARD SOME DAYS, I must confess, to see anything at all to be grateful about. That's when you nag me with stories of evil turned upside down. Then I have to laugh because I know all over again that you will have the last laugh, God of Life. And when you do, I'll be there laughing too.

GENESIS 50:19–21

¹⁹וַיֹּאמֶר אֲלֵהֶם יוֹסֵף אַל־תִּירָאוּ כִּי הֲתַחַת אֱלֹהִים אָנִי׃

²⁰וְאַתֶּם חֲשַׁבְתֶּם עָלַי רָעָה אֱלֹהִים חֲשָׁבָהּ לְטֹבָה לְמַעַן עֲשֹׂה כַּיּוֹם הַזֶּה לְהַחֲיֹת עַם־רָב׃

²¹וְעַתָּה אַל־תִּירָאוּ אָנֹכִי אֲכַלְכֵּל אֶתְכֶם וְאֶת־טַפְּכֶם וַיְנַחֵם אוֹתָם וַיְדַבֵּר עַל־לִבָּם׃

תִּירָאוּ v.2.m.p.impf.Q.pause [ראה]; חֲשָׁבָהּ v.3.m.s.pf.Q. [חשב] + 3.f.s.pr.sf.; עֲשֹׂה v.in.ab.Q. [עשׂה]; לְהַחֲיֹת prep. + v.in.cs.H. [חיה]; אֲכַלְכֵּל v.1.com.s.impf.Plpl. [כול] (supply); טַפְּכֶם (little child)

ROMANS 8:28–29

²⁸οἴδαμεν δὲ ὅτι τοῖς ἀγαπῶσιν τὸν θεὸν πάντα συνεργεῖ εἰς ἀγαθόν, τοῖς κατὰ πρόθεσιν κλητοῖς οὖσιν. ²⁹ὅτι οὓς προέγνω, καὶ προώρισεν συμμόρφους τῆς εἰκόνος τοῦ υἱοῦ αὐτοῦ, εἰς τὸ εἶναι αὐτὸν πρωτότοκον ἐν πολλοῖς ἀδελφοῖς·

συνεργεῖ (work together); πρόθεσιν (plan); κλητοῖς (called); προέγνω v.3.s.aor.act.ind. [προγινώσκω] (know beforehand); προώρισεν (predestine); συμμόρφους (similar in form); εἰκόνος (image); εἶναι v.pres.in. [εἰμί]; πρωτότοκον (firstborn)

3. Psalm 26:6–8; Hebrews 10:19–22

For Washing, We Give Thanks

WE ARE CLEAN—shout the news! Let us run gladly toward our God, the God of our salvation! Let us dance our way along, singing of his goodness. Let us worship him with gratitude, children of the Lord!

PSALM 26:6–8

⁶אֶרְחַ֣ץ בְּנִקָּי֣וֹן כַּפָּ֑י וַאֲסֹבְבָ֖ה אֶת־מִזְבַּחֲךָ֣ יְהוָֽה׃

⁷לַ֭שְׁמִעַ בְּק֣וֹל תּוֹדָ֑ה וּ֝לְסַפֵּ֗ר כָּל־נִפְלְאוֹתֶֽיךָ׃

⁸יְהוָ֗ה אָ֭הַבְתִּי מְע֣וֹן בֵּיתֶ֑ךָ וּ֝מְק֗וֹם מִשְׁכַּ֥ן כְּבוֹדֶֽךָ׃

בְּנִקָּיוֹן (purity); וַאֲסֹבְבָה cj. + v.1.com.s.coh.P. [סבב]; לַשְׁמִעַ prep. + v.in.cs.H.defective and contracted [שמע]; תּוֹדָה (thanks); מְעוֹן (dwelling)

HEBREWS 10:19–22

¹⁹Ἔχοντες οὖν, ἀδελφοί, παρρησίαν εἰς τὴν εἴσοδον τῶν ἁγίων ἐν τῷ αἵματι Ἰησοῦ, ²⁰ἣν ἐνεκαίνισεν ἡμῖν ὁδὸν πρόσφατον καὶ ζῶσαν διὰ τοῦ καταπετάσματος, τοῦτ᾽ ἔστιν τῆς σαρκὸς αὐτοῦ, ²¹καὶ ἱερέα μέγαν ἐπὶ τὸν οἶκον τοῦ θεοῦ, ²²προσερχώμεθα μετὰ ἀληθινῆς καρδίας ἐν πληροφορίᾳ πίστεως ῥεραντισμένοι τὰς καρδίας ἀπὸ συνειδήσεως πονηρᾶς καὶ λελουσμένοι τὸ σῶμα ὕδατι καθαρῷ·

παρρησίαν (confidence); εἴσοδον (access); ἐνεκαίνισεν v.3.s.aor.act.ind. [ἐγκαινίζω] (dedicate); πρόσφατον (new); καταπετάσματος (veil); ἔστιν v.3.s.pres.ind. [εἰμί]; ἱερέα (priest); ἀληθινῆς (genuine); πληροφορίᾳ (certainty); ῥεραντισμένοι v.m.p.nom.pf.pass.ptc. [ῥαντίζω] (sprinkle); συνειδήσεως (conscience); λελουσμένοι v.m.p.nom.pf.pass.ptc. [λούω] (wash); καθαρῷ (pure)

4. Psalm 100:4–5; Romans 7:24–25

Celebrate the Lord!

HOW CAN WE HELP BUT EXPLODE with music when we think of who you are? For out of you flows everything that is good and beautiful and sane and whole and true. And where does all that love flow, but into us? So we celebrate you, Jesus!

PSALM 100:4–5

⁴בֹּאוּ שְׁעָרָיו בְּתוֹדָה חֲצֵרֹתָיו בִּתְהִלָּה הוֹדוּ־לוֹ בָּרְכוּ שְׁמוֹ׃

⁵כִּי־טוֹב יְהֹוָה לְעוֹלָם חַסְדּוֹ וְעַד־דֹּר וָדֹר אֱמוּנָתוֹ׃

בֹּאוּ v.2.m.p.impv.Q. [בוא]; בְּתוֹדָה (thanksgiving); הוֹדוּ v.2.m.p.impv.H.
[ידה]; בָּרְכוּ v.2.m.p.impv.P. [ברך]

ROMANS 7:24–25

²⁴ταλαίπωρος ἐγὼ ἄνθρωπος· τίς με ῥύσεται ἐκ τοῦ σώματος τοῦ θανάτου τούτου; ²⁵χάρις δὲ τῷ θεῷ διὰ Ἰησοῦ Χριστοῦ τοῦ κυρίου ἡμῶν. ἄρα οὖν αὐτὸς ἐγὼ τῷ μὲν νοῒ δουλεύω νόμῳ θεοῦ τῇ δὲ σαρκὶ νόμῳ ἁμαρτίας.

ταλαίπωρος (miserable); ῥύσεται (rescue); ἄρα οὖν αὐτός pt.illative + cj.illative + pr.m.s.nom. (so then); τῷ μὲν d.a.m.s.dat. + cor.pt. (myself); νοῒ (mind); δουλεύω (serve)

5. Isaiah 35:10; Romans 14:17

Waiting with Thanksgiving

EVEN BEFORE I SEE IT, my Liberator, I will thank you for final free-dom, for deliverance from grief, for the healing of all wounds, for the promise of completion. Even as I watch through the eyes of your prophets of old, I will praise you, Redeemer. Surely your word will come to pass.

ISAIAH 35:10

וּפְדוּיֵי יְהוָה יְשֻׁבוּן וּבָאוּ צִיּוֹן בְּרִנָּה וְשִׂמְחַת עוֹלָם עַל־[10]
רֹאשָׁם שָׂשׂוֹן וְשִׂמְחָה יַשִּׂיגוּ וְנָסוּ יָגוֹן וַאֲנָחָה:

וּפְדוּיֵי cj. + v.m.p.cs.pass.ptc.Q. [פדה]; יְשֻׁבוּן v.3.m.p.impf.Q. [שוב] + para.;
וּבָאוּ v.c. + v.3.c.p.pf.Q. [בוא]; שָׂשׂוֹן (joy); יַשִּׂיגוּ v.3.m.p.impf.H. [נשׂג]; וְנָסוּ v.c.
+ v.3.c.p.pf.Q. [נוס]; יָגוֹן (grief); וַאֲנָחָה (sigh)

ROMANS 14:17

[17]οὐ γάρ ἐστιν ἡ βασιλεία τοῦ θεοῦ βρῶσις καὶ πόσις ἀλλὰ δικαιοσύνη καὶ εἰρήνη καὶ χαρὰ ἐν πνεύματι ἁγίῳ·

ἐστιν v.3.s.pres.ind. [εἰμί]; βρῶσις (eating); πόσις (drinking)

6. Isaiah 55:1; John 7:37-38

Lead Me to the Desert

LEAD ME TO THE DESERT, away from poisoned trickling streams of self-sufficiency. Take me by the hand to craggy wastes. Increase my thirst until I pant for Living Water, until nothing else will do.

ISAIAH 55:1

יהוֹי כָּל־צָמֵא לְכוּ לַמַּיִם וַאֲשֶׁר אֵין־לוֹ כָּסֶף לְכוּ שִׁבְרוּ וֶאֱכֹלוּ
וּלְכוּ שִׁבְרוּ בְּלוֹא־כֶסֶף וּבְלוֹא מְחִיר יַיִן וְחָלָב:

הוֹי (hey!); צָמֵא (thirst); לְכוּ v.2.m.p.impv.Q. [הלך]; שִׁבְרוּ (buy grain);
וֶאֱכֹלוּ cj. + v.2.m.p.impv.Q. [אכל]; וּלְכוּ cj. + v.2.m.p.impv.Q. [הלך]; מְחִיר (price); וְחָלָב (milk)

JOHN 7:37-38

³⁷Ἐν δὲ τῇ ἐσχάτῃ ἡμέρᾳ τῇ μεγάλῃ τῆς ἑορτῆς εἱστήκει ὁ Ἰησοῦς καὶ ἔκραξεν λέγων, Ἐάν τις διψᾷ ἐρχέσθω πρός με καὶ πινέτω. ³⁸ὁ πιστεύων εἰς ἐμέ, καθὼς εἶπεν ἡ γραφή, ποταμοὶ ἐκ τῆς κοιλίας αὐτοῦ ῥεύσουσιν ὕδατος ζῶντος.

ἑορτῆς (festival); εἱστήκει v.3.s.plup.act.ind. [ἵστημι]; διψᾷ (thirst); εἶπεν v.3.s.aor.act.ind. [λέγω]; ποταμοὶ (river); κοιλίας (belly); ῥεύσουσιν (flow)

7. Habakkuk 3:17–18; Matthew 5:11–12

God of Enough

WHAT I WANT, WHAT I NEED, really, is to uncomplicate my faith until it's just a matter of God being there and that being enough.

HABAKKUK 3:17–18

¹⁷כִּי־תְאֵנָה לֹא־תִפְרָח וְאֵין יְבוּל בַּגְּפָנִים כִּחֵשׁ מַעֲשֵׂה־זַיִת
וּשְׁדֵמוֹת לֹא־עָשָׂה אֹכֶל גָּזַר מִמִּכְלָה צֹאן וְאֵין בָּקָר בָּרְפָתִים:
¹⁸וַאֲנִי בַּיהוָה אֶעְלוֹזָה אָגִילָה בֵּאלֹהֵי יִשְׁעִי:

תְאֵנָה (fig tree); תִפְרָח (blossom); יְבוּל (produce); כִּחֵשׁ (fail); זַיִת (olive tree); וּשְׁדֵמוֹת (field); גָּזַר (cut off); מִמִּכְלָה (sheepfold); בָּרְפָתִים (stall); אֶעְלוֹזָה v.1.com.s.coh.Q.plene [עלז] (exult); אָגִילָה v.1.com.s.coh.Q. [גיל] (rejoice); יִשְׁעִי (salvation)

MATTHEW 5:11–12

¹¹μακάριοι ἐστε ὅταν ὀνειδίσωσιν ὑμᾶς καὶ διώξωσιν καὶ εἴπωσιν πᾶν πονηρὸν καθ᾽ ὑμῶν [ψευδόμενοι] ἕνεκεν ἐμοῦ. ¹²χαίρετε καὶ ἀγαλλιᾶσθε, ὅτι ὁ μισθὸς ὑμῶν πολὺς ἐν τοῖς οὐρανοῖς· οὕτως γὰρ ἐδίωξαν τοὺς προφήτας τοὺς πρὸ ὑμῶν.

ὀνειδίσωσιν (revile); διώξωσιν (persecute); εἴπωσιν v.3.p.aor.act.sub. [λέγω]; ψευδόμενοι (lie); ἀγαλλιᾶσθε (be glad); μισθὸς (reward); πρὸ (before)

Faithfulness

---

1. Deuteronomy 7:9; 1 Corinthians 1:9

The Faithfulness of God

ALL MY HOPE AND TRUST are pinned on this one truth: the faithfulness of God.

DEUTERONOMY 7:9

‎⁹וְיָדַעְתָּ כִּי־יְהוָה אֱלֹהֶיךָ הוּא הָאֱלֹהִים הָאֵל הַנֶּאֱמָן שֹׁמֵר
‎הַבְּרִית וְהַחֶסֶד לְאֹהֲבָיו וּלְשֹׁמְרֵי מִצְוֺתָיו לְאֶלֶף דּוֹר׃

1 CORINTHIANS 1:9

⁹πιστὸς ὁ θεός, δι᾿ οὗ ἐκλήθητε εἰς κοινωνίαν τοῦ υἱοῦ αὐτοῦ Ἰησοῦ Χριστοῦ τοῦ κυρίου ἡμῶν.

κοινωνίαν (fellowship)

2. Genesis 32:11a [10a]; 1 Timothy 1:13–14

Fit Subjects

OPEN MY HEART, JESUS, to see the blasphemers, persecutors, and violent ones as fit subjects for your merciful and faithful love. For the truth is, until I see them as fit subjects, I will not see myself as a fit subject and I will refuse the deepest love you offer me.

GENESIS 32:11A [10a]

¹¹קָטֹנְתִּי מִכֹּל הַחֲסָדִים וּמִכָּל־הָאֱמֶת אֲשֶׁר עָשִׂיתָ אֶת־עַבְדֶּךָ

קָטֹנְתִּי (be small); עָשִׂיתָ v.2.m.s.pf.Q. [עשׂה]

1 TIMOTHY 1:13–14

¹³τὸ πρότερον ὄντα βλάσφημον καὶ διώκτην καὶ ὑβριστήν, ἀλλὰ ἠλεήθην, ὅτι ἀγνοῶν ἐποίησα ἐν ἀπιστίᾳ· ¹⁴ὑπερεπλεόνασεν δὲ ἡ χάρις τοῦ κυρίου ἡμῶν μετὰ πίστεως καὶ ἀγάπης τῆς ἐν Χριστῷ Ἰησοῦ.

πρότερον (before); βλάσφημον (blasphemous); διώκτην (persecutor); ὑβριστήν (violent); ἠλεήθην v.1.s.aor.pass.ind. [ἐλεέω] (show mercy); ἀγνοῶν (be ignorant); ἀπιστίᾳ (unbelief); ὑπερεπλεόνασεν (overflow)

3. Psalm 25:10; Romans 3:3–4a

Faithfulness: The Glue

GOD IS PECULIARLY IMMOVABLE in faithfulness to his word, regardless of what we do. God's faithfulness is the glue that holds the universe together, the ultimate power that will make all things new.

PSALM 25:10

¹⁰ כָּל־אָרְחוֹת יְהוָה חֶסֶד וֶאֱמֶת לְנֹצְרֵי בְרִיתוֹ וְעֵדֹתָיו׃

ROMANS 3:3–4A

³τί γάρ; εἰ ἠπίστησάν τινες, μὴ ἡ ἀπιστία αὐτῶν τὴν πίστιν τοῦ θεοῦ καταργήσει; ⁴μὴ γένοιτο· γινέσθω δὲ ὁ θεὸς ἀληθής, πᾶς δὲ ἄνθρωπος ψεύστης,

ἠπίστησάν (lack belief); ἀπιστία (unbelief); καταργήσει (nullify); γένοιτο v.3.s.aor.mid.ind. [γίνομαι]; ἀληθής (true); ψεύστης (liar)

4. Deuteronomy 32:20–21; Matthew 17:17a

What Does It Take?

RELIGIOUS CLICHÉS AND PLATITUDES are like a bridge made up of paperclips and twine. The least bit of pressure from a real problem sends the whole mess plummeting into the abyss. Real faith, on the other hand, is relaxing in God's arms as he personally bears us across.

DEUTERONOMY 32:20–21

²⁰וַיֹּאמֶר אַסְתִּירָה פָנַי מֵהֶם אֶרְאֶה מָה אַחֲרִיתָם כִּי דוֹר תַּהְפֻּכֹת
הֵמָּה בָּנִים לֹא־אֵמֻן בָּם:
²¹הֵם קִנְאוּנִי בְלֹא־אֵל כִּעֲסוּנִי בְּהַבְלֵיהֶם וַאֲנִי אַקְנִיאֵם בְּלֹא־
עָם בְּגוֹי נָבָל אַכְעִיסֵם:

אַסְתִּירָה v.1.com.s.coh.H. [סתר]; תַּהְפֻּכֹת (perversity); אֵמֻן (faithful); קִנְאוּנִי v.3.c.p.pf.P. [קנא] (be jealous) + 1.com.s.pr.sf.; כִּעֲסוּנִי v.3.m.p.pf.P. [כעס] + 1.com.s.pr.sf.; בְּהַבְלֵיהֶם (idol); אַקְנִיאֵם v.1.com.s.impf. [קנא] + 3.m.p.pr.sf.; נָבָל (stupid); אַכְעִיסֵם v.1.com.s.impf. [כעס] + 3.m.p.pr.sf.

MATTHEW 17:17A

¹⁷ἀποκριθεὶς δὲ ὁ Ἰησοῦς εἶπεν, Ὦ γενεὰ ἄπιστος καὶ διεστραμμένη, ἕως πότε μεθ᾽ ὑμῶν ἔσομαι;

εἶπεν v.3.s.aor.act.ind. [λέγω]; γενεὰ (generation); ἄπιστος (unbelieving); διεστραμμένη v.f.s.vocative.pf.pass.ptc. [διαστρέφω] (pervert); πότε (how long); ἔσομαι v.1.s.fut.ind. [εἰμί]

5. 1 Samuel 2:9; Matthew 25:21

The Way to Prevail

WE DO NOT PREVAIL in the spiritual life by might, by success, by victory. We prevail by faithfulness, no matter what it costs.

1 SAMUEL 2:9

⁹רַגְלֵי חֲסִידָיו יִשְׁמֹר וּרְשָׁעִים בַּחֹשֶׁךְ יִדָּמּוּ כִּי־לֹא
בְכֹחַ יִגְבַּר־אִישׁ:

חֲסִידָיו (pious one); יִדָּמּוּ v.3.m.p.impf.N. [דמם] (be silent); יִגְבַּר (prevail)

MATTHEW 25:21

²¹ἔφη αὐτῷ ὁ κύριος αὐτοῦ, Εὖ, δοῦλε ἀγαθὲ καὶ πιστέ, ἐπὶ ὀλίγα ἦς πιστός, ἐπὶ πολλῶν σε καταστήσω· εἴσελθε εἰς τὴν χαρὰν τοῦ κυρίου σου.

Εὖ (great!); ὀλίγα (few); καταστήσω v.1.s.fut.act.ind. [καθίστημι] (put in charge); εἴσελθε v.2.s.aor.act.ind. [εἰσέρχομαι]

6. Psalm 36:6 [5]; Matthew 24:35

God's Promise Is the Refuge

O GOD, IT SEEMS TO ME that the very heavens and earth are passing away. There is so much violence, so much hatred in the world, so much exploitation. Are there safe places anywhere anymore? My refuge is your promise that your word will not pass away until every syllable is fulfilled. You have promised to make all things new. So I lift my heart to you again in gratitude and worship, for you are faithful. Amen.

PSALM 36:6 [5]

יְהוָה בְּהַשָּׁמַיִם חַסְדֶּךָ אֱמוּנָתְךָ עַד־שְׁחָקִים:⁶

אֱמוּנָתְךָ (faithfulness); שְׁחָקִים (cloud)

MATTHEW 24:35

³⁵ὁ οὐρανὸς καὶ ἡ γῆ παρελεύσεται, οἱ δὲ λόγοι μου οὐ μὴ παρέλθωσιν.

παρελεύσεται v.3.s.fut.mid.ind. [παρέρχομαι] (pass away); παρέλθωσιν v.3.p.aor.act.sub. [παρέρχομαι]

7. Psalm 136:1; 1 John 4:9

Prayer for the Day Ahead

MAY I LIVE THE HOURS AND MINUTES of this day in such abandon to your faithfulness and love, O God, that everyone around me will be convinced that Jesus is alive. Amen.

PSALM 136:1

¹הוֹדוּ לַיהוָה כִּי־טוֹב כִּי לְעוֹלָם חַסְדּוֹ:

הוֹדוּ v.2.m.p.impv.H. [ידה]

1 JOHN 4:9

⁹ἐν τούτῳ ἐφανερώθη ἡ ἀγάπη τοῦ θεοῦ ἐν ἡμῖν, ὅτι τὸν υἱὸν αὐτοῦ τὸν μονογενῆ ἀπέσταλκεν ὁ θεὸς εἰς τὸν κόσμον ἵνα ζήσωμεν δι᾽ αὐτοῦ.

ἐφανερώθη (reveal); μονογενῆ (unique); ἀπέσταλκεν v.3.s.pf.act.ind. [ἀποστέλλω]

Week 50

Play/Delight

1. Zechariah 8:4–5; Matthew 11:16–17

Playful Life

THE SURE SIGN OF LIFE, of wholeness, of joyous *being* is the ability to play. Laughter, creativity, the issuance of things made new—these are evidence that the Spirit is present.

ZECHARIAH 8:4–5

⁴כֹּה אָמַר יְהוָה צְבָאוֹת עֹד יֵשְׁבוּ זְקֵנִים וּזְקֵנוֹת בִּרְחֹבוֹת יְרוּשָׁלִָם
וְאִישׁ מִשְׁעַנְתּוֹ בְּיָדוֹ מֵרֹב יָמִים׃
⁵וּרְחֹבוֹת הָעִיר יִמָּלְאוּ יְלָדִים וִילָדוֹת מְשַׂחֲקִים בִּרְחֹבֹתֶיהָ׃

יֵשְׁבוּ v.3.m.p.impf.Q. [ישׁב]; בִּרְחֹבוֹת (street); מִשְׁעַנְתּוֹ (staff); מְשַׂחֲקִים (play)

MATTHEW 11:16–17

¹⁶Τίνι δὲ ὁμοιώσω τὴν γενεὰν ταύτην; ὁμοία ἐστὶν παιδίοις καθημένοις ἐν ταῖς ἀγοραῖς ἃ προσφωνοῦντα τοῖς ἑτέροις ¹⁷λέγουσιν,
   Ηὐλήσαμεν ὑμῖν καὶ οὐκ ὠρχήσασθε,
   ἐθρηνήσαμεν καὶ οὐκ ἐκόψασθε.

ὁμοιώσω (compare); γενεὰν (generation); ὁμοία (like); ἐστὶν v.3.s.pres.ind. [εἰμί]; ἀγοραῖς (market); προσφωνοῦντα (call out); ηὐλήσαμεν v.1.p.aor.act.ind. [αὐλέω] (play flute); ὠρχήσασθε v.2.p.aor.mid.ind. [ὀρχέομαι] (dance); ἐθρηνήσαμεν (lament); ἐκόψασθε v.2.p.aor.mid.ind. [κόπτω] (mourn)

2. Jeremiah 31:11–13; John 16:22

Dance of Delight

Lord of beauty, Lord of dance, I long for the day of all-things-new. I watch with the anticipation of a woman awaiting her wedding day. I watch with the certainty of Elizabeth, seeing her Lord approach even as an unborn child. I watch with dancing and with joy for the day of rejoicing will surely come.

Jeremiah 31:11–13

¹¹כִּי־פָדָה יְהוָה אֶת־יַעֲקֹב וּגְאָלוֹ מִיַּד חָזָק מִמֶּנּוּ׃

¹²וּבָאוּ וְרִנְּנוּ בִמְרוֹם־צִיּוֹן וְנָהֲרוּ אֶל־טוּב יְהוָה עַל־דָּגָן

וְעַל־תִּירֹשׁ וְעַל־יִצְהָר וְעַל־בְּנֵי־צֹאן וּבָקָר וְהָיְתָה נַפְשָׁם

כְּגַן רָוֶה וְלֹא־יוֹסִיפוּ לְדַאֲבָה עוֹד׃

¹³אָז תִּשְׂמַח בְּתוּלָה בְּמָחוֹל וּבַחֻרִים וּזְקֵנִים יַחְדָּו וְהָפַכְתִּי

אֶבְלָם לְשָׂשׂוֹן וְנִחַמְתִּים וְשִׂמַּחְתִּים מִיגוֹנָם׃

וּגְאָלוֹ v.c. + v.3.m.s.pf.Q. [גָּאַל] + 3.m.s.pr.sf.; וּבָאוּ v.c. + v.3.c.p.pf.Q. [בּוֹא];
וְנָהֲרוּ (stream); טוּב (good thing); דָּגָן (corn); תִּירֹשׁ (new wine); יִצְהָר (oil)
וְהָיְתָה v.3.f.s.pf.Q. [הָיָה]; רָוֶה (watered); יוֹסִיפוּ v.3.m.p.impf.H. [יָסַף]; לְדַאֲבָה
prep. + v.in.cs.Q. [דָּאַב] (languish); בְּמָחוֹל (dance); וּבַחֻרִים (youth); אֶבְלָם
(mourning); לְשָׂשׂוֹן (joy); וְנִחַמְתִּים v.c. + v.1.com.s.pf.P. [נָחַם] + 3.m.p.pr.sf.;
וְשִׂמַּחְתִּים v.c. + v.1.com.s.pf.P. [שָׂמַח] + 3.m.p.pr.sf.; מִיגוֹנָם (grief)

John 16:22

²²καὶ ὑμεῖς οὖν νῦν μὲν λύπην ἔχετε· πάλιν δὲ ὄψομαι ὑμᾶς, καὶ χαρήσεται ὑμῶν ἡ καρδία, καὶ τὴν χαρὰν ὑμῶν οὐδεὶς αἴρει ἀφ᾽ ὑμῶν.

νῦν (now); λύπην (sorrow); ὄψομαι v.1.s.fut.mid.ind. [ὁράω]

357

3. Psalm 133:1–3; John 13:35

You, My Love and My Joy

I LOVE YOU LORD, in my friends, in my family, in the joy of hugs exchanged, laughter shared, table talk, even in the disagreements. You are there, enfleshed in each of them, You—my Love and my Joy!

PSALM 133:1–3

¹שִׁיר הַמַּעֲלוֹת לְדָוִד הִנֵּה מַה־טּוֹב וּמַה־נָּעִים שֶׁבֶת אַחִים גַּם־
יָחַד:

²כַּשֶּׁמֶן הַטּוֹב עַל־הָרֹאשׁ יֹרֵד עַל־הַזָּקָן זְקַן־אַהֲרֹן שֶׁיֹּרֵד
עַל־פִּי מִדּוֹתָיו:

³כְּטַל־חֶרְמוֹן שֶׁיֹּרֵד עַל־הַרְרֵי צִיּוֹן כִּי שָׁם צִוָּה יְהוָה אֶת־
הַבְּרָכָה חַיִּים עַד־הָעוֹלָם:

הַמַּעֲלוֹת (ascent); נָּעִים (pleasant); שֶׁבֶת v.in.cs.Q. [ישב]; הַזָּקָן (beard); שֶׁיֹּרֵד rel.pr. + v.m.s.act.ptc.Q. [ירד]; כְּטַל (dew)

JOHN 13:35

³⁵ἐν τούτῳ γνώσονται πάντες ὅτι ἐμοὶ μαθηταί ἐστε, ἐὰν ἀγάπην ἔχητε ἐν ἀλλήλοις.

358

4. Isaiah 61:3; Luke 15:22–24

Shout the Jubilee!

WHAT GREATER JOY IS THERE than to see old scars transformed into catalysts of life? Mourning into dancing, ashes into beauty, water into wine. Shout the jubilee! Shout the jubilee!

ISAIAH 61:3

³לָשׂוּם לַאֲבֵלֵי צִיּוֹן לָתֵת לָהֶם פְּאֵר תַּחַת אֵפֶר שֶׁמֶן שָׂשׂוֹן תַּחַת
אֵבֶל מַעֲטֵה תְהִלָּה תַּחַת רוּחַ כֵּהָה וְקֹרָא לָהֶם אֵילֵי הַצֶּדֶק מַטַּע
יְהוָה לְהִתְפָּאֵר׃

לַאֲבֵלֵי (desolate); לָתֵת prep. + v.in.cs.Q. [נתן]; פְּאֵר (glory); אֵפֶר (dust);
שָׂשׂוֹן (joy); מַעֲטֵה (garment); כֵּהָה (dim); וְקֹרָא v.c. + v.3.m.s.pf.Pu. [קרא];
מַטַּע (garden)

LUKE 15:22–24

²²εἶπεν δὲ ὁ πατὴρ πρὸς τοὺς δούλους αὐτοῦ, Ταχὺ ἐξενέγκατε
στολὴν τὴν πρώτην καὶ ἐνδύσατε αὐτόν, καὶ δότε δακτύλιον
εἰς τὴν χεῖρα αὐτοῦ καὶ ὑποδήματα εἰς τοὺς πόδας, ²³καὶ
φέρετε τὸν μόσχον τὸν σιτευτόν, θύσατε, καὶ φαγόντες
εὐφρανθῶμεν, ²⁴ὅτι οὗτος ὁ υἱός μου νεκρὸς ἦν καὶ ἀνέζησεν,
ἦν ἀπολωλὼς καὶ εὑρέθη. καὶ ἤρξαντο εὐφραίνεσθαι.

εἶπεν v.3.s.aor.act.ind. [λέγω]; Ταχὺ (quickly); ἐξενέγκατε v.2.p.aor.act.impv.
[ἐκφέρω] (carry out); στολὴν (robe); ἐνδύσατε (wear); δακτύλιον (ring); ὑποδήματα (sandal); μόσχον (calf); σιτευτόν (fattened); θύσατε (kill); εὐφρανθῶμεν v.1.p.aor.pass.sub. [εὐφραίνω] (rejoice); ἀνέζησεν (be alive again); ἀπολωλὼς v.m.s.nom.2.pf.act.ptc. [ἀπόλλυμι]; Ἦν v.3.s.impf.ind. [εἰμί]; εὑρέθη
v.3.s.aor.pass.ind. [εὑρίσκω]; ἤρξαντο v.3.p.aor.mid.ind. [ἄρχω]

5. Exodus 23:12; Matthew 11:28–29

Spiritual Sludge

JESUS PROMISED THAT HIS SPIRIT within us would be a river of living water. So, how can it be that so many of us are stagnant ponds? I think the sludge is worst among pastors! The cure has to do with learning to *live* the Sabbath rest, yoking ourselves with Jesus not just when we're weary and heavy-laden, but all the time. Whenever we unyoke ourselves, we clog the life-giving stream. Then it's only a matter of time until there's nothing left to give.

EXODUS 23:12

¹²שֵׁשֶׁת יָמִים תַּעֲשֶׂה מַעֲשֶׂיךָ וּבַיּוֹם הַשְּׁבִיעִי תִּשְׁבֹּת לְמַעַן
יָנוּחַ שׁוֹרְךָ וַחֲמֹרֶךָ וְיִנָּפֵשׁ בֶּן־אֲמָתְךָ וְהַגֵּר׃

וְיִנָּפֵשׁ (refresh self)

MATTHEW 11:28–29

²⁸Δεῦτε πρός με πάντες οἱ κοπιῶντες καὶ πεφορτισμένοι, κἀγὼ ἀναπαύσω ὑμᾶς. ²⁹ἄρατε τὸν ζυγόν μου ἐφ᾽ ὑμᾶς καὶ μάθετε ἀπ᾽ ἐμοῦ, ὅτι πραΰς εἰμι καὶ ταπεινὸς τῇ καρδίᾳ, καὶ εὑρήσετε ἀνάπαυσιν ταῖς ψυχαῖς ὑμῶν·

κοπιῶντες (toil); πεφορτισμένοι v.m.p.nom.pf.pass.ptc. [φορτίζω] (burden); ἀναπαύσω (relieve); ἄρατε v.2.p.aor.act.impv. [αἴρω]; ζυγόν (yoke); μάθετε v.2.p.aor.act.impv. [μανθάνω] (learn); πραΰς (gentle); ταπεινὸς (humble); εὑρήσετε v.2.p.fut.act.ind. [εὑρίσκω]; ἀνάπαυσιν (rest)

6. Proverbs 8:1a, 27a, 30; 1 Corinthians 1:30–31

Wisdom in the Works

THE WISDOM OF GOD is most fully revealed in Jesus. There is a progressive revelation of his wisdom in my own life, too, in all the circumstances, forces, and influences that hold the potential of birthing wisdom in me. This, too, is a source of great delight.

PROVERBS 8:1A, 27A, 30

¹הֲלֹא־חָכְמָה תִקְרָא
²⁷בַּהֲכִינוֹ שָׁמַיִם שָׁם אָנִי
³⁰וָאֶהְיֶה אֶצְלוֹ אָמוֹן וָאֶהְיֶה שַׁעֲשֻׁעִים יוֹם יוֹם מְשַׂחֶקֶת לְפָנָיו
בְּכָל־עֵת:

בַּהֲכִינוֹ prep. + v.in.cs.H. [כון] + 3.m.s.pr.sf.; אָמוֹן (architect); שַׁעֲשֻׁעִים (delight); מְשַׂחֶקֶת (play)

1 CORINTHIANS 1:30–31

³⁰ἐξ αὐτοῦ δὲ ὑμεῖς ἐστε ἐν Χριστῷ Ἰησοῦ, ὃς ἐγενήθη σοφία ἡμῖν ἀπὸ θεοῦ, δικαιοσύνη τε καὶ ἁγιασμὸς καὶ ἀπολύτρωσις, ³¹ἵνα καθὼς γέγραπται, Ὁ καυχώμενος ἐν κυρίῳ καυχάσθω.

ἁγιασμὸς (holiness); ἀπολύτρωσις (redemption); καυχώμενος (boast)

7. Ecclesiastes 9:9–10; 1 Timothy 4:1, 3–4

Delight in Sexuality

THANK YOU, LORD, for the astonishing gift of sexual love, for the playfulness in our bodies. Surely in our lovemaking we experience fully how "the two shall become one."

ECCLESIASTES 9:9–10

⁹רְאֵה חַיִּים עִם־אִשָּׁה אֲשֶׁר־אָהַבְתָּ כָּל־יְמֵי חַיֵּי הֶבְלֶךָ אֲשֶׁר
נָתַן־לְךָ תַּחַת הַשֶּׁמֶשׁ כֹּל יְמֵי הֶבְלֶךָ כִּי הוּא חֶלְקְךָ בַּחַיִּים
וּבַעֲמָלְךָ אֲשֶׁר־אַתָּה עָמֵל תַּחַת הַשָּׁמֶשׁ:
¹⁰כֹּל אֲשֶׁר תִּמְצָא יָדְךָ לַעֲשׂוֹת בְּכֹחֲךָ עֲשֵׂה כִּי אֵין מַעֲשֶׂה
וְחֶשְׁבּוֹן וְדַעַת וְחָכְמָה בִּשְׁאוֹל אֲשֶׁר אַתָּה הֹלֵךְ שָׁמָּה:

רְאֵה v.2.m.s.impv.Q. [רָאה]; וּבַעֲמָלְךָ (toil); לַעֲשׂוֹת prep. + v.in.cs.Q. [עשׂה]; עֲשֵׂה v.2.m.s.impv.Q. [עשׂה]; וְחֶשְׁבּוֹן (planning)

1 TIMOTHY 4:1, 3–4

¹Τὸ δὲ πνεῦμα ῥητῶς λέγει ὅτι ἐν ὑστέροις καιροῖς ἀποστήσονταί τινες τῆς πίστεως προσέχοντες πνεύμασιν πλάνοις καὶ διδασκαλίαις δαιμονίων, ³κωλυόντων γαμεῖν, ἀπέχεσθαι βρωμάτων, ἃ ὁ θεὸς ἔκτισεν εἰς μετάλημψιν μετὰ εὐχαριστίας τοῖς πιστοῖς καὶ ἐπεγνωκόσι τὴν ἀλήθειαν. ⁴ὅτι πᾶν κτίσμα θεοῦ καλὸν καὶ οὐδὲν ἀπόβλητον μετὰ εὐχαριστίας λαμβανόμενον·

ῥητῶς (clearly); ὑστέροις (later); ἀποστήσονται v.3.p.fut.ind. [ἀφίστημι] (depart); προσέχοντες (follow); πλάνοις (deceitful); διδασκαλίαις (teaching); κωλυόντων (forbid); γαμεῖν (marry); ἀπέχεσθαι (abstain); βρωμάτων (food); ἔκτισεν (create); μετάλημψιν n.f.s.acc. (sharing); εὐχαριστίας (thanksgiving); ἐπεγνωκόσι (know); κτίσμα (creature); ἀπόβλητον (rejected)

Advent I: The Anticipated Messiah

1. Isaiah 11:1–2; John 1:32–33

The Coming of Baptism

IT WAS NOT ENOUGH FOR THE SPIRIT to rest on Messiah. It was not enough for John to see it and to say, "Here is the One!" It will only be enough when we, too, are baptized—immersed and overflowing with our God.

ISAIAH 11:2

¹וְיָצָא חֹטֶר מִגֵּזַע יִשָׁי וְנֵצֶר מִשָּׁרָשָׁיו יִפְרֶה:
²וְנָחָה עָלָיו רוּחַ יְהוָה רוּחַ חָכְמָה וּבִינָה רוּחַ עֵצָה וּגְבוּרָה רוּחַ
דַּעַת וְיִרְאַת יְהוָה:

חֹטֶר (twig); מִגֵּזַע (stem); וְנֵצֶר (shoot); מִשָּׁרָשָׁיו (root); יִפְרֶה (bear fruit);
וְנָחָה v.3.f.s.pf.Q. [נוח]; וּבִינָה (understanding); וְיִרְאַת (fear)

JOHN 1:32–33

³²Καὶ ἐμαρτύρησεν Ἰωάννης λέγων ὅτι Τεθέαμαι τὸ πνεῦμα καταβαῖνον ὡς περιστερὰν ἐξ οὐρανοῦ καὶ ἔμεινεν ἐπ᾽ αὐτόν. ³³κἀγὼ οὐκ ᾔδειν αὐτόν, ἀλλ᾽ ὁ πέμψας με βαπτίζειν ἐν ὕδατι ἐκεῖνός μοι εἶπεν, Ἐφ᾽ ὃν ἂν ἴδῃς τὸ πνεῦμα καταβαῖνον καὶ μένον ἐπ᾽ αὐτόν, οὗτός ἐστιν ὁ βαπτίζων ἐν πνεύματι ἁγίῳ.

Τεθέαμαι v.1.s.pf.mid.ind. [θεάομαι] (see); περιστερὰν (dove); ᾔδειν v.1.s.plupf.act.ind. [οἶδα]; εἶπεν v.3.s.aor.act.ind. [λέγω]; ἐστιν v.3.s.pres.ind. [εἰμί]

2. Psalm 110:1–3; Matthew 22:42–45

Come, Mystery!

LIKE THE SKEPTICS IN YOUR TIME, Lord, we chafe at mystery. We
want to know it all, explain it with a chart. Lead our darkened
minds into your heart. Help us to "offer ourselves freely" to
you at your coming, Son of David, precisely because we don't
know it all.

PSALM 110:1–3

¹לְדָוִד
מִזְמוֹר נְאֻם יְהוָה לַאדֹנִי שֵׁב לִימִינִי עַד־אָשִׁית אֹיְבֶיךָ הֲדֹם לְרַגְלֶיךָ:
²מַטֵּה־עֻזְּךָ יִשְׁלַח יְהוָה מִצִּיּוֹן רְדֵה בְּקֶרֶב אֹיְבֶיךָ:
³עַמְּךָ נְדָבֹת בְּיוֹם חֵילֶךָ בְּהַדְרֵי־קֹדֶשׁ מֵרֶחֶם מִשְׁחָר לְךָ טַל יַלְדֻתֶיךָ:

אָשִׁית v.2.m.s.impv.Q.;[יָשַׁב];לִימִינִי prep. + n.m.s. [יָמִין] + 1.com.s.pr.sf.;שֵׁב v.2.m.s.impv.Q. [יָשַׁב];
נְדָבֹת v.1.com.s.impf.Q. [שִׁית];הֲדֹם (footstool); רְדֵה v.2.m.s.impv.Q. [רדה];
(freewill offering);חֵילֶךָ (splendor);מֵרֶחֶם (womb); מִשְׁחָר (dawn); טַל (dew)

MATTHEW 22:42–45

⁴²λέγων, Τί ὑμῖν δοκεῖ περὶ τοῦ Χριστοῦ; τίνος υἱός ἐστιν;
λέγουσιν αὐτῷ, τοῦ Δαυίδ. ⁴³λέγει αὐτοῖς, Πῶς οὖν Δαυὶδ ἐν
πνεύματι καλεῖ αὐτὸν κύριον λέγων,
    ⁴⁴Εἶπεν κύριος τῷ κυρίῳ μου,
    Κάθου ἐκ δεξιῶν μου,
        ἕως ἂν θῶ τοὺς ἐχθρούς σου ὑποκάτω τῶν ποδῶν
        σου;
⁴⁵εἰ οὖν Δαυὶδ καλεῖ αὐτὸν κύριον, πῶς υἱὸς αὐτοῦ ἐστιν;

ἐστιν v.3.s.pres.ind. [εἰμί]; εἶπεν v.3.s.aor.act.ind. [λέγω]; θῶ v.1.p.s.aor.act.sub.
[τίθημι]; ὑποκάτω (under); ποδῶν (foot)

3. Daniel 7:13–14; Revelation 1:7

Coming in the Clouds

WHEN YOU FIRST CAME, God of our Salvation, it was in clouds of common Galilean dust. Only a few eyes saw you, and then but dimly. It shall not be so when you come again. Truly it will be the Day of your Appearing. And surely we shall wail together, the just and the unjust, for we have pierced you, Holy God.

DANIEL 7:13–14 (A.)

¹³חָזֵה הֲוֵית בְּחֶזְוֵי לֵילְיָא וַאֲרוּ עִם־עֲנָנֵי שְׁמַיָּא כְּבַר אֱנָשׁ אָתֵה הֲוָה
וְעַד־עַתִּיק יוֹמַיָּא מְטָה וּקְדָמוֹהִי הַקְרְבוּהִי: ¹⁴ וְלֵהּ יְהִיב שָׁלְטָן וִיקָר
וּמַלְכוּ וְכֹל עַמְמַיָּא אֻמַיָּא וְלִשָּׁנַיָּא לֵהּ יִפְלְחוּן שָׁלְטָנֵהּ שָׁלְטָן
עָלַם דִּי־לָא יֶעְדֵּה וּמַלְכוּתֵהּ דִּי־לָא תִתְחַבַּל:

הַקְרְבוּהִי v.3.m.p.pf.Ha. [קרב] + 3.m.s.pr.sf.

REVELATION 1:7

⁷Ἰδοὺ ἔρχεται μετὰ τῶν νεφελῶν,
    καὶ ὄψεται αὐτὸν πᾶς ὀφθαλμὸς
καὶ οἵτινες αὐτὸν ἐξεκέντησαν,
    καὶ κόψονται ἐπ᾽ αὐτὸν πᾶσαι αἱ φυλαὶ τῆς γῆς.
ναί, ἀμήν.

νεφελῶν (cloud); ὄψεται v.3.s.fut.mid.ind. [ὁράω]; οἵτινες rel.pr.m.p.nom.;
ἐξεκέντησαν v.3.p.aor.act.ind. [ἐκκεντέω]; κόψονται (mourn); φυλαὶ (tribe);
ναί (indeed)

4. Jeremiah 23:5–6; Acts 13:19, 22, 24

Our Righteousness, God's Justice

THE VERY NAME OF GOD is "Our Righteousness." Why is it that when we think of God's justice we forget that? That is what Advent is all about—the coming of Our Righteousness, the blotting out of our sin! This is the justice of God.

JEREMIAH 23:5–6

⁵הִנֵּה

יָמִים בָּאִים נְאֻם־יְהוָה וַהֲקִמֹתִי לְדָוִד צֶמַח צַדִּיק וּמָלַךְ מֶלֶךְ וְהִשְׂכִּיל

וְעָשָׂה מִשְׁפָּט וּצְדָקָה בָּאָרֶץ:

⁶בְּיָמָיו תִּוָּשַׁע יְהוּדָה וְיִשְׂרָאֵל יִשְׁכֹּן לָבֶטַח

וְזֶה־שְּׁמוֹ אֲשֶׁר־יִקְרְאוֹ יְהוָה צִדְקֵנוּ:

בָּאִים v.m.p.ptc.Q. [בוא]; וַהֲקִמֹתִי v.c. + v.1.com.s.pf.H. [קום]; צֶמַח (shoot); תִּוָּשַׁע v.3.f.s.impf.N. [ישע]; לָבֶטַח (security); יִקְרְאוֹ v.3.m.s.impf.Q. [קרא] + 3.m.s.pr.sf.

ACTS 13:19, 22, 24

¹⁹καὶ καθελὼν ἔθνη ἑπτὰ ἐν γῇ Χανάαν κατεκληρονόμησεν τὴν γῆν αὐτῶν ²²καὶ μεταστήσας αὐτὸν ἤγειρεν τὸν Δαυὶδ αὐτοῖς εἰς βασιλέα ᾧ καὶ εἶπεν μαρτυρήσας, Εὗρον Δαυὶδ τὸν τοῦ Ἰεσσαί, ἄνδρα κατὰ τὴν καρδίαν μου, ὃς ποιήσει πάντα τὰ θελήματα μου. ²⁴προκηρύξαντος Ἰωάννου πρὸ προσώπου τῆς εἰσόδου αὐτοῦ βάπτισμα μετανοίας παντὶ τῷ λαῷ Ἰσραήλ.

καθελὼν v.m.s.nom.aor.act.ptc. [καθαιρέω] (conquer); κατεκληρονόμησεν (give as an inheritance); μεταστήσας v.m.s.nom.aor.act.ptc. [μεθίστημι] (remove); εἶπεν v.3.s.aor.act.ind. [λέγω]; Εὗρον v.1.s.aor.act.ind. [εὑρίσκω]; προκηρύξαντος (proclaim before); εἰσόδου (coming); μετανοίας (repentance)

5. Zechariah 9:9; John 12:13–15

The Coming of Humility

IT IS HARD TO KEEP LOOKING AT YOU, Humble One, riding on that colt, because inevitably I will become like the God I really worship. And what will everyone think if I forget about my dignity and empty myself so that you may fill me with your Spirit of humility so that I can faithfully bear your likeness in my Jerusalem? What will become of me?

ZECHARIAH 9:9

⁹גִּילִי

מְאֹד בַּת־צִיּוֹן הָרִיעִי בַּת יְרוּשָׁלַ͏ִם הִנֵּה מַלְכֵּךְ יָבוֹא לָךְ צַדִּיק וְנוֹשָׁע
הוּא עָנִי וְרֹכֵב עַל־חֲמוֹר וְעַל־עַיִר בֶּן־אֲתֹנוֹת׃

גִּילִי v.2.f.s.impv.Q. [גיל] (rejoice); הָרִיעִי v.2.f.s.impv.H. [רוע] (shout);
וְנוֹשָׁע cj. + v.m.s.ptc.N. [ישע]; עַיִר (donkey colt); אֲתֹנוֹת (she-donkey)

JOHN 12:13–15

¹³ἔλαβον τὰ βαΐα τῶν φοινίκων καὶ ἐξῆλθον εἰς ὑπάντησιν αὐτῷ καὶ ἐκραύγαζον,

Ὡσαννά·
εὐλογημένος ὁ ἐρχόμενος ἐν ὀνόματι κυρίου,
[καὶ] ὁ βασιλεὺς τοῦ Ἰσραήλ.

¹⁴εὑρὼν δὲ ὁ Ἰησοῦς ὀνάριον ἐκάθισεν ἐπ᾽ αὐτό, καθώς ἐστιν γεγραμμένον,

¹⁵Μὴ φοβοῦ, θυγάτηρ Σιών·
ἰδοὺ ὁ βασιλεύς σου ἔρχεται,
καθήμενος ἐπὶ πῶλον ὄνου.

βαΐα (palm frond); φοινίκων (date palm); ἐξῆλθον v.1.s.aor.act.ind [ἐξέρχομαι]; ὑπάντησιν (approaching); ἐκραύγαζον (cry); Ὡσαννά (hosanna); εὐλογημένος (bless); εὑρὼν v.m.s.nom.aor.act.ptc. [εὑρίσκω]; ὀνάριον (donkey colt); ἐκάθισεν (sit); ἐστιν v.3.s.pres.ind. [εἰμί]; θυγάτηρ (daughter); πῶλον (foal); ὄνου (donkey)

6. Psalm 2:7–9; Matthew 3:16–17

Begotten and Beloved

SON OF GOD, BEGOTTEN AND BELOVED, let me stay here beside you and simply look into your face. In you the Father is well pleased. So I want to know you. And even though I tremble because your rod is iron and your domain is all the world, still draw me close. I need to know you.

PSALM 2:7–9

⁷אֲסַפְּרָה אֶל חֹק יְהוָה אָמַר אֵלַי בְּנִי אַתָּה אֲנִי הַיּוֹם יְלִדְתִּיךָ׃

⁸שְׁאַל מִמֶּנִּי וְאֶתְּנָה גוֹיִם נַחֲלָתֶךָ וַאֲחֻזָּתְךָ אַפְסֵי־אָרֶץ׃

⁹תְּרֹעֵם בְּשֵׁבֶט בַּרְזֶל כִּכְלִי יוֹצֵר תְּנַפְּצֵם׃

אֲסַפְּרָה v.1.com.s.coh.P. [ספר]; יְלִדְתִּיךָ v.1.com.s.pf.Q. [ילד] + 2.m.s.pr.sf.; וְאֶתְּנָה cj. + v.1.com.s.coh.Q. [נתן]; אַפְסֵי (end); תְּרֹעֵם v.2.m.s.impf.Q. [רעע] (break) + 3.m.s.pr.sf.; תְּנַפְּצֵם v.2.m.s.impf.P. [נפץ] (shatter) + 3.m.p.pr.sf.

MATTHEW 3:16–17

¹⁶βαπτισθεὶς δὲ ὁ Ἰησοῦς εὐθὺς ἀνέβη ἀπὸ τοῦ ὕδατος· καὶ ἰδοὺ ἠνεῴχθησαν [αὐτῷ] οἱ οὐρανοί, καὶ εἶδεν [τὸ] πνεῦμα [τοῦ] θεοῦ καταβαῖνον ὡσεὶ περιστερὰν [καὶ] ἐρχόμενον ἐπ᾽ αὐτόν· ¹⁷καὶ ἰδοὺ φωνὴ ἐκ τῶν οὐρανῶν λέγουσα, Οὗτός ἐστιν ὁ υἱός μου ὁ ἀγαπητός, ἐν ᾧ εὐδόκησα.

ἀνέβη v.3.s.aor.act.mid. [ἀναβαίνω]; ἠνεῴχθησαν v.3.p.aor.pass.ind. [ἀνοίγω]; εἶδεν v.3.s.aor.act.ind. [ὁράω]; ὡσεὶ (as); περιστερὰν (dove); ἐστιν v.3.s.pres.ind. [εἰμί]; εὐδόκησα (be well pleased)

7. 1 Samuel 2:1, 10; Luke 1:68–69

Shatter the Strongholds!

THERE IS NOT AN ADVERSARY ANYWHERE, within my soul or without, who is beyond the reach of God. There is no corner in the cosmos where the trumpet of the Lord cannot be the horn of his salvation. Redeemer is his name. Let us welcome the shattering of strongholds in our lives! Let us rejoice in the coming of the Lord!

1 SAMUEL 2:1, 10

¹וַתִּתְפַּלֵּל

חַנָּה וַתֹּאמַר עָלַץ לִבִּי בַּיהוָה רָמָה קַרְנִי בַּיהוָה רָחַב פִּי עַל־אוֹיְבַי

כִּי שָׂמַחְתִּי בִּישׁוּעָתֶךָ:

¹⁰יְהוָה יֵחַתּוּ מְרִיבָיו עָלָיו בַּשָּׁמַיִם יַרְעֵם יְהוָה

יָדִין אַפְסֵי־אָרֶץ וְיִתֶּן־עֹז לְמַלְכּוֹ וְיָרֵם קֶרֶן מְשִׁיחוֹ:

בִּישׁוּעָתֶךָ prep. + n.f.s. + 2.m.s.pr.sf.; עָלַץ (rejoice); רָחַב (expand); יֵחַתּוּ
v.3.m.p.impf.Q. [חתת]; יַרְעֵם v.3.m.s.jus.H. [רעם] (thunder); יָדִין (plead a
case); אַפְסֵי (end); וְיָרֵם cj. + v.3.m.s.impf.H. [רום]; וְיִתֶּן cj. + v.3.m.s.jus.Q. [נתן]

LUKE 1:68–69

⁶⁸Εὐλογητὸς κύριος ὁ θεὸς τοῦ Ἰσραήλ,
  ὅτι ἐπεσκέψατο καὶ ἐποίησεν λύτρωσιν τῷ
    λαῷ αὐτοῦ,
⁶⁹καὶ ἤγειρεν κέρας σωτηρίας ἡμῖν
    ἐν οἴκῳ Δαυὶδ παιδὸς αὐτοῦ,

Εὐλογητὸς (blessed); ἐπεσκέψατο (visit); λύτρωσιν (redemption); κέρας
(horn); σωτηρίας (salvation); παιδὸς (servant)

369

Week 52

Advent II: He Is Come

1. Isaiah 7:14–15, Luke 1:34–35

A Home for God

WHO WOULD DREAM THAT ALMIGHTY GOD would entrust his advent to a teenage girl? But you did. Dare I hope, dare I believe, that in my smallness, Holy One, you also seek a home?

ISAIAH 7:14–15

14לָכֵן יִתֵּן אֲדֹנָי הוּא לָכֶם אוֹת הִנֵּה הָעַלְמָה הָרָה וְיֹלֶדֶת בֵּן
וְקָרָאת שְׁמוֹ עִמָּנוּ אֵל: 15 חֶמְאָה וּדְבַשׁ יֹאכֵל לְדַעְתּוֹ מָאוֹס
בָּרָע וּבָחוֹר בַּטּוֹב:

וְקָרָאת v.3.m.s.impf.Q. [נתן]; הָעַלְמָה (young woman); הָרָה (conceive); v.3.f.s.pf.Q. [קרא]; חֶמְאָה (cream); לְדַעְתּוֹ prep. + v.in.cst.Q. [ידע] + 3.m.s.pr.sf.

LUKE 1:34–35

34εἶπεν δὲ Μαριὰμ πρὸς τὸν ἄγγελον, Πῶς ἔσται τοῦτο, ἐπεὶ ἄνδρα οὐ γινώσκω; 35καὶ ἀποκριθεὶς ὁ ἄγγελος εἶπεν αὐτῇ, Πνεῦμα ἅγιον ἐπελεύσεται ἐπὶ σὲ καὶ δύναμις ὑψίστου ἐπισκιάσει σοι· διὸ καὶ τὸ γεννώμενον ἅγιον κληθήσεται υἱὸς θεοῦ.

εἶπεν v.3.s.aor.act.ind. [λέγω]; ἔσται v.3.s.fut.ind. [εἰμί]; ἐπεὶ (since); ἐπελεύσεται v.3.s.fut.mid.ind. [ἐπέρχομαι] (come upon); ἐπισκιάσει (cover)

2. Isaiah 9:5–6 [6–7]; Luke 1:31–33

The Zeal of the Lord Will Do It!

WHEN I READ THE NEWSPAPER—even one day's worth of mayhem—my heart sags with the gravity of despair. Thank God that isn't the only news! I've heard *more* than rumors about the coming of the Prince of Peace. And because "the zeal of the *Lord* will do this," I watch with growing joy.

ISAIAH 9:5–6 [6–7]

5כִּי־יֶ֣לֶד יֻלַּד־לָ֗נוּ בֵּ֚ן נִתַּן־לָ֔נוּ וַתְּהִ֥י הַמִּשְׂרָ֖ה עַל־שִׁכְמ֑וֹ
וַיִּקְרָ֨א שְׁמ֜וֹ פֶּ֠לֶא יוֹעֵץ֙ אֵ֣ל גִּבּ֔וֹר אֲבִיעַ֖ד שַׂר־שָׁלֽוֹם׃
6לְמַרְבֵּ֨ה הַמִּשְׂרָ֜ה וּלְשָׁל֣וֹם אֵֽין־קֵ֗ץ עַל־כִּסֵּ֤א דָוִד֙ וְעַל־
מַמְלַכְתּ֔וֹ לְהָכִ֤ין אֹתָהּ֙ וּֽלְסַעֲדָ֔הּ בְּמִשְׁפָּ֖ט וּבִצְדָקָ֑ה מֵעַתָּה֙
וְעַד־עוֹלָ֔ם קִנְאַ֛ת יְהוָ֥ה צְבָא֖וֹת תַּעֲשֶׂה־זֹּֽאת׃

יֻלַּד v.3.m.s.pf.Pu. [יֶלֶד]; נִתַּן v.3.m.s.pf.N. [נתן]; וַתְּהִי v.c. + v.3.f.s.impf.Q. [היה]; הַמִּשְׂרָה (dominion); שִׁכְמוֹ (shoulders); פֶּלֶא (wonder); אֲבִיעַד (father of eternity); לְמַרְבֵּה (increase); לְהָכִין prep. + v.in.cs.H. [כון]; וּלְסַעֲדָה cj. + prep. + v.in.cst.Q. [סעד] (sustain) + 3.f.s.sf.; קִנְאַת (zeal)

LUKE 1:31–33

31καὶ ἰδοὺ συλλήμψῃ ἐν γαστρὶ καὶ τέξῃ υἱὸν καὶ καλέσεις τὸ ὄνομα αὐτοῦ Ἰησοῦν. 32οὗτος ἔσται μέγας καὶ υἱὸς ὑψίστου κληθήσεται καὶ δώσει αὐτῷ κύριος ὁ θεὸς τὸν θρόνον Δαυὶδ τοῦ πατρὸς αὐτοῦ, 33καὶ βασιλεύσει ἐπὶ τὸν οἶκον Ἰακὼβ εἰς τοὺς αἰῶνας καὶ τῆς βασιλείας αὐτοῦ οὐκ ἔσται τέλος.

συλλήμψῃ v.2.s.fut.mid.ind. [συλλαμβάνω] (conceive); γαστρὶ (womb); τέξῃ v.2.s.fut.mid.ind. [τίκτω] (bear); ἔσται v.3.s.fut.ind. [εἰμί]; ὑψίστου (exalted); τέλος (end)

3. Isaiah 42:6–8; Luke 1:42–45

Where Is Elizabeth?

WHO ARE THE ELIZABETHS in our midst today? People with God-vision, God-courage, and God-dreams, looking for Messiah, rejoicing when they find him. People whose age and gender and standing in the community are really beside the point. Whenever there is Advent, there is Elizabeth.

ISAIAH 42:6–8

⁶אֲנִי יְהוָה קְרָאתִיךָ בְצֶדֶק וְאַחְזֵק בְּיָדֶךָ וְאֶצָּרְךָ וְאֶתֶּנְךָ
לִבְרִית עָם לְאוֹר גּוֹיִם: ⁷ לִפְקֹחַ עֵינַיִם עִוְרוֹת לְהוֹצִיא מִמַּסְגֵּר
אַסִּיר מִבֵּית כֶּלֶא יֹשְׁבֵי חֹשֶׁךְ: ⁸ אֲנִי יְהוָה הוּא שְׁמִי וּכְבוֹדִי
לְאַחֵר לֹא־אֶתֵּן וּתְהִלָּתִי לַפְּסִילִים:

קְרָאתִיךָ v.1.com.s.pf.Q. [קרא] + 2.m.s.pr.sf.; וְאֶצָּרְךָ cj. + v.1.com.s.impf.Q. [נצר] + 2.m.s.pr.sf.; וְאֶתֶּנְךָ cj. + v.1.com.s.impf.Q. [נתן] + 2.m.s.pr.sf.; לִפְקֹחַ (open); עִוְרוֹת (blind); לְהוֹצִיא prep. + v.in.cs.H. [יצא]; מִמַּסְגֵּר (prison); אַסִּיר (prisoner); מִבֵּית כֶּלֶא (prison); אֶתֵּן v.1.com.s.pf.Q. [נתן]; לַפְּסִילִים (idol)

LUKE 1:42–45

⁴²καὶ ἀνεφώνησεν κραυγῇ μεγάλῃ καὶ εἶπεν, Εὐλογημένη σὺ ἐν γυναιξὶν καὶ εὐλογημένος ὁ καρπὸς τῆς κοιλίας σου. ⁴³καὶ πόθεν μοι τοῦτο ἵνα ἔλθῃ ἡ μήτηρ τοῦ κυρίου μου πρὸς ἐμέ; ⁴⁴ἰδοὺ γὰρ ὡς ἐγένετο ἡ φωνὴ τοῦ ἀσπασμοῦ σου εἰς τὰ ὦτα μου, ἐσκίρτησεν ἐν ἀγαλλιάσει τὸ βρέφος ἐν τῇ κοιλίᾳ μου. ⁴⁵καὶ μακαρία ἡ πιστεύσασα ὅτι ἔσται τελείωσις τοῖς λελαλημένοις αὐτῇ παρὰ κυρίου.

ἀνεφώνησεν (cry out); κραυγῇ (shout); εἶπεν v.3.s.aor.act.ind. [λέγω]; Εὐλογημένη (praise); κοιλίας (womb); πόθεν (why); ἔλθῃ v.3.s.aor.act.sub. [ἔρχομαι]; ἐγένετο v.3.s.aor.mid.ind. [γίνομαι]; ἀσπασμοῦ (greeting); ὦτα (ear); ἀγαλλιάσει (gladness); βρέφος (fetus); πιστεύσασα v.f.s.nom.aor.act.ptc. [πιστεύω]; v.3.s.fut.ind. [εἰμί]; ἔσται v.3.s.fut.ind. [εἰμί]; τελείωσις (fulfillment)

4. Ezekiel 37:26–27; Matthew 1:20–23

God with Us? Wait a Minute!

SOMETIMES, EMMANUEL, your being-with-us is not what we
expect. Or particularly want. Come anyway! Come now and
dwell in our midst! Let your covenant of peace undermine our
fear. Come and stay with us, Emmanuel.

EZEKIEL 37:26–27

²⁶וְכָרַתִּי לָהֶם בְּרִית שָׁלוֹם בְּרִית עוֹלָם יִהְיֶה אוֹתָם וּנְתַתִּים וְהִרְבֵּיתִי
אוֹתָם וְנָתַתִּי אֶת־מִקְדָּשִׁי בְּתוֹכָם לְעוֹלָם: ²⁷וְהָיָה מִשְׁכָּנִי עֲלֵיהֶם
וְהָיִיתִי לָהֶם לֵאלֹהִים וְהֵמָּה יִהְיוּ־לִי לְעָם:

וְכָרַתִּי v.c. + v.1.com.s.pf.Q. [כרת]; וּנְתַתִּים v.c. + v.1.com.s.pf.Q. [נתן] +
3.m.p.pr.sf.; וְהִרְבֵּיתִי v.c. + v.1.com.s.pf.H. [רבה]; וְנָתַתִּי v.c. + v.1.com.s.pf.Q.
[נתן]; וְהָיִיתִי v.c. + v.1.com.s.pf.Q. [היה]; יִהְיוּ v.c. + v.3.m.s.impf.Q. [היה]

MATTHEW 1:20–23

²⁰ταῦτα δὲ αὐτοῦ ἐνθυμηθέντος ἰδοὺ ἄγγελος κυρίου κατ'
ὄναρ ἐφάνη αὐτῷ λέγων, Ἰωσὴφ υἱὸς Δαυίδ, μὴ φοβηθῇς
παραλαβεῖν Μαρίαν τὴν γυναῖκα σου· τὸ γὰρ ἐν αὐτῇ
γεννηθὲν ἐκ πνεύματος ἐστιν ἁγίου. ²¹τέξεται δὲ υἱόν, καὶ
καλέσεις τὸ ὄνομα αὐτοῦ Ἰησοῦν· αὐτὸς γὰρ σώσει τὸν λαὸν
αὐτοῦ ἀπὸ τῶν ἁμαρτιῶν αὐτῶν. ²²τοῦτο δὲ ὅλον γέγονεν ἵνα
πληρωθῇ τὸ ῥηθὲν ὑπὸ κυρίου διὰ τοῦ προφήτου λέγοντος,
²³Ἰδοὺ ἡ παρθένος ἐν γαστρὶ ἕξει καὶ τέξεται υἱόν,
καὶ καλέσουσιν τὸ ὄνομα αὐτοῦ Ἐμμανουήλ,
ὅ ἐστιν μεθερμηνευόμενον Μεθ' ἡμῶν ὁ θεός.

ἐνθυμηθέντος (consider); ὄναρ (dream); ἐφάνη (appear); παραλαβεῖν
(receive); ἐστιν v.3.s.pres.ind. [εἰμί]; τέξεται v.3.f.s.mid.ind. [τίκτω] (give
birth); ῥηθὲν v.nt.s.nom.aor.pass.ptc. [λέγω]; παρθένος (virgin); ἐν γαστρὶ
(be pregnant [in the womb]); μεθερμηνευόμενον (translate)

373

5. Micah 5:1 [2]; Luke 2:15–17

Small-Town God

Isn't it just like you, God, to make your Big Appearance at some Godforsaken crossroads? The least of these, the small, weak and despised, the treasure hidden in the field God. Of course you chose little Bethlehem. Of course you chose a manger.

Micah 5:1 [2]

¹וְאַתָּה
בֵּית־לֶחֶם אֶפְרָתָה צָעִיר לִהְיוֹת בְּאַלְפֵי יְהוּדָה מִמְּךָ לִי יֵצֵא לִהְיוֹת
מוֹשֵׁל בְּיִשְׂרָאֵל וּמוֹצָאֹתָיו מִקֶּדֶם מִימֵי עוֹלָם:

צָעִיר (small); לִהְיוֹת prep. + v.in.cs.Q. [הִיה]; מִמְּךָ prep. [מִן] + 2.m.s.pr.sf.;
יֵצֵא v.3.m.s.impf.Q. [יצא]; וּמוֹצָאֹתָיו (exit); מִימֵי prep. [מִן] + n.m.p.cs. [יוֹם]

Luke 2:15–17

¹⁵Καὶ ἐγένετο ὡς ἀπῆλθον ἀπ᾽ αὐτῶν εἰς τὸν οὐρανὸν οἱ ἄγγελοι, οἱ ποιμένες ἐλάλουν πρὸς ἀλλήλους, Διέλθωμεν δὴ ἕως Βηθλέεμ καὶ ἴδωμεν τὸ ῥῆμα τοῦτο τὸ γεγονὸς ὃ ὁ κύριος ἐγνώρισεν ἡμῖν. ¹⁶καὶ ἦλθαν σπεύσαντες καὶ ἀνεῦραν τήν τε Μαριὰμ καὶ τὸν Ἰωσὴφ καὶ τὸ βρέφος κείμενον ἐν τῇ φάτνῃ· ¹⁷ἰδόντες δὲ ἐγνώρισαν περὶ τοῦ ῥήματος τοῦ λαληθέντος αὐτοῖς περὶ τοῦ παιδίου τούτου.

ἐγένετο v.3.s.aor.mid.ind. [γίνομαι]; ἀπῆλθον v.3.p.aor.act.ind. [ἀπέρ-χομαι]; ποιμένες (shepherd); Διέλθωμεν v.1.p.aor.act.sub. [διέρχομαι] (go); δὴ (then); ἐγνώρισεν (make known); ἦλθαν v.3.p.aor.act.ind. [ἔρχο-μαι]; σπεύσαντες (hurry); ἀνεῦραν v.3.p.aor.act.ind. [ἀνευρίσκω] (look for); βρέφος (baby); φάτνη (manger); ἰδόντες v.m.p.nom.aor.act.ptc. [ὁράω]

6. Micah 5:3–4a[4–5a]; Luke 2:13–14

Angel Songs

IF I LISTEN CAREFULLY on cold nights in dark places and lonely hours, I can hear the coming of the Shepherd. And when I do, there are always angels singing.

MICAH 5:3–4A [4–5A]

³וְעָמַד וְרָעָה בְּעֹז יְהוָה בִּגְאוֹן שֵׁם יְהוָה אֱלֹהָיו וְיָשָׁבוּ כִּי־עַתָּה יִגְדַּל
עַד־אַפְסֵי־אָרֶץ: ⁴ וְהָיָה זֶה שָׁלוֹם

בְּגְאוֹן (pride); אַפְסֵי (end)

LUKE 2:13–14

¹³καὶ ἐξαίφνης ἐγένετο σὺν τῷ ἀγγέλῳ πλῆθος στρατιᾶς οὐρανίου αἰνούντων τὸν θεὸν καὶ λεγόντων,
   ¹⁴Δόξα ἐν ὑψίστοις θεῷ
     καὶ ἐπὶ γῆς εἰρήνη ἐν ἀνθρώποις εὐδοκίας.

ἐξαίφνης (suddenly); ἐγένετο v.3.s.aor.mid.ind. [γίνομαι]; στρατιᾶς (army); αἰνούντων v.m.p.gen.pr.act.ptc. [αἰνέω]; ὑψίστοις (exalted); εὐδοκίας (good will)

7. Zechariah 14:9; Luke 2:29–32

The Coming

YOUR COMING IS FOR ALL PEOPLE, everywhere, through all time.
My head swims at the thought of it. How can God do this? Yet
how can you not? For you are Salvation. Your name is Lord.

ZECHARIAH 14:9

⁹וְהָיָה
יְהוָה לְמֶלֶךְ עַל־כָּל־הָאָרֶץ בַּיּוֹם הַהוּא יִהְיֶה יְהוָה אֶחָד וּשְׁמוֹ אֶחָד׃

LUKE 2:29–32

²⁹Νῦν ἀπολύεις τὸν δοῦλον σου, δέσποτα,
    κατὰ τὸ ῥῆμα σου ἐν εἰρήνῃ·
³⁰ὅτι εἶδον οἱ ὀφθαλμοί μου τὸ σωτήριον σου,
    ³¹ὃ ἡτοίμασας κατὰ πρόσωπον πάντων τῶν λαῶν,
³²φῶς εἰς ἀποκάλυψιν ἐθνῶν
    καὶ δόξαν λαοῦ σου Ἰσραήλ.

Νῦν (now); δέσποτα (master); εἶδον v.1.s.aor.act.ind. [ὁράω]; σωτήριον
(salvation); ἡτοίμασας v.2.s.aor.act.ind. [ετοιμάζω] (prepare); ἀποκάλυψιν
(revelation)

Celebration

1. Deuteronomy 12:5–7; Revelation 22:20

Blessed Endings

HOLY FATHER, THE YEAR ENDS AS IT BEGAN—in the fullness of your love. We praise you that, in spite of our shortfallings, your love is to be celebrated, today and every day. Hallelujah—come!

DEUTERONOMY 12:5–7

⁵כִּי אִם־אֶל־הַמָּקוֹם אֲשֶׁר־יִבְחַר יְהוָה אֱלֹהֵיכֶם מִכָּל־שִׁבְטֵיכֶם
לָשׂוּם אֶת־שְׁמוֹ שָׁם לְשִׁכְנוֹ תִדְרְשׁוּ וּבָאתָ שָׁמָּה:
⁶וַהֲבֵאתֶם שָׁמָּה עֹלֹתֵיכֶם וְזִבְחֵיכֶם וְאֵת מַעְשְׂרֹתֵיכֶם וְאֵת תְּרוּמַת
יֶדְכֶם וְנִדְרֵיכֶם וְנִדְבֹתֵיכֶם וּבְכֹרֹת בְּקַרְכֶם וְצֹאנְכֶם:
⁷וַאֲכַלְתֶּם־שָׁם לִפְנֵי יְהוָה אֱלֹהֵיכֶם וּשְׂמַחְתֶּם בְּכֹל מִשְׁלַח
יֶדְכֶם אַתֶּם וּבָתֵּיכֶם אֲשֶׁר בֵּרַכְךָ יְהוָה אֱלֹהֶיךָ:

וּבָאתָ .v.c. +v.2.m.s.pf.Q. [בוא];וַהֲבֵאתֶם v.c. +v.2.m.p.pf.H. [בוא];מַעְשְׂרֹתֵיכֶם
(tithe);וְנִדְבֹתֵיכֶם (freewill offering);וּבְכֹרֹת (firstborn);מִשְׁלַח (business);בֵּרַכְךָ
v.3.m.s.pf.P. [ברך] + 2.m.s.pr.sf.

REVELATION 22:20

²⁰Λέγει ὁ μαρτυρῶν ταῦτα, Ναί, ἔρχομαι ταχύ. Ἀμήν, ἔρχου κύριε Ἰησοῦ.

Ναί (indeed); ταχύ (quickly)

2. Job 29:2–4; Matthew 24:37–38

Special Days

FATHER, WE LOOK BACK AND SMILE at days that charm our memory, and look forward to that most awaited day of your return, which is going to erupt into our daily days. May this day, one in 1461, serve to remind us that every day is special in your presence, that you were there in all our yesterdays, and are already there in all of our tomorrows.

JOB 29:2–4

²מִי־יִתְּנֵנִי כְיַרְחֵי־קֶדֶם כִּימֵי אֱלוֹהַּ יִשְׁמְרֵנִי:

³בְּהִלּוֹ נֵרוֹ עֲלֵי רֹאשִׁי לְאוֹרוֹ אֵלֶךְ חֹשֶׁךְ:

⁴כַּאֲשֶׁר הָיִיתִי בִּימֵי חָרְפִּי בְּסוֹד אֱלוֹהַּ עֲלֵי אָהֳלִי:

יִתְּנֵנִי v.3.m.s.impf.Q. [נתן] + 1.com.s.pr.sf.; יִשְׁמְרֵנִי v.3.m.s.impf.Q. [שמר] + 1.com.s.pr.sf.; בְּהִלּוֹ prep. + v.in.cs.Q. [הלל] + 3.m.s.pr.sf.; נֵרוֹ (lamp); אֵלֶךְ v.1.c.s.impf.Q. [הלך]; הָיִיתִי v.1.c.s.pf.Q. [היה]; בְּסוֹד (intimate group)

MATTHEW 24:37–38

³⁷ὥσπερ γὰρ αἱ ἡμέραι τοῦ Νῶε, οὕτως ἔσται ἡ παρουσία τοῦ υἱοῦ τοῦ ἀνθρώπου. ³⁸ὡς γὰρ ἦσαν ἐν ταῖς ἡμέραις [ἐκείναις] ταῖς πρὸ τοῦ κατακλυσμοῦ τρώγοντες καὶ πίνοντες, γαμοῦντες καὶ γαμίζοντες, ἄχρι ἧς ἡμέρας εἰσῆλθεν Νῶε εἰς τὴν κιβωτόν,

ὥσπερ (as); ἔσται v.3.s.fut.ind. [εἰμί]; παρουσία (coming); ἦσαν v.3.p.impf.ind. [εἰμί]; κατακλυσμοῦ (flood); τρώγοντες (eat); γαμοῦντες (marry); γαμίζοντες (give in marriage); ἄχρι (until); εἰσῆλθεν v.3.s.aor.act.ind. [εἰσέρχομαι]; κιβωτόν (ark)

Subject Index

Scripture Index

David Baker is professor of Old Testament and Semitic Languages at Ashland Theological Seminary. The author of several books and articles, he is also the editor of the *Ashland Theological Journal,* The Bible Commentary series, and the Evangelical Theological Society Monographs. His Ph.D. is from the University of London. **Elaine Heath** is an ordained deacon in the United Methodist Church and the author of numerous articles on the spiritual life. She is pursuing a Ph.D. in systematic theology from Duquesne University.